Jacobean Pageant, or the Court of King James I
Shakespeare and the Earl of Southampton

Plate I.   Portrait of King James VI and I by D. Mytens.
              (By permission of the National Portrait Gallery, London)

LETTERS OF
King James VI & I

EDITED WITH AN INTRODUCTION
by G.P.V. Akrigg

University of California Press

Berkeley / Los Angeles / London

University of California Press
Berkeley and Los Angeles, California
University of California Press, Ltd.
London, England
©1984 by
The Regents of the University of California
Printed in the United States of America

1   2   3   4   5   6   7   8   9

Library of Congress Cataloging in Publication Data

James I, King of England, 1566–1625.
  Letters of King James VI and I.

  "A finding-list for other letters of James VI and I
available in print": p.
  Includes index.
  1. James I, King of England, 1566–1625. 2. Great
Britain—History—James I, 1603–1625—Sources.
3. Scotland—History—James VI, 1567–1625—
Sources. 4. Great Britain—Kings and rulers—
Correspondence. 5. Scotland—Kings and rulers—
Correspondence. I. Akrigg, G.P.V. II. Title.
DA391.J35   1984   941.06′1′0924   82–20135
ISBN 0–520–04707–9

To
Andrew Philip Martin
AND
Christopher J. B. Martin

CONTENTS

PLATES

ACKNOWLEDGEMENTS

I wish to thank all those who have helped me in the long task of preparing this edition, though they are so many that it is not practicable to list them all by name.

Among institutions, however, specific mention must be made of the James Ford Bell Library of the University of Minnesota, the Bodleian Library, the British Library, the Cambridge University Library, the Cumbria Record Office (Kendal), the University of Edinburgh Library, the Folger Shakespeare Library, the Good-wood Estate Company, the Historical Society of Pennsylvania, the Henry E. Huntington Library, the House of Lords Record Office, the Lambeth Palace Library, the National Library of Scotland, the National Register of Archives, the Northamptonshire Record Office, the Dean and Chapter of Peterborough Cathedral, the Public Record Office, the Scottish Record Office, the Somerset Record Office, and the West Sussex Record Office. To this list must be added those archives on the Continent which are noted on p. 21 of the general introduction.

The editor expresses particular thanks to those archives and libraries which, by permitting him to print letters in their collections, made this edition possible. The location notes appended to the letters indicate the specific debts.

Individuals who have assisted me, chiefly through helping with enquiries, reading drafts, or permitting me to print letters in their possession, include Professor T. G. Barnes, the Duke of

Buccleuch, Mr. Simon Digby, the Duke of Hamilton, Lady Dorothy Hothfield, Mr. P. I. King, Professor J. A. Lavin, the Earl of Mar and Kellie, Mr. David F. Metcalfe, the Duke of Montrose, the Earl of Moray, Professor Linda Levy Peck, Professor Ian Ross, Professor Conrad Russell, Dr. Grant G. Simpson, the Marquess of Salisbury and his archivists, first Miss Clare Talbot and later Mr. R. H. Harcourt Williams. My old friend the late Professor G. B. Riddehough helped me greatly by translating King James's Latin and running down his classical quotations. Later, Professor H. G. Edinger and my son, George M. Akrigg, assisted here. I owe a debt of long continuance to the Library of the University of British Columbia, my home institution, for support services, particularly to Mrs. A. Yandle, Head of Special Collections, and to Mrs. S. Dodson, Head of Government Documents, who presides over the microform section. I remember gratefully the zealous endeavours of Mr. James Carter, my research assistant during the first stages of this project.

The Canada Council, during the era when it dispensed the federal government's largesse to academics, granted me two leave fellowships, and it was during these that much of the work on this edition was done.

Finally, I must once again thank my wife, Helen B. Akrigg, who, with remarkable good spirits and endurance, played the chief sustaining role and did most of the typing.

G.P.V.A.

INTRODUCTION

INTRODUCTION

I

That King James VI of Scotland, who became King James I of England, was no ordinary monarch soon becomes apparent to any reader of his letters. This was a king who could address a courtier as "my little pork" and a Secretary of State as "my little beagle" or "my little wiffe-waffe," and who could warn a son in quest of a wife to think "as well upon the business of Christendom as upon the codpiece point."[1] It is not enough to salute King James as an original—he was also one of the most complicated neurotics ever to sit on either the English or the Scottish throne.

Believers in prenatal influences, once aware of King James's lifelong dread of naked steel, have found significant an event that occurred when he had still three months to spend in his mother's womb: David Rizzio, secretary to that mother, Mary Queen of Scots, was dragged screaming from her presence and stabbed to death while Mary's vicious young husband, Lord Darnley, stood by, approving. It is not necessary, however, to look to events before James's birth to account for the dread of physical violence which became a central and at times a humiliating part of the King's character. This, like others of his

[1]See Letters 34, 116, 209.

3

idiosyncrasies, can be sufficiently explained by events that came after his birth on 19 June 1566.

Eight months after James was born, his father was found strangled. Another three months, and the widow married the Earl of Bothwell, the man chiefly responsible for Darnley's murder. One month later, and a powerful faction of Protestant lords prevailed in a confrontation with the lovers. Queen Mary abdicated and, on 29 July 1567, at the age of one year, one month and ten days, James became King of Scotland. If James was a king who could not remember a time when he had not been a king, he was also a king without any memories of a mother. While Mary was a captive, first in Scotland and then for many years in England, her son grew up, in his own phrase, "alone, without father or mother, brother or sister."[2]

After the coronation of the infant James, his uncle, the Earl of Moray, governed his kingdom as regent. When James was three and a half years old, Moray was fatally wounded by an assassin and the little boy's grandfather, the Earl of Lennox, succeeded to the regency. During an attempted coup by supporters of Queen Mary, Lennox was shot in the back. One of King James's earliest memories was of himself at the age of five watching his dying grandfather being carried into Stirling Castle.

Lennox's place as regent was taken by James's guardian, the Earl of Mar, whose stern wife showed the boy only a part of the affection that he might have received from his mother. In a little more than a year Mar met a natural death (the only one of four successive regents to do so). The harsh Earl of Morton, all along the most dominant of the Protestant lords, then assumed the regency, an office he was to hold for the coming five and a half years.

Meanwhile the bright little boy who was king was being subjected to a truly formidable education—later he observed succinctly, "They gar [made] me speak Latin ere I could speak

[2]See Letter 36.

Scots."[3] Directing the royal education was old George Buchanan, a renowned classical scholar and a sour, mean-minded misogynist. James regarded him with something approaching terror. Fortunately Peter Young, the coadjutor who attended to the daily routine of James's schooling, was a much kindlier, younger man who became a friend for life.

His tutors' endeavours were not wasted on the youthful James. Sir Henry Killigrew, an English ambassador who had been permitted to visit him, chose at random a chapter from the Bible and was amazed at how the eight-year-old translated its Latin *ex tempore* into French and then the French into English.

Nearing the age of twelve, James, with no love for Regent Morton, was easily persuaded by the latter's enemies to dismiss him from office and to announce his own "acceptance of government." Outmanoeuvred, Morton acquiesced. About a month later, however, he was restored to power, though only as First Lord of the Council, by a coup which saw blood shed at Stirling Castle—several men were killed, and King James was terrified.

In the spring of 1579 the King invited his French kinsman Esmé Stuart, Seigneur D'Aubigny, to visit him in Scotland. D'Aubigny, a polished courtier in his late thirties, made a tremendous impression on the lonely boy of fourteen. He discussed diplomacy and politics with the young king. He opened new worlds for him, introducing him to poetry and possibly to homosexuality. Rewards were heaped upon this the first of the King's favourites. James created D'Aubigny first Earl and then Duke of Lennox—the only duke in all Scotland. He gave him command of that key fortress Dumbarton Castle. He made him Great Chamberlain of Scotland. Lennox was Morton's enemy, and soon the former regent was charged with complicity in the murder of the King's wastrel father and beheaded.

In the process of destroying Morton, James had to outmanoeuvre Queen Elizabeth and her ambassadors, supporters of

---

[3]T. F. Henderson, *James I & VI* (London, 1904), p. 8.

Morton's regime in Scotland. Astounded to find that young James could steal a march on her, Elizabeth could only exclaim, "That false Scotch urchin! What can be expected from the double dealing of such an urchin as this?"[4] James may have been coached in duplicity by Lennox, but he was already learning the arts of concealment. About this time he wrote a poem containing the following advice to himself:

> Since thought is free, think what thou will,
> O troubled heart, to ease thy pain.
> Thought, unrevealed, can do no ill;
> But words passed out come not again.
>   Be careful aye for to invent
>   The way to get thy own intent.[5]

Lennox's greatness in Scotland lasted only two years. For one thing, although he declared that he had been converted to Protestantism by King James, already an amateur theologian, the Kirk simply did not believe that Lennox was anything other than a covert Catholic and was determined that he must go. For another, lords who had been glad enough to topple Morton became increasingly angry when they found the outsider from France engrossing so much of the royal favour. In the end, the latter organized a faction and struck. When on 23 August 1582 the King sought to leave Ruthven Castle to join Lennox at Edinburgh, his way was blocked by the Master of Glamis and others of the "Lords Enterprisers" as they called themselves. Furious, James stormed and threatened. Then suddenly the sixteen-year-old monarch, overcome by fear and humiliation, burst into tears. "Better that bairns should weep than bearded men," growled the Master.[6] Years later, in his *Basilikon Doron,* King

---

[4]Antonia Fraser, *Mary, Queen of Scots* (London, [1969]), p. 457.

[5]James Craigie, ed., *The Poems of James VI of Scotland* (Edinburgh, 1958), II: 132.

[6]John Spottiswoode, *History of the Church of Scotland,* Bannatyne Club No. 93 (Edinburgh, 1850), II: 290.

James made his own comment on such exploits of his half-barbarous Scottish lords, speaking of their "feckless arrogant conceit of their greatness and power."[7]

The Lords Enterprisers had things their own way in Scotland for the next ten months. Lennox retired to France, where he died, a Protestant, in May 1583. (The Duke of Lennox referred to in the King's later letters was the first duke's son, brought to Scotland a few months later.) Then, on 27 June 1583, King James gave his Ruthven captors the slip. Hitherto he had generally been a pawn, used or manipulated by this or that powerful lord or faction. Now he directed events, and made his own arrangements with the supporters who met him at St. Andrews. Demoralized, the Ruthven lords fled the kingdom.

King James made a bad mistake when, after his escape from the Ruthven lords, he chose for the chief of his ministers the accomplished but arrogant and rapacious Earl of Arran. After Elizabeth and her councillors had engineered Arran's downfall late in 1585, the government of Scotland improved under the regime of Maitland of Thirlestane, the Secretary of State whom King James later created Lord Chancellor. Maitland adroitly furthered the King's policies and provided him with at least a skeletal civil service devoted to the monarch's interests rather than those of personal patrons.

While Arran was still in power, there arrived in Scotland an agent of Mary Queen of Scots. His name was Fontenay, and in a letter[8] to Mary's secretary he gives us a most interesting account of the young king. James seems to Fontenay clear in understanding and careful in judgement. He asks perceptive questions and gives solid answers. He stands by what he deems true and just. Moreover, he is as well educated in the languages, sciences, and affairs of state as any in his kingdom. True, brought up in fear ["nourry en crainte"], he often lacks courage,

[7] *Basilikon Doron*, ed. James Craigie (Edinburgh, 1944), I:8.
[8] *Calendar of the State Papers Relating to Scotland and Mary, Queen of Scots 1584–85* (Edinburgh, 1913), pp. 274–75 (hereafter cited as *CSP Scottish*).

though he would like to appear courageous. He has other deficiencies. For lack of good instruction, he is rough and uncivil in his speech, eating, attire, pastimes, and conversation in the presence of ladies. His voice is loud. He is addicted to hunting and yet his body, though not delicate, is not strong. He is an old young man. Fontenay can see three faults that may cause future trouble. One is James's failure to realize his own poverty and lack of strength, especially in relation to other princes. Another is the indiscreet way in which he chooses his favourites, disregarding the wishes of his people. The third is laziness and carelessness in his management of his affairs, the consequence of devoting himself too much to his pleasures.

As the sixteenth century drew towards its close, James increasingly emerged as an effective and skillful sovereign, more and more in control of his turbulent kingdom. The "popes of Edinburgh," the Presbyterian ministers, had had their arrogance abated and their claims confined. The danger to royal independence posed by the pro-English party had been ended in 1586 by a treaty with England which made King James himself "in effect the head of the English faction in Scotland."[9] In 1587 James had skillfully handled the crisis brought about by the sentence of death passed on his mother in England—retaining the allegiance of the Scots through the efforts that he made on her behalf, while never letting those efforts become so strong as to alienate Queen Elizabeth, whose heir he hoped to become. By 1590–1591 Scotland was sufficiently stable that James could be in Denmark with his bride for a number of months and still find his kingdom tranquil when he returned. There were still, of course, occasional alarms, but the threat to King James's personal safety posed by the wild Earl of Bothwell, nephew to Queen Mary's Bothwell, ended when he went into exile in 1594. As for the mysterious "Gowrie Plot" of August 1600—appar-

---

[9]Maurice Lee, Jr., *John Maitland of Thirlestane and the Foundation of Stewart Despotism in Scotland* (Princeton, 1959), p. 96.

ently an abortive attempt to kidnap the King—that ended with both the young Earl of Gowrie and his brother slain, their family name of Ruthven abolished, and King James more strongly established than ever. James had emerged on top. He was, in the view of Maurice Lee, "unquestionably the most successful king of Scotland since Robert Bruce."[10]

The opening months of the seventeenth century found the King of Scotland very much concerned about the aging Queen of England. He had, over the years, written her many letters— they constitute an important part of this edition—letters explaining, remonstrating, recommending, assuring, mollifying, emphasizing, ingratiating. Always he had sought Elizabeth's good opinion, for he yearned to have her recognize him as her heir. However, the best he had been able to obtain from her was a conditional promise that she would do nothing to prejudice his claim to the succession. Now, towards the end of Elizabeth's life, James lost patience and committed the folly of seizing on the unstable Earl of Essex as the man who would bring him to the English throne.

It is impossible to say how far James was party to the activities that culminated in the Essex Rebellion of February 1601 (before his arrest Essex apparently destroyed incriminating letters from James), but Letter 76 in the present collection seems to indicate that James was deeply implicated. Fortunately for the Scottish king, Sir Robert Cecil, Essex's enemy who under Elizabeth directed the government of England, saved His Majesty from the disaster that he had invited. Realizing that James was the person most likely and best qualified to succeed to the English throne, Cecil kept James's name out of the trial that brought Essex to the block. Then Cecil entered into a secret agreement with King James to do all that he could, while remaining loyal to Elizabeth, to prepare the way for his succession.

[10]Ibid., p. 79.

For two years, from early 1601 to early 1603, James and Cecil conducted a secret correspondence in which they referred to themselves and others by code numbers. To understand Letters 79–92, a reader needs the key to their cipher identities:

    0 = The Earl of Northumberland
    2 = Sir Walter Raleigh [?]
    3 = Lord Henry Howard
    7 = Lord Cobham
    8 = Edward Bruce
    9 = David Foulis
    10 = Sir Robert Cecil
    20 = The Earl of Mar
    24 = Queen Elizabeth
    30 = King James
    40 = The Earl of Nottingham [?]

Despite several risky moments, Queen Elizabeth never learned of the arrangements between King James and Cecil, and when she died on 24 March 1603, James succeeded to her throne as easily as he could have desired.

On 3 April 1603, after the sermon was concluded at St. Giles Church in Edinburgh, King James arose and delivered a farewell message to his Scottish subjects. Three days later he crossed into England at Berwick. Scotland was not to see him again until 1617.

The government of Scotland did not fall into disorder after the departure of its monarch. Credit for the continued stability of the kingdom must be given in part to the loyal lieutenants whom James left in authority there, but even more is due to the King himself, who worked out a successful means of governing Scotland *in absentia*.

To rule Scotland from England, King James needed a rapid means of communication. Hence, within a month of His Majesty's departure for his new capital, the Privy Council of Scotland set up a stage system for the royal mail, with postmasters at Edinburgh, Haddington, Cockburnspath, and Berwick-on-Tweed. Conveyed along these stages and others in England, a letter could travel between Edinburgh and London in a week (longer in winter). The postmasters, unlike most servants of the Crown, were paid with great regularity.[11] Prompt payment helped to produce an exceptionally efficient service, and King James could boast to the English parliament, "Thus I must say for Scotland . . . here I sit and govern it with my pen: I write and it is done."[12]

A glance at the flow of letters that passed between London and Edinburgh shows how close an eye King James kept on Scottish affairs—especially those involving the Kirk, whose propensity for creating trouble he well knew. Interesting is a letter of 22 September 1624 addressed to the Lord Chancellor and Privy Council of Scotland. It deals with an overly zealous Presbyterian minister who had been ordered banished to the north of Scotland to cool off. Reading its close, one can almost hear the voice of the King telling the clerk what to put in the letter to be prepared for the royal signature:

Whereas the Archbishop of St. Andrews hath been an humble suitor unto us on behalf of Mr. Robert Bruce, earnestly craving that (by reason of the indisposition and weakness of body of the said Mr. Robert) he may have a prorogation of the time limited for his return to his confining at Inverness, we are well pleased that the said Mr. Robert shall have liberty during the time of this ensuing winter to remain at his own house, provided always that during all the time aforesaid he neither preach, make feasts nor visits; and in case of breach to be presently [immediately] sent to Inverness in what weather soever it shall happen to be: for we

---

[11]W. Taylor, "The King's Mails, 1603–1625," *Scottish Historical Review* XLII (1963), 144.
[12]Quoted by A. G. R. Smith in *The Reign of James VI and I* [London, 1973], p. 1.

think it neither convenient nor tolerable that he, who opposeth himself against all bishops, should play the part of an universal bishop and like an Apostle go from place to place preaching the Gospel.[13]

James's continuing supervision of Scottish affairs helped obviate any really major crises until death ended his reign over his northern kingdom. With England it was rather a different story.

King James made a good impression on those who hastened to greet him when he arrived from Scotland in the spring of 1603. They met a stocky man of thirty-six, high-complexioned, with a short thin beard setting off a rather square face. His large eyes in repose seemed blankly protuberant, but an agile mind lay behind them, and a canny gleam or a worried glance would readily animate his features. Because of a weakness in his legs, he was awkward in his walk, but stationary he had a sufficiently impressive presence. A rather unfriendly observer conceded that he was "not uncomely." When he spoke, his voice was thick with a strong Scottish accent.

The first sixteen years of his reign in England were, on the whole, successful. When in 1606 widespread reports of his assassination proved to be untrue, the thanksgiving was general. The governance of England proceeded fairly smoothly, partly because King James retained Cecil as his first minister until the latter's death in 1612. Cecil, poised, sensitive, and industrious, was like James himself conservative, and the two men conducted what Archbishop Mathew has called "in some ways an old-fashioned government."[14] At least, with the conscientious and industrious Cecil looking after the routine of administration in London, the King was free to spend much of his time at his beloved hunting at Royston or Newmarket. Some historians have exaggerated the effects of James's absenteeism at his sport;

[13]*Original Letters Relating to the Ecclesiastical Affairs of Scotland,* Bannatyne Club No. 92 (Edinburgh, 1851), II: 837.
[14]*James I* (London, [1967]), p. 8.

actually he was more in touch than they seem to realize. He had a Clerk of the Signet in attendance upon him, and papers despatched from Whitehall at the end of a day's work normally reached the King at Royston early the next morning.[15] It is, of course, because of the time that James spent at his hunting in Cambridgeshire, away from Cecil, that we have those highly idiosyncratic "little beagle" letters to him which bulk large in this edition.

James's defence of the amount of time that he devoted to hunting was that his health required the exercise. Perhaps this explanation has been too cynically swept aside in the past, for King James did have problems with his health. Our source for detailed medical information about him is the memoir drawn up late in 1623 by Dr. Theodore Turquet de Mayerne, his personal physician.[16] According to Mayerne, James had a long history of insomnia, indigestion, chronic diarrhœa, kidney trouble, and almost daily bleeding from hæmorrhoids. When one remembers the sudden bursts of anger that James showed in his dealings with the House of Commons, one wonders if the royal hæmorrhoids may not have played a significant role in British parliamentary history.

A crisis in the King's health came in April 1619, one marked by vomiting, diarrhœa, fever, a reported "inequalitie, intermission and fayling of his pulse,"[17] and the passing of gallstones. James, expecting that death was coming for him as it had for his queen a month earlier, took his leave of Prince Charles and the principal lords in the court.

James recovered, but he would have cut a much better figure in

---

[15]Historical Manuscripts Commission, *Calendar of the Manuscripts of the Most Hon. the Marquess of Salisbury,* Part XVI (London, 1933), pp. 50, 219 (hereafter cited as HMC, *Salisbury MSS.*)

[16]See Norman Moore, *The History of the Study of Medicine in the British Isles* (Oxford, 1908), pp. 97–106 and appendix. The appendix contains Mayerne's notes in the original Latin.

[17]*The Letters of John Chamberlain,* ed. N. E. McClure (Philadelphia, 1939), II: 232.

the history books if he had died at this time. Heretofore, he had been, in the main, a successful monarch. He had been able to keep his court, made up of touchy English and Scottish grandees, in a state of reasonable harmony. He had ended the long war between England and Spain. He had kept as firm a control over the English Puritans as he had ultimately achieved over the Scottish Presbyterians. He had contrived to come through the greatest scandal to rock his court—that centring around the poisoning of Sir Thomas Overbury—with his personal honour untarnished in the eyes both of his own subjects and of the courts of Europe. And when in 1614 he had had a head-on collision with his parliament, it was that parliament and not the King whom the English had labelled as "addled." True, his finances had gone from bad to worse, and he had tolerated scandalous abuses by his officers, but his had been a passable record.

After 1619, more and more burnt out nervously, and weakened physically (though he would still rise at first light for his hunting), King James simply could not cope with the crises of the final years. He allowed the Spaniards to negate him politically by leading him into labyrinthine negotiations related to a fatuous plan to wed his son to a Spanish Infanta. Lacking military resources to aid his son-in-law to regain the territories that had been lost through the latter's rashness, James made himself absurd by his attempts to win back the Palatinate with words. Worst of all, he lost to Parliament the support and sympathy of the English people. The letters (near the end of this edition) written to his son and his favourite while they were in Spain, give us a fascinating view into the heart of the old king, and they reveal an abject emotional dependence upon his "boys" that must have made James almost ludicrous in the eyes of his own court. In the end, Prince Charles and Buckingham pushed him, intermittently protesting, towards the wings. Increasingly they themselves took over the direction of affairs. King James died on 27 March 1625.

Many have tried to delineate and appraise the character of

James VI & I.[18] During the long era of the Whig interpretation of history, especially after it became laced with Victorianism, King James was seen as a "mean and despicable" monarch, an inadequate and ineffective despot perversely hindering the powers of good in the form of parliamentary democracy. It is remarkable how long that view prevailed. One is startled to find N. E. McClure as late as 1939 dismissively referring to "James's weak and disgraceful rule."[19] A lot has changed since then. We now realize that, in the King's struggles with Parliament, it was more often Parliament than the King that was trespassing upon areas that precedent had given to the other. The alleged historical grounds for various parliamentary claims have appeared increasingly suspect. The case has been made that James in his first dealings with Parliament tempered firmness with moderation and conciliation, and that his troubles with the Commons were partly due to the ineptness of his councillors, who should have better instructed a new king unaccustomed to the workings of the English parliament. There is increasing realization that Parliament "wanted substantial administrative changes without paying the compensation to the Exchequer without which James would have been a fool to sanction such reforms."[20] King James has been found far more statesmanlike than the M.P.s in the negotiations concerning the union of England and Scotland. And there have been other changes. The repugnance caused by the aura of homosexuality that surrounds King James in his relationships with his handsome male favourites has now moderated somewhat, in consequence of the changing moral attitudes of the late twentieth century. We are looking at King James with clearer vision.

James was a man strikingly composed of strengths and weaknesses. His mental acuity is evident: he was a formidable

[18]Perhaps the best brief sketch has been that provided by Wallace Notestein in his *The House of Commons 1604–1610* (New Haven, 1971), pp. 15–23.

[19]*Letters of John Chamberlain*, I: 18.

[20]R. C. Munden, "James I and 'the growth of mutual distrust': King, Commons, and Reform 1603–1604," in Kevin Sharpe, ed., *Faction and Parliament* (Oxford, 1978), pp. 43–72.

opponent in political or theological debate. His substantial books established for him a merited reputation as a controversialist. And he was, for all his occasional uncouthness in manner and language, essentially a civilized man. James was a seventeenth-century king who could say of religious dissidents, "I would be sorry to punish their bodies for the error of their minds."[21] He was a king who tried to be just. Even the censorious S. R. Gardiner had to concede, "To do James justice, during the whole course of his reign he never allowed personal favour to shield anyone whom he had reason to believe guilty of actual crime."[22] Sir Anthony Weldon, bitter because James had deprived him of his office at court, still conceded, "He naturally loved honest men."[23] Good old Bishop Goodman recalled how at the beginning of his career, when he was little known to the King and had not sought out any patron in the court to recommend him, James sent word that he himself would attend to his advancement. His Majesty, according to Goodman, seemed even more joyful in giving him the deanery of Rochester than he himself was in receiving it.[24] One recalls how James looked after a more illustrious dean, John Donne, whom he recruited for the Anglican priesthood.

There was humanity and kindness in King James. When he believed that his old servant, John Gibb, had lost some important papers, in his anger he kicked him, but when he discovered that the fault was his own he went down on his knees to beg Gibb's pardon. Generally James was a pretty good judge of character. He could, said Sir Henry Wotton, peruse men as well as books. Wiser than his son, he refused to advance Laud beyond a petty bishopric.

---

[21] John Stow, *Annales, or A General Chronicle of England,* continued by Edmund Howes (London, 1631), p. 841.

[22] *History of England from the Accession of James I to the Outbreak of the Civil War 1603–1642* (London, 1883–1884), IV: 84.

[23] *The Court and Character of King James* (London, 1650), p. 183.

[24] Godfrey Goodman, *The Court of King James the First,* ed. J. S. Brewer (London, 1839), I: 356.

On the other hand, James had a seriously flawed character. There was a basic insecurity in him which made him more or less demand the flattery which surrounded him—not a commodity that honest men liked to provide. He was devious and partial. Queen Anne warned Lady Anne Clifford not to accept James's offer to arbitrate between her and her husband, for James would probably deceive Lady Anne. When James refused a suit, rather than openly accept responsibility for his denial he would confide to the loser that he had "very heavy enemies in the court." In his devious manoeuvres, quite as much as in his dislike for applauding crowds, he resembled the "old fantastical duke of dark corners" in *Measure for Measure*.[25]

James was a monarch who was both impulsive and indecisive. Clarendon took his measure:

> very quicksighted in discerning difficulties and raising objections, and very slow in mastering them and untying the knots he made: in a word, he knew not how to wrestle with desperate contingencies, and so abhorred the being entangled with such.[26]

James liked to have life and gaiety about him. He affected a manner of jaunty good humour. But when distractions failed and he was left vulnerable to black thoughts, he could turn unpleasant. A Venetian correspondent recalled the scene one night at court:

> Last of all they danced the Spanish dance ... and being well nigh tired they began to lag, whereupon the king, who is naturally choleric, got impatient and shouted aloud, "Why don't they dance? What did they make me come here for? Devil take you all, dance."[27]

---

[25]IV, iii, 164. For the suggestion that Shakespeare was fitting into the play a portrait of King James, see the New Cambridge Shakespeare edition of the play, p. 118.

[26]*The History of the Rebellion and Civil Wars* (Oxford, 1888), I: 14–15.

[27]*Calendar of State Papers, Venetian, 1617–1619*, pp. 113–14.

James could not endure the presence of death. Fleeing from Whitehall to Theobalds, he absented himself from the sick-room where his son, the Prince of Wales, was dying. He attended neither Prince Henry's funeral nor that of Queen Anne.

Very much the Scot, King James liked to have his cronies about him. That was part of his trouble—a court full of cronyism is less than conducive to good government. Yet despite his desire to have friends ranged about him, King James was not good at establishing rapport with people. Professor Notestein has commented on how the quiet, sensitive Cecil must have winced at times at the heavy-handed humour of the "little beagle" letters.[28] James seemed to feel that friends had to be bought. Weldon observed how, in order to win a place in the King's circle, one had first of all to be the recipient of some royal benefit.[29] James went on the assumption that largesse secured allegiance and affection. Sending a renewed message (Letter 175) to the Lord Treasurer of Scotland to pay three thousand pounds—a great sum in those days—to the Marquess of Hamilton, he hopefully observed, "I assure myself his service will repay my liberality with a double interest." Of course, rich gifts too often brought only repining in others and, from the recipient, petitions for more.

There was another reason why King James poured forth his treasure: in his heart he felt that it was his duty to do so. Thoroughly a Renaissance prince, he believed in the role of the ruler as the fountain of honour and reward. He saw himself as losing honour—and honour was a constant theme with him—if he were not generous in bounty. In Letter 173 James issued a clarion call for economy in the royal household. But there is a fatal qualifying clause in that letter: the economizing must be so done as "to agree with honour." Real economies, by eclipsing his state, would dishonour him. It has been pointed out that, had James

[28]*House of Commons 1604–1610*, p. 18.
[29]*Court and Character of King James*, p. 183.

given his Lord Treasurers the powers and support that Henri IV gave to Sully and Louis XIV gave to Colbert, he could have escaped from the quagmire of debt.[30] But to have asked King James to use such rigour would have been to ask the impossible.

King James was a man who, in his own twisted fashion, loved profoundly. Brought up without kin, disappointed in a frivolous and rather difficult wife, he turned chiefly to his male favourites for love. He endured anguish when they denied him their affection. Once he had given his heart, he found it a torment to withdraw it. All this is spelt out for us in that long, agonizing Letter 159, in which he pleads for Somerset's love. A colder monarch would have dealt summarily with Somerset long before. The favourite's arrogance had become intolerable. The whole court had been thrown miserably out of joint. Only James could have let things drag on in this excruciating manner. But still he pleaded with the man to whom he had given so much.

No verdict passed on King James's reign should be sweepingly unfavourable. After all, until his final years, James did in rather a ramshackle way contrive to hold things together. He maintained peace. He got the Scots and English living together. He tried to deal reasonably with Parliament and the Puritans. He attempted some reforms. Despite the strains that had been building up in the social structure ever since the middle years of Elizabeth, he managed to avoid the cataclysm which came in his son's time. Twenty years ago, in an earlier book on King James and his court,[31] the present editor occasioned some mild dissent by maintaining that James was not such a bad king after all. Since then, "revisionist" historians have done a lot to rehabilitate King James. The danger now is that we may overestimate him. The verdict in the writer's earlier book still seems to him

[30]Menna Prestwich, "English Politics and Administration," in A. G. R. Smith, ed., *Reign of James VI and I*, pp. 143–44.
[31]G. P. V. Akrigg, *Jacobean Pageant, or The Court of King James I* (Cambridge, Mass., 1962).

the right one—agreement with Sir Robert Cotton when he said that he would be content that England should never have a better king, provided that she should never have a worse one.

II

If by a "royal letter" one means any message carrying the signature of a king, the number of royal letters surviving from the reigns of King James in Scotland and England is enormous. Once started in quest of them, one finds them everywhere. Many hundreds, even thousands, survive in the Public Record Office in London and a multitude more in the British Library. County record offices swell the total. The calendars of the Historical Manuscripts Commission list many in private collections, with pride of place taken by the Marquess of Salisbury's tremendous wealth of material at Hatfield.[32] Though Cambridge has a number of James's letters, Oxford is much richer in them. Among the many volumes of manuscripts in the Bodleian that contain letters by James, one (Ashmol. 1729) preserves the text of forty-one letters, nearly all written during the first six weeks of his reign in England. Among the extensive holdings of the Scottish Record Office in Edinburgh are the letters of King James to the Earl of Mar; the years 1621–1625 account for no fewer than seventy-nine of these letters, none of them unfortunately of a personal nature. The National Library of Scotland, incorporating the old Advocates' Library, is another prime source.

As if there were not material enough in Britain, there is more abroad. Some of the King's letters have migrated to the United States, including six of the most interesting printed in this vol-

---

[32]Special thanks are due to Lord Salisbury, not only for giving the editor permission to print the letters of King James in his possession but also for allowing him to work with them in the muniment room at Hatfield.

In this edition the original manuscripts are referred to as the Cecil Papers. The multivolume calendar of these papers, prepared by the Historical Manuscripts Commission, is referred to as HMC, *Salisbury MSS.*

ume. A quite surprising number survive in various archives on the Continent. About two hundred letters in Latin and two in English are in the Rigsarkivet in Copenhagen. One hundred and thirty-nine of these Latin letters, written after James became King of England, were published in microfiche in 1977 by Professor Ronald M. Meldrum. At least forty letters, some originals and others copies, survive in the Bibliothèque Nationale in Paris. Back in 1931, J. H. Baxter reported his discovery of thirty-five of James's letters in the Archivio di Stato in Turin.[33] Hitherto unreported are forty-two of his letters in the Archivio Mediceo (F. 4183) of the Archivio di Stato in Florence. Nine letters surviving in the Archivio di Stato in Venice are noted in the volumes of the *Calendar of State Papers (Venetian)*. In the course of an admittedly hurried search in the Archivo General at Simancas in Spain, the present editor could find only two original letters and a few copies (Legajos 2849, 2850). Three minor Latin letters were found in the Archives Générales du Royaume de Belgique at Brussels. It was simply not practicable to dig for letters from James in the enormous mass of uncatalogued material in the Algemeen Rijkarchief in The Hague. There was nothing in the Koninklijke Bibliotheek but, with the gracious permission of Her Majesty the Queen of the Netherlands, the keeper of her personal library, a most courtly and distinguished gentleman, came up with a single letter from King James. Unfortunately this, like so many of the King's letters found during this reconnaissance on the Continent, proved to be just one more of those innumerable vapid Latin letters of compliment that the sovereigns and princes of Renaissance Europe despatched to each other.[34]

[33]"Unpublished Letters of James VI," *Scottish Notes and Queries* Series 3, IX (1931), 114.

[34]These letters did serve certain diplomatic purposes. They afforded a convenient pretext for the despatch of a messenger who could transact business in a court where there was no British agent. They helped to keep alliances in repair and to preserve contacts. For a good specimen of the genre see R. M. Meldrum, ed., *The Letters of King James I of England to King Christian IV of Denmark* (Harvester Press microfiches, 1977), pp. 51–52.

Those wishing to examine in Britain specimens of King James's Latin foreign correspondence are referred to MS. Ff. 4.25 in Cambridge University Library, where they will find the texts of seventy-three letters written between 1603 and 1609 to recipients ranging from the King of Poland to "The Grand Signor" (the Sultan Achomet). For further royal correspondence in Latin one may turn to Add. MS. 12485 in the British Library, a register containing copies of over three hundred Latin letters sent over the King's signature to such diverse persons as the Archduke Albert and his wife in Brussels, the King of France, assorted French dukes, the city of Strasbourg, the canton of Berne, Marquis Spinola, the Prince of Piedmont, and the Assembly General of Reformed Churches at La Rochelle. The foregoing list does not indicate anything like the full scope of the royal correspondence. King James also sent letters to the rulers of Russia,[35] Abyssinia,[36] China,[37] Japan,[38] Persia,[39] Sumatra, and Turkey.[40] A grandiloquent reply from Sumatra can be found in the Bibliothèque Nationale.[41]

After this brief survey of King James's foreign correspondence, let us turn to his multitudinous surviving letters to persons within his domains. These exhibit a remarkable range: intimate letters to members of his own family and to his favourites and cronies, letters of instruction to his principal ministers, testimonial letters for returning foreign ambassadors, letters of credence and instruction for departing English ambassadors, letters summoning recipients to attend Conventions of the Estates and General Assemblies in Scotland, sum-

[35]For James's sixteen letters to Muscovy, see I. Lubimenko, "The Correspondence of the First Stuarts with the First Romanovs," *Transactions of the Royal Historical Society* Series 4, I (1918), 77–91.

[36]British Library, Cotton MSS., Nero B XI: 138.

[37]Now in the James Ford Bell Library of the University of Minnesota (MS. 1614 oJa), this letter was formerly in the More MSS. at Linley Hall in Shropshire. Its text is printed in HMC, *10th Report*, Part 4: 407–8.

[38]Letter 152.

[39]India Office Records, MSS., Persia I: 1620–1710, No. 632.

[40]Letter 170.

[41]*Fonds Français*, No. 16141, ff. 263ᵛ–266ʳ.

mons also to appear before the Council of Scotland or the Council in England, letters of commendation to meritorious subjects and letters of rebuke to offending ones, letters ordering arrests, imprisonment, or release, letters granting posts or pensions, letters asking support for litigants, letters requesting loans, letters of thanks for gifts of dogs, horses, hawks, partridges, and wine.

No matter seemed too small for a royal letter. We have, for instance, a letter from Scotland to James Hudson in London asking him to assist the bearer, George Smith, to secure twelve tuns of double London beer "becaus it is nocht unknawin to yow that o^r dairest spouse is daylie accustumed to drink of the same."[42] One royal letter asks the Earl of Mar for two couple of fox terriers, and another asks him to supply the Marquess of Buckingham with young fir trees. A royal letter instructs Justices of the Peace in Northumberland to repair Haydon Bridge. A royal letter asks the Mayor of Exeter to permit the Bishop of Exeter to cut a doorway through the city wall so that the latter may have more easy access abroad for his health. A royal letter to the Lord Deputy in Ireland asks that the fines for attaching ploughs to horses' tails be strictly levied. A royal letter to Sir William Curteen informs him that he would do well to marry one of his three daughters to the son of Sir Richard Fleetwood, Baron of Newton, and he is told that the King will look with favour upon any increase in dowry given to the girl at the expense of her sisters. A royal letter asks Lord Chandos to abate his displeasure at his daughter's marriage to Sir John Kennedy, who enjoys the King's regard. A royal letter asks the Mayor of Coventry to renew the lease of Cowden Farm to one of His Majesty's chaplains. Another royal letter asks the Company of Fishmongers of London to lease two tenements to Gilbert Penven, a Yeoman of the Guard. Still another royal letter asks the Lord Mayor of London to let Julian Miccote, an Italian, run a lottery for four months. And on and on the list could be continued.

[42]Public Record Office , SP 52/55/28.

Certain things are obvious. Only a small proportion of the letters signed by the King were actually either composed or dictated by him. Most were drafted by clerks or secretaries and perfunctorily signed by the King with hardly a glance. (Significantly, in 1608 an embarrassing letter from King James to the Pope was explained away by a declaration that Secretary Balmerino had treacherously slipped it into a pile of letters which His Majesty had signed without reading.)[43] Certainly the advantages of having "a friend at court" become manifest when one sees how easily a suitably placed friend could obtain for a man a royal letter to help him get anything from a bride to a university fellowship.

Occasionally the King's lack of awareness concerning the piles of papers presented for his signature could have amusing or embarrassing consequences. Thus in January 1604, Richard Caple obtained a letter from the King to the President of Magdalen College, Oxford, asking him to admit Caple to a fellowship previously held by a Mr. Pocock. Unfortunately, a certain Mr. Warner also obtained a letter from the King recommending him for this fellowship. The result was that the President of Magdalen was put in the unpleasant position of having to ask His Majesty whom he really wanted. The result was a third letter saying that Caple was the man.

III

Some sort of pattern can be imposed upon King James's correspondence if we view it in terms of the following categories:

1. Letters under the sign manual

A *sign manual* is defined by the *Oxford English Dictionary* as "an autograph signature (esp. that of the sovereign) serving to

---

[43]See Letter 141 and headnote.

authenticate a document." King James's signature when it serves as a sign manual appears at the head of a letter, not its foot. Most of those very minor letters which we have just mentioned are sign-manual letters. Clearly they were a routine means of dealing with petty government business. The procedure involved in the preparation of a sign-manual letter is suggested by a 1604 preliminary draft preserved in the Public Record Office (SP 14/7/26a). Its text has been neatly engrossed by a scribe. One clause has been struck out, and in the lower left-hand corner is a bold notation, "ex T. Lake," indicating that Sir Thomas Lake, Clerk of the Signet, had approved the amended text for submission to the King.

It would be a mistake to dismiss all sign-manual letters as routine government paperwork. Important instructions to ambassadors would be sent under the sign manual, and the King's very friendly and quite personal note to the Earl of Cumberland a few days before the latter's death (Letter 126) went to him under the sign manual.

2. *Secretarial letters signed at the close by the King*

These are generally, but not invariably, of more importance and greater status than the much more numerous sign-manual letters. Occasionally the identity of the secretaries who drafted these letters can be discovered. Thus we know who composed a whole series of Latin letters between 1619 and 1623 because Thomas Read, Latin Secretary to the King, kept copies in a letterbook which has survived.[44]

Rarely did King James follow Henry VIII's practice of going over letters drafted for him and making alterations.[45] The

---

[44]British Library, Add. MS. 38597.

[45]A copy of Letter 99 (PRO SP 14/5/8) has been identified (*CSP Dom. 1603–10*, p. 57) as a draft bearing corrections in the King's hand, but such is not the case. The writing hardly resembles that of the King, the *th* combination, for example, being markedly different. According to Stow, James wrote this letter entirely in his own hand. The PRO letter is a copy in which the original Scottish

checking of drafts of important letters seems to have been generally left to one or another of the Secretaries of State. Thus the draft for a royal letter of 22 May 1603 to the Privy Council exhibits changes made in the hand of Cecil (Cecil Papers 100: 30). Of course, important letters intended for the royal signature could be drafted entirely by the Secretaries of State themselves.

After Cecil's death in 1612, the King's favourite, Robert Carr, who became Earl of Somerset, served for a while as an unofficial Secretary of State. Letter 153 in this volume survives in the hand of Carr. The greatest of all James's favourites in England, George Villiers, whom he made Duke of Buckingham, also wrote letters for him. Thus we have in Buckingham's hand the King's letter of 25 October 1622 preserved in the Digby Papers at Sherborne (Vol. I: f. 134).

3. Holograph letters

One cannot always assume that letters that survive in King James's own hand were composed by the monarch himself. Wishing to pay an eminent person the compliment of a letter in the royal hand but shirking the labour of authorship, James was not above having an underling compose a letter which he would then copy out himself. Evidence is supplied by Sir James Melville, who proudly notes in his *Memoirs:*

> Vnto this lettre [a holograph from Elizabeth in 1583], his Maieste commandit me to minut ane answer in his hyenes name, that he mycht wret it over again with his awen hand.[46]

---

spellings have been anglicized. Somebody has amused himself by restoring Scottish spellings: it is very doubtful that James would ever have indulged in so picayune an exercise.

[46]Bannatyne Club No. 18 (Edinburgh, 1827), p. 297.

The vast majority of King James's holograph letters are, however, truly and completely his.

An impressive number of royal holographs survive. The present editor has personally examined 227 holographs, of which 154 are included in the present edition. These surviving letters represent only a fraction of those which the King penned. Thus in Letter 194, written in March 1623, James reports that he has written five letters to Buckingham's wife, two to his sister and one to his mother, "all in my own hand"—yet none of these can be found today.

Why did King James so often do his own letter-writing even when, in his later years, arthritis had made penmanship so painful that at the last he was using a stamp[47] to affix his signature to minor letters? Part of the answer is that James was a literary man who clearly found pleasure in writing letters. Strongly moved, he would grab a pen and find relief in dashing off a letter of his own rather than waiting for one to be prepared by a subordinate. Sometimes after signing a letter presented for his signature he would add a postscript in his own hand (e.g., Letter 158). Sometimes, when a letter was to deal with a very sensitive matter, King James made and revised his own first draft, then sent a polished final draft to the recipient. An example is Letter 27, with which James replied to Queen Elizabeth's own letter informing him that his mother had been beheaded. The draft with its alterations is reproduced as Plate II.

To the everlasting gratitude of his present editor, the King, who as a boy had been trained to write a beautiful italic script, maintained a very legible hand throughout his life even though his writing coarsened with the progress of time. One curious mannerism marks it: over the indefinite article "a" the King habitually placed an acute accent.

---

[47]For the order of 8 July 1624 authorizing the making of this stamp, see PRO SP 14/169/32. For a sign-manual letter with a stamped signature, see Huntington Library MS. 7161.

Madame & dearest Sister ~~I have receaued~~ youre letir be ~~youre~~

~~youre seruand & ambassadoure~~ ... ye purge

youre sels of yone unhappy fact as on the one pairt

consiodering youre rank & sexe, consanguinitie & longe pro

fessed goode will to the defunct together with youre many

& solemnie attestationis of youre innocentie I darr not

wronge you so farre as not to iudge honorablie of youre un

spotted pairt thairin So on the other syde I wishe that

youre honorable behavioure in all tymes heirafter may

fully perswaide the quhole worlde ~~of youre innocent~~ of the same

~~pairt thairin~~ & as for my pairt I looke & if that ye will

~~at this tyme litle~~ geve me at this tyme suche a

fall satisfaction in all respectis ~~a priefe of youre honorable & kynde dealing toua~~

this bearere

hath sumquhat

to informe you   ~~dis me~~ as sall be a meane to strenthin & unite this

of in my name   yle, establishe & maintaine the trew religion, & oblis

quhom I neid noce   me to be as of before I was youre most louing

desyre you to credit

for ye knou sto... him

Apart from the King's very distinctive hand, there are other means of identifying a letter personally written by King James. For one thing, whereas in letters drafted for the King by others the traditional "kingly we" is used throughout, James invariably uses the first person singular in letters which he wrote himself. Another characteristic of the letters penned by the King is the curtailed or informal nature of the salutation. A scribal letter to Queen Elizabeth begins elaborately "Right excellent, right high and mighty princess, our dearest sister and cousin, in our heartiest manner we recommend us unto you"; James, penning a letter of his own to her, begins simply "Madame and dearest sister." Similarly the King, when writing in a familiar vein, will dispense with formulary openings such as "Right trusty and right well-beloved cousin, we greet you well," and plunge into his letter with "Sandy" or "My little beagle."[48]

4. *Holograph letters that survive only in copies*

Because of features such as those just noted above, no great penetration is needed to identify various manuscripts as copies that preserve for us the texts of lost holograph originals. Quite a number of such copies survive, thanks partly to seventeenth- and eighteenth-century antiquaries who ardently collected royal letters and often acquired copies of holographs in each other's collections. The present edition contains a number of letters which, although scrupulously noted as "apparently" copies of lost holographs, are in the editor's own mind quite obviously such.

King James has a number of idiosyncratic spellings. Some of these are Scotticisms, of which we must take note shortly. Others are forms such as "ame" for "am," "ather" for "either," "bearare" for "bearer," "cace" for "case," and the use of "kk" for "ck" in such forms as "Bukkingham," "bakkward," and "quikke." Unfortunately, since copyists usually anglicized King James's letters and used their own spelling for his words, the

---

[48]Cf. Letters 38 and 105.

royal spelling is of little use in detecting copies of lost holographs. While on the subject of the royal spelling, we may note that James, in an age before orthography became standardized, regarded some spellings as preferable to others. Having written "broche," he carefully corrected it by inserting a caret mark and an "a" between the "o" and "c" (Harl. 6987, f. 30^r and again on f. 30^v). Having written "presente," he thoughtfully put a stroke through the final "e" (Harl. 6987, f. 1^v).

IV

Since King James holds a secure position in the ranks of secondary figures in English literature,[49] one turns with some eagerness to judge the literary quality of his letters. Not surprisingly, the King could write good letters, terse pithy ones such as Letters 172 and 173, amusing good-natured ones such as Letters 109 and 123, ones skillfully constructed with the elaboration of statement admired in the author's day, such as Letter 80. On the other hand, with the rare exceptions of Letters 71 and 176, James did not write his letters as additions to his literary corpus. Only in letters calculated to impress did he trouble himself with literary polish. Paradoxically, for one who prided himself on "the concised shortness of my style," James (possibly relaxing after a day of hunting) could write long slovenly letters, confusing in syntax and anything but precise in phrasing. Fortunately, even in these rather meandering missives a sudden gleam of humour, a pungent comment, or a vivid phrase lightens the way.

Whereas the twentieth century uses clichés for stock-in-trade, the seventeenth century fell back on proverbs. James's letters are constantly reinforced with proverbs, not only the Latin maxims to be expected of a Renaissance prince but

---

[49]See G. P. V. Akrigg, "The Literary Achievement of King James I," *University of Toronto Quarterly* XLIV (1975), 115–29.

homely Scottish and English adages. "According to the old proverb," he reminds Queen Elizabeth, "it is better late thrive than never,"[50] and in a dedicatory letter to Buckingham he observes "old men are twice babes, as the proverb is."[51]

Some readers may be surprised that, even in his most intimate letters, the King still signs with his customary "James R." This invariable use of the kingly form is not a peculiarity in James but a matter of tradition. Byrne notes that Henry VIII signed even the most personal of his letters "Henry R."[52]

For an editor who has followed James and his letters from the early boyhood note to the Countess of Mar to the last blotched scrawls, there is a certain pathos to the final years. Failing energies and crippling arthritis made it harder and harder for him to write. Possibly the latest of James's holograph letters to survive is one at Windsor, the briefest of notes to the King of France.[53] This is so blotted and corrected that apparently somebody decided that it would be an insult to send it to the French king and so it was put aside to become the only letter of James, in his own hand, to enter into the personal possession of Elizabeth II.

V

King James could, when he wished, write using the vocabulary accepted in England, and his letters to Queen Elizabeth from early youth onwards, though they use Scottish spellings, are comparatively free from Scotticisms. On the other hand, during the greater part of his life James was a Scot living among Scots, and various of his letters to his fellow countrymen are written in good homely Lallan. In these latter letters we find an abundance of Scottish words such as "allanerlie" (alone), "buddit"

[50]Letter 54.   [51]Letter 176.
[52]*The Letters of King Henry VIII*, ed. M. St. Clare Byrne, (2nd ed. New York, 1968), p. xviii.
[53]Royal Archives, Stuart Add. MSS. 1/120.

(bribed), "sensyne" (since then), "fascherie" (trouble), "lippen" (to trust), "horneris" (outlaws), and "maun" (must). Typical of James's Scottish letters is the following unaddressed and undated holograph:

> I uas at á lang conference uith yone erl of ouris efter youre depairting yistrein surelie he hes delt uerie plainlie uith me & ye sall find that he sall recompence yone bairnlie conceatis uith obedient deidis patrike murraye is presentlie to be at you & thairfore be freindlie plaine uith him & in the mene tyme kepe all oure folkis on starting ouir meikill at yone man quhill ye heir mair of me. faireueill,
>
> JAMES R.[54]

In England James remained faithful to the Scottish "quh," writing "quho," "quhen," and "quhat" for "who," "when," and "what," but apart from these forms the King more and more used English English even in his informal correspondence, though he did not quickly purge himself of words and forms such as "fashit," "thoch," "richtlie," "micht," and "sleichtlie." Gradually, however, the partial anglicization of James Stuart proceeded. In a letter to the Earl of Mar in May 1618, he wrote "thoght" (not "thocht"), "owin" (not "awin"), and "knowe" (not "knaw"). By 1623 King James was beginning to waver even in his allegiance to "quh" and, meeting the English halfway, addressed a letter from "qwhitehall."

VI

Letters from King James have been published in a number of collections, and the most important of these must be noted here. Henry Ellis printed careful Old Spelling texts for eighteen of King James's letters in his *Original Letters Illustrative of English*

---

[54]British Library, Add. MS. 23241, f. 11.

History (1824–1846). Ellis was followed in 1848 by J. O. Halliwell (later Halliwell-Phillipps), who included eighty-three letters by James in his two-volume *Letters of the Kings of England*. Since Halliwell's is the most comprehensive selection of James's letters hitherto available, it has been the one most frequently used. Unfortunately it is completely unreliable, being one of the horrors of Victorian "scholarship." Halliwell, for instance, dealing with what becomes Letter 198 in the present edition, lops off two-thirds and unblushingly prints the remaining third as a complete letter.[55] He makes silent excisions left and right. Many of these are inspired by Victorian notions of propriety. "We regret," says Halliwell, "to add that, in some instances, the extreme grossness of the originals has compelled us to make a few inconsiderable omissions."[56] If only the omissions had been few and inconsiderable! But Halliwell, when he comes to King James's blessing upon Buckingham and his pregnant wife "and the sweet little thing that is in her belly" (Letter 182), removes these last ten words without any sign of omission.[57] As for Letter 209 in which, as we earlier noted, James urges his son, negotiating for a marriage in Spain, to think "as well upon the business of Christendom as upon the codpiece point," Halliwell makes the King speak vaguely of "the [other] point."[58]

Halliwell's slipshod transcripts are riddled with errors. Thus James's greeting, "Sweete hairte," addressed to Buckingham in Letter 226, becomes not "Sweet heart" but "My Sweet Hearty"[59]—though here we may have censorship rather than carelessness. Halliwell sets something of a record with his text for Letter 227, supplying seven misreadings within its total length of some two hundred words. It is here that he reads "the big rich man" for "the bigge irishe man."[60] Dealing with Letter 205, in which King James reports the arrival from Spain of the Earl of Carlisle, "todos Castillanos" (i.e., having everything

[55] *Letters of the Kings of England* (London, 1848), II: 192.
[56] Ibid., I: xxxi.   [57] Ibid., II: 150.   [58] Ibid., II: 220.
[59] Ibid., II: 155.   [60] Ibid., II: 158.

about him Castilian), the ineffable Halliwell presents us with "Carlisle came yesterday to Dos Castellanos,"[61] leaving his readers to wonder who or where Dos Castellanos may be. Halliwell is hopeless with proper names. Sir Robert Carr (Letter 191) becomes "Sir Robert Cave," Buckingham's sister Sue (Letter 190) becomes "Sal," and his infant daughter Mary, nicknamed "Mall" (Letter 224), becomes "little Mawde." It hardly comes as a surprise to find Secretary Conway (Letter 211) presented as Secretary Coventry.

In 1849 John Bruce published his *Letters of Queen Elizabeth and King James VI of Scotland,* in which he gave Old Spelling texts for sixty-two of Elizabeth's letters to James and thirty-three of James's letters to Elizabeth. In 1861 Bruce followed this with his *Correspondence of King James VI of Scotland with Sir Robert Cecil and Others in England,* in which he gave fourteen letters by King James, thirteen being part of the secret correspondence of 1601–1603. Bruce occasionally makes a slip in his transcriptions, but his errors are few compared with those of Halliwell. Bruce, like Ellis, must be treated with respect.

Turning to the calendars published by the Historical Manuscripts Commission, we find that the most important volumes as far as King James's letters are concerned are those devoted to the Marquess of Salisbury's Cecil Papers at Hatfield. The work of the HMC editors is remarkably uneven. Sometimes they offer Old Spelling texts, sometimes modernized ones. Without warning they switch to paraphrases or cut versions. Thus they give us what appears to be the complete text of Letter 141 but it is really only a paraphrase half the original length.[62] Moreover, the outwardly impressive tomes of the Historical Manuscripts Commission contain a surprising number of misreadings. In the HMC text (XVI: 393–94) of Letter 121, for example, "parforme" is given as "pay for me," "fewaire" as "swear," and "intercessouris" as "intercession."

---

[61]Ibid., II: 203.   [62]HMC, *Salisbury MSS.,* XX: 253.

The volumes of the *Calendar of the State Papers Relating to Scotland and Mary Queen of Scots, 1547–1603,* published at intervals since 1903, bear the identifying phrase "Preserved in the Public Record Office, the British Museum, and Elsewhere in England." The "elsewhere" was never very extensive, and the twelfth volume amends the phrase to read simply "Preserved in the Public Record Office and the British Museum." Even where these two archives are concerned, *CSP Scottish* has numerous omissions as far as the letters of James VI are concerned. As in the HMC volumes, the work is decidedly uneven. We are given, for instance, only a truncated version of Letter 54, one which renders "renounced any further dealing with thaim but by extremitie" as "vowed to pursue them by extremity."[63]

VII

The present edition contains two hundred and twenty-seven of the more important and representative letters of King James. Over four hundred other letters, available in print elsewhere, are noted in a finding-list, the appendix to this volume.

Most of the letters in this edition survive in holograph. Some fifty-four of the letters chosen for inclusion are now printed for the first time. Except in half a dozen instances where no manuscripts survive, new transcripts have been made and these have been checked against existing printed texts.

The choice between an Old Spelling text and a modernized one was difficult. Whatever way that decision went, it would find disfavour in some quarters. Originally this was to have been an Old Spelling edition. A review, however, of several hundred indigestible pages preserving the original spelling and punctuation (or lack of it) emphasized the virtues of a modernized text. After all, why should readers have to pause to deduce

[63]*CSP Scottish, 1593–95,* p. 437.

that "uou" means "vow"? Moreover, a laboriously preserved Old Spelling would keep for many of the letters not the spelling of King James but that of sundry clerks. Cogent, also, was the warning against Old Spelling given by the Yale editors of Horace Walpole's correspondence:

> What is amusing and "flavoursome" in small doses becomes wearisome in large, and it imparts an air of quaintness to a text which is not apparent to the correspondents themselves.[64]

Those who wish to see what the King's letters looked like when they left his pen are referred to Plates II and III.

King James's Scottish spellings have been anglicized: thus "awin" appears as "own" and "thocht" as "thought." Whenever, however, James uses distinctively Scottish words such as "al-lanerlie," "lippen," "fashid," these have been kept, marked with an asterisk, and explained in the book's glossary. Whenever it has seemed particularly desirable to place the original spelling of the manuscripts before the reader, quotation marks have been used to signal the brief departure from a modernized text.

Though spelling, punctuation, and capitalization have been modernized, King James's syntax has been preserved. One consequence is that the reader may feel that James made a remarkable number of errors in the agreement of his subjects and verbs. It must be remembered, however, that where inflected or uninflected present-tense verbs are concerned, Middle Scots differed significantly from English.[65] We must guard against mistaking Scotticisms for solecisms.

The dating of the letters has presented a number of problems. Though the King carefully dated most of his early letters, with the passage of time he became increasingly careless about

---

[64] *Horace Walpole's Correspondence with the Rev. William Cole*, ed. W. S. Lewis and A. Dayle Wallace (New Haven, 1937), p. xxxvi.

[65] See G. Gregory Smith, *Specimens of Middle Scots* (Edinburgh, 1902), pp. xxxv–xxxviii.

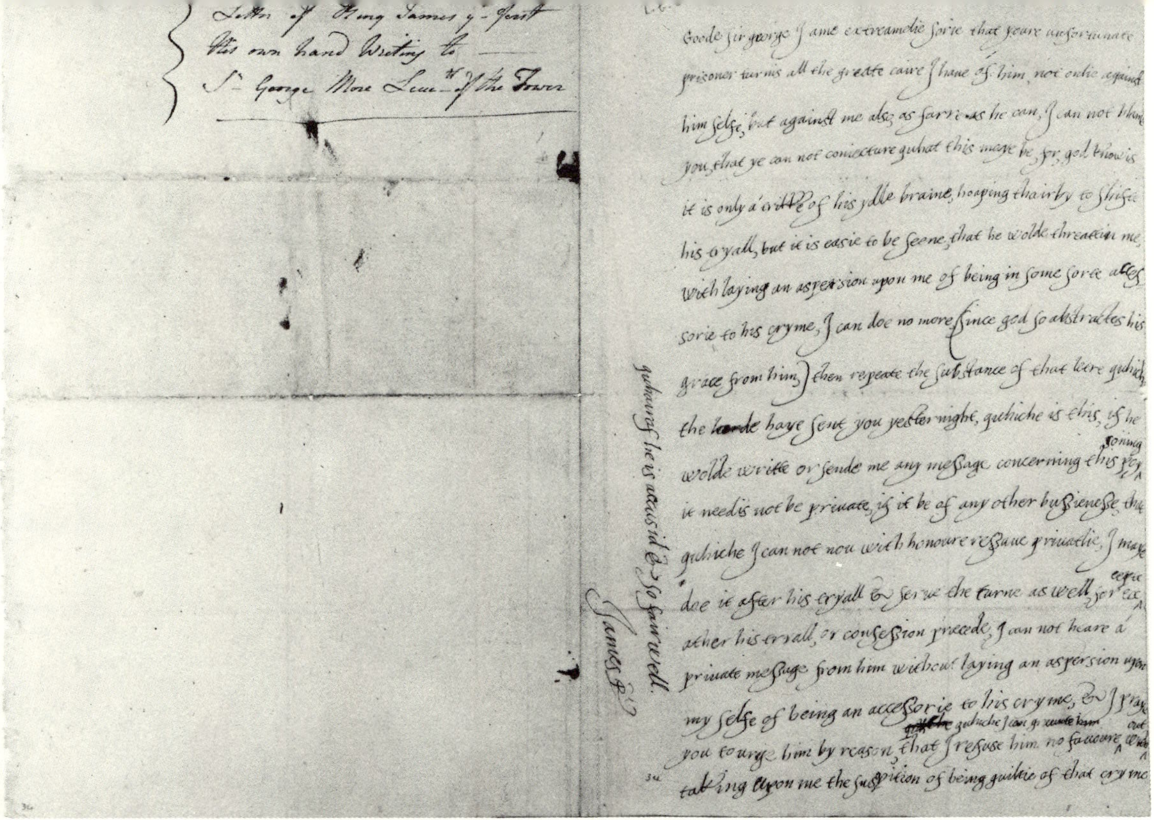
Letter of King James ye first
His own hand Writing to
Sr George More Lieut of the Tower

Goode sir george I ame extreamlie sorie that youre unfortunate
prisoner turnis all the greate caire I haue of him, not onlie against
him selfe, but against me also, as farre as he can, I can not blame
you, that ye can not coniecture quhat this maye be, for, god knowis
it is only a tricke of his ydle braine, hoaping thairby to shifte
his tryall, but it is easie to be seene, that he wolde threattin me,
with laying an aspersion upon me of being in some sorte acces
sorie to his cryme, I can doe no more (since god so abstractes his
grace from him) then repeate the substance of that lettre quhiche
the ~~lorde~~ haye sent you yesternight, quhiche is this, if he
wolde writte or sende me any message concerning this poysoning
it needis not be priuate, if it be of any other busienesse that
quhiche I can not nou with honoure resaue priuatelie, I maye
doe it after his tryall & serue the turne as well, for except
either his tryall, or confession preceade, I can not heare a
priuate message from him without laying an aspersion upon
my selfe of being an accessorie to his cryme, & I praye
you to urge him by reason that I refuse him no favoure which I can grante him
taking upon me the suspicion of being guiltie of that cryme
quhairof he is accusid & so fairwell.
James R.

Plate III. Letter 167, Original Manuscript in the King's Hand.
(By permission of the Folger Shakespeare Library)

dates and in his familiar letters he generally gives no dates at all, leaving his editor to do the best he could with internal evidence. Of major assistance in dating a number of the letters are the endorsed dates which they carry, but these seem generally to be dates of receipt rather than of despatch. As was noted earlier, usually a day would elapse between James's writing of a letter at his hunting lodge at Newmarket or at Royston and its arrival in London. Letter 163, one from Newmarket that carries at its close the date 12 November, has been endorsed by a clerk:

Novemb. 13, 1615
ffrom his Matie to M^{r}
Secretary winwood.

Where endorsed dates have been used for letters, the reader's attention is drawn to the fact. The Old Style dating of the letters has been preserved, though modern usage has been followed in beginning each year on 1 January, not on 25 March.

G.P.V. Akrigg
Celista, British Columbia

THE LETTERS

Letter 1

To Annabel Erskine, Countess of Mar

Born in Edinburgh Castle on 19 June 1566, James VI of Scotland was crowned in Stirling on 29 July 1567. His mother, Mary Queen of Scots, had crossed into England the previous May. There she was to spend the rest of her life in captivity and never to see her son again. The Earl of Moray became the first of a series of regents to govern Scotland, and the infant king was entrusted to the care of Annabel, Countess of Mar. The following letter is probably the earliest surviving in the boy-king's hand.

[*mid 1570s*]

Lady Minny,[1]

This is to show you that I have received your fruit and thanks you therefore, and is ready for mee*[2] when ye please to send them, and shall gif* as few by me as I may. And I will not trouble you farther till meeting which shall be as shortly as I may, God willing. And so fare ye well as I do, thanks to God.

JAMES R.

Scottish Record Office　　　　　　　　　　　　　　　*Holograph*
GD 124/10/45

[1]"Minny" is a familiar Scots word for "mother."
[2]Though not recorded in the *Dictionary of the Older Scottish Tongue*, "mee" is probably, like "mea," a variant of "ma," meaning "more." Words marked with an asterisk are explained in the glossary to this edition.

Letter 2

To George Buchanan

The supervision of the education of the boy-king was entrusted to that redoubtable and cantankerous scholar George

41

Buchanan. This letter to him is best regarded as a form of school exercise. The sentiments expressed must have been entirely insincere, for James so feared Buchanan that many years later, as King of England, he was shaken by a nightmare in which Buchanan, long dead, appeared and severely rebuked him.

TRANSLATED FROM THE LATIN

[mid 1570s]

King James to his most worshipful teacher,
George Buchanan, greeting.

Since, O my father, nothing can be more profitable or more welcome to me than your presence and, on the other hand, nothing can happen more unfortunate or more regrettable than your absence, I beseech you again and again that you will not allow me any longer to lack so great a good or to be distressed by this misfortune. Wherefore please be so good as to do your utmost, as soon as those matters are finished on account of which you set forth, to free yourself therefrom and to hasten to us; and may you come no less safe and sound than you are longed for. Farewell!

Bodleian Library   *Copy, apparently*
MS. 15680 (Smith 74),   *of a lost holograph*
p. 169

Letter 3

To Captain Thomas Crawford of Jordanhill

Crawford figures in various military actions of the period. The nature of the services that elicited the following letter from the young king, with its subsequent reaffirmations, is not known.

15 September 1575

Captain Crawford,

I have heard such report of your good service done to me from the beginning of the wars against my onfreindis* as I shall some day remember the same, God willing, to your great contentment. In the meanwhile be of good comfort, and reserve you to that time with patience, being assured of my favour. Farewell. 1575. xv September.[1]

Your good friend,
JAMES R.

We approve these four lines above written with our own hand by this present. At Falkland the fifth day of September 1584.

JAMES R.

I ratify this man's evident[2] being now of perfect years and past all revocation.[3] At Linlithgow the xx3 of March 1591.

JAMES R.

Letter in possession of the Duke of Montrose; on deposit in Scottish Record Office (Lennox Charters, No. 197)

All three notes holograph and on the same sheet of paper.

[1]The day and the month have been added in a different hand.
[2]A variant of "evidence."
[3]I.e., revocation of grants given during the King's minority.

Letter 4

To Mary Queen of Scots

In September 1579 there arrived in Scotland King James's distant French kinsman Esmé Stuart, Seigneur D'Aubigny. Urbane, sophisticated, ingratiating, the newcomer soon became the first of King James's favourites; in March 1580 he was created Earl of Lennox. Strongly influenced by Lennox, James inclined increasingly towards his mother and countenanced the enemies of Regent Morton, leader of the pro-English faction in Scotland. On 31 December 1580 Morton was accused of involvement in the murder of Lord Darnley, the King's father, and was promptly arrested. These developments explain sufficiently the anger of Queen Elizabeth who, it would seem, prevented delivery of those messages from the King's mother which are referred to at the beginning of the following letter.

TRANSLATED FROM THE FRENCH

29 January 1581

Madame,

I beg you very humbly to believe that it was not with my goodwill that your secretary has returned without having given me your letter and making me aware of what you had commanded him to tell me, I having, alas, much regret for what has passed— for I should be infinitely distressed if anyone should think that I was unwilling to bear you the honour and the duty that I owe you, having hope that with time God will grant me grace to give you proof of my good and affectionate friendship, I well knowing that, after him, I hold from you all the honour that I have in this world. I have received the ring which you have been pleased to send me, which I shall carefully keep out of honour for you, and I send you another, which I very humbly beg you to receive as gladly as I received yours. You have indeed shown me by the remarks that it has pleased you to give me in your last letters how much you are a good mother to me, and I beg you very humbly that if you hear more to give me notice thereof that I may put things in the best order that will be possible for me, which I have already commenced as you will hear from the Earl of Lennox. Begging you to be helpful to me and to give me your good counsel and advice, which I wish to follow to the end to render you more certain that, in every matter wherein it pleases you to command me, you will always find me your very obedient son.

Very humbly kissing your hands, praying God, madame, that he give you a very happy and long life. From Lislebour[1] this xxix[th] day of January, 1580.

Your obedient son always,
JAQUES R.

Madame, I recommend unto you the fidelity of my little monkey, who stirs not from my side, by whom you will often send me news about yourself.

Public Record Office   *Last four words, signature,*
SP 53/11/44   *and postscript holograph*

[1]For this French name for Edinburgh see T. G. Law, "Lislebourg and Petit Leith," *Scottish Historical Review* I (1904), 19–26.

Letter 5

To Mary Queen of Scots

Early in 1581, Mary, through the Duc de Guise, proposed to her son an act of "Association," under which she would become joint sovereign of Scotland with James. This stipulated that she would give him the title of King and appoint him to rule the country in the names of both of them. In October she drew up instructions for the Archbishop of Glasgow to negotiate the "Association." There were attractive aspects to this scheme for James since, especially in the eyes of his Catholic subjects, his right to the throne was questionable during his mother's lifetime. Certainly in the following letter James assures Mary of his readiness to proceed with this scheme.

TRANSLATED FROM THE FRENCH, ORIGINAL SENT IN CIPHER[1]

28 May 1582

Madame,

I have received your letters which it has pleased you to do me the honour to write me dated the 9th of January and 23rd of February, on the 16th of April, which have been delivered to me by the Duke of Lennox[2] and George Douglas,[3] and have learnt from them what you have commanded them to make me understand. On your part I beg you very humbly to believe that I have never had nor will have other will than to recognize you as my mother and as the one from whom all the honour that I can receive in this world will come, and with the aid of God and time you will recognize that all my affection does not tend to anything but to honour and respect you and execute your commandments, and to follow the overtures that it has pleased you to make touching our union and association. I have already begged you by my last of last month to be willing to send me the form of the said association by writing, which I begged you to do as soon as possible and having it I will endeavour to content you, and cause the lords of my Council to consent thereto, having hope that you will know by what will happen and by the care that I shall take to execute your will that mine is above all dedicated to obey you, as it is my duty to do. And as to the said machinations which are made against us, it is a thing from which by your means and advertisement I have been preserved and hope to be still, and that it will not be in the power of hostile kings to carry out their evil designs, and even those that they have devised in the dissension that they have caused between the Duke of Lennox and the Earl of Arran,[4] who are at this time as good friends and better than they have ever been, and will both strive for the accomplishment of our union, you being able to assure yourself of not having anyone in Scotland who may be more affectionate.

46

My horses that Monsieur de Guise my cousin was to send me have arrived which are exceedingly beautiful, and I know by his letters that he bears me a very affectionate goodwill which he will find reciprocated in me; and I am intending to send him one of my esquires express with his to thank him and to take him some hackneys and some gold seals. . . . Making an end, kissing you very humbly on the hands praying God madame that he will give you happy and long life.

Dalkeith, May 28th, 1582

Madame, since my letters were written I have received 20 miliers of powder that Monsieur de Guise sent me, also I have received the letter that you have written me that was sent from Berwick which it will not be necessary to put in execution and I will write to the Queen of England as you ask me. Always your very humble and obedient servant.

Madame, there is the Lord of Fiancares, brother of Lord Paul, equerry of Monsieur de Guise, who owes you some payment by reason of his marriage, which is for the land of Vurmille near Vutry in Arthois. And inasmuch as he will remain here near me some time to give into my hands these horses I beg you very humbly to do me the honour to give him, for love of me, his payment and send it to your ambassador and to your Chancellor, and believing that as much for the very humble request that I have made you as for the love he bears to Monsieur de Guise at whose devotion he is that you will grant him this. . . . I will not importune you further except to assure you that in everything that it pleases you to command me you will find me always your very humble and obedient son.

Public Record Office   *Original cipher letter*
SP 53/12/12   *with interlined decoding*

---

[1]The translation that follows is that of the *Calendar of State Papers, Scottish, 1581–83*, pp. 125–26.
[2]Esmé Stuart, 1st Duke of Lennox.
[3]"Pretty Geordie," brother of the Laird of Lochleven. Romantically devoted

to Queen Mary, he followed her into exile. In July 1583 he is mentioned as very familiar and "inward" with King James.

[4]James Stewart, 5th Earl of Arran, the King's favourite, who held the title from 22 April 1581 until his attainder in November 1585.

Letter 6

To Queen Elizabeth

On 2 June 1581, despite the representations of Queen Elizabeth's ambassador, Morton the former Regent of Scotland was put to death. The government of the fourteen-year-old king's realm was entrusted to his favourite, the headstrong and unscrupulous Earl of Arran. English disquiet grew while King James, despite statements of his unwavering Protestantism, became increasingly friendly with the Catholics. A crisis came in the spring of 1582, when James refused to accept a letter of expostulation and advice from Elizabeth. In an attempt to moderate the English queen's anger, James despatched the following letter.

19 June 1582

Most excellent, right high and mighty princess, our dearest sister and cousin, in most heartiest manner we recommend us unto you.

The understanding which, by your knowledge and permission, we receive from the Queen our dearest mother of her disposition to send to visit us, whereof indeed we accept very gladly, and your stay and hinder of the following forth thereof proceeding, as appeareth, upon occasion of our refuse* of your late message sent us in time of Parliament, hath moved us to purge us to you by the present [letter] of any other meaning or intention in that behalf but alanerlye* the surety of our person and quietness of our country as the states of our affairs required at that time. Praying you effectually to conceive of it no otherwise, and to assure you that without any great or urgent cause we will be loath to do in any sort but that thing which may tend to the continuance of the amity by all good offices that may be looked for of any affectionate and loving brother, according to the good advice and counsel which we have of our dearest mother to the same effect, whose estate and preservation we recommend unto you above all earthly things. Therewithin you shall most oblige us unto you and do us greatest pleasure. And so right excellent, right high and mighty princess, our dearest sister and cousin, we commit you to the protection of the Almighty from our Castle of Stirling this xixth day of June 1582 and of our reign the xvth year.

Public Record Office   *Copy*
SP 52/30/10

Letter 7

To Queen Elizabeth

The summer of 1582 found King James in a highly dangerous situation. The anger of the Kirk and the Protestant nobility was intense against James's French favourite the Duke of Lennox, even though the latter had declared his conversion to Protestantism. James's other favourite, Arran, had alienated almost everybody. James's lame letter of excuse of 19 June (Letter 6) had achieved nothing with Queen Elizabeth. England was ready to countenance, if not to instigate, a change of government in Scotland. Accordingly, in August in "the Ruthven Raid," James was seized by a powerful group of Protestant lords headed by the Earls of Angus and Gowrie. Lennox was forced to leave Scotland, and a pro-English government was set up. James quietly bided his time and, on 29 June 1583, contrived to escape from the lords who had captured him at Ruthven Castle. Anxious to head off any English military intervention to reinstate the Ruthven government, James hastened to send the following letter to Queen Elizabeth.

49

Right excellent, right high and mighty princess, our
dearest sister and cousin, we recommend us unto you in
our most hearty manner.

Doubting of the least impression which the report of this late
accident about us, being carried to your ears by other means,
might give you opinion of some alteration in us from that good
course which we have taken us to, we have thought meetest to
prevent it by our own letter simply to let you understand how it
fell out, on what occasion, and what is the effect intended
thereof. Upon the 28 of June last, having appointed a convention of our nobility and Council here in our City of Saint Andrew of intention to have acquainted them with the answers
lately returned to us from you by our late ambassadors, minding
to have procured their approbation and liking of them; and,
being come to that effect, we were advertised that some speciallis* of our nobility, divided in particularities among themselves,
had trysted their friends and dependeris* to accompany them in
arms to our said presence where being disposed (as they were
indeed) likely to draw on our whole nobility, convened in their
two factions, we fearing the event of it and understanding their
nearness to us, we were advised by so many of our Council as
were present for the time to withdraw us to our castle of our
said city where our person might be in best surety till some good
order might be taken for removing of the inconvenient [*sic*] ap-
pearing to ensue thereof. This is our only meaning and intent in
this behalf assuring you that in so doing neither mind we to
control nor remove any of our nobility or others that has faithfully given their dependence on us heretofore, nor prejudge
them in their honours, lives, nor livings in any sort, except they
give us special occasion hereafter to the contrary. Wherewith
always we mind to make you first acquainted before we proceed
against them, and always to conform us to your good advice
and counsel in that behalf; it being our special meaning and
intention to use all our good subjects indifferently and to grant
them equally access unto our presence except so many as are
debarred therefrom, whom we intend not to call again unto us

without your special consent and privity, nor do in any sort whereby you may conceive jealousy (justly) of any our actions or proceedings. But that as most deservedly you possess our special liking and goodwill before all princes in the world, so mean we to continue to you and afauldlie* to follow forth that good course which we have both professed sincerely and solemnly promised to you by our former letters. And whereas heretofore it has been liked of but by ourself and two or three of our nobility that were about us, we shall be now about to qualify it ourself, in such sort to the whole as we are in good hope to be the mean of a more frequent approbation of it, at least by so many as will depend upon our own good liking. Praying you, therefore, dearest sister, to conceive no otherways of us and our intention in this behalf nor we have here set down, and in our princely word shall keep unto you, for so it is, and so shall it appear by the course of our whole actions to be testified unto you from time to time by your ambassador here resident, whom we have at more length by our own speech assured of our continuance and constancy in this behalf. And so right excellent, right high and mighty Princess, our dearest sister and cousin, we commit you in the protection of the Almighty God. Off our Castle of Saint Andrew the second day of July and of our reign the seventeenth year 1583.

Your most loving and affectionate brother and cousin.

JAMES R.

Madame, I have stayed Master Spencer[1] upon the letter which is written with my own hand, which shall be ready within two days.

British Library, Cotton MSS., *Last eight words, signature*
Caligula C VII, f. 257 *and postscript are holograph.*

[1]Richard Spencer, the messenger who was to take various letters to England.

Letter 8

To Sir John Maitland

On 18 May 1584, King James appointed Sir John Maitland of Thirlestane as his Secretary of State. Maitland, the "Burghley of Scotland," was to school James in politics and to provide him with something approaching a properly functioning civil service. In this undated letter, which commences with the abruptest of salutations, "Secretaire," the King relieves himself of some of the anger and frustration which the Kirk too often aroused in him.

[1584?]

Secretary,

John Andro [Andrew][1] has informed me what the session of the Kirk in Edinburgh has mintid* at, and sensyne* revoked in a part. Their spite in this has more offended me than ever I was, since God created me, at that unworthy sort of people. Neither have ye done your duty in this matter, for your duty had it been to have discharged their communion and also their session till I had taken farther order for the repressing of that proud contempt. And therefore, to teach you that when ye count without your host in these matters ye maun* count twice, I have directed a proclamation which ye maun* cause solemnly to be published. And since they have kindled up *sopitos cineres*[2] I swear they shall never fail on my side till I find anis* as great proof of their obedience as I have ever had of their contemptuous rebellion.

I write sharply for when my proper actions are called in question *tunc mea res agitur*.[3] I have given John Andro [Andrew] his despatch as his letter will inform you.

Farewell in haste,
JAMES R.

British Library   *Holograph*
Add. 23241, f.5

[1]Clerk of the Privy Council of Scotland.

[2]"Inactive ashes."

[3]The complete passage from Horace *Epistles* 1.18.84–85 reads, "nam tua res agitur, paries cum proximus ardet, et neglecta solent incendia sumere vires" ("for it is your interest that is at stake when the wall next door is ablaze, and fires, if neglected, generally gather strength").

Letter 9

To the Fugitive Ministers of the Kirk

In April 1584 the Ruthven lords again moved to seize control of Scotland. However, this time they failed and fled to England. In May, King James appointed the Earl of Arran as Chancellor, and this same month a parliament dominated by the latter's faction passed the "Black Acts." These denounced presbyterianism and reasserted the authority of bishops. A number of Scottish divines then went into exile in England. The next month the following letter was sent to various fugitives, inviting them home. No other letter by King James survives in a greater number of contemporary copies. Possibly the flight of the ministers and the writing of this letter (conceivably for wide distribution by royal agents) should both be seen as parts of a campaign to mould English opinion.

9[?] *June* [1584]

Trusty and beloved,

Forasmuch as, since the accepting of the regiment in our person, we have chiefly endeavoured to establish a godly and perfect order of policy in the church of our realm for the sincerity of the gospel being professed in our kingdom, and the troubles wherewith this realm hath been vexed in our minority not permitting a solid and established order of policy, we, coming to years of maturity, have chiefly disposed our intention (by the grace of God) to maintain the truth, set forth his glory (by whose mercy we govern and reign), and to establish sic* order whereby the posterity hereafter may find the comfort. And

53

because this work of God cannot duly be accomplished without instruments, and that we are certainly informed of your good gifts and long time bestowed in godly learning, especially in the scriptures, and that chiefly to perform this work we have need of men endued with sic* virtues, therefore we have given commission to our well-beloved Mr. Archibald Herbertson,[1] whom ye shall trust in our name, that ye may with possible diligence address yourself hither to your native country and king, that we may have your counsel, assistance, and concurrence to so godly a work—assuring you upon our honour, and in the word of a prince, that upon your returning to your native country ye shall find us disposed not only to consider the pains of your journey but also to respect you likewise in your placing, and providing for you in honourable rooms which we desire to be furnished with godly, learned, and quiet spirits. And like as we protest before God to mean sincerely, so we wish you to render that obedience to us whereby ye shall have good proof of our favour.

We have also commanded our well-beloved chaplain and councillor, the Bishop of St. Andrews,[2] to write unto you in these matters, to whose writing, and the declaration of the bearer (whom ye shall credit and whom we have specially directed for that purpose), we commit the rest.

And thus we commit you and your labours to God, and wish you not to be negligent in his work. From our palace of Falkland, the 9th of June.[3]

JAMES R.

British Library, Cotton MSS.,   Copy
Caligula C VIII, f. 58

[1]Herbertson was chosen by Archbishop Adamson to approach the refugee ministers. Later he was deemed to have been insufficiently discreet in his mission.
[2]Patrick Adamson (1537–1592). His title was Archbishop of St. Andrews.
[3]Other copies of this letter (Harl. 6897 f. 43 and Harl. 291 f. 123) give its date as 10 June.

Letter 10

To Mary Queen of Scots

The "Association" proposed by Mary in 1581, under which she and her son would share the sovereignty of Scotland, had inevitably become a dead issue during the regime of the Protestant Ruthven lords. Now, in 1584, Mary was once more urging the scheme, but circumstances had changed and Queen Elizabeth, increasingly suspicious of Mary's motives, was no longer prepared to countenance it. The following letter by James on the subject shows something less than the enthusiasm for "Association" that had marked his earlier statements. By August it was plain that James himself had decided against "Association."

TRANSLATED FROM THE FRENCH, ORIGINAL SENT IN CIPHER

[*July 1584*]

Madame,

The little leisure that I have hinders me from writing this time anything else to Your Majesty except that I thank you very humbly for the honour and infinite favour that you have done me in sending to visit me Fontenay,[1] brother of Nau,[2] Secretary of your Commandments, being the first that I have had from you since your captivity. I do not know how to express the extreme consolation that I have received from it, having heard from him several particularities of your estate, and especially the incomprehensible maternal affection that it pleases you to continue in my respect, by which I am forced more than ever to render myself by all duties of humility and obedience to the accomplishment of your commandments. The choice that it has pleased Your Majesty to make of the said Fontenay, and the manner in which he has proceeded until now, has made me hope all contentment on his part.

Beyond generally he has as yet declared to me but few of the particularities of your intentions, especially for our perfect union and association, which without fail I shall pass after the return of my Lord Seton,[3] as Fontenay tells me he has recovered from Monsieur de Glasgow[4] the letter patent and the Articles of the same to serve him there in the charges and negotiations that I have committed to him. However I will prepare as much as possible the minds of my common subjects to ratify and hold as agreeable the conclusion of our said Association. Without other recommendation on your part the sympathy and conformity of our affections with the sentiment that I have of the injuries and treasons committed in respect of you by my Lord Lindsay[5] have already made me resolve to make exemplary punishment, as I hope, of his fellows, without that that there may escape from me a single one of those that I could catch.

Immediately that Fontenay has made known to me the other particulars of his negotiation, especially of the secret instructions that Your Majesty forbids me to ever reveal to any one, I will not fail to write to you briefly my advice on the whole, and to follow such directions that it will please you to appoint to me. As to your deliverance according to the deliberation that for so long I have taken over it, Your Majesty can assure yourself that shortly I will send with Fontenay some of mine to receive your holy benediction and to inform you of divers of my intentions, as also to require of the Queen of England your deliverance, for which I wish above all the happiness of this world. Above all I promise Your Majesty that you will receive from me all the contentment that a good mother can hope for from a very humble and obedient son, such as I will be to you all my life. In this mind, having very humbly kissed your hands, I pray God the Creator, madame, to give to Your Majesty very long and happy life in perfect health. Falkland.

Public Record Office   *Original cipher letter*
SP 53/13/37   *with interlined decoding*[6]

[1]M. de Fontenay, brother-in-law to Nau and one of Mary's agents, described himself as Secretary to her Council.
[2]Jacques (Claude?) Nau de la Boisselière, Mary's secretary.
[3]George Seton, 5th Lord Seton (1531–1586), Scottish ambassador to France 1583–1585. Although he had entered King James's service, he remained attached to Queen Mary's interests.

⁴Robert Montgomery, Archbishop of Glasgow.
⁵Patrick Lindsay, 6th Lord Lindsay of the Byres (1521–1589). One of the murderers of Rizzio, he was an implacable enemy to Mary. As one of the Ruthven Raiders who had fled to England, he was expected to be executed now that he was back in Scotland.
⁶The above text has been reprinted from *CSP Scottish, 1584–85*, pp. 233–34.

Letter 11

To Henry Carey, Lord Hunsdon

In July 1584, Queen Elizabeth, increasingly concerned about King James's conduct, sent Lord Hunsdon to Berwick, there to take up with James's own emissary such important issues as James's prosecution of Elizabeth's friends in Scotland, his refusal to let banished Scots go to England, his failure to turn over to Elizabeth's officers Jesuits and other fugitives, his sending of messengers to the Pope and to the Kings of Spain and France, and his secret negotiations with his mother. Informed of Hunsdon's arrival at the border stronghold of Berwick, James sent him the following letter.

26 July 1584

My lord and cousin,

The good endeavours and honest offices you have done me since first I employed you at the Queen, your sovereign, our dearest sister's hand hath moved me now by these few lines of mine own hand to thank you heartily of all these foresaid. And since you are come down to Berwick to the effect that, remaining there so near my realm, you may the more commodiously perform and put to happy end that inward and sincere amity which by your travails and foresaid good offices doth already begin, I will therefore in an homely manner desire you earnestly, since you have already taken the pains to travel, for the goodwill you bear me, so near the borders of my country, that you will take so much more pains as to visit me. In which doing you shall as well know by myself the great contentment I have of your good and honourable offices—which I cannot so well express by letters or message—as also you shall know my mind anent those matters that you have in commission to deal in more fully and plainly than you can do by message. Notwithstanding, in case your commission permit you not so to do (as I would be sorry it should) I have commanded the Earl of Arran to be in readiness to wait upon your diet,[*] who according to my direction is ready to meet with you upon your next advertisement. But assuring myself you will grant my so reasonable request above written I commit you to God. From my Palace of Falkland the 26th of July 1584.

Your loving and assured
friend and cousin,
JAMES R.

The good liking we have conceived of our young cousin your son Robert[1] when we saw him makes us now to desire you earnestly to bring him with you to us if he come.

British Library, Cotton MSS.,   *Copy, apparently of a*
Caligula C VIII f. 94   *lost holograph*

[1]In 1603, as Sir Robert Carey, he would make his famous ride to Edinburgh to inform King James of his accession to the English throne. Carey first attracted the monarch's favourable attention in 1583 when he accompanied Sir Francis Walsingham on the latter's Scottish journey.

Letter 12

To William Cecil, Lord Burghley

In the wake of the Hunsdon–Arran conversations, James decided that it was very much in his interest to give some satisfaction to Queen Elizabeth. Accordingly, in October he sent Pat-

*rick, Master of Gray, as his ambassador to London to intimate
that he was prepared to abandon his mother and reveal her secrets in order to secure an English–Scottish alliance. Aware of
the central role old Lord Burghley would play in any further
negotiations, James provided Gray with a letter of compliment
to deliver to the venerable Lord Treasurer.*

14 October 1584

My lord and cousin,

Alexander the great conqueror of the world reading one day,
according to his accustomed manner, on the *Iliads* of Homer,
which he ever carried about with him, he did burst forth in these
words following: "I esteem not," said he, "Achilles to have been
so happy for the good success he had in the wars as he was in
having so worthy a trumpeter to blow abroad and immortalize
to all posterities and ages his worthy fame as Homer was."[1] My
lord, albeit indeed Achilles was ornit* with so diverse and rare
virtues as, in that case, I can in no ways be justly compared unto
him, and that on the other part ye do far excel such a blind
begging fellow as Homer, yet in one thing I may be compared
unto him (I mean Achilles) to wit that there is so wise and trusty
a counsellor as ye are about her of whose amity I have made
choice above all other princes if she will accept of me who may,
and I am assured will, further that amity which now, by the
bearer hereof, my ambassador, I do crave of her—whom I have
commanded not only to impart his commission unto you but
also to use your prescript in all these matters. The cause that
moves me so to do is the report I have heard how ye have been
the man about your sovereign these times bygone who has had
the chief and only care of the well-doing of my affairs there.
And having directed this bearer with more special and secret
commission than any I ever directed before, I have given charge
therefore to deal most specially and secretly with you, next the
Queen our dearest sister, as he will show you more at length,
whom earnestly desiring you to credit as myself, with assurance
of your continuance in the furthering of all my adoos* there,

and specially this present, I commit you my lord and cousin to God's holy protection.

From my palace of Holyroodhouse the 14 of October 1584.

Your assured friend and cousin,

JAMES R.

Public Record Office   *Holograph*
SP 52/36/85

[1] For this anecdote see Cicero *Pro Archia* 24; also Plutarch *Alexander* 15.9.

Letter 13

To Sir Lewis Bellenden

By April 1585, when Sir Lewis Bellenden had taken over the negotiations successfully commenced by the Master of Gray, it was clear that there was a real prospect of an Anglo–Scottish accord. James, who was haunted by the fear that the Ruthven lords might launch an invasion from their English asylum, was elated at the prospect of robbing them of Elizabeth's covert protection. His feelings about these "rebels" emerge strongly in this letter to Bellenden, now his ambassador in London.

12 April 1585

Right trusty and well-beloved counsellor, we greet you heartily well.

Your letters of the first of this instant was by this bearer delivered to us the sixth of the same. We cannot but like of your honest behaviour and discreet proceeding in your negotiation, whereby ye have given effectual proof with what earnest zeal ye are devoted to our service, whereof ye shall not have occasion to repent you; and, as we doubt not ye will always continue, so may ye remain fully assured to be acknowledged as your affection and fidelity have deserved.

We are not a little rejoiced to hear of the reciproque* goodwill professed by our dearest sister towards us, which (withersoever these foreign commotions do tend) shall be sincerely acquit on our part, without respect to consanguinity or whatsomever sequel or event. And, since we have entered in this happily begun amity *non casu sed iudicio*[1] and made special choice thereof, we have vowed to prosecute the same with all integrity and to prefer it to all other, without either scruple of incidents that may fall out or doubt of mutual sincerity on the part of our dearest sister.

Ye did rightly in pressing our said dearest sister to banish our rebels her realm and dominions, and yet, since John Home[2] is fugitive, or rather subduced* by them from trial, their guilt is thereby manifest, being their servant, partaker in their treasons and conspiracies, fugitive with them, their messenger often employed, returning to them and living at their charges—no doubt directed by them to fly and withdraw himself from examination lest the late and many other their treasons should be detected. It is more nor certain they are culpable of the unnatural practice of our intended murder wherewith they are charged, which, against us and other princes by them and others their like, is almost commonly attempted as the fittest expedient to alter estates—as our said dearest sister has lately discovered [such wickedness] has been often intended against her own person, though God of his mercy has stayed the execution of so devilish enterprises. Ye shall therefore with all instance press our said dearest sister to cause apprehend our said rebels and cause them to be committed to the Tower there or other straight ward, till after John Home be found out and delivered to us, or that either by their mean or other inquisition knowledge may be had where he lurks. And thereafter, let the said rebels (if she think it dishonourable to deliver them according to the articles of the peace) at least be exiled and kept out of her whole dominions.

Ye shall also signify to our said dearest sister that some disordered persons of her West March have assisted to some broken men of our Border, stirred up by the Lord Maxwell,[3] made

61

hostile incursions on certain our subjects, committed some murders, and raised fire, and burnt the Laird of Johnstone's house. Which her subjects insist ye to cause be used according to the laws of the Marches and conditions of peace between the two realms—as also that none of our outlaws, rebels, or disobedients of our Border be received or suffered to remain within her realm.

Give thanks to Sir Philip Sidney for his lyme-hound.[4] We have given order for your furniture, as this bearer will declare you, of whom when occasion serves we shall not be unmindful.

Thus we commit you to the protection of the Almighty.

From Holyroodhouse this xii of April 1585.

JAMES R.

Edinburgh University Library   *Scribal text, signed*
Laing MSS. I: 12   *by the King*

[1]"Not through chance but judgement."

[2]The fugitive Ruthven lords had employed Home in their plots and, lest he testify against them, had persuaded him likewise to flee Scotland. See *CSP Scottish, 1584–85*, pp. 100, 564.

[3]John Maxwell, 7th Lord Maxwell (1554–1593), a Catholic Border magnate, was long involved in a feud with the Laird of Johnstone, a feud which finally cost him his life.

[4]A species of bloodhound.

Letter 14

To Queen Elizabeth

The negotiations begun by the Master of Gray and Bellenden were carried a stage further at the end of May, when Edward Wotton arrived in Edinburgh to arrange an alliance, both offensive and defensive, among England, Scotland, and other Protestant powers. The following letter from James indicates his approval of the proposed terms.

Right excellent, right high and mighty princess, our
dearest sister and cousin, in our heartiest manner we
recommend us unto you.

The articles of a new treaty and league which your ambassador here has delivered in our hands to be advised with, we like
well of, and thinks them fittest and most likely grounds for our
mutual sureties to be built on—the necessity of this time, touching us alike, so craving, and the motion of the same being that
religion in the profession whereof, we both have, since our very
coronations, found the favour of our God effectually assisting
and preserving us against so many dangers wherewith both our
persons and estates have been extremely threatened. For the
abolishing whereof, seeing the long-covered pretenses of the Pope
and other Princes his adherents begin now to disclose their meaning, we think us bound in Christian duty to prevent the prosecution thereof by opposing thereunto the remedies granted to us of
God, both for the surety of so great a benefit in our times and the
continuance thereof to our posterities. Wherefore when as you
shall think good to direct some express messenger to any foreign
prince for his concurrence in this cause we will request you very
earnestly to let us be acquainted both with the man and with so
much of his commission and instructions as concern that errand,
to the intent that upon sight thereof we may authorize him with
the very like from us and thereby give demonstration to the world
of the sincerity of our meaning and afauld * joining in that cause.
And thus right excellent, right high and mighty princess, our
dearest sister and cousin, we commit you in the protection of the
Almighty God. From our palace of Falkland the ninth day of July
1585 and of our reign the eighteenth year.

Your most loving and affectionate
brother and cousin,
JAMES R.

I doubt not, madame, but ye will suspend your judgement of
me notwithstanding any fellow's reports till you be informed by

myself, for you may be assured to be fully resolved according to my promise in whatsomever you inquire of me.

British Library, Cotton MSS.,   *Last eight words, signature*
Caligula C VIII, f. 302   *and postscript holograph*

Letter 15

To Queen Elizabeth

The tentative Anglo–Scottish alliance was jeopardized when on 27 July Lord Russell, son of the Earl of Bedford, was slain in a scuffle during a meeting of the English and Scottish wardens of the Middle March. As soon as he heard of Lord Russell's murder, a profoundly agitated King James dashed off the following letter to Queen Elizabeth.

[*3 August? 1585*][1]

Madame and mother,

Since haste, anger, and extraordinary sorrow will not permit any long letter, this present shall only serve to assure you of my honest innocence in this late mischief, and of my constancy in that course mentioned in my last letter unto you, not doubting but your ambassador[2] hath written to you at large both of the one and the other. I have also directed expressly the bearer hereof unto you to know your mind and desire for the repairing of this foresaid mischief whom, praying you firmly to credit, and to esteem still of my truth, I commit you, madame and mother, to God's holy protection. From Saint Andrews the 3 day of July. 1585.

Your most loving and devoted
brother and son,
JAMES R.

I doubt not madame but ye have kept one ear for me notwithstanding of many malicious tongues that now do boldly speak.

Cecil Papers(Hatfield House)   *Holograph*
133: 45

[1] The date at the close of this letter is "the 03 day of iulie," with a blot filling the centre of the zero. The letter cannot have been written on 3 July, however, since its contents obviously refer to the murder of Lord Russell in late July. James in his haste and perturbation must either have inverted the numerals of 30 July, or written 3 July in error for 3 August. John Bruce in his *Letters of Queen Elizabeth and James VI* (London, Camden Society, Vol. 46, 1849, p. 18) inclined, like the present editor, to 3 August.

[2] Edward Wotton (knighted 1592, Lord Wotton 1603) was Elizabeth's envoy to Scotland May–October 1585.

Letter 16

To Queen Elizabeth

At the time of the affray of 27 July 1585, Elizabeth and her ministers had decided that the arrogant and tempestuous Catholic Earl of Arran, who was becoming more and more powerful, must be removed from his position as Chancellor of Scotland. Even his assassination was considered. Lord Russell's murder was seen by Elizabeth and her ministers as a means of getting rid of Arran, and her ambassador in Edinburgh, using assertions where he lacked evidence, accused the Chancellor of complicity in Russell's death. When the Queen learned that James had imprisoned Arran, she wrote approvingly that she did "perceive that you have not spared your well-favoured to cause him to answer to such a suspicion." Pleased with the young King's compliance, she did not break off the treaty negotiations. These are the subject of the following letter.

Madame and mother,

In great haste ready to ride. Your ambassador's present despatch hath moved me to write these few words to assure you that, although my articles that the ambassador sends you desires the league to concern only religion, yet my plain intention is that the league shall be offensive and defensive for all invasions upon whatsomever pretext. And therefore I will pray you to keep this present in token and testimony of my plain assent thereunto and that I will employ my crown and country to resist to whatsomever invasions upon yours. Thus praying you to appardone* this scribbling in haste and to continue still my loving mother as I shall be your devoted son, I commit you, madame and mother, to God's holy protection. The xix day of August from Stirling. 1585.

> Your most loving and devoted
> brother and son.
> JAMES R.

Cecil Papers   *Holograph*
133: 55

Letter 17

To Queen Elizabeth

James should have accepted the implicit deal of an Arran for a Russell but, unfortunately, his inability to deal harshly with a favourite now asserted itself. After a few days of imprisonment in St. Andrews Castle, Arran was allowed to withdraw to his mansion in Ayrshire. The consequences were foreseeable. On 24 August the English ambassador reported to Elizabeth that James was incapable of dealing with Arran and that, until the latter was driven from office, there was no point in concluding an alliance. He advised Her Majesty to "let slip" the Ruthven lords and their allies who were biding their time in England.

Elizabeth finally accepted this last piece of advice. Late in October the Ruthven lords entered Scotland with eight thousand men, and were completely victorious. Arran was stripped of his titles and offices. James, trimming his sails, declared that he found the Ruthven lords, those "outlaws" he had so denounced, to be true and loving subjects. He resumed his correspondence with Queen Elizabeth, lightly referring to the overthrow of his former chancellor as "this late accident."

26 November 1585

Madame and dearest Sister,

Ye have so far kythed* at this time, as ever before, your constant favour towards me as I am ashamed since I can by no means acquit the same, as well in respect of your most loving letter as of the hasty and careful despatch and direction of the gentleman bearer hereof, your ambassador;[1] whom with, according to your desire, I have dealt plainly concerning this late accident and all other things he inquired of me. Surely I find the gentleman correspondent to your expectation both in honesty and secrecy. He hath kept also your command so strictly in dealing only with myself as in very deed some men here finds it not a little strange. And now, madame, ye have dealt so plainly and honestly with me as I am beholden to do the like: as upon the one side I trust firmly your declaration of your own part concerning this late accident which, as God is my witness, I never otherwise suspected; so, on the other part, I say for myself that, notwithstanding I must confess I was hourly earnestly dealt with to run some foreign course, yet Almighty God bears me record that since my promises made unto you I never have directly nor indirectly dealt in any foreign course to this hour. And to the end that I may give you a reciproke* proof of my honesty, I will earnestly desire you that these matters left off betwixt us may of new be fallen to and finally perfected, that your goodwill may be so far acquitted by me as your part may be mine in all cases, as I swear on my part ever to prefer you to all kin and friendship I have in any country. Ye have so far heaped your good deservings upon me and, to the effect that these foresaids may be the better performed, I will withal speed direct one of mine own unto you who will also amply inform you of all proceedings here. In the meantime I will remit me to the foresaid bearer whom to whatsomever I have spoken it is freely and without any compulsion, for never shall I for compulsion either speak, promise, or write otherwise than I think, and that which is honest.

Thus praying you ever to esteem of me as of one careful to acquit the manifold obligations he hath unto you, I commit you, madame and dearest sister, to God's Holy protection. From Linlithgow the xxvi day of November 1585.

Your truest and lovingest friend
and brother,
JAMES R.

Je vous prie, madame, de faire ce porteur entendre que j'ai bonne opinion de lui et que j'estime qu'il est bien aquitté de sa charge, tant envers vous qu'envers moi.[2]

British Library, Cotton MSS.,   *Holograph*
Caligula C VIII, f. 379

[1] William Knollys, who had arrived at Linlithgow on 22 November.
[2] "I pray you, madame, to inform this bearer that I have a good opinion of him, and that I think he has acquitted his errand well, as towards you so towards me."

Letter 18

To Queen Elizabeth

Early in March 1586 a new English ambassador, Thomas Randolph, arrived in Edinburgh, and negotiations were resumed for the long-proposed Anglo–Scottish treaty. King James was bitterly disappointed at the English terms. There would be no mention of his "title" to the English succession. He was to be paid an annuity of only £4000, not the £5000 to which Elizabeth really stood committed. Moreover, the Queen would not sign an "instrument" or equivalent letter safeguarding what James regarded as his vital interests. Provoked, James wrote the following letter, no doubt hoping for concessions. His hopes were unrealized, but in July James, outmanoeuvred, signed the treaty rather than imperil his claim to the English succession.

10 May 1586

Madame and dearest sister,

I have from your ambassador received your last letter. And as it hath pleased you to write plainly and roundly in the same, so I doubt not but ye will accept in good part my plain sincerity in answering—as well for that round dealing is interpreted to the best among inward friends as also considering how rare and delicate among great princes is the discovering of the simple truth unto them.

Whereas in the beginning of your letter, after that ye have at length dilated how honourable it is for me, in straitest times of crossing, to continue my professed goodwill towards ye, then [ye] exhort me by many arguments to perform the same, as if I yet were in doubt what course to run. Surely, madame, if I had not been and still were not fully resolved (notwithstanding of whatsomever alteration in the world) to continue and augment (if possible were) my great and irrevocable goodwill towards you, I would never have entered so far in this course [i.e., the treaty negotiation] as I have done already. For sure, nearness of blood, bound up with so many obligations, vicinity of realms, conformity of language, and religion, which is most of all (and not your greatness, more than other princes have for the same been in amity with my predecessors), since these causes, I say, have moved me to enter in such inward amity with you, ye may then rest assured this my affection, built upon so sure and godly grounds, is never able to fall.

And whereas ye seem to marvel and mislike so far of the sending of yon instrument to be subscribed by you, surely I must blame your other weighty affairs that have made you somewhat forget how both first by Wotton[1] and now last by Randolph, ye have desired me to form [draft] a letter to be passed by your

69

hand writ and seal, tending to the same effect [as] that instrument which I sent you does—these two clauses being always specially inserted, to wit, this word "pretended" being always added to the word "title" and, in case I altered my course, that letter to avail me nothing. And, being thus moved by your ambassador, I sent that letter unto you which I look ye should rather have corrected than rejected, and therefore I complain of you to yourself, appealing *a regina male consulta ad reginam bene consultam.*[2]

And now I must pray you for one thing, that hereafter ye will use me mutually as ye remember by William Keith[3] ye desired me to use you. Thus praying you to excuse my rude plainness, since I protest it proceeds neither of pride nor malice but of mere love and affection, and praying you to make ever account of me as of your most steadfast and most devoted friend, I rest from troubling you with any more scribbling, but commits you, madame and dearest sister, to God's holy protection who mote* long continue your flourishing reign in despite of all your adversaries.

From Holyroodhouse the xth day of May 1586.

As concerning the delivery of yon men for the repairing of your honour, the same, according to your ambassador's information, shall be fully accomplished with all possible diligence.

Your most loving and steadfast
brother and cousin,
JAMES R.

Public Record Office   *Copy*
SP 52/39/71

[1]Edward Wotton, created Lord Wotton by King James in 1603, was Elizabeth's envoy to Scotland from May to October 1585.

[2]"From a queen badly advised to a queen well advised."

[3]Sir William Keith had been sent on an embassy to the English court in late December 1585. James is apparently referring to the reply Keith brought back to Scotland.

Letter 19

To Queen Elizabeth

King James was, of course, a poet as well as a monarch: he published collections of his verse in 1584 and 1591. On one occasion he wrote a sonnet for Queen Elizabeth in which he developed the thought that their occasional differences led only to warmer friendship. Apparently the Queen did not condescend to reply, and the hurt pride of an author is obvious in this letter with which he sent her a second copy of his sonnet.

[c. 1586]

Madame and dearest sister,

Notwithstanding of my instant writing one letter unto you yet could I not satisfy my unrestful and longing spirit except by writing of these few lines, which, albeit they do not satisfy it, yet they do stay the unrest thereof while the answer is returning of this present.

Madame, I did send you before some verse. Since then Dame Cynthia has oft renewed her horns and innumerable times supped with her sister Thetis. And the bearer thereof returned, and yet void of answer. I doubt not ye have read how Cupid's dart is fiery called because of the sudden ensnaring and restless burning; thereafter what can I else judge but that either ye had not received it, except the bearer returned with the contrary report; or else that ye judge it not to be of me because it is *incerto authore*.[1] For which cause I have insert[ed] my name to the end of this sonnet here enclosed. Yet one way am I glad of the answer's keeping up, because I hope now for one more full after the reading also of these presents and hearing this bearer dilate this purpose more at large according to my secret thoughts. For ye know dead letters cannot answer no questions; therefore I must pray you, how unapparent soever the purpose be, to trust him in it as well as if I myself spake it unto you face by face (which I would wish I might) since it is specially and in a manner only for that purpose that I have sent him. Thus, not doubting of your courtesy

71

in this far, I commit you, madame and dearest sister, to God's holy protection, the day and date as in the other letter.

> Your more loving and affectionate
> brother and cousin than (I fear)
> yet ye believe.
> JAMES R.

Cecil Papers   *Holograph*
133: 48

[*Sonnet enclosed with letter*]

> Full many a time the archer slacks his bow
> That afterhend it may the stronger be.
> Full many a time in Vulcan'[s] burning stow
> The smith does water cast with careful ee.*
> Full oft contentions great arise, we see,
> Betwixt the husband and his loving wife
> That sine* they may the firmlyer agree
> When ended is that sudden choler strife.
> Yea, brethren, loving other as their life,
> Will have debates at certain times and hours.
> The winged boy dissentions hot and rife
> Twixt his[2] lets fall like sudden summer showers.
> Even so this coldness did betwixt us fall
> To kindle our love as sure I hope it shall.

> Finis   J.R.

Cecil Papers   *Holograph*
133: 49

[1]"By an unknown author."
[2]Lines 11–12 are unintelligible as they stand. Apparently the King, when copying his poem, carelessly left out some word such as "joys" after "his."

Letter 20

To Sir Francis Walsingham[?]

At the end of June 1586 an ardent young Catholic, Anthony Babington, smuggled a message to Mary Queen of Scots that six gentlemen were about to murder Queen Elizabeth while others would hasten to release Mary from her captivity. On 17 July Mary wrote a reply warmly approving the planned assassination. This letter she sent to Babington through the same secret channel. That action was to cost her her life, since Walsingham's agents were intercepting and deciphering her correspondence. In August, Walsingham, supplied with all the evidence he required, made known the plot and arrested the conspirators. From Scotland King James sent the following letter, almost certainly to Walsingham.

9 September 1586

Right trusty friend,

The bearer hereof, your countryman and my servant, having to do in these parts for some his particular affairs, I have thought good to hasten his voyage, to the effect he might visit the Queen, your sovereign, and send me assured word of her health and welfare in the midst of this wicked age fulfilled with [i.e. filled full with] foul conspiracies as have been of late haply discovered amongst you. I have also thought meet to accompany the said bearer with these few lines unto you, hereby heartily to request you that ye will further his adoose * with the best speed you can, whereof, since I have directed the Master of Gray[1] to write to you more at large, I will end this present, committing you, right trusty friend, to God's most holy protection. From my palace of Falkland the ix of September 1586.

Your most loving assured friend
JAMES R.

British Library
Harl. 6986, f. 43

Holograph

[1]Patrick Gray, Master of Gray, who in 1608 became 6th Lord Gray.

Letter 21

To William Keith

On 14 October 1586, following the execution of Babington and his fellow conspirators, Mary was placed on trial at Fotheringhay Castle. On 25 October her judges reconvened at Westminster to declare her guilty of seeking the death of Queen Elizabeth. On 12 November the English parliament petitioned Elizabeth to order Mary's execution. While Scotland seethed with fury born of frustrated national pride, James prepared to send two special ambassadors, the Master of Gray and Sir Robert Melville, to intercede for his mother. Meanwhile he despatched the following letter to William Keith, one of the two agents he already had in London.

[27? November 1586]

I perceive by your last letter the Queen my mother continueth still in that miserable strait that the pretended condemnation of that parliament has put her in. A strange example indeed and so very rare, as for my part I never read nor heard of the like practice in such a case. I am sorry that by [beyond] my expectation the Queen hath suffered this to proceed so far to my dishonour, and so contrary to her good fame as by subjects' mouth to condemn a sovereign prince descended of all hands of the best blood of Europe. King Henry the Eighth's reputation was never prejudged* in anything but in the beheading of his bedfellow. But yet that tragedy was far inferior to this if it should proceed as seemeth to be intended; which I can never believe, since I know it the nature of noble princes at that time chiefly to spare when it is most concluded in all men's minds that they will strike. Always [in any event] I am presently upon the directing of a very honourable ambassade thither for the same purpose, in which commission shall be one man[1] that the Queen will well like of and who both hath and deserveth great credit at her hand, and therefore fail not to insist with the Queen that all

74

farther may be stayed while [until] their arrival, which shall be as soon as possible they may post thither.

This far I promise to myself will be granted, since I no way merit at that queen's hands such hard using as to disdain to hear my overture and reasons, which, when she hath heard, she may weigh as best pleaseth her. Fail not to let her see all this letter. And would God she might see the inward parts of my heart where she should see a great jewel of honesty toward her locked up in a coffer of perplexity, she only having the key which by her good behaviour in this case may open the same.

Guess ye in what strait my honour will be in this unhapp* being perfected, since before God I already dare skath* go abroad for crying out of the whole people. And what is spoken by them of the Queen of England it grieves me to hear, and yet [I] dare not find fault with it except I would dethrone myself, so is whole Scotland incensed with this matter. As you love your Master's honour, omit no diligence in this request. And let this letter serve for excuse to the Queen my dearest sister of my not writing to her at this time in respect of this bearer's sudden departure. Farewell.

JAMES R.

Public Record Office
SP 52/41/74

Copy, apparently of a lost holograph

[1]The Master of Gray.

Letter 22

To Robert Dudley, Earl of Leicester

On 30 November 1587, Queen Elizabeth called home from the Netherlands her favourite, the Earl of Leicester, who had been serving there as Governor of the United Provinces. King James must have addressed the following letter to Leicester as soon as he learned of his imminent return. In this appeal to Leicester to interest himself in Queen Mary's case, James seems concerned more with monarchical immunity than filial feeling.

4 December 1586

Right trusty and well-beloved cousin,

I cannot but be very glad of your absence out of England this time past, since so rare an example, as is of late there practised, was not worthy of the presence of such a one as you be—I mean the pretended condemnation of the Queen my mother. And as I cannot deny but her course was to be hated by all good Christians and lovers of this isle, so will I affirm that such a fashion of proceeding by subjects against a free prince of the best blood in Europe is greatly slanderous to all the princes in the same, and most dishonourable to the Queen your sovereign. As for my own part, it is far by [out of keeping with] my expectation or deserts that your countrymen, in so using the mother, should have borne so small respect to the offspring, always [in all events] I could not omit, upon the knowledge of your return, immediately to write this present [letter] unto you, hereby most earnestly to desire you according to the trust I have in you that by your means the rest of this tragedy may be unperfected till the arrival of my ambassador is there, which shall be in as few days as possibly can be. At what time, if my overtures and offers be not found reasonable, the Queen may then do as shall seem to her best; but to proceed before she hear it, could come of no wisdom—and what strait I would be put in thereby I doubt not ye can well judge, since ye have all these times past been a professor at the very school of honour. My extremity if so should be [i.e., if his mother is executed] is greater than I can express; and therefore I pray you once again, as ever ye would do me any pleasure or honour, so to behave yourself in fulfilling my expectation in this matter as the deliverer hereof will more amply inform you, whom praying you heartily to trust as myself, I commit you, trusty and well-beloved cousin, to the holy protection of the Most High. From my palace of Holyroodhouse the 4 day of December, 1586.

Your most loving and
assured friend,
JAMES R.

I had long since despatched Sir Alexander Stewart[1] with my answer unto you but the uncertainty of your return moved me to stay him here. Always [in any event] he shall be shortly with you.

British Library   *Holograph*
Add. 32092, f. 56

[1]For the King's subsequent annoyance with "Sir Alexander Stewart's dealing," see *CSP Scottish, 1586–88*, pp. 275–76.

Letter 23

To Robert Dudley, Earl of Leicester

In 1584, for the greater protection of their queen, thousands of Englishmen had signed a "bond" pledging not only personally to take the life of any assassin who struck down Elizabeth but to keep from the throne anyone who (even without knowledge of that fact) had been intended by the conspirators to be Elizabeth's successor. Parliament passed its own act, based on the bond, excluding from the succession all persons who had plotted against the Queen and all their descendants who had been privy to such plotting. Now, with Mary convicted of plotting against Elizabeth's life, James was fearful that his enemies might contrive to use this parliamentary act to bar him from the English throne. In the following letter he makes the strongest possible statement that, though he seeks mercy for his mother, he had never known of the plot in which she was involved and can only "hate her course."

Right trusty and well-beloved cousin,

I have no time, through the hasty despatch of this bearer, to answer in this letter to that which Master Archibald[1] wrote to me in your name. But the full answer thereof ye shall receive with the Master of Gray, who parts from here upon Saturday precisely, and shall not fail to part the said seventeenth day of this month, all excuses set aside. And therefore, as ye love my honour, deal for the stay of all proceeding till he be heard. And I pray you procure that a passport for him and another gentleman may meet him by the way.

But to my first purpose: this far shortly may I say, I am honest, no changer of course, altogether in all things as I profess to be. And whosoever will affirm that I had ever intelligence with my mother since the Master of Gray's being in England, or ever thought to prefer her to myself in the title, or ever dealt in any other foreign course, they lie falsely and unhonestly of me. But, specially, how fond and inconstant I were if I should prefer my mother to the title let all men judge. My religion ever moved me to hate her course, although my honour constrains me to insist for her life. Therefore I pray you suspend your judgement of me, lest your credulity in such reports do harm us both.

I cannot also omit to thank you for your careful excusing to the Queen the plainness of my letter written to William Keith, which she did very far misconstrue.

And thus, right trusty and well-beloved cousin, I commit you to the holy protection of the Most High. From my palace of Holyroodhouse, the xv day of December 1586.

Your most loving and
assured friend,
JAMES R.

Scottish Record Office   *Copy, apparently of*
GD 1/371/3, f. 337   *a lost holograph*

[1]Apparently a reference to Archibald Douglas, one of James's agents in London. D. H. Willson described him as "a corrupt lawyer" (*King James VI and I*, p. 73).

Letter 24

To Queen Elizabeth

With the approach of the decision that would mean life or death for Mary, James on 17 December despatched to England two special envoys, the Master of Gray and Sir Robert Melville, to make last, desperate pleas for his mother's life. He could not have made a worse choice for his principal spokesman; Gray had long since sold out to the English, and the previous August had confidentially advised Elizabeth to execute Mary, remarking "Mortui non mordent" (The dead don't bite). In the following letter James tries to calm Elizabeth's anger at the letter he had told William Keith to show her (see Letter 21) and informs her of his despatch of Gray.

16 December 1586

I am from my heart sorry, madame and dearest sister, that ye should so far have misconstrued my letter written to William Keith as to have thought I meant thereby to threaten you and your estates; whereas, by the contrary, my meaning was only (as God knows) to inform you what bruit these proceedings made to be spread through all this country, wherethrough [the] whole [of]Scotland is indeed so incensed as the bearer hereof, your own countryman, can inform you what his own ears and eyes have heard and seen herein.

As for me, I know well enough how hardly ye are pressed by the objecting the peril of your own life unto you [i.e., the urgings of her advisers that she was in danger as long as Mary lived], and therefore I never blamed yourself directly of these proceedings. I pray you then, madame, to account me your most honest and steadfast friend, since I never did, nor shall, deserve any other opinion to be conceived by you of me.

Now, madame, I must heartily pray you for my sake to continue any proceeding against my mother while [until] my overtures be heard, which the Master of Gray shall bring unto you, who I promise to you upon my honour shall part from hence on

Saturday next, all excuses set aside; and therefore I also pray you that your passport for him and another gentleman may meet him by the way. This far I assure myself ye will do for my sake, as I shall ever press to deserve it at your hands. And thus, not omitting to thank you for the delay already granted, I commit you, madame and dearest sister, to the holy protection of the Most High.

From Holyroodhouse the x6 day of December 1586.

Your most loving and affectionate
brother and cousin,
JAMES R.

Scottish Record Office   *Copy, apparently of*
GD 1/371/3, f. 336   *a lost holograph*

Letter 25

To Patrick Gray, Master of Gray

The Master of Gray and Sir Robert Melville arrived in London on 31 December to join Archibald Douglas and William Keith in a last fight to save Mary's life. Not surprisingly, since both Gray and Douglas had sold out to the English, their representations were ineffective. James, somehow alerted as to the faintness of their efforts, wrote practically identical letters to the two men, demanding greater exertions to save Mary. For the companion holograph to Archibald Douglas, see British Library, Cotton MSS., Caligula C IX, f. 574.

[*January 1587*]

Reserve up yourself no longer in the earnest dealing for my mother, for ye have done it too long. And think not that any dealing will do good if her life be lost, for then adieu with my dealing with that estate. And therefore, if ye look for the continuance of my favour, spare no pains nor plainness in this case, but

read my letter written to William Keith and conform yourself
wholly to the contents thereof. And in this request let me reap
the fruits of your great credit there, either now or never. Farewell.

JAMES R.

Scottish Record Office   Holograph
GD 1/371/1, f. 189

Letter 26

To Queen Elizabeth

*There is no reason to think that James did not sincerely wish
to save his mother's life, even though her death would make his
own status as King of Scotland entirely unequivocal. What inspired him in his endeavours on Mary's behalf was not filial
affection—it would have been absurd for him to pretend such
feeling for a woman he could not remember ever having seen.
His motives were political: he would lose status and honour if
his mother were executed, and her execution would be a
flagrant violation of the Law of Divine Right, so dear to James,
that made sovereigns accountable only to God. These two arguments provide the substance for the turgid letter he wrote to
Elizabeth in his final attempt to save Mary's life.*

26 January 1587

Madame and dearest sister,

If ye could have known what divers thoug[hts] have agitated
my mind since my directing of William Keith unto you for the
soliciting of this matter whereto nature and honour so greatly
and unfeignedly binds and obliges me; if, I say, ye knew what
divers thoughts I have been in and wh[at] just grief I had weighing deeply the thing itself if so it should proceed (as God forbid)
what events might follow thereupon, what number of straits I
would b[e] driven unto and, amongst the rest, how it might

peril my reputation amongst [my sub]jects—if these things, I yet say again, were known unto you then [doubt] I not but ye would so far pity my case as it would easily make you at the first to [re]solve your own best into it.

I doubt greatly in what fashion to write in [this] purpose, for ye have already taken so evil with my plainness as I fe[ar if] I shall persist in that course ye shall rather be exasperated to passio[ns in rea]ding the words than by the plainness thereof be persuaded to consider r[ightly] the simple truth. Yet justly preferring the duty of an honest f[riend] to the sudden passions of one who, how soon they be past, can wiselier weigh the [reasons] than I can set them down, I have resolved in a few words and plain to give y[ou my] friendly and best advice appealing to your ripest judgement to discern t[here]upon. What thing, madame, can greatlier touch me in honour that [am] a king and a son than that my nearest neighbour, being in straitest [friend]ship with me, shall rigorously put to death a free sovereign prince and my natural mother, alike in estate and sex to her that so uses her, albeit subject I grant to a harder fortune, and touching her nearly in proximity of blood. What law of God can permit that justice shall strike upon them whom he has appointed supreme dispensators of the same under him, whom he hath called gods[1] and therefore subjected to the censure of none in earth, whose anointing by God cannot be defiled by man unrevenged by the author thereof, who, being supreme and immediate lieutenants of God in heaven, cannot therefore be judged by their equals in earth? What monstrous thing is it that sovereign princes themselves should be the example-givers of their own sacred diadems' profaning!

Then what should move you to this form of proceeding (supposing the worst, which in good faith I look not for at your hands)? Honour or profit? Honour were it to you to spare when it is least looked for; honour were it to you (which is not only my friendly advice but my earnest suit) to take [sic: make?] me and all other princes in Europe eternally beholden unto you in granting this my so reasonable request and not (pardon, I pray you, my free speaking) to put princes to straits of honour where through your general reputation and the universal (almost) misliking of you may dangerously peril both in honour and utility your person and estate. Ye know, madame, well enough how small difference Cicero concludes to be betwixt *utile* and *honestum* in his discourse th[ere]of and which of them ought to be framed to the other.[2] And now, madame, to conclude, I pray you so to weigh these few arguments that as I ever presumed of your nature so the whole world may praise your subjects for their dutiful care for your preservation and yourself for your princely pity, the doing whereof on[ly] belongs unto you, the performing whereof only appertains unto you, and the prai[se] thereof only will ever be yours. Respect them, good sister, this my first, so long con[ti]nued and so earnest request despatching my ambassadors with such a comfortable answer as may become your person to give, and as my loving and honest heart unto you merits to receive. But in case any do vaunt themselves to know further of my m[ind] in this matter than my ambassadors do, who indeed are fully acquainted therewith, I pray you not to take me to be a chameleon but, by the contrary, [them] to be malicious imposters as surely they are.

And thus praying you heartily to ex[cuse] my too rude and longsome letter, I commit you, madame and dearest sister, to the blessed protection of the Most High, who mott* give you grace so to resolve in this matter as may [be most] honourable for you and most acceptable to him. From my palace of Holy-[roodhouse], the 26 day of January 1586.

Your most loving affect[ionate]
brother and cousin
JAMES R.

British Library, Cotton MSS.,   *Holograph*
Caligula C IX, f. 192

[*Note:* *The outer edges of this manuscript having been charred in the fire that wrought such havoc on the Cotton MSS., it has been necessary to supply in square brackets the syllables or words that appear to be missing.*]

[1] Many years later, in his *Trew Law of Free Monarchies*, the King was to write,

"Kings are called Gods by the prophetical King David," citing Psalm 82:6 as his authority (*Political Works*, C. H. McIlwain ed., Cambridge, Mass., 1918, p. 54).

[2]The identity of the *utile* (useful) and the *honestum* (honourable) is stressed in Cicero's *De Officiis*, a typical instance being 3.8.35: *Quicquid honestum id utile*.

Letter 27

To Queen Elizabeth

On 8 February 1587, Mary Queen of Scots was executed at Fotheringhay Castle. Men looked to see what action her son, the King of Scotland, would take. Would he act on his veiled threats and terminate the recent Anglo—Scottish treaty of alliance? To the young king Elizabeth wrote a letter on 14 February denying that she had ever intended his mother's death. (Although she had signed Mary's death warrant, she dismissed Secretary Davison alleging that he had not had her permission to have it carried into effect.) When Elizabeth's kinsman Robert Carey arrived at Berwick with Elizabeth's exculpatory letter he was refused entry to Scotland, but he was allowed to hand over the Queen's letter for transmittal to King James. In reply His Majesty wrote the following letter. There would be no crisis with England, and James would not risk his claim to be Elizabeth's successor.

[*Late February 1587*]

Madame and dearest sister,

Whereas by your letter and bearer Robert Carey,[1] your servant and ambassador, ye purge yourself of yon unhappy fact, as on the one part considering your rank, sex, consanguinity, and long professed goodwill to the defunct, together with your many and solemn attestations of your innocency, I dare not wrong you so far as not to judge honourably of your unspotted part therein. So, on the other side, I wish that your honourable behaviour in all times hereafter may fully persuade the whole world of the same. And as for my part I look that ye will give me at this time such a full satisfaction in all respects as shall be a

84

mean to strengthen and unite this isle, establish and maintain
the true religion, and oblige me to be, as of before I was, your
most lov*ing and dearest brother.*

J.R.

This bearer hath somewhat to inform you of in my name, whom
I need not desire you to credit for ye know I love him.

British Library   *Holograph*
Add. 23240, f. 65

[*Note: The above-noted manuscript [Plate II] is James's draft and is
marked by a number of cancellations and some interlining of added
phrases. James did not bother to complete the complimentary close or
add his signature to this draft. These (in italics) have been supplied
from a copy of the letter sent to the Queen (Harl. 4004, f. 142).*]

[1]See Letter 11, n. 1.

Letter 28

To James Stewart, Earl of Moray

*Popular feeling in Scotland ran so high after the execution of
Mary, and the affront to the King himself appeared so apparent,
that James felt that he had to take some sort of action, however
nominal. Accordingly, he ordered the Estates to meet but set a
date that left national passions an interval in which to moderate. The summons reminded the turbulent Scottish lords that
they were not allowed to bring troops of armed men to such
meetings.*

15 March 1587

Right trusty cousin, we greet you well.
    The strait wherein this recent news of the Queen our moth-
er's most dolorous and cruel death has cassin* us, both in

honour and estate being the greatest that befell us ever since our nativity, and wherein we have greatest need of the assistance and advice of our nobility and Estates to take such resolution as may be to the preservation of God's true religion, our honour, and the quietness of our estate, we have therefore thought meet to assemble our Estates at Edinburgh, upon the 20th day of April next, and to the same effect will desire you most affectuislie* that in any ways ye fail not to be present with us the said day and place, as ye will testify unto us your willing mind to do us service and will deserve therefore our special thanks.

Thus we commit you to God, from Dalkeith, the xv day of March, 1586.

JAMES R.

We look that ye will come accompanied with 24 persons allanerlie,* according to our proclamation.

Moray MSS., Darnaway Castle (no catalogue number, but calendared HMC, Sixth Report, Part I, 1877, p. 639)

Scribal text, signed by the King

Letter 29

To Sir John Maitland[?][1]

Accounts differ as to King James's reaction when, on 23 February 1587, he received news of his mother's execution. According to one report, he was so upset that he went to bed without supper and the next morning "he past [sic] solitarlie to Dalkeithe, desiring to be solitar."[2] *James's reference in the following letter to making a "pilgrimage" may refer to this withdrawal from his court. On the other hand, the mention of keeping Gray where he is may date the letter from the imprisonment of Gray on 20 April after the Earl of Leicester had revealed the perfidy of Gray in secretly advocating Mary's death. On 15 May, after a full confession, Gray was sent into exile.*

[early 1587]

Because I am making now to my pilgrimage, I must remember you that is resident to garr* keep good order and watch in this town during my absence and have good intelligence of any folk is "steiring be south oure hande."[3] As for me, "I will flit every two or three days anis* as I told you yestereen."[4] Retain all folks by public or pri[vate] command from coming to trouble me. And garr* them await upon my coming every two or three days anis* to this town for doing of business. As for the horsemen, let them wait on in some places near me, but forbid them to remain directly with me. I recommend to your memory and diligence all my affairs, especially remember the stay of Gray where he is.

JAMES R.

British Library   *Holograph*
Add. 23241, f. 13

[1]The provenance of this letter (in a volume of Maitland Papers) and its date and contents all suggest that it was addressed to Secretary Maitland.
[2]David Moysie, *Memoirs of the Affairs of Scotland*, Bannatyne Club No. 39 (Edinburgh, 1830), p. 60.
[3]"Stirring to the south of us." (The reference is probably to the Border.)
[4]The sense is: "As I told you last night, I will make a quick trip to town once every two or three days."

Letter 30

To Queen Elizabeth

On 31 July 1588 the English ambassador to Scotland, William Ashby, received a despatch from Secretary Walsingham informing him that the Spanish Armada had entered the English Channel. That evening Ashby passed on the information to King James, who was, of course, under the terms of his alliance with Elizabeth bound to support her militarily. In case James might be tempted to renege on this treaty, Ashby offered him, in return for his participation in the war, an English dukedom, an increase in his annuity to £5000, and sufficient extra money to maintain a royal bodyguard of fifty men and a force of a hundred horse and a hundred foot to police the Border. After a few days' thought, James wrote the following letter.

4 August 1588

Madame and dearest sister,

In times of straits true friends are best tried. Now merits he thanks of you and your country who kythis* himself a friend to your country and estate; and so this time must move me to utter my zeal to the religion and "quhou" [how?] near a kinsman and neighbour I find myself to you and your country. For this effect then have I sent you this present hereby to offer unto you my forces, my person, and all that I may command, to be employed against yon strangers in whatsomever fashion and by whatsomever mean as may best serve for the defence of your country. Wherein I promise to behave myself not as a stranger and foreign prince but as your natural son and compatriot of your country in all respects.

Now, madame, to conclude, as on the one part I must heartily thank you for your honourable beginning by your ambassador in offers for my satisfaction, so on the other part I pray you to send presently down commissioners for the perfecting of the same, which I protest I desire not for that I would have the reward to precede the deserts, but only that I with honour, and all my good subjects with a fervent goodwill, may embrace this your godly and honest cause, whereby your adversaries may have ado not with England but with the whole isle of Britain.

Thus praying you to despatch all your matters with all possible speed, and wishing you a success convenient to those that are invaded by God's professed enemies, I commit, madame and dearest sister, your person, estate, and country to the blessed protection of the Almighty.

From Edinburgh the fourth of August, 1588.

Your most loving and affectionate
brother and cousin as
time shall now try,
JAMES R.

Cecil Papers
133: 85

Holograph

Letter 31

To George Gordon, Earl of Huntly

One of the most powerful of James's lords was George Gordon, Earl of Huntly, the Catholic magnate who dominated much of northern Scotland. James was attracted to the earl, a young man about his own age. Although experience should have taught James that Huntly was unreliable and unscrupulous, the King received a considerable shock when, on 27 February 1589, the English ambassador gave him intercepted letters which revealed that Huntly was one of a group of Scottish Catholic leaders who had written to Philip II promising assistance should the Spaniards decide to invade Scotland. Huntly was lodged in prison. There he received this reply to a letter in which he had begged for an interview with the King. (In fact, James dined with him on 28 February, and visited him each day during the following brief week of imprisonment.)

[February? 1589]

I am moved, my lord, upon the earnest desire of your letter somewhat to satisfy the request thereof by these presents, in resolving you hereby what is the best course ye can take for reparation of these things past.

I would wish you then, first, to consider wherein ye have offended, wherefrom ye are fallen, and what is your present state that thereby, entering in deep consideration thereof, there may the easelier appear unto you the only way of remedy. As for your offences, I will not at this time aggrege* them unto you. But this far only will I remember you of: how far ye have promised obedience unto me in following my will in all things, in doing whatsomever I directed you, which ye affirmed to be your right honour; how far promised ye to give proof as well in religion and course; how far promised ye to contempne* all friendship or fellowship but such allanerlie* as I should make you.

As for particular men about me, how far, and how innumerable times bade ye me answer for you unto them. And with what solemn oaths persuaded ye me thereto. And was it not your hardest speech that, in case they could no ways be put out of suspicion of you, ye would be in general friendship with them, but mell* in no matters fur[ther] than awaiting upon me and quhylis* dwelling at home. And since your parting from me, what promised ye to George Home¹ that day upon the fields, in case any man had dealt with you to withdraw you? What wrote ye to me after that out of Dunfermline? And what friendship promised ye in that letter to them that were about me whom with I had joined you in friendship? What wrote ye likewise out of Montrose? And as for any contrary persuasion ye could since have gotten, how many million of times, and specially that night in the cabinet, after that suspicion among you in the abbey, did I not then, I say, amongst innumerable other times resolve you that ye could not both trow* me and those busy reporters about you, and assured I you not that I could not be your friend if ye trusted these practisers [plotters]. This far for your offences.

Now as to that estate wherefrom ye are fallen. Consider only this one thing, which is "ower mekle the allane":² what favour and credit ye had of me, how far I assured of you to all honest men both in religion and course, and how surely I builded upon the last promise of yours—I will twiche* no more of this. And as to your present estate, look not (I pray you) to your present detention, uncouth form of entreatment, or any unsell* particularity following thereupon, for these are but effects flowing from a cause, and so but a part of the fruits of your present estate. But cast your eyes upon your estate indeed. First, consider what I, and next what all other honest men, must think of you. As for me, what further trust can I have in your promises, confidence in your constancy, or estimation of your honest meaning? I whom to, particularly as a man whom to ye was most obliged, and generally as a Christian king, ye have so inexcusably broken unto. And as for all other honest men, what can they think of you? Are these the fruits of your well conversion? Is this a likely purgation of your letters intercepted by England? Or is this a good proof of your honest course in my service? What, then, is the only remedy of all this? Nothing but this: as ye have offended two persons in me, a particular friend and a general Christian king, so must ye make amends to both these. As for the general king, ye must aggrege* and not diminish your offences. Conceal nothing of your pretense. Be not ashamed to declare how and whomby ye was moved thereunto. Discover plainly the butt ye shot at. And if any further was intended by any others, how far precisely ye agreed unto, what further ye knew of, or was meant or intended by any other.

And because ye desire to speak with me, that it may be to this effect only, and so your speech may be profitable to us both, as for my satisfaction as a particular man, willingly (without irking) to be content with whatsomever form I shall please to use you in. To remit fully to my discretion your contentment in all things. To use yourself in whatsomever thing as I shall direct you. To deliver the band [bond] if ye have it or may obtain it. Never to trust hereafter but such as I trust. And finally to repent you of all your faults, that in heart and mouth with the "forlorne" [prodigal] son ye may say "Peccavi in caelum et contra te."[3]

JAMES R.

Public Record Office   Copy, apparently of a
SP 52/43/15   lost holograph

[1]Knighted in 1590, Home was created a baron in 1604 and Earl of Dunbar in 1605.

[2]"Too much by itself."

[3]A misreading of the Vulgate text for Luke 15:18, "Peccavi in caelum, et coram te" ("I have sinned against heaven and before you").

Letter 32

[To Jean Douglas, Dowager Countess of Angus]

The next two letters, preserved in the same volume of manu-scripts, are undoubtedly addressed to the same lady. She is named in the address on the reverse of Letter 33, "Countesse of Angus douarier." A link with her is indicated by an endorsed phrase on the present letter: "The Kings M^{ty} letter anent ye Lordship of Spynie." Apparently it was in May 1590 that Jean, widow of Archibald Douglas, Earl of Angus, married James's crony, Alexander Lindsay, soon to be created Lord Spynie. In this letter James seems to be holding out this promotion as an inducement to the lady to accept the match which he has ar-ranged for her.

[1589]

Madame,

As I have no new occasion so have I no new thing to write at this present, except a new toot in an old horn, as they say; thereby to renew unto you that which I ever wish to be new in your breast. Till the performance thereof I can use no other arguments unto you than I used at my last speaking with you. And I trust I need not to repeat the same since I take you to be as well-willing in that matter as ever ye was. And, in a word, as he[1] merits whose blood, whose affection, and whose credit with me, I hope, be nothing inferior to any that can suit you. And in a thing, am I sure, he overpasses them all that "quhaire" [?]. In other folks bestowing I am but a consenter or acsistaire.* In this I am the only actor, solicitor, and bestower, whom as I have out of my own "bedl" [bed?][2] been willing to bestow upon yours, so need ye not to doubt I will advance him to such degree as that place merited.

Madame, as my sonnet says, I am and must continue best friend to you both "sen sa is."[3] For all others ye need the less to care; ye are come to perfect age and can govern yourself. Now, since I am so constant in this matter and his affection so lasting,

92

I look the constancy shall not inlayke* at the third hand, which otherwise (as God forbid) this matter, being so publicly broken forth as it is, would turn to my scorn, his scathe, and your small honour. Farewell.

He that will and can best
in this cause,
JAMES R.

National Library of Scotland   *Holograph*
MS.33.1.1 (Vol. I, item 13)

[1]Apparently a reference to Alexander Lindsay, the future Lord Spynie.

[2]In April 1588, Lindsay was described as "the King's only minion ... his nightly bed-fellow": *CSP Scottish 1586–88*, p. 558.

[3]"Since so it is." The poem is not in Craigie's edition of *The Poems of James VI of Scotland* (Edinburgh, Scottish Text Society, 1955, 1958). Apparently it has been lost.

Letter 33

[*To Jean Douglas, Dowager Countess of Angus*]

A further letter concerning the lady's marriage to Alexander Lindsay.

[1589]

Madame,

Although the straitness of this time so occupies me with affairs as I can never obtain one idle hour, yet in the very midst thereof I am compelled in haste to write to you these few lines that time be not tint* on any hand. According to my promise, I am resolute to advance this man of mine, whom for I have now so long dealt with you, to the rank that ye was last joined withal, that ye may be matched with that rank which ye presently possess and this will I do, without fail, at the time of the solemnization of my marriage as the properest time for such an action and

93

for providing him of a living correspondent to that estate.[1] I promise you I shall omit no possibility of time for doing the one as well as the other, whereof the performing of this first shall be a certain pledge. Now, madame, since I am thus ways to play my part on the one side, I look ye will not tyne* time on the other part as I have already said; and therefore I must most earnestly request you if ye will so far oblige me as to testify that ye do all this for my sake as ye wrote unto me, that then ye will presently subscribe the contract and cause proclaimed the banns, which thing (as I assure myself) ye will for my sake at this time perform. So may ye lay full account that, as I have oft promised unto you, I shall ever remain best friend to you both, be your patron in all your adoes,* and revenger of all torts* that any dare offer to either of you. And thus in haste I bid you farewell.

Your best friend,
JAMES R.

National Library of Scotland   *Holograph*
MS. 33.1.1 (Vol. I, item 14)

[1]With Lindsay in his retinue, King James returned to Scotland with his Danish queen on 1 May 1590. This same month Lindsay received the promised estate and, apparently, married the Countess. However, not until November of the same year was he created Lord Spynie.

Letter 34

To George Keith, Earl Marischal

Ever since James had attained his majority in 1587 there had been intermittent negotiations for his marriage. Queen Elizabeth, for political reasons, wanted James to marry Princess Catherine of Navarre, and the merchants of Edinburgh, for commercial reasons, wanted him to marry a Danish princess. Finally the choice was made, and in June 1589 the Earl Marischal was despatched to Denmark to negotiate a match with the Princess Anne. On 20 August James was married to her by proxy at Copenhagen. At the end of the month the bride sailed for Scotland but contrary winds forced her to turn back. James, knowing only that he was now married, languished for Anne and, impatient for tidings, sent the following letter to his emissary in Denmark.

28 September [1589]

My little fat pork,

    The continual languor I have had of your company's delay in coming, and the fear I have of longer protracting of time yet through the contrariousness of the winds, has at last constrained [me] to post away the bearer hereof to seek in whatever part of the world ye be in, as well to bring me certain nouelles* of your estate as to inform you of some things concerning your coming—whom willing you to credit and praying God to speed well your voyage, I bid you heartily farewell, in haste this last Sunday of September.

JAMES R.

    I pray you excuse to the ambassadors my not writing to them at this time, sen* your presence there may supply that default and, besides, I know not their names and styles.

Mr. David F. Metcalfe   *Holograph*
Cardiff, Wales

Letter 35

To John Maitland, Lord Thirlestane[1]

Increasingly impatient to be united with his Danish bride, James prepared in mid-October to fetch her to Scotland himself. He was in a state of romantic euphoria and, as the following letter indicates, impatient with those who sought to direct his attention to routine business when his mind was full of Anne.

The King's prohibition in this letter of all gatherings such as law days during his absence sprang from a canny awareness of how quarrels at such "convocations" could quickly ignite into violence that might unsettle the realm.

[*19 October 1589*]

I thought not to have written to you at this time but to have remitted all my directions to the sufficiency of this bearer, were not the inconsiderate importunity of this Master of Glamis,[2] who, as a man careless of me and only lover of himself, presses by all means, with his convocations, for days of law to interrupt and trouble this time only dedicated for my honour. Well, these faconis* are intolerable in subjects whose prince merits so well at their hands alluaye.* This and all other things I remit to the sufficiency of this bearer, as I have said, whom ye may fully credit, for I have amply enough informed him in all things. And as for silver, in good faith I am making all the shift I can, but I dare promise nothing, this world is so false.

Forget not to make presently, even the morn [i.e. tomorrow morning], a proclamation to be proclaimed through all Scotland discharging under pain of "deade" [*sic*] all convocations either for days of law, teinds,[3] turfs,[4] possessions of corns or commountie,* as well in respect of my order taken the last year in a convention thereabout as by reason of this extraordinary time. And this to endure till the twenty day of October next betwixt; and the which [proclamation] it shall promise in the word of a prince that I shall set down a solid order to be followed in all times coming by the subjects, herein assuring all the contraveners hereof that I will account them as hinderers of my marriage and evil-willers of any succession that ever I should have. And let this be proclaimed in Edinburgh the morn without fail. Farewell.

Written this Sunday at night in haste.

JAMES R.

John Gibb[5] remember on me at this time, now or never.

British Library   *Holograph*
Add. 23241, f. 29

[1]On 29 July 1587, Sir John Maitland of Thirlestane was appointed Chancellor, while retaining the post of Secretary. He received his peerage on 17 May 1590. The provenance of this letter and its contents indicate that it was written to Maitland.

[2]Sir Thomas Lyon, uncle of the 8th Lord Glamis. When he died in 1608, James reportedly exclaimed that "the boldest and hardiest man of his dominions was dead." The Master had played a prominent part in the Ruthven Raid.

[3]The teinds were a part of the agricultural produce of a parish; in some cases they were paid in kind but in others in money. Basically the teinds were intended for the support of the clergy, but part of them had passed into secular hands.

[4]Apparently the symbolic taking possession of land "by turf and twig."

[5]John Gibb was one of the King's Grooms of the Chamber.

Letter 36

To the People of Scotland

On 22 October 1589 King James sailed from Leith, with a retinue numbering about three hundred, to bring Queen Anne to Scotland. Behind him he left not only very detailed instructions as to how the government of the kingdom was to be carried on during his absence, but also the following general letter to his subjects explaining at length why he was embarking on this voyage.

[22? October 1589]

In respect I know that the motion of my voyage at this time will be diversely skansit* upon, the misinterpreting whereof may tend as well to my great dishonour as to the wrangous* blame of innocents, I have thereupon been moved to set down this present declaration with my own hand, hereby to resolve all good subjects, first, of the causes briefly that moved me to take this purpose in head and, next, in what fashion I resolved myself thereof.

As to the causes, I doubt not it is manifestly known to all how far I was generally found fault with by all men for the delaying so long of my marriage. The reasons were that I was alone, without father or mother, brother or sister, king of this realm and heir apparent of England. This my nakedness made me to be weak and my enemies stark.* One man was as no man, and the want of hope of succession bred disdain. Yea, my long delay bred in the breasts of many a great jealousy [suspicion] of my inability, as if I were a barren stock. These reasons and innumerable others, hourly objected, moved me to hasten the treaty of my marriage; for, as to my own nature, God is my witness I could have abstained longer nor the weal of my patrie* could have permitted. I am known, God be praised, not to be intemperately rash nor concety* in my weightiest affairs, neither use I to be so carried away with passion as I refuse to hear reason.

This treaty then being perfected, and the Queen my bedfellow coming on her journey, how the contrarious winds stayed her and where she was driven it is more nor notorious to all men. And that it was necessarily concluded by the Estates that it behooved necessarily to be performed this year, I remit to themselves, who concluded the same in the spring at the Earl Marischal's[1] directing.

The word, then, coming to me that she was stayed from coming through the contrarious tempests of winds and that her ships were not able to perfect their voyage this year through the great hurt they had received (remembering myself of her inability on the one part to come, and of the foresaid resolution of the Estates on the other, the like whereof I had often solemnly avowed), I, upon the instant, yea the very moment, resolved to make possible on my part that which was impossible on hers. The place that I resolved this in was Craigmillar, not one of the whole Council being present there. And, as I took this resolution only of myself, as I am a true prince so [I] advised with myself only what way to follow forth the same. Whereupon I thought first to have had the colour of the Earl Bothwell's[2] parting, whom first I employed to have made this voyage, as well in respect of his office as likewise the rest of the Council being absent all that whole day after I came to Edinburgh—the

98

Chancellor[3] and the Justice Clerk[4] being yet unreturned out of Lauder, and the whole rest of the officers of estate being all at their own houses, the Clerk of Register only excepted. But, fra* I saw this voyage impossible to be perfected by the Earl Bothwell in respect of the costs he had bestowed upon the preparations of my marriage, whereby he was unable to make it with such expedition and honour as the estate of that affair and his person did require, I was then forced to seek some other way and to abide the Council's assembling.

Who, being convened, found such difficulties in reiking* out a number of ships for her convoy (for so I gave it out who should be the persons of the ambassade) as I was compelled, to make them the more earnest, to avow in great vehemency that, if there could be gotten no other to go, I should go myself alone, if it were but in one ship. But if all men, said I, had been as well-willed as became them, I needed not be in that strait. These speeches moved the Chancellor, upon three respects, to make his offer of going: first, taking these speeches of evil will unto him, because all men knows how he has been this long time slandered for overgreat slowness in the matter of my marriage; next, his zeal to my service, seeing me so earnest; and last, the fear he had that I should have performed my speeches if no better could have been. From the time of the making of this offer, I have ever kept my intention of my going as close as possibly I could from all men, because I thought ay[e]* it was enough for me to put my sute* in the ship when all things were ready, without speiring of* further.

As I kept it generally close from all men so I say (upon my honour) I kept it so from the Chancellor, as I was never wont to do any secrets of my weightiest affairs, two reasons moving me thereto. First, because I knew that if I had made him "on the counsaill thairof" he had been blamed of putting it in my head, which had not been his duty (for it becomes no subjects to give princes advice in such matters). And therefore, remembering what envious and unjust burden he daily bears for leading me, by the nose as it were, to all his appetites, as if I were an unreasonable creature or a bairn* that could do nothing of myself, I thought pity then, to be the occasion of the heaping of further

99

unjust slander upon his head. The other reason was that, as I perceived, it was for staying me that he made the offer of his going, so was I assured that, upon knowledge of my going, he would either altogether have stayed himself or at least lingered as long as he could, thinking it overgreat a burden to him to undertake my convoy—as I knew upon the rumours of my going he has said no less to sundry of his friends. This far I speak for his part as well [as] for my own honour's sake, that I be not unjustly slandered as an irresolute ass who can do nothing of himself, as also that the honesty and innocency of that man be not unjustly and untruly reproached.

And as for my part, what moved me ye may judge by that which I have already said, besides the shortness of the way, the surety of the passage (being clean of all sands, forelands, or suchlike dangers), the harbours in these parts so sure, and no foreign fleets resorting upon these seas.

It is my pleasure, then, that no man grudge or murmur at these my proceedings; but let every man leave [lead?] a peaceable and quiet life, without offending of any, and that all man conform to himself[5] to the directions in my proclamation till my return, which I promise shall be, God willing, within the space of twenty days, wind and weather serving. Let all men assure themselves that whatsoever contravenes my directions in my absence I will think it a sufficient proof that he bears no love in his heart towards me. And, by the contrary, those will I only have respect to, at my return, that reverences my commandment and will in my absence. Farewell.

JAMES R.

Clerk of Register: It is my will that this declaration be registered for the more force and authenticness.

Scottish Record Office　　　　　　　　　*Copy of a lost holograph*
Register of the Privy Council of
*　　Scotland (original manuscript)*
Acta 1587–89, 22 October 1589

¹George Keith, 5th Earl Marischal (see Letter 34).
²Francis Stewart, Earl of Bothwell, Lord Admiral of Scotland from 1583 to 1591.
³John Maitland, Lord Thirlestane.
⁴The office of Justice Clerk was held by Sir John Bellenden.
⁵Possible corruption of the text here—one would expect "all men conform themselves" or "every man conform himself." "Man" may be a variant of "maun." *

Letter 37

To Lord John Hamilton

On 28 October King James landed safely in Norway, then part of Denmark. On 23 November he and Anne were married at Oslo. Shortly afterwards the King wrote the following letter to Lord John Hamilton, the powerful Lowland magnate whom James, during his absence abroad, had left as lieutenant of the south of Scotland.

1 December 1589

Good my lord,

What constant good opinion I had of you and what trust I have in you I declared by my letter unto you at my parting; and now by this bearer, Colonel Stewart,¹ my trusty servant and your friend, I send unto you the certainty of that good news that ye have long looked for. For, in a word, all things are succeeded with me since my parting according to wish and have [*sic*] praised be God. As to the particulars of all things, I remit to the said bearer the ample declaration thereof, whom I pray you to credit in such directions as I have burdened him with to deliver unto you, who will inform you of my diet* and mind in all things. In the meantime make your full account that I shall never forget the promise I made you in the bishop's yard in the abbey, oft renewed since according to your wish and sure hope when ye was a banished man. Thus since the hastiness of my

despatch will not permit me to write any farther I bid you heartily farewell, from Oslo the first of December 1589.

Your master in the old manner,
JAMES R.

I must, my lord, importune you for a man here that I am so
mekill* beholden to at this time, I mean the Justice Clerk,[2] that
for my sake ye will end that particular unto him that he has
been so long in suit of. Good faith, I will count it as done to
myself and therefore I assure myself I will not be refused.

Hamilton MSS., Lennoxlove,   *Holograph*
The Red Book, Letter 12
(Marshall catalogue no. C1/12)

[1]Colonel William Stewart, Commendator of Pittenweem, used by King James
as a confidential messenger, was involved in negotiating James's marriage.
[2]See Letter 36, n. 4.

Letter 38

To Alexander Lindsay

*At Hamlet's Elsinore stands Kronborg Castle and here the
honeymooning James and Anne took up residence on 21 January 1590. From here James wrote the following letter to Alexander Lindsay, the future Lord Spynie, who had accompanied
him from Scotland but, apparently because of illness, had not
been able to travel with the royal couple to Kronborg Castle.*

[February ? 1590]
Sandy,

Till your good hap furnish me some better occasion to recompense your honest and faithful service, uttered by your dili-

gent and careful attendance upon me specially at this time, let this assure [you] in the inviolable word of your own prince and master that, when God renders me in Scotland, I shall irrevocably and with consent of Parliament erect you the temporality of Murray[1] in a temporal lordship with all honours thereto appertaining. And let this serve for cure to your present disease. From the castle of "croneburg" [Kronborg] where we are drinking and driving "our" [o'er] in the old manner.

J.R.

Holograph

*The original of this letter, once in The Advocates' Library (now part of the National Library of Scotland), was lost when a book of royal papers was stolen some fifty years ago. Fortunately, a lithographed facsimile had been provided as a plate at the head of the Bannatyne Club's Volume XXVI (*Papers Relative to the Marriage of King James VI)*

[1]On 6 May 1590 Lindsay received lands belonging to the suppressed bishopric of Moray, which were "erected" into the free barony of Spynie. In November 1590 Lindsay was created Lord Spynie. (See Letters 32 and 33.)

Letter 39

To Robert Bruce

Robert Bruce, an eminent minister in the Kirk in Edinburgh and one of Chancellor Maitland's friends, was at this period in favour with the King. Possibly on his chancellor's advice, James ordered that, while he and Maitland were away in Denmark, Bruce was to be kept informed of all government decisions, so that he could protest against any misconduct. In this letter of instructions concerning his return, James amuses himself by

echoing the biblical parable of the wise and the foolish virgins
who awaited the bridegroom's coming (Matthew 25: 1–13).

19 February 1590

Good Master Robert,

Besides the welcome news that by your last letter ye sent unto me ye painted out so viflie* therein your honest meaning to my service, beside the good report I have otherwise heard of your daily travails for that effect now during my absence, as I think myself beholden while I live never to forget the same. And now, Master Robert, since by the season of the year ye may perceive that (God willing) your fascherie* in that is near an end, ye may fight out the rest of your battle with a greater courage, *nam perseveranti in finem*[1] etc.

I pray you waken up all men to attend my coming and prepare themselves accordingly, for my diet* will be sooner able nor is laikid* for and (as our Master says) I will come like a thief in the night, and whose lamps I find burning, provided with oil, these will I cunn* thank to and bring into the banquet house with me but those that lack their burning lamps provided with oil will be barred at the door, for then will I not accept their crying "Lord! Lord!" at my coming, that has forgot me all the time of my absence. How properly this metaphor convenes with my purpose I leave to your judgement.

For God's sake take all the pains ye can to toone* our folks well now against our home-coming, lest we be all shamed afore strangers; and exerce [exercise] diligently your new office of Reader and Componer. I think this time should be a holy jubilee in Scotland, and our ships should have the virtue of the ark in agreeing [reconciling] for a time at least *naturales inimicitias inter feras,*[2] for if otherwise it fell out (*quod deus avertat*)[3] I behooved to come home like a drunken man amongst them, as the prophet says,[4] which would well keep decorum to, coming out of so drinking a country as this is. I pray you recommend me heartily to the good provost[5] of your town and, in anything he can, pray him to assist my affairs as I have ever been certain of his goodwill in my service. Especially desire him to further all he can the reiking* out of three or four ships to meet me here and convoy me home, as more particularly the Council's directions will inform him, and likewise I doubt not he will assist the Master of Work in getting as many good craftsmen as may be had for ending out the half-perfected abbey[6] that lies in such a dead thraw* as did the Host of *hoc est enim cor*[7] betwixt the Spanish priest's hands; thus, recommending me and my new rib to your daily prayers, I commit you to the only All-Sufficient. From the castle of "croneburg" [Kronborg] the xix of February 1589.

JAMES R.

Recommend me heartily to my three ministers, and show Master Patrick my man I am sorry he has been so long hained* here from Court, but he may the better wait on hereafter.

Scottish Record Office   *Holograph*
GD 1/240/2

[1]"For one persevering unto the end."
[2]"Natural enmities among wild beasts."
[3]"May God prevent it!"
[4]A nice example of King James's pawky sense of humour. The passage, Jeremiah 23: 9–10, reads: "I am like a drunken man, and like a man whom wine hath overcome, because of the Lord, and because of the words of his holiness. For the land is full of adulterers."
[5]John Arnott, Provost of Edinburgh.
[6]Holyrood Abbey, adjacent to the royal palace. In 1547 the English had stripped the lead off the roofs. In 1569 the transepts and their chapels, the quire and presbytery, had been demolished by order of the General Assembly of the Reformed Kirk, and only the nave was repaired.
[7]"For this is the heart." One would expect *hoc est enim corpus* ("for this is the body"), but there is no mark in the manuscript to suggest that *cor* is an abbreviation. Possibly James made a slip which went unnoticed.

Letter 40

To Robert Bowes

Robert Bowes, the English ambassador to Scotland, corresponded with James during the latter's months in Denmark. To a complaint about Scottish raiders crossing the Border, James sent the following good-natured reply.

31 March 1590

Good Bowes,

Since this is the last messenger that is (God willing) to be sent to Scotland before my own coming, I have thought good to write unto you these few lines with him, but the faithfulness of the bearer, known to you, will make me the shorter.

Since the writing of my last unto you I received your letter whereby, amongst other things, I perceive there has been some roads [inroads] on the Borders by some on my side. Well, what is possible to an absent man to do therein I have given order with this bearer to the Council there. I do still continue in matters of justice and keeping of amity twixt the two realms in that same mind that ye have found me of beforetimes.

I have likewise heard of the relief of those that were apprehended in the Spanish bark,[1] whereof I wonder not a little; but what direction upon the first advertisement of their apprehension I sent there I trust ere now is come to your ears. Always care not how evil any there, against their promise, do behave themselves, for ye may assure yourself my goodwill is tied to no man in Scotland any longer than he swerves from following me in that course and profession that I wrote of in my last letter unto you.

I pray you trust the bearer (for therefore have I chosen him) in such things as I have directed him to deal with you into concerning my state, either in general or particular, for I doubt not of your forwardness in my affairs. But remitting the particulars of all things to his report, I bid you heartily farewell. From the stately castle of "crouneburge" [Kronborg] the xxxi of March 1590.

Your loving friend,
JAMES R.

What is amiss in absence I assure you shall be repaired in presence.

Public Record Office   *Holograph*
SP 52/45/11

---

[1]A ship, commanded by "John de Mereda," seized while illegally in Scottish waters. (See *Register P.C. Scotland* IV, 1585–92, pp. 830–31.)

Letter 41

To Robert Bruce

This letter from Kronborg Castle was probably one of the last that James wrote before his return to Scotland. On 1 May he and Queen Anne landed at Leith.

4 April 1590

I have received, Master Robert, from "coronell"[1] a letter of yours, the counsel whereof (as I thank you heartily for it) so I promise you I am resolved deliberately to follow it at my home-coming.

I pray you continue careful in all my affairs, as ye have been, till my home come, for now your fascherie*[2] (God willing) will last you but few days. I have heard of all the General Assembly's proceedings, whereof I like very well. As to the contents of their letter I shall, God willing, satisfy all your expectations at my home-coming. I doubt not of your diligence to persuade the town of Edinburgh to guard themselves in such form as the bearer hereof has in direction unto them. I hope by [the time] this letter come to your hands it shall be time for you to pray for a good wind to us. So farewell till meeting, from the castle of "crouneburghe" [Kronborg] the fourth of April 1590.

JAMES R.

I pray you let not this calm lull the town of Edinburgh asleep, for in deadest calms ye know sudden and perilous puffs and whirlwinds will arise.

Scottish Record Office   *Holograph*
GD 1/240/3

[1]Colonel William Stewart (see Letter 37, n. 1).
[2]The trouble of scanning the government's actions (see Letter 39).

Letter 42

To Queen Elizabeth

One of James's most trusted servants was Roger Aston, a native of Cheshire who had lived in Scotland since boyhood. Aston having some private business to attend to in England, James used him as a courier[1] to deliver this reply to Elizabeth's request for the surrender of O'Rourke, an Irish rebel who had fled to Scotland.

22 March 1591

The parting of this bearer my servant, madame and dearest sister, towards your country, his native soil, for certain particular affairs, have moved me to accept the occasion for writing these few lines unto you.

I received a letter of yours within these few days, requesting me for the delivery of an Irish rebel of yours, fugitive in this realm. How I behaved myself in that matter before I received your letter, from the first hour I heard of that man's arrival in this country, I remit to the information of your ambassador here resident—for I did nothing therein without first acquainting him and forewarning thereof always.

Upon the receipt of your letter I willingly yielded unto your request, and am sorry I could not have the man himself to accompany this letter. But I have given order for his apprehension with all speed and means possible and, if success succeed my unfeigned goodwill, he shall be delivered at Berwick;[2] but, if I had known it ere the receipt of your letter, you had been satisfied ere now in this turn.

I would to God your greatest enemies were in my hands—if it were the King of Spain himself, he should not be long undelivered to you—for that course have I taken me to, and will profess it till I die, that all your foes shall be common enemies of us both, in spite of the Pope, the King of Spain, and all the Leaguers, my cousins[3] not excepted, and the Devil their master.

As to the affairs of the Borders, I remit likewise to your ambassador's information, wherewith I trust you shall be well satisfied, as you may assure yourself to be in all things that shall lie in my power.

As to the particular discourse of the state of all things here, and especially of my behaviour concerning your Irishman, I remit to be largely declared unto you by this bearer, for that he knew somewhat more particularly than others did, whose honesty and faithfulness to us both I recommended to you of before, so I cannot cease to renew it unto you at this time, which, I pray you, may find the due effects at your hands, for my sake, in anything wherein you may reasonably further him.

And thus, madame and dearest sister, I commend you to the tuition [protection] of the Almighty in the prosperous preservation of your estate and person, and utter confusion of all your enemies and so common to us both.

From Dalkeith the 22 of March 1590.

Public Record Office
SP 52/47/29

Copy, apparently of a
lost holograph

[1] This letter is endorsed, "The k of Scotts lre to the Q. Matie by Roger Ashton."
[2] King James made good this promise. Brian O'Rourke, convicted at Westminster of high treason, was executed on 3 November 1591 with all the horrors provided by the law.
[3] James's Guise kindred, who were particularly identified with the Catholic League.

Letter 43

To Queen Elizabeth

As part of his program for strengthening the royal authority, Chancellor Maitland worked for cooperation between the King and the Kirk. He must have felt heartened when in 1591 James, to please the ministers, sent[1] *the following letter to Queen Elizabeth on behalf of some of their allies, eminent but extremist English Puritans who had been arrested for their nonconformity. Elizabeth probably resented James's intervention on behalf of Cartwright and Udall. In any event, she kept them in prison for approximately a year after he wrote this letter.*

12 June 1591

Right excellent, right high and mighty princess, our dearest sister and cousin, in our heartiest manner we recommend us unto you.

Hearing of the apprehension of Master Udall[2] and Master Cartwright[3] and certain ministers of the Evangel within your realm, of whose good erudition and fruitful travails in the Kirk we hear a very credible commend, howsoever their diversity from the bishops and others of your clergy in matters touching them in conscience hath been a mean by delation to work them your mislike at this present, we cannot (weighing the duty

110

which we owe to such as are afflicted for their conscience in that profession) but by our most effectuous* and earnest letter [interpone*]† us at your hand to forbear any harder usage of them for that cause, requesting you most earnestly that, for our cause and intercession, it may please you to let them be relieved of their present strait and whatsoever further accusation or pursuit depending on that ground—respecting both their former merit in the forth [setting] of the Evangel in the simplicity of their conscience in this defence, which cannot well be thralled by compulsion, and the great slander which could not fail to fall out upon their streighting* for any such occasion, which we assure us your zeal to religion, besides the expectation we have of your goodwill to pleasure us, will willingly accord to our request, having such proof from time to time of our like disposition to you in any matter which you recommend unto us. And thus right excellent, right high and mighty princess, our dear sister and cousin, we commit you to God's good protection.

From Edinburgh the 12 of June 1591.

British Library　　　　　　　　　　　　　　　　　*Copy*
Harl. 787, f. 66

†[Note: Bracketed words, lacking or corruptly reproduced in Harl. 787, are supplied from other contemporary copies of this letter.]

[1]David Calderwood, compiling in the mid-seventeenth century his *History of the Kirk of Scotland*, included this letter, prefixing it with the following note: "Upon Fryday, the 11th of June, a letter was purchased [i.e., procured] from the king, by my Lord Lindsay and Mr. Robert Bruce, to the Queene of England, in favours [sic] of Mr. Udall. The letter was penned by Mr. George Young." (Edinburgh, Wodrow Society, 1842–49, V: 131–32.) The letter, as printed by Calderwood, makes no mention of "Master Cartwright and certain ministers of the Evangel."

[2]John Udall, the Puritan preacher and author, was a particular friend of the Scottish Presbyterians. He had preached before James on 20 June 1589. After his return to England, he settled at Newcastle, where he was arrested sometime in early 1590. He died almost immediately after his release in June 1592.

[3]Thomas Cartwright, the most notable of the English Presbyterians, had been deprived in 1570 of the Lady Margaret Professorship of Divinity at Cambridge. The next year he was in Geneva, along with Andrew Melville. Returning to England in 1572, he fled to the Continent in 1573. Back after eleven years of exile, he energized the English Presbyterians until his arrest in 1590. After his

release in 1592 he withdrew to Guernsey. At one time he was expected to be a Puritan spokesman at the Hampton Court conference, but in December 1603, before it met, he died. In any event, the Puritans had decided he was too controversial to make a good representative. See Patrick Collinson, *The Elizabethan Puritan Movement* (Berkeley, [1967]), pp. 110–11 and passim.

Letter 44

To John Maitland, Lord Thirlestane

Seeing that King James, with the skillful aid of Chancellor Maitland, was gradually consolidating the royal power and reducing that of the nobility, the erratic Earl of Bothwell became the irreconcilable enemy of both James and Maitland. The King, in consequence of Bothwell's rebellion, imprisoned him and planned his banishment. Aghast to learn that Bothwell had dealt with warlocks and witches against him, the King determined upon their death.

A few days after the King wrote the following letter, Bothwell escaped from Edinburgh Castle. For the next three years he would make James's life miserable with plots and attempted coups. James, a neurotically insecure man, became obsessive about this reckless and irresponsible enemy.

[*Spring 1591*]

Chancellor,

I marvel that so wise a man and old a counsellor as ye are should have done so unwise a turn as to have found fault with the generality of my revocation,[1]—especially considering the purpose I spake to you, at my last going over, in your own yard. *Sat sapienti.*[2]

As to the offending of any by this revocation—either it may prejudge* them or not. If it may not, it is nothing; and nothing can offend nobody. If it may, have I not enough ado with my own? And if the people knew who would offend with that they needed no more but hiss till* him.

112

I have offended the whole country, I grant, for prodigal giving fra* me. But when I take to me none can be offended but the particular person. But of all men it set least the Council or Chequer to have found fault with this turn, for by this way the vulgar opinion conceived of them these many years, that they were better friends to my person nor my purse, will not only be confirmed but holden now as confessed. It is ill to be called a thief and syne* found stealing. If I had been present when these articles were read to the Council, as Scoggin[3] bade the greatest ghooke* lay on the first stripe, so would I have bidden him that was most claggit* with the king's gear find the first fault, and it would then have been answered *cum alto silentio.*[4] But if your public offer had been performed by every one, this would not have been skarrid* at.

As for your own part, keep yourself from "well danced and well played." Your felicity, worldly man, depend only upon one and consist only by and in him. This far I writ only to yourself for that goodwill ye know I bear you. Let the uprightness of your meaning be unspottable by any, as well in bearing with as in doing. This far I recommend to your own only reading. The rest following ye may communicate it to the Council or sic* as it appertains unto. If I have been sharp, blame the sharpness of the humour that has troubled my head and bred sic impatience. The incessant labour I have taken upon affairs all this year, with the residence in ill-aired Edinburgh this time of year, has so weakened my complexion and so subjected me to sundry showers of diseases as it is unable to [impossible for] me to mell* in affairs till I be somewhat rested, and therefore I recommend unto you these principal points to be remembered in my absence. My wife's eleven hundred pounds must be here the morn [morrow] at even, without tryst-breaking. Maclean[5] is now relieved, and the gentlemen, I doubt not, ere now has kept their promise. This must be done and either yon sun or never, *car elle mesme y assigne ce temps.*[6]

I gart* the Secretary write yesterday a question to you about the clothes of some Dutch fellows—either money or clothes, choose you which of them. But I think rather clothes.

The two aides of the kitchen ran out yesterday and would not make the supper ready, saying condition was not kept. The Master Cook and his boy behooved to dress the meat. Call for the rou.* See what is conditioned and yet unaccomplished. Let it be presently mended since it is but so pigraill* a matter. Suppose we be not wealthy, let us be proud poor bodies. Remember your promise made to the Queen of Denmark. Take the thanks and honour of it yourself. The man that got the hundred crowns the last year is come here again the [this] year. Advise what to do with him. The Secretary shall tell you the particulars of that the morn [tomorrow].

Since there can no present trial be had of the Earl Bothwell, I think best he prepare himself to depart within thirty or forty days—his absence to be no nearer hand nor Germany or Italy—that he remain where he is till the ship be ready to pull up sails—only such persons as mells* with that preparation, by special licence at times to be admitted unto him. Great souertie* to be taken, Lothian barons being cautioners for his departing at that day, for his not returning without licence, for "practising nathing uithout" [plotting nothing outside] the country, and for leaving some principal man to be answerable for Liddisdale. In my opinion Buccleuch[7] were meetest for that charge. Let the man and ship's names that transports him be notified within fifteen days that burgess caution may be taken of him for transporting of him to sic* or sic ports, and for that cause let that man be warned to be master of his own ship. What letters my lord craves of recommendation to other princes, grant them, so being they be honourable. As for the coloured cause of his departure, advise upon some honourable excuse, for there is no want of matter.

Try, by the mediciners' oaths, if Barbara Napier[8] be with bairn* or not. Take no delaying answer. If ye find she be not, to the fire with her presently and cause bowel [disembowel] her publicly. Let Effie Makkaillen [Euphame MacCallum][9] see the stoup* two or three days and upon the sudden stay her in hope of confession if that service adverts. If not, despatch her the next oulke* anis* [next week sometime] but not according to the rigour of the doom. The rest of the inferior witches, off at the nail

114

with them. But gar* see that Richie Grahme [Ritchie Graham][10] want not his ordinary allowance till I take farther order with him. Remember yon action before the Council between the Grays and the Athol men.

Farewell, for I am weary of writing.

JAMES R.

British Library
Add. 23241, f.40   Holograph

[1] I.e., the revocation of grants made during his minority.
[2] "Enough for a wise man."
[3] John Scogan was the court fool of Edward IV. *Scoggin, his Jestes* was entered in the *Stationers' Register* in 1566, but the earliest edition to survive is that of 1613 (STC 21851).
[4] "With deep silence."
[5] Lachlan Maclean of Dowart, who had been imprisoned about a year earlier for employing shipwrecked Spaniards in an attack on one of his enemies.
[6] "For she herself assigns this time for it."
[7] Walter Scott of Buccleuch.
[8] On 15 April 1591 the Earl of Bothwell had been brought before the King and Council and charged with trafficking with the sorcerer Ritchie Graham and various witches, including Barbara Napier and Euphame MacCallum. Barbara Napier was arraigned on 8 May 1591 and, to James's great annoyance, acquitted of planning his destruction. She was, however, convicted of consulting with witches and left to the King's pleasure.
[9] Found guilty on nine counts of witchcraft, including two of treason against the King's person, Euphame MacCallum met death by burning on 26 June.
[10] Ritchie Graham was strangled and burnt at the Cross, Edinburgh, 28 February 1592.

Letter 45

To the Clerk Register[1]

Partly because of the King's extravagance, partly because so many of the Crown's sources of income had been alienated, and partly because of the government's inefficiency in collecting taxes, King James was always in debt and existed by means of one financial expedient after another. Royal officers, their salaries in arrears, were often slack in their duties. The following pungent letter, which unfortunately survives only in a most un-satisfactory copy,[2] *illuminates a financial crisis that apparently had everybody at their wits' end. The letter had the effect of goading the Lords of the Exchequer into such drastic retrench-ment that they stopped the King's quart of wine in the afternoon and his pint "after collation."*

[December 1591]

Clerk of the Register,

Because the Chancellor[3] is occupied in his despatches, I maun* address my complaint to you. I have been Friday, Satur-day, and this day waiting upon the direction of my affairs and never maun* command. Them of the Chequer that was or-dained to take the accounts waits "neveron".[4] The turns* of the house [hold] should have been ended this day—no man comes down. I sent for the Advocate both Friday and Saturday —nei-ther meet[ing] nor answer. Siclike* after the baillies of this town for the matter of the "tocher"[5]—the like answer. I ordered, as ye heard, a certain number to make overtures for reforming of the session—no sic* thing meditat.* I ordained the Treasurer to garr* make charges about the "horneris"[6]—I have heard nothing of that as yet. In short, no tryst or dayet* is kept. What is spoken this night late is forgotten [in] the morn. In the morn-ing I see nothing is menid* but to "gurne,"[7] weary of this work beholding of as long as I am earnestly waiting on. And when I am compelled to rest myself then to lay the . . . .[8] None cannot be always *vené*[9] and so let this writ be a witness for my part whenever it beis* called in question. I protest I may do no more nor I may, if I were then wait[ing?] on as long [as?] I cannot be waited.[10] Farewell.

Show this letter to the Chancellor and as many of our folks as ye meet withal.

National Library of Scotland   *Copy, apparently of*
Adv. MS. 34.2.17, f. 148   *a lost holograph*

¹The Clerk Register (Alexander Hay of Easter Kennet), was the official in charge of the clerks and responsible for the records. He had competence in parliament, court of session, council, and exchequer.

²Sir William Purves, who printed an Old Spelling text of this letter (*Revenue of the Scottish Crown, 1681,* Edinburgh, 1897, pp. xxxvii–xxxviii), found it partly illegible. The present editor, while correcting some misreadings by Purves, likewise finds a portion of the letter either illegible or garbled.

³Chancellor Maitland, who on 17 May 1590 had been created Lord Thirlestane.

⁴I.e., never wait on the business.

⁵The dowry, presumably of Queen Anne.

⁶Outlaws. In Scotland men who were outlawed were said to be "put to the horn."

⁷The general sense is that all the King can do is to snarl, or make a face, in frustration.

⁸The six omitted words are unintelligible.

⁹*Sic.* The original reads "uene," which Purves rendered as "vené," which does not really help. R. Cotgrave, *A Dictionarie of the French and English Tongues* (London, 1611) f. Kkkk5ᵛ, notes "vené" as a variant of "veiné," which he defines as "veined, or full of veins."

¹⁰The King's meaning seems to be that there is a limit to what he can do personally even if he were to attend to matters himself all the while that his negligent servants should be attending to them.

Letter 46

To Queen Elizabeth

On 28 June 1592 the Earl of Bothwell, with an armed force, launched a sudden attack on Falkland Castle when James and his queen were staying there. In the following letter Queen Elizabeth is asked to deny refuge to those responsible for this unsuccessful foray.

5 July 1592

Madame and dearest sister,

The residence of your ambassador here, whomby ye are as well advertised of every accident falls out here, as likewise informed what my request or desire is that ye should do at this time, this I say is the cause that stays me untroubling you so oft with my own letters as otherwise I would do.

117

In special, I doubt not ye are sufficiently informed of this late rare and rash attempt[1] confirming now at Falkland that treason which in winter they committed at Holyroodhouse.[2] But God be praised, who gave the last the worst success. Now it rests for me to hunt them the best I may, and therein to spare no pains nor travail; and for your part of concurrence, as well that none of these traitors shall find refuge in any part of your dominions as also that ye will, according to your own laws and their just deserts, punish such of your own lewd [base] subjects as were induced by them to assist them at this deed. I doubt not in this case of your good will in respect of the strait bond of amity betwixt us; and besides that I leave it to your consideration if this be not a perilous precedent for all princes.

And because this turn will of necessity drive me to extraordinary charges, I must heartily pray you at this time to send me that whole sum of annuity which I did the last year require of you; not that I am ignorant of the greatness of your present adoes,* but that I trust ye will, in this turn, turn your eyes a little from looking upon your own estate to blink upon the necessary case of your friend.

But remitting this and all other things to her loving consideration who never yet failed me in any my adoes; I commit you, madame and dearest sister, to the protection of the Almighty. From Edinburgh the fifth of July 1592.

Your most loving and affectionate
brother and cousin,
JAMES R.

British Library, Cotton MSS.,   *Holograph*
Vespasian F III, f. 83

[1]Bothwell's foray of 28 June 1592.
[2]Bothwell's raid on Holyroodhouse, 27 December 1591.

Letter 47

To Thomas Burgh, Lord Burgh

Late in December 1592, a Catholic courier was arrested while bearing the notorious "Spanish Blanks," empty pages signed by the Earls of Huntly, Errol, and Angus, on which their emissaries might write any terms they could negotiate with Philip II for an invasion of Scotland. In February 1593, King James headed into northern Scotland and there seized lands owned by these traitorous lords. Queen Elizabeth suspected, however, that once more James would deal too leniently with his Catholic nobles. Accordingly, she sent an English agent to confer with the Earl of Bothwell, who posed as a Protestant champion. Such was the ticklish situation when, on 16 March, a new English ambassador, Lord Burgh, presented his letters of credence to King James.

Having heard Burgh's representation, James drafted, in his own hand, an eight-point reply which may be summarized thus:

1. *The King is glad that Elizabeth has sent Lord Burgh to see what steps he is taking.*
2. *He is resolved to punish the vile plotters.*
3. *He will follow Elizabeth's advice as far as his parliament will agree.*
4. *He will maintain a council committed to Anglo-Scottish amity.*
5. *He will hazard his crown in support of Protestantism but must have Elizabeth's aid against traitors.*
6. *He will appoint as his wardens of the Border marches persons committed to friendship with England.*
7. *Elizabeth is, however, to consider her own need for James's assistance.*
8. *She should punish those who have given Bothwell asylum in England.*

This very important holograph document has been lost except for a single sheet (containing only the last two articles),[1] which survives in Scotland. This, complete with the dividing line that James drew between the clauses, reads as follows:

[Late March 1593]

We thank most heartily our dearest sister of her friendly offer in this case, and wishes her to consider if she have not as great need to help to stay the Spaniard from putting his foot in this country as either in France or in any part of the Low Countries, and to help to enable us for entertaining a sufficient number of guards to be employed: a part of them upon the guarding of our person, having so many great men now to be our rebels; a part of them to lie in such parts of the country as these rebels have greatest friendship in, both for repressing their insolence in case they would make any stir, as likewise to take up their levingis* according to her friendly advice; and the third part of these guards continually to be employed in hunting out of the conspirators, and the whole number to be employed to resist, as far as in them lay, to the landing of any foreign forces in case they came. And what my particular desire herein is I shall make her, with all speed, to be certified by one of my own [i.e., an ambassador of his own to England].

We pray her earnestly to follow forth the due punishment of such as have plainly received Bothwell, as she tenders her own honour, my contentment, and as the ingratitude towards me of these base-minded fellows does deserve, whereof we have at large informed you by our own mouth. And touching that vile man himself, as his foul offences towards me are unpardonable and most to be abhorred for example's sake by all sovereign princes, so we most earnestly pray her to deliver him in case he have refuge any more within any part of her dominions, praying you to inform her plainly that, if he be received or comforted hereafter in any part of her country, I can no longer keep amity

120

with her but, by the contrary, will be enforced to join in friendship with her greatest enemies for my own safety.

Scottish Record Office   *Holograph*
GD 1/371/3

[1]For the missing six clauses we are dependent on a copy at Hatfield endorsed: "The king of Scots answers with his own hand" (Cecil Papers 133: 101). This has been printed in HMC, *Salisbury MSS.*, IV: 296–97.

Letter 48

To Lord John Hamilton

On 24 July 1593 occurred one of those bizarre, complicated, and mysterious episodes that mark Scottish history. The Duke of Lennox, temporarily supporting Bothwell, effectively took over control of Holyroodhouse and signalled Bothwell that he could safely enter it. James, emerging from the privy with his clothing in some disarray, found Bothwell in his presence chamber offering his sword in surrender and loudly calling for the King's pardon. What he wanted, it turned out, was a purely nominal trial on the charge of treason and witchcraft, with a subsequent restoration of his estates. James met Bothwell's pretended submission with pretended forgiveness. For a few weeks Bothwell was able to have things his own way, but adroitly King James was able to regain the direction of events.

In the following letter, written immediately after the coup and almost certainly at Bothwell's insistence, James assures Lord John Hamilton, one of Bothwell's bitterest enemies, that all is well and that he need not raise any forces. (The original letter is in a very decayed condition, with some of the phrasing lost.)

121

24 July 1593

Right trusty cousin and counsellor, we greet you well.

Forsomuch as Francis, Earl Bothwell, this xxiiij of July, accompanied with Master John Colville,[1] and sundry others that were under danger of laws, came to our palace of Holyroodhouse and there, in all humility, on their knees craved our pardon for their extraordinary accomplots* here at our palace of before, [and] at Falkland, and at this time offering themselves for other crimes to trial, to be used as they shall be found innocent or guilty. Which humble petition we could not but of princely humanity admit and ... for in case any would inform you to the contrary that we are detained and pressed against our will and heart's liking you shall give no [ear?] ... unto but keep yourself quiet and peaceable ... [for] since there is no ... to your distr[ust] ... this we trust ye will do ... a good subject and as ye would do us acceptable service.

From the said palace, the day foresaid.

JAMES R.

My lord, these folks have promised all humility. Suppose the form was violent and indeed presently there is no force here but mine.

Hamilton MSS.,   *Only the signature and*
The Red Book, Letter 15   *postscript are holograph.*

---

[1]Originally a Presbyterian minister, Colville neglected his duties to his parishes and plunged into political intrigue, serving as an English spy. On 11 December 1593, with Bothwell, he was declared an outlaw. His last years were spent in exile.

Letter 49

To Queen Elizabeth

*In September, having "come out of the hands" of Bothwell,
James wrote the following letter to Queen Elizabeth, advancing
specious reasons why neither the lords involved in the Spanish
Blanks affair nor Bothwell would be tried for treason. The real
reason was that James, caught between two forces, the Protestant and the Catholic, at this point deemed it politic to move
against neither.*

19 September 1593

Madame and dearest sister,

It was no negligent unthankfulness on my part that made me,
ever since my late ambassador's return, keep silence towards
you till now, but only because that never till now I could both
with honour and surety advertise you of the truth of my estate
since the falling out of this late accident here.[1]

I cannot enough thank you of your so kindly accepting of my
late ambassador and for the loving and friendly despatch ye
gave him, especially for that privy and most familiar dealing ye
had with him even without the privity of any of your own Council; but most of all for your honourable promise never to hurt
my title notwithstanding of the many assaults given you
therein. I also thank you for that aid ye have sent me of the
annuity; wherein I consider the great charges ye are presently at
and doubts not but, when it shall please God to lessen them, ye
will be mindful of your promise in that matter. I am also obliged
unto you for your promise to assist me with two ships whensoever I shall take occasion to prosecute the rebels of the isles,
who are also assisters of your rebels in Ireland.

Now, madame, as to the estate of my affairs here, I received
lately a letter of yours together with some doubts delivered by
your ambassador, wherein ye desire to be fully satisfied. Whereunto for eschewing of tedious longsumnes,* I answer summarily and to the substance, though not point by point as it is

123

proponed. And first, concerning the papist rebels, according to my promise made to the Lord Burgh.[2] I was fully resolved to have proceeded to their forfeiture at the last parliament if two lets had not intervened; the one that, taking the Advocate's oath whether he thought we had sufficient law for us or not to proceed against them, we found plainly our law would not permit it; wherein, if our Advocate had been a flatterer, he had betrayed the cause if that matter, being put to judgement, had gone against us, as surely it would have done. The other was the said rebels had so travailed by indirect means with every nobleman as, when I felt their minds first apart and then being convened together, they plainly and all in one voice refused to yield to any forfeiture. Whereupon I was forced to continue that matter to the next parliament and they to remain "relaxit"[3] in the meantime, otherwise their summons behooved to have deserted. And although their relaxation gave full liberty to every man to intercommoun* and ressett* them, yet they never kythit* themselves publicly in any place till this late accident of Bothwell's surprising of my person. And now of late they incessantly make petitions unto me, not only offering but craving a trial, promising faithfully humbly to confess whatever they have committed, but denying the chief point which they remit to trial, and offering to give what surety I please to devise for good order in times coming, not only for this country but likewise concerning your part and the whole isle. As for me, I have ever yet refused to hear of them till first ye were made acquainted therewith, not only because that matter concerns you as well as me but also because of your secret and friendly message with Sir Robert[4] that, if I could not find the means presently how to pursue them with rigour ye would then for the respect ye had to my weal and safety, deal and give your advice what conditions of surety might be taken of them. Therefore, madame, since I cast still a deaf ear to all their offers till I hear your answer, I pray you hasten it as speedily towards me as goodly ye may, and make me obliged in giving me that advice which ye have obliged me in making so kindly an offer of already.

And as to Master George Kerr's[5] escape or Angus's[6] either if they had been in the Tower of London and had had as false

124

knaves to their keepers (whom they buddit* and made to flee with them) they had played the like, for since that time sour experience hath taught to myself that the thickness of no walls hold out treason. And as for Bothwell's coming about me I cannot surely wonder enough that ye, being so wise a prince and of so great intelligence, should have been so evil and uncertainly advertised thereof; for, as Bothwell's first incoming was violent and altogether without my privity or consent, so was his behaviour thereafter violent and irreverent, not respecting nor remembering in the end what he promised at the beginning—guarding me as I had been his lawful prisoner and apprehending divers of my most special domestic servants, whose custody he committed to the greatest of the Border thieves, till at last I was forced (not only for my own safety but also for the safety of my whole country in me, for the which I am born more than for myself) to grant him almost whatever he required. And now of late, since I came out of his hands, after convening of my estates, although I could not by any law or reason be obliged to observe that which at so unlawful a time I had promised, yet partly for that I would not incur the slander of the breaking, if it were but the shadow of a promise, and partly at the humble suit of the said estates for quieting of the country, that therethrough justice might be equally ministered hereafter upon all other enormities, I was content to grant him in substance, though in a more honourable form, that which of late he had unlawfully purchased of me. These were the causes, madame, of my pardoning him and not any change of my opinion towards him, whom indeed in most things I perceive to be the same man he [was] wont to be. If he behave himself well hereafter, the better will it be for him: if otherwise, ye and all the Christian princes in the world shall be witnesses of my part. And whereas ye was informed that he and his complices had craved of me the prosecuting of the papists, alleging that for an excuse of their irreverent behaviour, upon my honour it was neither intended, nor alleged, nor no other cause but the bare seeking of his own relief and security. And, by the contrary, all his complices have, ever since his incoming, dealt with me for agreeing him and Huntly,[7] with promise of conformity on Bothwell's part. And Colville[8] has offered himself to be the doer of it unto me and,

that which resulted in the birth of their first child, Prince Henry,
on 19 February 1594.

[*June 1593?*]

M. Robert,

My wife has this day given command to her servants to make
all things ready for her riding against Tuesday next, and she has
said to myself flatly that she will ride—and that for the cause
that ye "uaite" [wit?] of. How she is moved since your speaking
with her God knows and not I, for when I speirid at* her what
was betwixt you and her she said ye could tell, and would say no
farther. Therefore I pray you come down here the morn [tomor-
row] afternoon and warn M. David to be here likewise that I
may speak with you, for I would be sorry that she should travel
in this weather, she being in the case that she is thought to be in,
which I fear makes her the more wilful. Farewell.

JAMES R.

Scottish Record Office   *Holograph*
GD 1/240/5

Letter 51

To Queen Elizabeth

*In early 1594, King James and Queen Elizabeth were close
to a major crisis. Angry and apprehensive at James's failure to
put on trial his Catholic lords involved in the Spanish Blanks
affair, Elizabeth sent a special ambassador, Lord Zouche, to demand action, and wrote James a very forthright letter in which
she told him he was a "seduced" king. Elizabeth may have contemplated a new Ruthven Raid to impose a more wholeheart-
edly Protestant regime upon James. The chosen instrument this
time would have been the Earl of Bothwell, who with other
Protestant Scottish lords was allowed to rally his forces on the
English side of the Border. Thus using England as his base,*

Bothwell with several hundred men launched the Raid of Leith. Attacking a force under the direct command of James, Bothwell compelled them to retreat and almost captured Edinburgh.

To head off any more English aid for Bothwell, James sent two special ambassadors to Elizabeth—James Colville, Laird of Easter Wemyss, and Edward Bruce, the Commendator of Kinloss. With them they carried the following letter. Either as a result of their negotiations or of growing awareness of the unreliability and folly of Bothwell, Elizabeth abandoned him, leaving him to his ruin.

13 April 1594

So many unexpected wonders, madame and dearest sister, have of late so overshadowed my eyes and mind and dazzled so all my senses as, in truth, I neither know what I should say nor whereat first to begin. But thinking it best to take a pattern of yourself since I deal with you I must (repeating the first words of your last letter, only the sex changed) say I rue my sight that views the evident spectacle of a seduced queen: for when I enter betwixt two extremities in judging of you, I had far rathest* interpret it to the least dishonour on your part, which is ignorant error.

Pardon me, madame, for long approved friendship requires a round plainness, for, when first I consider what strange effects have of late appeared in your country, how my avowed traitor hath not only been openly received in your realm but plainly made his residence in your proper houses, ever plainliest kytheth* himself where greatest confluence of people was and, which is most of all, how he hath received English money in a reasonable quantity, waged both English and Scottish men therewith, proclaimed his pay at divers parish churches in England, convened his forces within England in the sight of all that border, and therefrom contemptuously cummid* and camped within a mile of my principal city and present abode, all his trumpeters and divers waged men being English, and, being by myself in person repulsed from that place, returned back in England with displayed banners and since that time with sound of trumpet making his troops to muster within English ground. When first, I say, I consider these strange effects, and then again I call to mind, upon the one part, what number of solemn promises, not only by your ambassadors but by many letters of your own hand, ye have both made and reiterated unto me that he should have no harbour within your country, yea, rather stirring me further up against him than seeming to pity him yourself, and, upon the other part, weighing my deserts towards you—how, for being a friend to you, I have ever been an enemy to all your enemies (and the only point I can be challenged in, that I take not such form of order and at such time with some particular men of my subjects as peradventure ye would do if ye were in my room)—when thus I enter in consideration with myself I cannot surely satisfy myself with wondering enough upon these above-mentioned effects. For, to affirm that these things are by your direction or privity, it is so far against all princely honour as I protest I abhor the least thought thereof. And again that so wise and provident a prince, having so long and happily governed, should be so sylid* and condemned by a great number of her own subjects, it is hardly to be believed, if I knew it not to be a maxim in the state of princes that we see and hear all with the eyes and ears of others, and if these be deceivers we cannot shun deceit.

Now, madame, I have refuge to you at this time as my only pilot to guide me safely betwixt these Charybdis and Scylla. Solve these doubts and let it be seen ye will not be abused by your own subjects who prefers the satisfying of their base-minded affections to your princely honour.

That I wrote not the answer of your last letters with your late ambassador,[1] and that I returned not a letter with him, blame only I pray you his own behaviour who, although it pleased you to term him wise, religious, and honest, had been fitter in my opinion to carry the message of a herald[2] than any friendly commission betwixt two neighbor princes; for as no reason could satisfy him, so scarcely could he have patience ever to hear it offered. But if ye gave him a large commission, I dare answer for it, he took it as well upon him and therefore have I rather "choosid" to send you my answer by my own messengers. Suffer me not, I pray you, to be abused with your abusers, nor grant no oversight to oversee

Right trusty and well-beloved cousin,

Although I have this long time forborne the writing unto you because of the wrong ye received therethrough, suppose not in my default but in the default of them that were employed betwixt us. Yet now, having directed these two gentlemen ambassadors to the Queen your sovereign upon weighty and urgent occasions importing no less than the preservation or break of the amity so long and happily continued betwixt the two crowns, I would not omit this occasion unsending these few lines unto you, hereby to pray you favourably to hear and (according to the friendship I look for at your hand) to further them, as far as in you lies, to a good and speedy despatch.

I look, my lord, that a nobleman of the rank ye are of will move and assist the Queen with your good advice not to suffer herself to be syled* and abused any longer with such as prefer their particular and unhonest affections to the Queen's princely honour and peace of both the realms, but I refer the particulars of all to the bearer's report whom I have commanded to use your advice in all their proceedings. And thus, right trusty and well-beloved cousin, I bid you heartily farewell. From Edinburgh the xiii of April 1594.

Your very loving friend,
JAMES R.

National Library of Scotland   *Holograph*
MS. 33.1.7 (Vol. XXI, Item 9)

Letter 53

To Queen Elizabeth

Although, in replying to James's letter of 13 April (Letter 51), Elizabeth had declared she would not allow her subjects to give Bothwell any future help or refuge, she also had made it plain that she very much resented what she regarded as a threat couched in the Virgilian reference in that letter. Having received the assurances he wanted about Bothwell, James here tries in a remarkably awkward manner to extricate himself from his unhappy Virgilian allusion.

5 June 1594

Because I perceive by your last letter and the report of my ambassador, madame and dearest sister, that ye have far mistaken the meaning of my last letter, I am forced to let this present serve for a short apology thereof. For in two principal points I perceive ye have mistaken me; and first, whereas ye interpret my imitation of your words in the beginning of my letter to mean that ye are seduced[1] by trusting false reports made of me, if ye please to consider the following discourse of my letter ye will find I meant by some of your own subjects who, in receiving and assisting my avowed traitor in divers parts of your kingdom without your allowance or privity, seduced you in abusing your princely honour and will—which appears to be but over true since by your own letter ye grant it and avows to make them to be duly punished for the same. And surely, madame, it appears your subjects do not yet weary to abuse you since, notwithstanding your late proclamations, he [Bothwell] is still received within your own country. But in this I trust I need not to move you, since the hurting of your princely honour by the contempt of your laws will, I doubt not, stir you up to take order therewith.

Now the other point of mistaking is of yon Latin verse in the hinder end of my letter, which I perceive ye interpret to be a threatening of you, but I doubt not ye will conceive far otherwise of my meaning thereby if ye will be pleased to weigh first the meaning of the author that first wrote it and syne* consider what precedes and follows in my letter that alleges it: for Virgil feigneth that Juno, being in a rage that the rest of the gods through Venus's persuasion would not consent to the wrack of Aeneas, whom against she bore an inveterate hatred as against all Troy, she not only pronounceth these words of my letter but immediately goes to Alecto, one of the hellish furies, and persuades her to stir up Turnus in Italy to war against Aeneas, thereby to hinder his conquest there. Now to make the allusion then (suppose *omnis comparatio claudicat uno pede*),[2] I am Juno, ye are the rest of the gods, Bothwell is Aeneas, and other foreign princes are Acheron; Juno seeking aid of Acheron, then, was only for the wrack of Aeneas and no ways either for the invading or threatening of the rest of the gods. On the other part, where this verse is set down in my letter I say not that I am of mind so to do but, by the contrary, I say I trust you will not constrain me so to do and the very next words I subjoin are "and to give you a proof of my honest affection," etc. Thus madame my intention was to complain unto you, not to threaten you, thereby seeking your aid and neither seeking nor leaning to the aid of others. So, in a word, my prayer was to you as we all pray to God, "Lead us not into temptation." But, as ever it be, suppose in this I interpret my intention, yet I ever bear the reverence to all virtuous ladies, but above all to you whose blood, long and trusty friendship, and manifold virtues requires such loving and kind reverence of me as I am not so to stand in my defence. But if ye think it a fault I will crave pardon for it and only claim to my homely rudeness, which I hope ye will accept in the better part since what I wrote of you I wrote only to you. And therefore, madame, I trust never to deserve the least thought of your suspicion of any dealing of mine with your enemies, for I protest before God I never, to this hour, had dealing directly or indirectly with any of them, either to the prejudice of you or your state, or the state of religion; and am content, besides my many bypast promises, that this letter remain a pledge of my faith herein as well for times to come as bypast, aye and till (as God forbid) I discharge myself honestly[3] unto you, which shall never be except ye constrain me unto it—but *absit omen!*[4] I also trust that before this time your ambassador has informed you of some of my proceedings at this parliament to your satisfaction.

As to the despatch given to my ambassadors, whereas ye are general in time of payment and quantity of the support craved by them, yet I doubt not ye will consider my present adoes,* having now begun and entered in action, wherein I crave an answer according to the proverb *qui cito dat bis dat.*[5] Of one

133

sary, addressed a strong protest to the Queen against the way in
which the English, despite having denied Bothwell asylum, were
still allowing his Scottish supporters to take refuge in England.
For the Queen's comfort James declared that, at long last, he
was preparing to strike at his "Spanish lords," those who had
signed the Spanish Blanks. This declaration was entirely genu-
ine. James had been forced into action by their leader, the Earl
of Huntly, who, with outrageous contempt for the royal author-
ity, had used a threat to burn down Aberdeen to force the
townspeople to release his Jesuit uncle and the papal gold that
the latter had been trying to smuggle in from Spain.

11 September 1594

I could not permit, madame and dearest sister, now after the
ending of this solemn time, the nobleman bearer hereof[1] to depart without returning with him unto you my most hearty thanks
for the honouring me with so noble a substitute gossip [god-
parent] in your place, and where[as] ye excuse his youth, surely he
was the fitter for a young king and feasting days. But I cannot
enough commend unto you his extreme diligence in coming, and
courteous and mild behaviour here, which moves me to request
you to cherish so noble a youth now after his first employment.

As for the other part of his commission and your letter which
concerns the Spanish lords[2] here, ye can be no earnester now in
that matter than I am, who has now renounced any further dealing with them but by extremity. And presently have I vowed myself only to that errand and never to take rest till I put some end
thereunto. And suppose ye may justly accuse (as ever ye do) my
deferring so long to put order unto them, yet, according to an old
proverb, it is better late thrive than never. And surely I will think
my fault the more excusable if the example thereof make you to
eschew the falling in the like error in making your assistance not
to come as far behind the time as my prosecution does. But in this
I remit you to your own wisdom, for ye are not ignorant how
occasion is painted.

And now I cannot omit to lay before you some incident griefs
of mine, but lest I weary you too much with the reading of my

ragged "hande writte" I remit the particulars thereof to the report of this nobleman, only touching this far by the way: I think ye have not given commission to any of your Council to treat with Bothwell's ambassador, nor yet allows that his agent, and one guilty of all his treasons, should use his public devotion in the French kirk in presence of my ambassador, who, indeed, was better furnished with a patience at the sight thereof than he is likely to get thanks for at my hands. Ye know, madame, none can brook me and Bothwell both. Examine straitly your councillors and suffer them not to behave themselves more to your dishonour than my discontentment. Only *honestum utile est præcipue regibus*,[3] and if James Forret[4] or any other Bothwellists be at this present within your country, I crave, by these presents, delivery according to the treaties, your many handwritten promises, and my good deserts by O'Rourke.[5] And thus, not doubting but, as it hath been your fortune to be godmother both to me and my son, so ye will be a good mother to us both, I commit you, madame and dearest sister, to the protection of the Almighty. From my palace of Holyroodhouse the xi of September 1594.

Your most loving and affectionate
brother and cousin,
JAMES R.

Public Record Office   *Holograph*
SP 52/54/38

[1]Robert Radcliffe (1569?–1629) who on 4 December 1593 became 5th Earl of Sussex.

[2]The Earls of Huntly, Errol, and Angus, and others involved in the Spanish Blanks affair.

[3]"The honourable is useful, especially to kings."

[4]James Forret of Burrowfield, denounced by the Council at Edinburgh on 29 March 1594 as a rebel who had failed to clear himself of "treasonable practices and conspiracies."

[5]See Letter 42.

Letter 55

To John Erskine, Earl of Mar

King James's finances, always precarious, became much worse after the expensive ceremonies at the time of Prince Henry's baptism. Accordingly, he asked his faithful friend Mar, son of his former guardian, to head a commission to propose reforms.

11 September 1594

Because, my lord, your house has been so honest to my forebears, yourself had the honour to be brought up with me, since married my aunt and gotten the keeping of my two greatest strengths, and (which is most of all) of my eldest and only son, I think of reason I can lippin* more to none, and none can be more obliged to me. And, therefore, being utterly wearied and ashamed of the misgovernment of the country for lack of concurrence of noblemen on the one part, and of my extreme want on the other part, through the mishandling of my rents by my careless and greedy officers that intromets* therewith, I am forced to burden you to travail with such noblemen as I have already named unto you, that they would bestow their pains and presence for putting me in some better estate, and that ye would take their promises to come to Edinburgh the twenty of November next and remain till they see me put to some certainty in both these points. And that they may know that, as I am no more a minor, so I apprehend deeply the straits I am cast in and am resolved to follow constantly their counsel, back their conclusions, and thankfully (whenever occasion shall serve) requite their travails. I have both written and subscribed this your warrant with my hand. At Holyroodhouse the xi of September 1594.

JAMES R.

Scottish Record Office
GD 124/10/65

Holograph

Letter 56

To Queen Anne

Bothwell, finding himself abandoned by England, threw in his lot with the rebel northern "Spanish lords"—the Earls of Huntly, Errol, and Angus—thereby finally revealing himself as the unprincipled opportunist he was. At the end of September the young Earl of Argyll led a royal army north to use fire and sword against Huntly and his friends. On 4 October James himself started north also, only to be greeted with news of the defeat of Argyll with the loss of some seven hundred men. In this letter, James comments upon the Battle of Glenlivat, correctly remarking that, through their casualties, the rebels had lost more than they had won in their "victory."

TRANSLATED FROM THE FRENCH

15 December [1594]

My heart,

According to the desire expressed in your letter, I have wished to accompany the bearer with the enclosed.

As for the news from here, I am sure that you have already heard all the account of the battle between Argyll and these papist lords. To put it in a word, the rebels have inflicted the defeat but have received the greater loss, through the death and wounding of many of their principal gentlemen. And for my part it is only two days since I arrived here, with the most prodigious and deadly tempest ever seen. And still, since these papist lords have retired alone into some hiding-places, nobody knows where, at this hour I am proceeding to make secret enquiry concerning them and their associates in order to strike at them, just as I do against Bothwell and his associates when I am over there.

And because I am resolved never to return without having put some good and honourable end to things, I pray you to prepare to come here if the slowness of my affairs gives me occasion to send for you. But postponing the decision (which of us

138

for a proof of my course by my actions that thereby, all cause of doubting being removed, a common danger might by a common assistance be prevented. But, upon the one part, finding you slower herein than either your well [weal] or your vows do require of you; and, on the other, imputing it to no lack of your goodwill but of true information, I have now at last made choice of the bearer hereof, my servant, to inform you truly of all these things, as the fittest messenger to inform you of the whole progress of my actions in this great cause,[2] since by him I did also advertise you of my first proceeding therein by law.

Surely, madame, if it shall please you to weigh it, ye will find that we both are but at truce and not at peace with the Romish and Spanish practices. These Spaniolized rebels of mine that are fled the country are but retired to fetch a greater fairde* if they may; and, believe me, if any would persuade you otherwise, they but abuse you for their own gain (or at least thinking it sufficient gain to them to annoy whom they hate). How can I wonder enough that ye, who was so watchful for my weal at the first breeding of these practices as ye never wearied from time to time to forewarn me of my peril, resenting it as vivelie* as if it had been your own, should now, in the very height and ripeness thereof, be fallen in so lethargic a sleep as ye are, so far from either advertising or aiding that ye do not so much as once to enquire what hath been here adoing these nine months past.

But pardon me, I pray you, to complain of you to yourself for, use me as ye list, ye shall never shake me off, by so many knots am I linked unto you. Neither shall your slowness this while past be able to blot out of my thankful memory your manifold proofs of kindness shown towards me in all times past. Only I crave that ye remember we have a common enemy, and that now we must either concur to hold them under our feet as long as we are treading upon them or else, if they get leisure to rise again, it will but learn them experience to wrestle the more cunningly the next time. I trust my part be now past *fieri;* I pray you let your assistance appear now in *esse.*[3]

But remitting the more large discourse of all things to the bearer, whom I pray you favourably to hear and firmly to trust, I commit you, madame and dearest sister, to the protection of the Almighty. From my palace of Falkland, the viii of July 1595.

Your most loving and affectionate
brother and cousin,
JAMES R.

Cecil Papers   *Holograph*
133: 137

¹Sir Richard Cockburn of Clerkington.
²Dealing with those incriminated by the discovery, in December 1592, of the Spanish Blanks.
³"I trust my part be now past the 'becoming' phase; I pray you let your assistance appear now in actuality."

Letter 58

To John Erskine, Earl of Mar

James's queen vehemently objected to his decision to place Prince Henry in the keeping of the trusted Earl of Mar. In fact, sound political reasons dictated that the heir should be kept in Mar's care at Stirling Castle. Aware of the danger that the Earl might give way to the Queen's importunity or be deceived into letting a group of malcontent lords get possession of the prince and use him for their own ends, James wrote the following unequivocal letter to Mar.

24 July 1595

My lord of Mar,

Because in the surety of my son consists my surety, and that I have concredited* unto you the charge of his keeping upon the trust I have of your honesty, this present therefore shall be a warrant unto you not to deliver him out of your hands except I command you with my own mouth, and being in such company

141

as I myself shall best like of—otherwise not to deliver him for any charge or message that can come from me. And, in case God call me at any time, that neither for Queen nor Estates' pleasure ye deliver him till he be eighteen years of age and that he command you himself. At Stirling the xxiiii of July 1595.

JAMES R.

Scottish Record Office   *Holograph*
GD 124/10/70

Letter 59

To Robert Devereux, Earl of Essex [?]

The following letter is addressed to "My goode friend SHB." Probably these initials, like the "u.u." in the text, are code identifications used to protect particular persons. SHB was probably the Earl of Essex. The Queen had been angered when she had discovered that Essex had been carrying on an unauthorized correspondence with King James, and this fact helps to explain the precautions that James was now taking to conceal his letters from the "Argus eyes" of Elizabeth's intelligence service.

Certainly, in his eagerness to recruit friends in England who would support him as successor to Elizabeth, James was paying a good deal of attention to Essex.

6 October 1595

My good friend,

Since the writing of my last unto you I have seen your letter written to u.u. whereby I find the constant continuance of your loving goodwill towards me; but I can use no thanks towards you, since deeds and no words must be a just requittal of your deserts. I am glad of all the heads of your letter except one, whereof I am sorry, for I am glad of your diligent "unwayting" [*sic*] there upon all occasions, wherein I wish you heartily to continue. I am also glad that he who rules all there[1] is begun to be loathed at by the best and greatest sort there, since he is my enemy (though undeserved, as God knows). And I thank you most heartily for your wise and honest counsel in Border causes for, as God shall judge me, I never behaved myself, nor shall do, otherwise but as *communis parens*[2] and that all your country borderers can bear me witness. My enemies are ever busy to trouble and I to quiet it. Think not that the bad deserts towards me of any particular men of your country can ever divert my fatherly friendship to that state. But I am sorry that ye have so much longed for my answer, whereby I perceive ye had not at the writing thereof received my letter. But, as I wrote to you in my last, I pray you think not that either sloth or negligence breeds my slowness in answering, but only the care I have that my letters be surely convoyed since there is so many Argus eyes that watches over me. To end now, ye may freely write all news with this bearer, and I doubt not ye will not omit no occasion to do me all the good ye can there and, God willing, I shall not omit no fair occasion unwriting unto you, and further I will not hazard it. Farewell my good friend.

Your beholden and constantly
assured friend,
JAMES R.

From "Saint Ionstoune"[3] the vi of October 1595.

National Library of   *Holograph*
Scotland MS. 1.2.2., Item 28

[1]Almost certainly Sir Robert Cecil, who was increasingly taking over from his ailing father, Lord Burghley.
[2]"The common parent."
[3]Perth, by an earlier name which is sometimes given as St. Johnstown and sometimes as St. Johnstone.

Letter 60

To Queen Elizabeth

Early in 1596, when a truce had been declared for resolving Border feuds, the English deputy warden of the West March violated that truce by seizing a notorious Scottish freebooter, William Armstrong (better known as "Kinmont Willie"), and lodging him in Carlisle Castle. On 13 April, after the English had refused requests for Kinmont Willie's release, Sir Walter Scott of Buccleuch, the Keeper of Liddesdale, and his men broke into the castle and rescued him. Queen Elizabeth was furious. In this letter James, doing his best for Buccleuch, urges the Queen to see the freeing of Kinmont Willie in the context of his wrongful seizure.

4 June 1596

Madame and dearest sister,

In respect of the hard impression that ye have conceived concerning Buccleuch's late attempt at Carlisle, I have taken occasion by these few lines to pray you most heartily to consider aright and take in good part my answer therein. And first I must pray you to consider that your information proceeds from your officer,[1] who is not only partial but direct party in that matter, who as well (for the excuse of his own sloth at the time of the committing of that deed, as of his former injury whereupon the other did succeed) cannot choose but agredge* and aggravate that deed as far as in him lies. But, madame, I need not to exhort a prince of so long and happy experience in government as ye are, to stop the one ear till ye hear the other party; and then, all passion being removed, wisely and justly to judge. For I am fully persuaded that when ye shall be rightly informed of that injury which made this other deed to follow, the preceding [event] shall (though not purge) yet qualify very much the other in your just censuring mind.

Always, whatever the quality be of that deed, my answer and request both is that ye will be content to appoint commissioners on your part, as I shall be most ready upon mine to try as well the turn* itself as the occasion whereupon it did proceed, and to give order therein according to the leagues of amity and treaties of peace established betwixt us, which I vow and promises upon my honour shall be fully accomplished and put in execution on my part in that case. For who can be so fit judges of offences fallen betwixt your subjects and officers and mine as commissioners from us both who, according to the laws of neighbourhood, ought to discern amongst neighbours. And whereas it appears ye are persuaded by some to think that your hard using me in other matters will be a mean to procure your satisfaction in this turn at my hands, surely, madame, as my conscience bears me witness that I never wilfully offended you in any time past, so shall I never hereafter omit any part of constant and true friendship towards you. But I am sure that ye will not love [me] the worse that as I am otherwayes* near of blood unto you so to be your cousin in that quality also to do twice more for courtesy than hard usage. But, touching that purpose, I have spoken more at length to your ambassador[2] therein.

This time requires greater diligence in us both against the common enemy than to trouble ourselves with the base particular quarrels and debates betwixt our subjects. And thus praying you to take in good part these homely and rude lines, I commit you, madame and dearest sister, to the protection of the Almighty. From my palace of Linlithgow, the 4 of June 1596.

Your most loving and affectionate
brother and cousin,
JAMES R.

Public Record Office   *Holograph*
SP 52/58/95

[1]Lord Scrope, Warden of the West Marches.
[2]Robert Bowes.

Letter 61

To Queen Elizabeth

Negotiations continued over the Kinmont Willie affair. James conceded that Buccleuch had blemished Elizabeth's honour by forcibly entering her castle and, accordingly, he put him under arrest. Elizabeth responded favourably to James's suggestion that an Anglo-Scottish commission keep peace on the Border.

17 August 1596

Madame and dearest sister,

I perceive by your last letter that the only thing ye stick at concerning Buccleuch's attempt is that your honour may only be repaired therein, and for all other questionable matters ye are content that with all expedition they may be handled by commissioners. Surely, madame, my mistaking your meaning until now in that matter hath been the cause of my so long delay to satisfy you therein; for, in respect of your ambassador's first complaint in that matter, craving first fyling* and then delivery, I could not but think that, according to the custom ever observed in Border causes, an ordinary form of trial behooved to precede an ordinary punishment. But since I do now find it is only your honour ye respect herein, hurt by the breach of your castle, surely, as I would be loath to grant to any inequity in the form of equal justice or mutual redress betwixt our two realms, so will I be as loath on the other part to give you cause to think that any prince in Europe would be so careful to preserve your honour from all blemish as I, without regard to the appetite of whatsomever the best subject in my land. Both nearness of blood and thankfulness binds me so to do. And, since I have never been either actor or consenter to your harm or dishonour in any sort, I would be sorry to begin so badly at this time. And to give you some proof thereof, I have without (yea, rather against the advice of any) commanded in wairde* the party whomwith ye are offended (that it may be seen I will not allow of anything that ye might interpret to be an offence unto you) till I may be farther informed of your mind herein, which I pray you to haste together with some speedy and undelayed order for commissioners, as I wrote to you in my last, for I doubt not it grieves your conscience to hear the smart that the poor ones daily receives of all hands, and this insolence of Borderers can never be stayed but by commissioners. Wherefore I once again pray you to hasten them, with as few ceremonies as may be, that all delay may be eschewed.

And thus, praying you to excuse and take in good part my long delay of satisfying your honour, which I heartily pray you to impute to my mistaking, as I have already declared, I commit you, madame and dearest sister, to the protection of the Almighty who motte* still continue to give you a victorious success over all your enemies. From Dunfermline the 17 of August 1596.

Your most loving and affectionate
brother and cousin,
JAMES R.

Cecil Papers   *Holograph*
133: 150

Letter 62

To George Gordon, Earl of Huntly

The Earls of Huntly and Errol, exiled in 1595 (see Letter 57), returned to Scotland without permission the following year. James, out of his great partiality for Huntly, was not inclined to create difficulties. The following letter probably refers to the General Assembly of the Kirk and the Convention of the Estates, which at its meeting at Dundee in May 1597 would decide what action should be taken about the earls. In the end, after they had confessed their guilt and declared themselves now to be Protestants, no penalties were exacted. King James's postscript to Huntly proved prophetic.

I trow ye are not so unwise, my lord, as to misinterpret my exterior behaviour the last day; seeing what ye did ye did it not without my allowance and that (by your humility in the action itself) your honouring of me served to countervail the dishonouring of me by others before. But perceiving by my expectation that both noblemen and councillors thought to wash their hands of that turn* and lay the whole burden upon me, I thought the hurting of myself and their louping* free could be no pleasure nor weal unto you; for, if that impediment had not been, assure yourself I would fainer have spoken with you than ye would with me for many causes that were longsome to write. Always assure yourself and the rest of your marrows* that I am earnester to have your day of trial to hold forward than yourselves, that, by your services thereafter, the tyranny of these mutinies may be repressed. For I protest before God in extremity, I love the religion they outwardly profess and hates their presumptuous and seditious behaviour. And for your part in particular, I trow ye have had proof of my mind towards you at all times. And, if of my favour to you ye doubt, ye are the only man in Scotland that doubts thereof, since all your enemies will needs bind it on my back. To conclude, hold forward the suiting* of your trial as the bearer will inform you, and use the advice that I have commanded him to give you in your proceedings, and move your marrows* to omit no diligence in holding forward this dyet.* Let none see this letter. Farewell.

Your old friend,

J. R.

I hope to see you ere this month be ended (if ye use yourself well) in as good estate as ever ye was in.

West Sussex Record Office   *Holograph*
Goodwood MS. 1427, no. 5

Letter 63

To Queen Elizabeth

The final result of the Kinmont Willie episode (Letters 60 and 61) was the signing at Carlisle, in May 1597, of a treaty intended to prevent future Border clashes. A clause in this treaty provided that certain persons should surrender themselves to the English as pledges for the future peaceful behaviour of Buccleuch, who had led the attack on Carlisle Castle. Unfortunately for Buccleuch, his pledges failed to present themselves and so he had to place himself in English custody. In this letter James does the best he can for Buccleuch, proposing the terms that some little while later secured his release.

20 October 1597

Right excellent, right high and mighty princess, our dearest sister and cousin, in our heartiest manner we recommend us unto you.

We doubt not but ye are advertised, by report as well of your ambassador, officers, and commissioners as otherwise, of our sincerity and goodwill toward the prosecuting of justice upon these lewd [base] and broken people of our borders, troublers of the peace and amity standing betwixt our realms, and toward the effectuating of our promise made both by our letters to yourself and your ambassador for delivery of the pledges designed by the commissioners in their late treaty or of our wardens and officers for them, and of our beginning at the delivery of our officer, the laird of Buccleuch, for his pledges (betraying him and now become fugitives), which being unable to be trapped for delivery but by himself and his own presence in the country.

For his relief, who has kythed* so loyal and obedient and given so good proof of his sincere meaning toward the tranquility and peace of our realms, we have taken occasion to recommend him to your courteous and favourable regard, requesting you, our dearest sister and cousin, that according to the customable form of these Borderers (yea, used toward the most notorious thieves) he may be freed upon his bond or the entry of his only son as a pledge in his place for a certain space, that in the meantime he may be enabled to search [for] and trap these his pledges for his own relief, which may produce a better and more effectual satisfaction to you and us both than his retention, being a gentleman obedient, entered only for his pledges, and so well affected toward the continuance of the amity betwixt our realms. Thus right excellent, right high and mighty princess, our dearest sister and cousin, we commit you in God's most blessed tuition [protection]. From our palace of Linlithgow, the xx of October 1597.

Your most loving and affectionate
brother and cousin,
JAMES R.

Madame, it is my honour to request for one that so willing yielded himself a prisoner at my command, and it is honourable for you to use with courtesy him who hath put himself in your hands without any condition.

Public Record Office   *Last eight words, signature,*
SP 52 / 61 / 46   *and postscript are holograph.*

Letter 64

To Queen Elizabeth

To pressure James into giving her satisfaction about the attack on Carlisle Castle, Queen Elizabeth had withheld payment of his annuity of £4000. Now that the offending Buccleuch had been handed over to her, James lost no time in asking for his money.

Madame and dearest sister,

Although that since the writing of my last I never until now interrupted you with my handwrit for excusing my part in all such accidents as since that time fell upon the Borders, yet the uprightness of my conscience makes me to rest assured that, according to the equity that God hath planted in your mind, ye are fully persuaded of my honest intention in that turn, as I doubt not your ambassador hath truly and honestly informed you from time to time.

And therefore I would earnestly entreat you that, according to equity and justice, ye would give order that all things may be speedily performed on your part (as I shall be ready to have the like done upon mine) whereby the intention of such wicked people as thought to have stayed it may be disappointed, and peace and justice established according to both our honest intentions. For, since we both shoot at one mark, a plain way must appearandlie* lead us best to the same, and not curiously to dispute upon terms and circumstances as peradventure some would advise us. For, a good order being once now settled, my wardens are so nipped at this time that I dare promise for their peaceable behaviour in all times coming. In the meantime I most heartily pray you that at all occasions ye may make known to the world your honourable and loving opinion of me notwithstanding of all these unhappy crosses. And specially that (since I have a man waiting there upon the receipt of the annuity) ye would be pleased to give him a good and speedy despatch, that it may be seen ye have conceived no thoughts of me but such as I shall ever deserve. And thus, madame and dearest sister, I commit you to the protection of the Most High.

Your most loving and affectionate
brother and cousin,
JAMES R.

Public Record Office   *Holograph*
SP 52/61/54

Letter 65

To Queen Elizabeth

The preceding letter and subsequent ones pressing for payment of his annuity having gone unanswered, James wrote to Elizabeth as follows.

24 December 1597

Madame and dearest sister,

Your silence hath been so long, and I have so long awaited upon your breaking thereof, that I am forced now at last to remember you again by these few lines. I have written three letters unto you and have never as yet received answer of any of them either by word or writ, which moves me to think that my letters never came to your hands—especially my last wherein I wrote as plainly and as lovingly unto you as I could.

What can I think except that either ye have been by some greatly abused, or else in other weighty affairs greatly distracted? Howsomever it be, I am sure ye could not have taken a greater trial of my patience. But, presupposing that my letters came never to your hands, yet could ye not be ignorant of the subject of them as well by Buccleuch's detaining in Berwick as by Robert Jowssie's[1] endless detaining there. As for Buccleuch, I thought the great care and pains that all this year I have taken in the Border matters, together with his delivery, had given as much proof of my goodwill as deserved at the least an answer (if not thanks). For my part I am ready to perfect the entry of the whole pledges;[2] but if that course like you not (as it appears by your long delay), I would likewise know it. And as for Robert Jowssie's errand, it is turned from an honourable annuity to a voluntary uncertainty almost after long begging, and now at last to as much worse than nothing, as there is time spent in the seeking of it. I pray you, madame, excuse my impatience in this. It is no wonder I weary to be a longsum* suitor as one who was not born to be a beggar but to be begged at. A short refusal had less displeased me than an answerless and disdainful delay. Remember that, as I am your kinsman, so am I a free prince. The disdaining of me can be no honour to you. The use of tempting your friends so sore can turn you to no advantage. If ye think my friendship worthy that annuity, remember *qui cito dat bis dat*.[3] Let not the circumstances of the giver disgrace the gift, for I weary to be a suitor. And, for your pleasure, I will promise never to challenge that debt any more if you will not be content as freely to pay it as freely ye promised it.

I must once again pray you to excuse my impatience, for there cannot a greater grief come to an honest heart than to be lightled* by them at whose hands he hath deserved so well as my conscience bears me upright record I have ever done at yours. My fault is the less that I complain of you to yourself, and I will yet hope that ye will give forth a just sentence in my favour and appardon* my free speaking in pleading my just cause.

And thus, madame and dearest sister, I commit you to the tuition [protection] of the Almighty. From Holyroodhouse the xxiiij of December 1597.

Your most loving and affectionate
brother and cousin,
JAMES R.

Cecil Papers   Copy, apparently of a
133: 176   lost holograph

[1]"Robert Jowsie, merchant of Edinburgh," was apparently the agent whom James had sent to Berwick to receive his annuity.
[2]See Letter 63.
[3]"Who gives quickly gives twice."

Letter 66

To Queen Elizabeth

Elizabeth's failure either to answer his letters or to pay his annuity, along with her earlier refusal to recognize him as her heir, drove James to make some critical and threatening remarks about her when addressing parliament in December 1597. These were reported to Queen Elizabeth, who wrote to James in scathing terms. In the following letter James tries to abate the tempest which he had raised.

[February? 1598]

Madame and dearest sister,

Although I had sufficiently purged to your late ambassador, Sir William Bowes, the calumnious and untrue reports that came to your ears of me, yet I could not satisfy myself without sending one of my own [ambassadors] unto you, as well to inform you more amply of the truth thereof as to turn over most justly on yourself that over-hasty credulity which in your letter ye lay so sharply to my charge. No farther will I answer particularly to your letter since it becomes me not to strive with a lady, especially in that art wherein their sex most excels. But, believe me, I take not unkindly your passionate letter: both because it was but privily written to myself, as likewise because I perceive sparks of love to shine through the midst of the thickest clouds of passion that are there set down. And indeed I must confess, if I had any ways been guilty of that wherewith ye charged me, I had deserved worse at your hand than so kind and homely a reproof as it was, although it was bitter. But *amantium irae amoris redintegratio*,[1] which makes me to trust that the fruits of our contesting shall be sweet although the buds thereof were sour. And for my part I am only to continue with you in that old contention of honest amity, for which effect I have sent unto you my ambassador, the Abbot of Kinloss,[2] whom I heartily pray you favourably to hear and trust as one for whose honesty and plainness I will be answerable.

And thus with my earnest prayers to the Almighty for your prosperity I heartily pray you, madame and dearest sister, ever to make full account of me as of your most loving and affectionate brother and cousin,

JAMES R.

Cecil Papers   *Holograph*
133: 184

[1]"The quarrels of lovers are the renewal of love." The King is misquoting Terence's *amantium irae amoris integratio* (*Andria* 555).

[2]Edward Bruce (1548–1611), the secular Abbot of Kinloss, would on 2 February 1602 receive a charter giving him Kinloss and granting him the rank of "Free Baron" with the title of Lord Kinloss. He was to play an important part in the manoeuvring that finally brought James to the English throne.

Letter 67

To Queen Elizabeth

In the spring of 1598, when Elizabeth was confronted with rebellion in Ireland, James sent her the following assurances of friendship and alliance.

[June? 1598]

Madame my dearest sister,

    I must claim to your courtesy, and not to any excuses I can make, for pleading my pardon at your hands that I have so long delayed by my handwrit to witness the thankfulness of my heart both for your liberal and ready satisfaction of the last term of the gratuity, as likewise for your gracing so far with your good countenance both Aston and Foulis[1] at their being there. But as I am more and more strengthened and confirmed in the persuasion of your love by the proof I have of your courtesies and benefits, which daily are augmented and heaped upon me, so am I obliged to increase in thankfulness in the same measure, whereof I shall, with God's grace, ever be ready to give proof at all occasions wherein my ability may reach, for procuring the weal for your person and state.

I am heartily glad of the safe return of your ships out of Spain that carried the Spaniards there from Ireland.[2] I am also glad to hear of your preparation to sea lest ye be taken at unawares, for now is providence to be used before the enemy make any attempt. As for my part, I shall ever be ready upon your advertisement to assist you in what sort of service it shall please you to employ me. And that your rebels get no assistance from my Highlands I am presently to give order.

And thus, lacking all other means wherewith to requite worthily your many favours and benefits, I most heartily pray you to accept the renewed offer of the constant affection and thankful heart of

> Your most loving and affectionate
> brother and cousin,
> JAMES R.

I must not also forget to thank you for your clement order given for more mild using of the Scottish pledges,[3] which is but presently "comd" to my ears. For this and all your other courtesies I acknowledge only to proceed from your own favour.

Public Record Office   *Holograph*
SP 52/62/33

---

[1] For Roger Aston see Letter 42, headnote. David Foulis served the King as an agent in London. Sir William Bowes, Elizabeth's ambassador to Scotland, had no great regard for him: "I thought him too ordinary a man to carry matters, if they were of extraordinary weight. For his behaviour in his former employments, some speeches had deserved little good acceptance; neither for my own part did I take him for very studious of good offices between the Princes" (letter of 22 Aug. 1598, HMC, *Salisbury MSS.* VIII: 315–16).

[2] In May 1598 there was an exchange of Spanish and English prisoners. Actually, only one ship was involved, the *Unicorn*.

[3] In June 1598 the Laird of Cessford handed over to Lord Willoughby the Scottish pledges required in consequence of the Kinmont Willie affair.

Letter 68

To Queen Elizabeth

In the early spring of 1598, Valentine Thomas, an audacious criminal to whom James had once unfortunately granted an interview, was in trouble with the English law. Possibly hoping to ingratiate himself with the authorities by a spurious revelation, Thomas alleged that James had suggested that he assassinate Queen Elizabeth. The English government declared it did not believe Thomas. King James, however, was thrown into great agitation, fearing that Thomas's story might at some future date rob him of his anticipated succession to the English throne.

30 July 1598

Madame and dearest sister,

That I have been so long unanswering your last letter I most heartily pray you not to impute it to any swearnesse* or fault of courtesy in me, whereunto my nature (I thank God) is no ways inclined. But, in truth, I bear so little regard to so vile and treacherous lies proceeding from so base a fountain¹ as I, through my only innocence, should have force enough to bear me through the foggy mist of such groundless calumnies, and therefore had remitted the answer of your letter to have been carried by a messenger of my own whom I am shortly to send unto you. Always ye may assure yourself that I have obeyed the contents and desire of your letter, for before God it never entered in my heart to suspect that a prince endowed with such rare graces as ye are could ever give ear to such shameless fictions. My suit only is that until you hear farther from me (which shall be with all diligence) ye would favour me so far as to delay the fellow's execution (if he be yet alive) to the effect that by some honourable means, wherein I am to deal with you, my undeserved slander may be removed from the minds of all men. Which assuring myself of your princely honour and love towards me ye will gladly do, I commit you, madame and dearest sister, to the tuition [protection] of the Almighty. From my palace of Falkland the xxx of July 1598.

Your most loving and affectionate
brother and cousin,
JAMES R.

How unjustly I am blamed anent Irish matters ye shall likewise be informed by one of mine.

British Library, Cotton MSS.,   *Holograph*
Caligula D II, f. 358
(portions lost through fire
are supplied from a copy,
Titus C VII, f. 19)

[1]Valentine Thomas.

Letter 69

To Queen Elizabeth

In this letter, sent with the messenger promised in Letter 68, James seeks further to convince Elizabeth that he is innocent of the plot attributed to him by Valentine Thomas.

[August 1598]

Madame and dearest sister,

I have now, according to my promise in my other letter, directed unto you the bearer hereof, my servant,[1] whomby ye shall be informed what I crave for clearing of my honour anent these slanders which that base villain[2] hath raised upon me; wherein I doubt not but your honour and love towards me will move you not to see me innocently wronged. The particulars hereof I will not trouble you with by longsome letter but remits them to his declaration, together with sundry other things wherewith I am

158

likewise falsely charged, as God shall judge me. For on my honour I would wish that all the direct or indirect dealing that ever I had that might concern your person or state were in a book laid open before you, and then ye would see that no subject of England hath kept himself clearer of any guilt against you than I have done ever since I was born. I have likewise commanded him to deal with you in divers other things wherein I also pray you to give him favourable ear and trust.

As for this foul attempt upon the Borders, whereof I lately wrote unto you, I doubt nothing of the equity of your judgement in case ye be truly informed, but I know your officers on that border will make the fault to seem unto you as small and light as they can. But consider they are parties and determine according to right. And thus, madame and dearest sister, I recommend you to the tuition [protection] of the Almighty.

> Your most loving and affectionate
> brother and cousin,
> JAMES R.

Cecil Papers   *Holograph*
133: 138

[1]David Foulis—see Letter 67, n.1. For the financial problem that delayed his departure until late August, see *CSP Scottish, 1597–1603*, p. 245.
[2]Valentine Thomas.

Letter 70

To Queen Elizabeth

In the end Elizabeth and her ministers, deciding that the less publicity given to Valentine Thomas's story the better, held him in the Tower and did not let him come to trial. To reassure James, Queen Elizabeth issued on 20 December 1598 a declaration stating, "We do give no credit to such things as the said Valentyne Thomas has affirmed against our good brother." This unequivocal statement was not sufficient for James, who seems to have been bent on Thomas's execution. In the following letter he vents his frustration in various cavils. After he became King of England he lost little time in having the wretched man hanged, drawn, and quartered.

[*August? 1598*]

Madame and dearest sister,

Since the return of my servant Foulis[1] I found myself incessantly pricked, by the law of that honest friendship which I bear unto you, to hasten unto you, how soon my leisure might anyways permit me, the true portrait of my thoughts upon that answer to my most just petitions which it pleased you by the hands of [the] said servant to return unto me. The ground of my request was to be freed of that as untrue as vile imputation and calumny laid against me by so infamous a villain seduced thereto either by his own self-love, seeking thereby "the furthest of thoch most detestable death" [*sic*] or else by my malicious though undeserved haters; not that I meant or needed to crave to be made clear of any such treacherous attempts (whereof, indeed, I ever was most clear) but that my effectual innocency might be made known, which now may in some measure be obscured by murmuring surmises flowing from this filthy spring. But as for the means for attaining to the same, I remit you to your own memory what choice and diversity of them I made to be proponed unto you, and in end relayed* my chiefest surety therein upon your own device, which out of your own wisdom, tempered with your kindest love towards me, I looked ye would find out. But now when I have ripely considered, and weigh in the just balances of a reasonable and unpassionate judgement, the true force and pith of your answer, I must plainly confess (except I would feign with you, which is the foulest error that in a mutual friendship can be committed) that I cannot find in any point thereof anything near to my just satisfaction. For first, in your letter patent, the narration therein declares it to be only obtained by importunity, and the conclusion thereof to be rather an allowance of your own good conceit that it hath pleased you to take of me than any

160

acknowledge[ment] of my many good and honourable deserts at your hand.

And whereas ye declare therein that ye ought to give account of any of your actions to no mortal creature,[2] I know very well that it becomes none that enjoys such places as we both do either to give account [or] be judged by any. And therefore, as I never thought to crave the one, so think I never to submit myself in the other. So that whereas my expectation was that, by your patent, ye should have declared that as by the laws of all nations the bare and s[ingle] alleging of so infamous and base a villain could bring forth no blemish to the honour and fame of one of any rank and calling, so had your experience of my kind and honest behaviour towards you at all times justly preserved you from harbouring in your heart the least jot of suspicion of me in such a case; wherewith as ye rested fully persuaded within yourself, so wished ye all to whose knowledge that patent would come to rest in that full assurance of my honourable innocence which the good of all nations, and the proof of my bypast behaviour would in all reason obtain of them. I can, by the contrary, collect nothing of your patent but as the ground thereof seems to be drawn out by importunity, and not willingly obtained by goodwill; so, by the dilating of the virtuous merits of your own inclination and of your manifold benefits bestowed upon me, the substance thereof seeming rather to tend to the aggravating of my ingratitude (in case I were guilty) than to the clearing of my innocence, since neither your virtuous inclination in judging others by the measure of your own qualities, nor yet your own knowledge of your good deserts towards me, can carry any further proof than what of reason I should do, but not what indeed I have done; otherwise all virtuous and innocent persons would ever be as free from the peril of receiving as deserving any causeless injuries.

And next, whereas I craved that, by some act or statute, order might be given for the cancelling and razing of anything in his indictment or depositions that might concern me (that as I assure myself ye put no doubt in your own heart of my innocence, so ye might thereby remove all occasions whereby I might be calumniated at any time hereafter), I have only received a copy of his indictment, and a general sum of his depositions, a favour which by no law could be refused to the caitiff himself at his leading out to the execution. And as for the omission of my name out of the indictment which, notwithstanding, contains the specialities of the alleged practices and places where the same was devised, which is fully relative to his depositions wherein my name is plainly mentioned, I can think it no greater grace than that my name is (for the fashion) scraped out of the text, but well retained in the gloss or commentary. He is indicted for practising according to his own confession, and in the same confession (by which means only this practice is revealed) I am plainly named and accused. And for answer to my last petition, wherein I craved that if my satisfaction could not presently be agreed upon, the person of the caitiff might at least be detained unexecuted until some more sure and honourable way of his trial and my clearing might be found out, ye have only, into the midst of a privy letter written to your agent, made him a general promise therein as long as ye shall find me continue in my good behaviour towards you.

Thus far have I thought good truly and hone[st]ly to communicate my mind unto you concerning your late answer, which I protest is no ways done for building up grounds of miscontentment thereby, but only lest ye should deceive yourself in thinking me (if I had remained silent) satisfied with your answer. For as a prince it becomes me not to feign, and as your friend I were faulty if I should dissemble. My request then is only that ye would patiently and gravely consider upon the premises, and let me by your direct answer be resolved if in your judgement ye think my petitions reasonable. And since the ground of my request is only that ye would help not to clear me of this false and filthy calumny but only to declare me to be the thing I am indeed, vouchsafe then by some honourable means to give me only that which of myself I fully do possess, persuading so the world to believe that which in your own conscience and knowledge ye are surely persuaded of. Consider it is craved by him who hath ever been your most constant friend, who never at any time did so much as once conceal anything that might import the harm of your person or state, and that your granting of my request will tend as well to the honour of the granter as the craver. And thus craving pardon for my faschous* longsomeness and rude plainness as proceeding from an honest and friendly heart, I commit you, madame and dearest sister, to tuition [protection] of the Almighty.

> Your most loving and affectionate
> brother and cousin,
> JAMES R.

Cecil Papers   *Holograph*
133: 140

¹David Foulis—see Letter 67, n. 1.
²In her declaration of 20 December 1598, Elizabeth had said, "We are no way bound to yield account to any person on earth of any our actions more than in love and kindness" (*CSP Scottish, 1597–1603*, p. 358).

Letter 71

To Prince Henry

In 1599, in a secret edition of just nine copies, King James published his Basilikon Doron, *a treatise which he had composed the previous year on the duties and skills required of a king. Since he had written the work for the future guidance of his heir, King James prefaced it with the following dedicatory epistle addressed to Prince Henry.*

[*September 1598?*]¹
To Henry, my dearest son and natural successor,
    Whomto can so rightly appertain this book of the institution of a prince in all the points of his calling, as well general (as a Christian towards God) as particular (as a king towards his people): whomto, I say, can it so justly appertain as unto you my dearest son? Since I, the author thereof, as your natural father maun* be careful for your godly and virtuous education as my

eldest son and the first fruits of God's blessing towards me in my posterity; and, as a king, maun timously* provide for your training up in all the points of a king's office since ye are my natural and lawful successor therein, that (being rightly informed hereby of the weight of your burden) ye may in time begin to consider that, being born to be a king ye are rather born to *onus* than *honos,*[2] not excelling all your people so far in rank and honour as in daily care and hazardous painstaking for the dutiful administration of that great office that God has laid upon your shoulders; laying, so, a just symmetry and proportion betwixt the height of your honourable place and the heavy weight of your great charge; and consequently in case of faillie* (which God forbid) of the sadness of your fall according to the proportion of that height.

I have therefore, for the greater ease to your memory, and that ye may at the first cast up any part that ye have to do with, divided this whole book in three parts. The first teaches you your duty towards God as a Christian; the next your duty in your office; and the third teaches you how to behave yourself in indifferent things, which of themselves are neither right nor wrong but according as they are rightly or wrong[ly] used and yet will serve, according to your behaviour therein, to augment or impair your fame and authority at the hands of your people.

Receive and welcome this book, then, as a faithful preceptor and counsellor unto you, which (because my affairs will not permit me ever to be present with you) I ordain to be a resident faithful admonisher of you. And because the hour of death is uncertain to me as to all flesh, I leave it as my testament and latter will unto you, charging you, in the presence of God and by the fatherly authority I have over you, that ye keep it ever with you as carefully as Alexander did the *Iliad* of Homer. Ye will find it a just and impartial counsellor, neither flattering you in any vice nor importuning you unseasonably at unmeet times. It will not come uncalled nor speak unspearid* at. And yet, conferring with it when ye are quiet, ye shall say with Scipio that ye are *numquam minus solus quam cum solus.*[3]

To conclude, then, I charge you, as ever ye think to deserve my fatherly blessing, to follow and put in practice (as far as lies in you) the precepts hereafter following. And if ye follow the contrary course I take the great God to record that this book shall one day be a witness betwixt me and you, and shall procure to be ratified in Heaven the curse that, in that case, here I give you. For I protest, before that great God, I had rather be not a father and childless nor be a father of wicked children. But hoping, yea even promising unto myself, that God who in his great blessing sent you unto me shall, in the same blessing, as he hath given me a son so make him a good and a godly son (not repenting him of his mercy shown unto me).

I end this preface with my earnest prayer to God to work effectually into you the fruits of that blessing which here, from my heart, I bestow upon you.

British Library   *Holograph (unsigned)*
Royal 18 B XV, f. 3

[1]For the evidence that *Basilikon Doron* "was written in the summer or early autumn of 1598" see J. Craigie's ed., Vol. II (Edinburgh, 1950), p. 4.
[2]"Rather born to a burden than an honour." The play on words is not original: Ovid has "*Non honor est sed onus*" (*Heroides* 9. 31).
[3]"Never less alone than when alone." The King's source is Cicero, either *De republica* 1. 27 or *De officiis* 3. 1.

Letter 72

To Various Scottish Lords

On 22 February 1600 John Chamberlain, in London, wrote to his friend Dudley Carleton: "The Scottish nobilitie find themselves greeved that theyre king is no more respected, and have lately made an association among themselves against all those that shall hinder his right and succession."[1] James, in fact, had decided to draw his nobility into his preparations to secure the English throne. The "association" that Chamberlain mentions probably consisted of those who had responded to James's following request for funds to be used in recruiting and assisting supporters in England.

[1600?]

We by these presents, both written and subscribed with our own hand, faithfully promises in the word of a prince that how soon it shall please God to possess us in the crown of England according to our just and undoubted title, we shall, within the space of a year thereafter, thankfully pay and content every one of these persons that have advanced us at this time with such sums as the Duke of Lennox has in ticket for the furtherance of our honourable adoes* in foreign parts; like as we also faithfully promise to employ the said sums and every part of them for the furtherance of our attaining to the said crown allainerlie* and, for the further surety hereof, will retain them in our own keeping privily in a little coffer whereof the said duke shall keep the key, and will also favourably gratify the persons advancers at all good occasions that shall be presented.

JAMES R.

Letter in possession of the   *Holograph*
Duke of Montrose, on deposit
in Scottish Record Office
(Lennox Charters and Letters,
Item 186)

¹*The Letters of John Chamberlain,* ed. N. E. McClure (Philadelphia: American Philosophical Society, 1939), I: 87.

Letter 73

[To James Hamilton]¹

Seeking to create an atmosphere in England that would be favourable to his succession, King James tried to inspire good expectations among both Catholics and Puritans there. The following letter seems to have been intended for Hamilton, one of James's agents, to show to Puritans.

Mr. Hambleton,

Although I never doubted and was ever sufficiently informed of the goodwill borne towards me in all lawful sort (for otherwise I never did nor shall require them) by all the honest subjects of England that sincerely profess the only true religion, professed and by laws established in both these countries (the bond of conscience being the only sure bond for tying of men's affections to them whom to they owe a natural duty), yet, having the same renewed and confirmed unto me by your late advertisements, I have thought good by this present, all written with mine own hand, to set you down a meeting for them in this point. That is, that ye shall, in my name, assure all the honest men ye can meet with that are affected that way, and that in the princely word of a Christian king: that, as I have ever without swerving professed and maintained the same religion within all the bounds of my kingdom, so may they assure themselves that how soon it shall please God lawfully to possess me with the crown of that kingdom wherein they are subjects, I shall not only maintain and continue the profession of the Gospel there, but withal not suffer or permit any other religion to be professed and avowed within the bounds of that kingdom. But because you have been, at your last being with me, particularly acquainted with my intentions in this point, as also that yourself is so well known and approved unto them there, ye shall by tongue more particularly inform them of my mind herein, resolving them of such malicious calumnies and unjust imputations as have been from time to time, by my undeserved enemies, contrived against me. And thus I bid you heartily farewell.

JAMES R.

British Library   Copy of a lost holograph
Harl. 787, f. 1

[1]For Hamilton (Hambleton) see D. H. Willson, *King James VI and I* (London: [1956]), p. 149.
[2]This copy is headed "K James his L[r] to one of his Seru[ts] here Anno 1600."

Letter 74

To Queen Elizabeth

James, most unwisely, had chosen the Earl of Essex as his ally in forming in England a faction that would support the King's claims to the throne when Elizabeth died. In early February 1601, in good measure to maintain liaison with Essex, James appointed the Earl of Mar and Edward Bruce, secular Abbot of Kinloss, as ambassadors to the court of Queen Elizabeth. With them he sent the following letter to the Queen.

10 February 1601

Madame and dearest sister,

As the strait bonds of our so long continued amity do oblige me, so your daily example used towards me in the like case does invite me not to suffer any misconstrued thoughts against any of your actions to take harbour in my heart but, by laying open all my griefs before you, to seek from yourself the right remedy and cure for the same. And since that I have oft found by experience that evil-affected or unfit instruments employed betwixt us have oftentimes been the cause of great misunderstanding amongst us, I have therefore at this time made choice of sending unto you this nobleman, the Earl of Mar, in respect of his known honesty and constant affection to the continuance of our amity, together with his colleague, the Abbot of Kinloss (a gentleman whose uprightness and honesty is well known unto you) that, by the labours of such honest and well-affected ministers, all scruples or griefs may on either side be removed and our constant amity more and more be confirmed and made sound. Assuring myself that my ever honest behaviour towards you shall at least procure that justice at your hands to try ere you trust any unjust imputations spread of me, and not to wrong yourself in wronging your best friend; but, in respect of the faithfulness of the bearers, I will remit all particulars to their relation who, as they are dir[ected] to deal with you in all honest plainness (the undisseverable compan[ion] of true friendship), so do I heartily pray you to hear and trust them in all things as it were myself and to give them a favourable ear and answer as shall ever be deserved at your hands by

Your most loving and affectionate
brother and cousin,
JAMES R.

From Holyroodhouse the tenth of February 1601[1]

Public Record Office   *Holograph*
SP 52/67/11

[1]James had marked the beginning of the seventeenth century by commencing the New Year on 1 January not, as was still the case in England, on 25 March.

Letter 75

To the Earl of Mar and Edward Bruce

The following letter of instruction was probably written about the same time as the preceding letter. The friends in England whose advice the ambassadors were to follow were, of course, Essex and his associates, of whose ineffectual rebellion the King had not yet heard.

[*Early February 1601*]

A private instruction to the Earl of Mar and the
Abbot of Kinloss, my ambassadors towards the
Queen of England.

Ye shall temper and frame all your dealing with the Queen or Council by the advice of my friends there, whose counsel ye shall directly follow in all your behaviour there, with these reservations only which by tongue I delivered unto you. And if that actually they perform their promises on their part, I give you by

169

these presents of my own hand ample power to give them full
assurance of my assisting them accordingly.

JAMES R.

National Library of Scotland   *Holograph*
MS. 33.1.7, Vol. XXI, Item 8

Letter 76

To the Earl of Mar and Edward Bruce

*News of the Essex Rebellion probably reached Edinburgh
on 12 or 13 February, in time for King James to give his ambassadors to England these revised instructions before they set out
on their journey.*

[*Mid-February 1601*]

Notes for my ambassadors anent this accident[1]

1. If turns be remediable and that my friends think it the best
   appearance for their safety that I lie still and that ye kythe*
   not, follow their advi[ce] but beware to be prevented ere ye
   look for it.
2. But if they think your kything* in it may do good, stand not
   then upon terms and I shall avow you bravely.
3. And if they be resolved that they lack nothing but a head to
   enter in plain action with it, assure them I shall be as willing
   and ready to supply that place as they can be to desire me,
   only with that old reservation of the safety of the Queen's
   person, which ye maun* take them sworn t[o].
4. But if, as God forbid, it be past redding* ere ye come there,
   use then all the means ye can to get me a party there and
   assure them that I can neither with honour nor surety disguise myself any longer.

5. And if when ye come to Berwick ye find any peril of preventing your coming, post up with all speed tua* and yourself and be not a ble[...] ambassador, but remember of little lomini.²

JAMES R.

National Library of Scotland   *Holograph*
MS. 33.1.7, Vol. XXI, Item 6

¹The Essex Rebellion.
²*Sic.* Since James rarely used capitals, we should perhaps read "Lomini." The allusion here is probably irrecoverable, but may refer to Antoine Loménie de Brienne (1560–1638). After serving Henri IV on various missions, including one to England late in 1595, he became Secretary of State in 1606.

Letter 77

To Sir Michael Balfour

Hoping to have the Pope and various Italian rulers support him rather than a Spanish claimant to the throne of England, James in 1598 sent a secret envoy to the Grand Duke Ferdinand of Tuscany to seek the latter's good offices. This envoy was a tempestuous little Scot, Sir Michael Balfour, Laird of Burley, who passed himself off as a mere tourist. In the spring of 1601, Sir Michael revisited Florence, this time to propose a match between James's heir, Prince Henry, and one of the Grand Duke's daughters. The following letter dates from this second visit. It is here printed slightly out of chronological order so that Letters 78–91 can be given en bloc.

[*27 June? 1601*]¹

My little Sir Michael,

That the bearer your brother returned no sooner unto you, you may wyte* the wind which until yesterday never changed out of the east, almost past memory of man.

171

Now as for answer to your letter, I have the copy of the Queen of England's brave instructions for Florence and I know what use to make of them. And, where now ye are, ye may help to prevent such hen wiles by filling the Duke's head with true informations which will serve to hold out all such feckless calumnies in times to come. As for the men that the Duke craves, ye shall most lovingly grant them unto him as your Latin letter[2] (which is formed according to your desire) will testify, which ye may acquaint him with. As for your commission that ye crave, it cannot be gotten done without hurt to the secrecy of this errand, wherein chiefly consists the good success thereof. But I think that secret taikin* set down betwixt you and Secretary Vinta[3] may serve that turn in times to come well enough. Always, if ever the necessity of the errand shall so require, ye shall offer to lay yourself in wed* there until that commission be returned you upon your sending for. And as for the letter of credit presented by the Master of Gray,[4] the letter, credit, and all is alluterlie* false and feinzeid,* upon my honour, which in my name ye shall answer for. And last, for your captainship, ye never needed to doubt that I would prefer any other to any part of the honour of your labour, whereunto praying God to grant as good a success and happy event as ye have in the very beginning thereof had a fortunate rencontre [meeting], I bid you heartily farewell, hoping that *Caesarem vehis et eius fortunam*.[5]

JAMES R.

National Library of Scotland   *Holograph*
MS. 33.1.13, Item 46

[1]The date is that proposed by J. D. Mackie in his *Negotiations between King James VI and I and Ferdinand I, Grand Duke of Tuscany* (Oxford, 1927), p. 35.

[2]For this see Mackie, *Negotiations*, pp. 36–37.

[3]Belisario Vinta, secretary to the Grand Duke.

[4]In his banishment, Gray had misused a blank letter of credit which, before his downfall, he had obtained from James.

[5]"You may bear off Caesar and his fortune." (James's most likely source is Plutarch, *Vitae*, "Julius Caesar," 38.5.)

hairtelie* devotion. And if it be after the last, then are ye to be resolved of their course therein and by what means they are able to effectuate the same, upon the knowledge whereof I shall then determinate what your part shall be. For above all ye must in this errand learn to be well fensid,* the chief property whereof is to take the time right, which will make you to eschew the two extremities: either by precipitation to mar all for lack of good backing, or else by starting too late (if they groan so under the burden that they are like to faint) to give the people a ground of excuse that, by suffering them to be overthrown for not declaring myself in time, they were forced to sue to other saints for shunning of their present overthrow. But, in this last point, beware with the facility of the people and the craft of the Council, for I know they concluded before that ever they saw you to deny you whatever ye craved, thereby to force me to kythe* in my own colours as they call it.

As to your next doubt, it touches the main ground of your commission, which, if ye deeply consider, ye cannot misbehave yourselves therein. For at the time of your despatch (things were so miscarried by that unfortunate accident)[1] as I was out of all hope that ye could come any speed at the Queen and Council's hand anent the main point. And therefore your whole commission was divided in two parts: to wit, to deal with the Queen and [her] present guiders, and to deal with the people—with the first publicly and for the present time, with the next privately and for the future time; with the first to obtain a surety for holding off of evil (since there was small appearance of the grant of any good), with the next to obtain a certain assurance for the furtherance of future hopes. And therefore the particular points that ye was to crave of the Queen and Council were, first to release or give just punishment for known and proved offences to all such as are detained only for speaking with me, and specially for poor Ivers.[2] The next is to give out a plain declairaitoure,* which must be enacted in her own records, that I am untouched in any action of practice that ever hath been intended against her, especially in this last[3] (wherein I wonder that, according to your former letter, ye have written nothing in this last). The third is that hereafter a difference be put betwixt

174

such honest men of her subjects as shall be known to love and deal with me and those that practises with her greatest enemies or rebels. The fourth is that she would liberally consider of my necessities, holding forth in that point your suit already begun for the lands of my grandmother.[4] And the last, and of most importance, is that it would please her to renew her old promise that nothing shall be done by her in her time in prejudice of my future right nor no "cheue under cure"[5] reserved against me (excepted always if she be not to endure as long as the sun and the moon).

In these heads ye must so deal with Master Secretary[6] and her principal guiders as ye may assure them that, as I find my requests answered in these points, I will make account of their affections towards me accordingly, and (if in these points I be satisfied) that ye have power to give them full assurance of my favour, especially to Master Secretary, who is king there in effect.

And as to your doubt in what sort to leave there, it must be according to the answers ye shall receive to these former demands. For if ye be well satisfied therein, then must ye have a sweet and kind parting. But, if ye get nothing but a flat and obstinate denial, which I do surely look for, then are ye in both the parts of your commission to behave yourselves thus: first ye must be the more careful, since ye come [can?] so little speed in your public employment with the Queen, to set forward so much the more your private negotiation with the country. And if ye see that the people be not in the highest point of discontentment (whereof I already spake) then must ye by your labours with them make your voyage at least not alluterlie* unprofitable, which doth consist in these points: first, to obtain all the certainty ye can of the town of London that in the due time they will favour the right; next, to renew and confirm your acquaintance with the Lieutenant of the Tower; thirdly, to obtain as great a certainty as ye can for the fleet by the means of 3 nephew[7] and of some seaports; fourthly, to secure the hearts of as many noblemen and knights as ye can get dealing with and to be resolved what every one of their parts shall be at that great day; fifthly, to foresee anent armour for every shire, that against that day my enemies have not the whole commandment of the armour and my friends only be unarmed; sixthly, that (as ye have written) ye may distribute good seminaries through every shire that may never leave working in the harvest till the day of reaping come; and generally to leave all things in such certainty and order as the enemies be not able in the meantime to lay such bars in my way as shall make things remediless when the time shall come.

Now as to the terms ye shall leave in with the Queen, in case of the foresaid flat denial: let your behaviour ever be with all honour, respect, and love to her person; but at your parting ye shall plainly declare unto her that she cannot use me so hardly as it shall be able to make me to forget any part of that love and respect that I owe to her as to my nearest kinswoman, and that the greatest revenge that ever I shall take of her shall be to pray to God to open her eyes and to let her see how far she is wronged by such base instruments about her as abuses her ear, and that (although I will never give her occasion of grief in her time) yet the day may come when I will crave account at them of their presumption when there will be no bar betwixt me and them. And ye shall plainly declare to Master Secretary and his followers that, since now when they are in their kingdom they will thus misknow me, when the chance shall turn I shall cast a deaf ear to their requests; and whereas now I would have been content to have given them, by your means, a full assurance of my favour if at this time they had pressed to deserve the same, so now, they condemning it, may be assured never hereafter to be heard, but all the Queen's hard usage of me to be hereafter craved at their hands. And thus shall ye part without any just offence to the Queen, please the humour of the people, and use no greater threatenings than such as I shall be very able to perform in the owin* time.

But above all, ye must not forget to deal as earnestly as ye can for obtaining of yon declairaitoure* that I am clear and untouched in any of these practices, which if by no means ye can get granted unto you, then must ye desire to be publicly heard before the nobility and whole Council and, if it can be possible, in the Star Chamber, where, having delaitid* how many vile and untrue calumnies have from time to time been spread of me, that I should have been upon the counsel of divers practices against the Queen's person and state, notwithstanding of my ever upright and honourable dealing with her, that ye are come there to declare unto them how, in my name, ye have earnestly craved of the Queen and Council that I might now be cleared of all these imputations, which being denied unto you, ye could do no less than publicly there to protest ye are and ever was ready to answer in case she would have accused you of such practices; otherwise, if nothing be laid to my charge during your presence, that ye protest that I shall be counted clear of any such imputations for all times hereafter and this for fear of after checcis,* and that ye desire this protestation to be enacted in their records, and this *ex iure gentium*[8] cannot well be refused unto you.

Ye see now how your doubts, obscurely proponed without making me particularly acquainted how matters goes, hath forced me against my nature to write rather in a historical than logical style. I wish ye may be as sore wearied in reading as I was in writing hereof, but I must conclude now with giving you a checce* that ye are so hasty to return as ye begin to count the day thereof before ye see the end of your errand, which is of that weight that I, as master, and ye, as servants, must set our whole rests upon the well-going thereof, respecting not *quam cito* but *quam bene*[9] ye may put an end to your affairs there. It shall not also be amiss that ye impart such parts of this letter to such known and trusty friends as ye know shall have a sympathy with their humours, making end with my hairtelie* wishes to God that he may so prosper your labours as the fruits thereof may yield contentment to me, a security to that afflicted estate and country, and honour to yourselves that are employed ministers therein. And thus I bid you heartily farewell.

From Linlithgow the viii of April.

JAMES R.

National Library of Scotland   *Holograph*
MS. 33.1.7, Vol. XXI, Item 40

[1]The Essex Rebellion.

[2]Sir William Evers, or Eure, imprisoned by Elizabeth for being in secret communication with King James (*v.* Chamberlain, *Letters,* I: 113).

[3]Another reference to the Essex Rebellion.

[4]Margaret Stuart, Countess of Lennox.

[5]Lord Hailes, in his *Secret Correspondence of Sir Robert Cecil with James VI* (Edinburgh, 1766, p. 6), modernized this as "check under cure," but in a footnote observed, "The sense is not obvious"—a notable understatement.

[6] Sir Robert Cecil, Principal Secretary of State.

[7]We have here the earliest use of the numerical code employed in ensuing letters. By "3" is meant Lord Henry Howard. His nephew is probably Lord Thomas Howard.

[8]"By the law of nations."

[9]"Not how quickly but how well."

Letter 79

To "10" [Sir Robert Cecil]

While in England, the Earl of Mar and Edward Bruce learned that Queen Elizabeth's Principal Secretary, Sir Robert Cecil, was prepared to smooth the way for James's succession to the English throne. A more powerful and useful ally could not have been found, but there were complications. James had allowed Essex, the Secretary's great enemy, to prejudice him against Cecil. On the other hand, that devious politician Lord Henry Howard, already working closely with James and enjoying his trust, had earlier proposed that James seek the aid of Cecil. After considering the situation, James decided to accept Cecil's offered alliance, and he sent the following letter.

In opening an unauthorized correspondence with the King of Scotland on a subject as sensitive as the succession, Cecil was risking the Queen's severest displeasure and the ruin of his entire career. For this reason code numbers[1] were used to designate him and others in the secret correspondence from which the next thirteen letters come.

[*May? 1601*][2]

I am most heartily glad that 10 [Cecil] hath now at last made choice of two so fit and confident ministers[3] whom with he hath been so honourably plain in the affairs of 30 [King James], assuring 10 that 30 puts more confidence in them, according to the large and long proof that he hath had of them, than in any other that follows him. Like as 10 is most beholden unto them for the honourable report that they have made of him to 30, whom to they have upon the peril of their credit given full assurance of the sincerity of 10. And because 30 cannot have the occasion to speak face to face with 10, that out of his own mouth he may give him full assurance of his thankful acceptance of his plain and honourable dealing, he therefore prays 10 to accept of his long approved and trusty 3 [Lord Henry Howard] both as a surety of his thankfulness and his constant love to him in all times hereafter, as also to be a sure and secret interpreter betwixt 30 and 10 in the opening up of every one of their minds to another, whom 10 hath the better cause to like of and trust since long before this time 3 dealt very earnestly with 30 to take a good conceit of 10, offering himself to be a dealer betwixt them. Whereupon 30 was contented that 3 should deal betwixt Essex and 10 for a conformity betwixt them for the weal of 30 in the owin* time. But that 10 mistrusted the aspiring mind of Essex, 30 cannot but commend, taking it for a sure sign that 10 would never allow that a subject should climb to so high a room and that he should ever be thrall to a subject, that hath from his childhood been trained up in the service of a free prince. And yet 30 doth protest upon his conscience and honour that Essex had never any dealing with him which was not most honourable and avowable. As for his misbehaviour there, it belongs not [to] 30 to judge of it for, although 30 loved him for his virtues, he was no ways obliged to embrace his quarrels but to accept of every man according to his own deserts. This far hath 30 thought good to commit to paper to be a witness to 10 of his inward disposition towards him, assuring him that he takes in very good part his warenes* in dealing, like as he doth promise upon his honour that, in all times hereafter, the suspicion or disgracing of 10 shall touch 30 as near as 10. And, when it shall please God that 30 shall succeed to his right, he shall no surelier succeed to the place than he shall succeed in bestowing as great and greater favour upon 10 as his predecessor doth bestow

179

Right trusty and well-beloved 10,

If, at my first dealing with you by my late ambassadors, I had not been settled in that assurance that the party I dealt with was wise and that my favour was to be grounded upon a fixed star and not a mobile or wavering planet, I could not (I must confess) have thought myself fully secure of a thankful meeting until from yourself I had been certified of your thankful acceptance of my letter by a direct and dutiful answer thereunto, as lately ye have done. But being (as I have already said) well acquainted with your qualities, and resolved that I dealt with a wise man, I no sooner was certain that my letter was put in your hands but as soon I laid my count ever after *dormire securus in utramque aurem*[1] for your part; and therefore may ye assure yourself that I do accept of your most wise and kind answer as only proceeding from the fervency of your affection, which hath made you to surmount all doubts of incurring such hazards thereby as one in your place is ever subject unto, accounting now your honest affection so much the more precious unto me that ye have never untimously* and undutifully snatched at future fortunes, which unlawful form of doing might some day tend as far to my own discontentment; protesting in the presence of God that with his grace I shall ever keep that alike Christian as politic rule to measure as I would be measured unto; and since (God be praised) my claim is both just and honourable, ever to join the adverb to the name in using *bonum bene*.[2]

It is indeed true, as in your own letter ye confess, that if your silence had continued any longer it might have bred some hazards to the fortunes of both the princes (besides your own particular) for, as princes must hear and see with other ears and eyes than their own, so (to deal plainly with you) it was continually beaten in my ears that your silence did proceed not of duty to your sovereign but out of unquenchable malice against me; for, although I thought it ever the part of a wise man to judge by certain effects and not by outward and deceivable appearances, yet too many impressions might in the end have proved it to be true that *gutta cavat lapidem non vi sed sepe cadendo*,[3] so as by your breaking of silence at this time ye have not only reaped the

181

full assurance of my constant favour but also done most honest service to your own sovereign by removing such jealousies as might otherwise have brangled* our amity, which, although it be not convenient that she know (by reason of her jealousy), yet is it most avowable how soon it shall come to light. Promising to you, for my part, in the honour of a king, that not only shall I never by any untimous* impatience press in the least jot to divert you from your dutiful fidelity to your sovereign but shall also, in all times coming, rule all my actions for advancing of my lawful future hopes by your advice even as ye were one of my own counsellors already, being justly moved to this confidence in you as well by the experience of your wisdom and sincerity in her service as by the wise and honest advice ye give me how to behave myself towards her in your late most kind and wise letter. Assuring you that I will not only use your honest advice in my behaviour towards her (as I protest to God I was never otherwise inclined), but I will also use and follow your other advice concerning my behaviour with her people.

No, ye need not to think that I am so evil acquainted with the histories of all ages and nations that I am ignorant what a rotten reed *mobile vulgus*[4] is to lean unto, since some in your country have very dearly bought the experience thereof of late. I am no usurper; it is for them to play the Absalom.[5] Yea, God is my witness that I shall ever eschew to give the Queen any just cause of jealousy through my too busy behaviour; and besides that I ever did hold this maxim that a few great spirits were the ordinary instruments and second causes that made the world to be ruled according to their temperature. Otherwise I behoved by favouring democracy [to] fichte* against myself. But yet is it true indeed that the hearts of the people are not to be rejected, but not to be compassed by any particular insinuation with every one of them, which would breed greater jealousy in the Queen than good success with them. But good government at home, firm amity with the Queen, and a loving care in all things that may concern the weal of that state are the only three steps whereby I think to mount upon the hearts of the people. And surely I am importuned by sundry there more than I could wish for fear they bewray themselves, for I could be very well contented to be sure of their goodwill without the renewing of many messages. And in special I could wish the ditty of "I say nothing" might have a good sympathy with the owner thereof. As for my part, I shall follow the advice of my faithful 3 [Lord Henry Howard] therein.

And thus, having unfolded before you the anatomy of my mind, I heartily pray you to rest assured that although to mercenary men I would keep promise for my own respect, but without any care for their well-doing, yet the only respect that can move you and my faithful 3 to love me being for the love of virtue, I shall ever acquit it in that virtuous sort that I shall need no other remembrancer for you both than my inward gratitude to stir me to be careful both for present reservedness and future favours in the owin* time.

Your most loving friend,

30

Cecil Papers   *Holograph*
135:59

[1]"To sleep without anxiety." The King is misquoting Terence *Heautontimoroumenos* 342.

[2]"Using good well."

[3]"The drop hollows out the stone not by force but by the repeated falling" (Latin proverb).

[4]"The fickle mob."

[5]Absalom rebelled against his father, David, but James will never rebel against his "mother," Elizabeth. In Letter 82 we find James referring to himself as "the son of the present queen."

Letter 81

To "10" [Sir Robert Cecil]

Normally, important services to a king were rewarded with jewels, pensions, grants of land, and titles. James regrets that because of the secrecy of their connection he can reward Cecil only with letters of thanks.

[1601–1602]

My dearest 10,

I am ashamed that I can as yet by no other means witness my thankfulness for your daily so honourable, judicious, and painful labours for the furtherance of my greatest hopes than by bare ink and paper, and that your travails of so great worth and inestimable value should be repaid with so poor a recompense. But the best excuse is that these papers are but witnesses of that treasure of gratitude which by your good deserts is daily nourished in my heart. I am not a little encouraged by the letter of 24 [Queen Elizabeth] which discovers a great integrity in her affection, and plainness in her dealing. Whom I ought to thank for her good temper ye may easily guess. I have answered her in the best sort I could, as by the copy thereof ye will perceive.

And that ye may have proof that my confidence is fully settled upon you, I have sent you the substance of two messages that Sir Anthony Shirley hath lately sent me, without keeping up one jot thereof, whose errors appear rather to proceed from ignorance than malice. Ye cannot do me a greater service than to move 24 [Elizabeth] to continue this inward and privy form of intelligence, whereby I hope ye shall in the end prove an honest and happy minister. To faithful 8 [Edward Bruce] his letter I remit all particulars, and specially my opinion how ye shall behave yourself in that matter which, God knows, is more grievous unto me than any temptation that Satan by God's permission could have devised to have afflicted me with. But here I end with the assurance of the continuance of my constant love to my most faithful 3 [Lord Henry Howard], assuring him that, as I

184

am infinitely sorry for that defluxion fallen upon his eye, so would I think a hospital a reward that would keep no proportion either for a king's honour to give or by him for so well meriting services to be received. And thus, my dearest 10, I bid both you and 3 most heartily farewell.

Your most loving and
assured friend,
30

Cecil Papers   *Holograph*
135: 71

Letter 82

[*To Henry Percy, Earl of Northumberland*]

Sometime in the early spring of 1602 an important new development took place. The northern magnate Henry Percy, Earl of Northumberland, belatedly followed Cecil's course and let James know that he could count on his support in seeking the English crown. In a letter Northumberland made much the same assessment of the situation in England and offered much the same advice as Cecil had a year earlier. As Northumberland was not regarded as a friend by either Lord Henry Howard or Cecil, he was not admitted into the secret of their arrangement with James. Northumberland, however, was much too important a person to be openly rebuffed, so James wrote him the following letter which, while professing exemplary sentiments, gives nothing away.

Right trusty cousin,

I have received your most wise, plain, and honest letter from the hands of the gentleman bearer hereof, and I have conferred with him at as great length as the opportunity of the time could, with safety from the hazard of his discovery, permit. And although I never doubted of the integrity of your affection towards me for many reasons, which to the bearer I have communicated, yet am I infinitely glad that you have, by so honourable a letter and so well a chosen messenger, made the first discovery thereof.

To the two main points of your letter, which you confirm with many well grounded and infallible reasons: for the first of them, although it be a maxim in the schools that *De futuris contingentibus non est determinanda veritas*,² yet by all probable appearance your opinions are well grounded. And I do assuredly hope that God, who hath by lineal descent clad me with an undoubted right to your crown, will also in the due time make the possession thereof, and entry thereinto, pleasant and peaceable to me and unto you all although, as you wisely confess, I ought notwithstanding hereof omit no lawful provision in case of the worst,† that becomes a wise and provident prince to do in so grave a matter.

And as for your advice in the other point, if my constant resolution were not agreeable to your advice, I could neither be religious, wise, nor honest. For how could I be religious to prevent God's leisure by unlawful anticipation, and to do that wrong to my neighbour the like whereof I would be loath to suffer in my own person? It were very small wisdom, by climbing of dikes and hedges for pulling of unripe fruit to hazard the breaking of my neck when, by a little patience and abiding the season, I may with far more ease and safety enter at the gate of the garden and enjoy the fruits at my pleasure in the time of their greatest maturity. Yea, what a foolish part were that in me, if I might do it, to hazard my honour, state, and person, in entering that kingdom by violence as a usurper which God by lawful right hath provided for me, to the which I am called as a lawful heir, as the

186

son of the present queen, without inverting, innovating, or making any alteration in the state, government, or laws. And besides, what confidence could I ever have in those that for pleasure of me had betrayed their present sovereign? No, since the old proverb is most true, that, though princes make sometimes use of treason yet they ever hate the traitor, with what security could I think to make my residence in a kingdom so full of traitors? And last, for the point of honesty, with what mask or veil could I cover that blot to mine honour in being the first breaker off, for untimely ambition, of that long continued friendship betwixt the Queen and me—especially at this time when, by my long honest behaviour towards her, I have at last attained to a more inward and confident amity with her than ever was betwixt us heretofore.

For conclusion then of this letter, as by the choice of this messenger you have given a testimony both of your honest intention in employing a gentleman whom nature must bind you to love, and so not to engage him further than you may well warrant him, as also of your wisdom, he being either something to you or nothing to himself, and therefore do I heartily wish you to employ hereafter no other Mercury[3] in your dealing with me. Yea, further, would I wish you to be wary with sending of any message to me at all except some great occasion shall require it, lest if any misfortune fell out, it might breed harm to us both: to me in stirring anew the Queen's jealousies, at this time so far quenched, and to you in respect of the jealous state you once stood in.

Assure you, ye can by no means so far enable yourself for my service against the lawful time as by not only maintaining but also advancing your credit at her hands, that whenever it shall please God to call her to his mercy, you may be a chief instrument to assist my settling in that seat which I honour as the apparent heir, in all quietness, without the alteration or prejudice of any that will not wilfully resist to my right.

And thus remitting the more particular discourse of all things to the bearer's sufficiency, of whose honesty I have ever heard a sound report, with assurance to yourself of my thankful acceptance of this your so honourable a resolution, and so I bid you heartily farewell.

Your loving
and affectionate friend,
J.R.

Cecil Papers   *Edward Bruce's copy,*
135: 92   *apparently of a lost*
holograph

[†*Note:* A few obvious errors in this copy have been corrected from another copy at Hatfield, one in Cecil's own hand, MS. 135: 93. The words from the Cecil copy have been marked by underlining dots.]

[1]In a letter dated only 1 May but obviously written in 1602, Lord Henry Howard mentions that Northumberland had shown Cecil this letter. (See Hailes, *Secret Correspondence*, p. 105.)
[2]"Concerning future contingencies, the truth is not to be determined."
[3]Messenger.

Letter 83

[*To Henry Percy, Earl of Northumberland*]

Although, in Letter 82, King James had discouraged further correspondence, Northumberland sent a second letter suggesting that James seek an ally in Cecil. In the following letter, a model of bland duplicity, the King keeps Northumberland in ignorance of the connection already forged with Cecil, while lulling the earl with smooth and flattering phrases.[1]

[*1602?*]

Right trusty cousin,

I am heartily glad that it is my good fortune to be acquainted with a noble man carrying so honourable a mind, as also that doth rightly interpret and discern of my honest intentions as you do. In both your letters may clearly be seen the upright sincerity of your affection towards me, which if I do not requite

188

with thankfulness I should more wrong myself than you. And as to your last, wherein you give your censure of divers men's affections in particular, I think it not possible to find more apparent probabilities in a case of that nature, wherein nothing of certain can be concluded (*ante eventum*) but specially concerning the chief agent[2] of that state. I protest I will ever hope for the best of him so long as he truly serves the present and shall work nothing derogatory to the future, and therefore I cannot but very well allow of your inward friendship with him, as one who can best enable you to make your power to have a correspondence with your affection in my service *cum veneret dies ille*.[3] If otherwise he deceive my expectation, I leave it to your caution to make him deceive himself and none of us. But although I know that of all men in England he will be the hindmost to make himself known unto me during the Queen's breath (so great is his caution for his own hazard), yet if he serve truly the present and wrong me not in her time, as I have already said, I can think no otherwise of him nor of a very honest man.

As for his favourable behaviour to such persons in particular as in your letter you have reckoned out and observed: although divers men may diversely judge thereof, yet do I well allow of your charitable interpretation and so it fits best a Christian king to think. But your observing of their names in particular puts me in mind of one of them, poor Southampton, who lives in hardest case[4] of any of them, and if in any sort your means may help to procure him further liberty or easier ward, pity would provoke me to recommend it unto you.

I do very well allow of your wariness to write or send unto me, for a king cannot be without many eyes upon him as one exalted on a height and eminent place. And although I perceive both by your letters to me and the Earl of Mar that their intelligences are false and contrived, yet among many guessings at circumstances something may run counter that will foster jealousies, and one small discovery may mar a great game. And therefore as I wrote before so I maun* repeat the same, since my course is honourable and avowable in substance: beware to offend the Queen with shadows and send no more messengers except some great and urgent occasion of sending be accompanied with some sure and safe means of convoy, in the meantime settling yourself in that certainty that by your honourable and faithful dealing you have acquired the sincere and constant affection of your loving and assured friend.

Cecil Papers
135: 97

Copy in the hand of Edward
Bruce, apparently of a lost
holograph

[1]The use of "0" as the symbol for Northumberland in their secret correspondence may partly indicate the view that Cecil and James took of him. (Edward Bruce, copying this letter, headed it "30 letter to 0.")
[2]Sir Robert Cecil.
[3]"When that day [i.e., of James's accession to the English throne] shall come."
[4]Henry Wriothesley, 3rd Earl of Southampton, had been a prisoner in the Tower ever since his participation in the Essex Rebellion.

Letter 84

To "3" [Lord Henry Howard]

Essex's foolhardy advice that James actively recruit and propagandize in England was discarded and the King followed the much wiser course, proposed by Cecil, of biding his time and being agreeable to the Queen until her death permitted Cecil and his colleagues to bring him quietly to the English throne. Meanwhile, as this letter indicates, James had a continuing problem with zealous offers of support from Englishmen who could not be told the reason for James's apparent aloofness.

[May 1602][1]

My dear 3,

Because I perceive by your answer, that either ye have mistaken the meaning of 8 [Edward Bruce], or else he mine, anent my sending of one to 24 [Queen Elizabeth], I have therefore thought good in my own laconic style to answer all your ample Asiatic[2] and endless volumes upon that subject, all your discourse being founded upon that question whether or no it be fit for me to have a resident[3] lying there. Whereof surely I never meant to doubt, for I have daily large experience that no resident sent from me could accomplish the hundredth part of that service which by the means of my worthy 10 [Cecil] is performed unto me there, except (as a fool) I would ever be desirous of change. No, my meaning was only to have directed to 24 [Elizabeth] either 8 [Bruce] or 9 [David Murray], as the necessity of some apparent occasion had required a greater or meaner messenger, by that means once for all to put a stay to the longing curiosity of men there, not of one or two discontented spirits but of the most part of the wisest and honestest subjects of all ranks, that wonders they never hear from me and cannot guess at the cause of my silence; and, since it is not fit that they know what rock I have built upon, it is most requisite that by some fair shift I advise them to secure themselves upon my watchful providence against the due time, lest otherwise my long flat silence be misinterpreted by them to proceed either from a carelessness of my own state or a contempt of them; and my meaning is that the messenger should by 10 his advice [Cecil's advice] frame this answer unto them and upon the despatch of his public errand with 24 [Elizabeth] to return again.

I am from my heart sorry for this accident fallen to Arbella,[4] but as nature enforces me to love her as the creature living nearest of kin to me, next my own children, so would I for her own weal that such order were taken as she might be preserved from evil company and that evil-inclined persons might not have access unto her to supplant[5] her, abusing of the frailty of her youth and sex; for if it be true (as I am credibly informed) that she is lately moved by the persuasion of Jesuits to change her religion and declare herself Catholic, it may easily be judged that she hath been very evil attended on by them that should have had greater care of her, when persons so odious not only to all good Englishmen but to all the rest of the world, Spain only excepted, should have had access to have conferred with her at such leisure as to have disputed and moved her in matters of religion. And now to conclude, I must not forget to take notice of that new obligation I have to my dearest 10 [Cecil] for his so

to vary from these grounds and transcend these limits which first were promised and agreed upon betwixt us, in drawing on a more affectionately familiar, though lawful, correspondence betwixt us than was at our first dealing promised by me to be urged or by you to be performed. But ye may, notwithstanding hereof, boldly repose in that security of his upright and honourable intention that deals with you that, although sundry intervening accidents may in some sort change my style of writing, yet shall I never in substance vary one jot from these main points which at our first acquaintance I did promise and vow unto you.

For I must plainly confess that both ye and your faithful colleague 40 [Nottingham?] have by your vigilant and judicious care so easily settled me in the only right course for my good, so happily preserved the Queen's mind from the poison of jealous prejudice, so valiantly resisted the crooked courses of some seditious spirits who can never weary secretly to sting the heels of honest men whom they only envy for virtue's sake, and so carefully laboured to further all my reasonable and lawful ends, as the great proof I have had of your happy and honest concurrence for my weal doth force me, out of the abundance of a thankful mind, to write in a more loving, plain, and familiar style than ever I was wont to do before; but not that hereby I have any intention to desire you or 40 (whom I always and ever shall account as one) anyways to alter either in form or substance your accustomed form of answering me. For although that I, in respect of my birth and place, cannot fall under the censure of any dangerous constructions (though I never with God's grace shall do anything in private which I may not without shame proclaim upon the tops of houses) yet, so dangerous is your state as subjects that, although your intention to your sovereign be never so upright, yet if the lion think your ears to be horns there will be no place admitted you for excuse. It shall therefore suffice me that ye rest in a full and certain persuasion of my love and thankful mind to you both, whereof this my handwrit shall serve for a witness unto you, assuring 40 that with God's grace he shall never be disappointed of his confidence in my honesty upon your relation. And as it never was nor shall be my course to press him or any beyond the bounds of their dutiful allegiance to their sovereign, so do I protest in God's presence that if I had wronged any of you so far as to have suspected you guilty of so great unworthiness, I would not have so far stained my conscience and honour as to have fostered so vile a motion, not for the gaining of the whole world's monarchy unto me.

I cannot also omit to display unto you the great contentment I receive by your so inward and united concurrence in all the paths that lead to my future happiness, most heartily wishing you to continue in that happy course as ye may be sure of my thankfulness towards you, whom I know to be only moved, for the respect of conscience and honour, to deserve so well at the hands of a lawful, natural and loving successor to your queen and country. And thus, praying 40 to be assured that by your means only he shall hear from me, that he may thereby discern if any other word come to him in my name that it is but false and adulterate coin, and persuading him of my entire affection towards him as to yourself, I bid you heartily farewell.

Your most assured loving friend,
30

From Falkland the third of June 1602

Cecil Papers   *Holograph*
135: 63

Letter 86

To "40" [Charles Howard, Earl of Nottingham?]

King James assures the new recruit (noted in Letter 85) that he gratefully accepts his services. If that new recruit was Nottingham, this letter must have made him the more confident that

194

James, who regarded Essex as his "martyr," did not hold it against him that he had commanded the force that had put down the Essex Rebellion.

29 July 1602

Trusty and well-beloved cousin,

Although your readiness and favourable furtherance to any suitors recommended by me, in anything concerning your office ever since your entry thereunto,[1] did long ere now sufficiently persuade me of your honest and lawful affection to my service, yet having lately the assurance thereof confirmed, both by the faithful testimony of 10 [Cecil], as likewise by your own words uttered in enigma to my servant Ashton,[2] I would not omit to send you these few lines of my own hand, as witness of my thankfulness. And as by my letter to you and 10 conjunctly ye are already certified of my honest and upright course with your sovereign, and that I am no ways to employ you beyond the bounds of your allegiance, so have I for the present no other recompense to send you for your goodwill but my faithful promise that all my dealing with you shall ever be accompanied with these three qualities: honesty, secrecy, and constancy. But as I will deal with you by no other way but by the means of 10, so may ye assure yourself that your strait and steadfast conjunction with him in my service is the only way to enable you both therein, and to disappoint all my malicious and undeserved adversaries. And thus, trusty and well-beloved cousin, I bid you heartily farewell. From Falkland the xxix July 1602.

Your loving friend,
30

Cecil Papers   *Holograph*
135: 101

[1]Nottingham (as Lord Howard of Effingham) on 8 July 1585 was appointed Lord High Admiral for life.
[2]See Letter 42, headnote.

Letter 87

To "3" [Lord Henry Howard]

To reduce the risk of detection, the correspondence between James (30) and Cecil (10) was often conducted via Lord Henry Howard (3) in England and Bruce and Mar (8 and 20) in Scotland. The following letter shows the network in operation and serving a useful secondary function as an intelligence-gathering device for both Cecil and James.

29 July 1602

My dear and trusty 3,

The cause of my delay of writing until now was only that I stayed upon the parrot's coming, who repeated his lesson of "*Ave Caesar*" so coldly, so carelessly, and above all so imperfectly that he might have been safely made to have carried his own death folded up in such an enigma.[1]

The deep and restless care that both worthy 10 [Cecil] and ye have of my safety I shall never be able to recompense, as well for that honourable and loving dealing of 10 in persuading the Queen to give order for the banishment of unquhile* Gowrie's[2] brethren as for his circumspect dealing in the other great point whereof ye wrote in your last to 8 [Edward Bruce]. But, as my upright and guiltless conscience hath ever been my greatest guard and strong brazen wall, so am I most sure that there is a treacherous deceit and most unjust imputation of the innocent used in that errand; and therefore, as from the bottom of my heart I thank 10 for his watchful care herein, so do I pray you most earnestly to insist with him in my name that I may be informed from what fountain such news are derived unto him, for by the knowledge thereof I presume I shall be able to guess at the whole mystery.

I do also perceive by your letters to 8 that 10 is very desirous to know the knight's name that dealt betwixt the Duke of Lennox[3] and Raleigh. And therefore, although the knight himself be a very honest plain gentleman for so far as I can learn, yet knowing that confident trust can no more be severed from true friendship than the shadow can be cut from the body, I will give to 10 this further proof of my confident trust in him by discovery of this gentleman's name unto him, which is Sir Arthur Savage. Not doubting but 10 will conserve this as a friend's secret, without suffering the gentleman to receive any harm hereby, which more would interest me in honour than him in person. Especially since the gentleman's nature appears to be far different from Raleigh's though, out of zeal to me and affection to his friend, he could not refuse to be trucheman* unto him.

Ye shall also inform 10 that I have never heard word yet from Hamilton,[4] neither directly nor indirectly, since his return. Whereby I do guess that he is not well pleased with his answer. Mercury[5] is also come down to the border. How soon I receive his letter I shall answer it in every point according to the advice set down by 10. I hope Mackenzie[6] shall be an instrument of some good service to be done against Tyrone, for I find him very willing, but this and all other particulars I remit to the fidelity of 8 his pen, and do commit both 10 and you to the protection of the Almighty. From Falkland the xxix of July 1602.

Your constantly assured friend,

30

Cecil Papers   *Holograph*
135: 85

[1]What the King is saying, apparently, is that, like a parrot unaware of the meaning of the human speech it reproduces, Howard's messenger showed no sign of comprehending the oral message, with an inner secret meaning, that he had addressed to that Caesar (monarch) King James. He could have been used to carry a message importing his own execution, so oblivious was he of any concealed significance.

For the story (a good one) of the raven, parrot, magpie, and crow that were trained to greet Augustus with "Ave Caesar," see Macrobius *Saturnalia* 2.4.29–30. Erasmus borrowed the anecdote, and subsequently Skelton, Lyly, Lupton, and Nashe made allusions to a bird saying "Ave Caesar." (See McKerrow's edition of Nashe, IV: 105.)

[2]I.e., the former Earl of Gowrie. After the Gowrie conspiracy of August 1600 the title had been extinguished.

[3]The Duke of Lennox had visited London in November 1601.

[4]John Hamilton, 1st Marquess of Hamilton.
[5]A joking or code name. For the King's use of "Mercury" as a generic name for any messenger, see Letter 82 and n. 3.
[6]Kenneth McKenzie of Kintail, who had earlier been charged to provide a hundred men for service in Ireland (*v. CSP Scottish, 1597–1603*, p. 942).

Letter 88

To "10" [Sir Robert Cecil]

As his correspondence with Cecil progressed, James had increasing opportunities to appreciate the moderation, integrity, and wisdom of Queen Elizabeth's Principal Secretary. In the following letter the King offers to review his letters to Queen Elizabeth in the light of Cecil's advice, cannily binding the Secretary more closely to him by this gesture of trust and regard.

[*Autumn 1602?*][1]

My dearest and trusty 10,

My pen is not able to express how happy I think myself for having chanced upon so worthy, so wise, and so provident a friend as 10 is, which ye could not better have manifested than by that honest advice ye give me for writing to xxiiii [Queen Elizabeth]. And although I have very lately written unto her somewhat concerning that subject yet have I now again written this other according to your advice. Only this far I wish you to be acquainted with, that in truth such remonstrances as ye sent me were never presented unto me.

And as for the French ambassador,[2] he hath often upon his oath purged himself unto me that he hath no direction to move any such matter, for it was much noised amongst our ministry that his only errand to Scotland was to crave liberty of conscience, and therefore I had no will to put myself in use of lying. But as indeed I was lately advertised by some subjects of my own out of France that great offers were to be sent me from Spain, and that upon condition of granting liberty of conscience, so did I truly advertise the Queen thereof as well in my last as in this. Wherein I have followed your grounds, only leaving out some phrases that in my opinion smelled of flattery and some others that seemed too sharp and to accuse her of mistrusting me. Always when ye have read the copy of my letter I leave it to your discretion, who best knows her humour, whether to present it or not; wherein I must repose upon your discreet fidelity, that if it may please her and work good effects it may be put in her hands, otherwise that ye may freely advertise me what ye would have to be mended therein.

As for your course in time coming with the Master of Gray, I remit my opinion therein to 20 [Mar] his letter. But this far I heartily pray you to assure yourself, that ye can have no dealing with whatsomever Jew, gentile, or heathen that ever will breed the least suspicion in me of any crack in your integrity towards me. But, by the contrary, the further ye are upon their secrets, the more able will I be to sit as a god upon all the imaginations of their hearts, and the more secure will my state be from all their practices, whereof ye have already given me so large a proof that if ever I needed any more apologies or excuses in that matter I were not worthy of the place I possess. Nay, by the contrary, ye may assure yourself that I trust no more in the fidelity of 20 [Mar], that of a child was brought up with me, than I do in you, protesting that these words do only proceed *ex abund[ant]ia cordis*,[3] and not of any intention to pay you with Italian complementoes, and therefore I do wholly remit it to your own discretion and, as ye shall find the necessity of time to require it, to use greater or less frequency of advertisements. And thus, with my most hearty commendations to my dear and faithful 3 [Lord Henry Howard], I bid you heartily farewell.

Your constantly assured friend,

30

Cecil Papers   *Holograph*
135: 69

[1]Evidence for the date is supplied by the mention in this letter of "the French ambassador." There was no French ambassador in Scotland between the

inception of James's secret correspondence with Cecil, in the spring of 1601, and the arrival, late in July, 1602, of Charles Cauchon de Maupas, Baron du Tour. This letter, then, must have been written after Tour's arrival. In connection with the suspicions that the ambassador had been sent to seek religious toleration, and that James was ready to make concessions in favour of the Catholics, see Thomas Douglas's letter of 27 October 1602 to Sir Robert Cecil (*CSP Scottish* XIII: 1064).

[2]See n. 1 above.
[3]"Out of the abundance of the heart."

Letter 89

To "10" [Sir Robert Cecil]

King James had an abiding fear that some Catholic claimant might appear and snatch the English crown from his grasp. At this time, as he indicates in the following letter, he was opposed to both a peace between England and Spain and to any form of tolerance of Catholicism in England.

[*December? 1602*]

My dearest 10,

In regard that my trusty 3 [Lord Henry Howard] in a letter of his to 8 [Edward Bruce] wisheth him in your name to make me acquainted of the late wakening up again of a communing for a treaty of peace betwixt England and Spain, craving my advice how to behave yourself therein, I have taken occasion by these few lines, first most heartily to thank you for your timous* advertisement hereof, and next to set you down as shortly as I can my opinion there anents.

When I have advisedly considered and deeply looked in this matter, I cannot surely but think that, the time being weighed and the present state of things, such a peace at this time must be greatly prejudicial, first to the state of religion in general, secondly to the state both in religion and policy of this isle in special, and lastly most perilous for my just claim in particular. Amongst many, three principal gates for procuring these forenamed mischiefs by this peace would apparently be opened. First, *liberum com[m]ercium*[1] betwixt these nations would so soundly conciliate and extinguish all former rancours as it would no more be thought odious for an Englishman to dispute upon a Spanish title; secondly, the King of Spain would thereby have occasion by his agents of all sorts, loadenit* with golden arguments, who (if so were) would have free access in England to corrupt the minds of all corruptible men for the advancement of his ambitious and most unjust pretenses, besides the settling sure means for intelligence at all occasions; and lastly, Jesuits, seminary priests, and that rabble wherewith England is already too much infected would then resort there in such swarms as the caterpillars or flies did in Egypt, no man any more abhoring them, since the Spanish practices was the greatest crime that ever they were attainted of, which now by this peace will utterly be forgotten.

And now, since I am upon this subject, let the proofs ye have had of my loving confidence in you plead for an excuse to my plainness if I freely show you that I greatly wonder from whence it can proceed that not only so great flocks of Jesuits and priests dare both resort and remain in England but so proudly do use their functions through all the parts of England without any controlment or punishment these divers years past. It is true that for remedy thereof there is a proclamation lately set forth,[2] but blame me not for longing to hear of the exemplar[y] execution thereof *ne sit lex mortua*.[3] I know it may be justly thought that I have the like beam in my own eye but, alas, it is a far more barbarous and stiff-necked people that I rule over. Saint George surely rides upon a towardly riding horse where I am daily burstin* in daunting a wild unruly colt. And I protest, in God's presence, the daily increase that I hear of popery in England, and the proud vanterie* that the papists make daily there of their power, their increase, and their combined faction that none shall enter to be king there but by their permission, this their bragging, I say, is the cause that moves me, in the zeal of my religion and in that natural love I owe to England, to break forth in this digression and to forewarn you of these apparent evils. For though ye must know all these things far better than I can, yet it is a true old saying that another man will better see a

My dear 3,

Since my pen is not able to express the least part of that in-finite thanks which my heart doth yield to my dearest 10 [Cecil] for his so great and daily deserts at my hand, I am forced to em-ploy you as the trustiest friend to us both to descryve* unto him, the most vifly* that is possible unto you, what inward gratitude both ought to be and, indeed, is reserved in my heart towards him. But especially when I consider the greatness of his care and vigilance for my preservation by his offer for maintenance of an ordinary guard, I must say with our Saviour that in the last day he shall stand up and accuse my own subjects of ingratitude and too little care of me, who being born my subjects by nature, bound to me by many obligations and benefits, and daily conversant with me, are negligent of that which he, born a stranger, never bound to me by any benefit, and with his eyes never having seen me, can take no rest without he offer it unto me, but of this, as of all other things, ye will by the letter of 8 [Bruce] be particularly acquainted with my mind.

I cannot also thank 10 enough for acquainting me so vifly with the cogging of Gray,[1] but I have commanded 20 [Mar] to make you acquainted with such a juggling trick of his as may make both 10 and you hold in a great while your expenses upon physic by a half hour's good laughter.

And thus, my dear 3, being for lack of leisure compelled to be short, I bid you heartily farewell, ever praying you to rest more and more assured of the constant affection of

Your most loving friend,
30

Cecil Papers
135: 87

Holograph

[1]Patrick Gray, Master of Gray. For Cecil's relations with Gray see H. G. Staf-ford, *James VI of Scotland and the Throne of England*, pp. 262–67.

Letter 91

To "10" [Sir Robert Cecil]

*King James sets forth in detail his views concerning the treat-
ment of Catholics in England.*

[*March? 1603*][1]

My dearest 10,

The fear I have to be mistaken by you in that part of my last
letter[2] wherein I discover the desire I have to see the last edict
against Jesuits and priests[3] put in execution, the fear, I say, of
your misconstruing my meaning herein (as appears by your answer) enforceth me in the very throng of my greatest affairs to
pen by post an answer and clear resolution of my intention. I
did ever hate alike both extremities in any case, only allowing
the middes* for virtue, as by my book now lately published doth
plainly appear.[4] The like course do I hold in this particular. I
will never allow in my conscience that the blood of any man
shall be shed for diversity of opinions in religion, but I would be
sorry that Catholics should so multiply as they might be able to
practise their old principles upon us. I will never agree that any
should die for error in faith against the first table, but I think
they should not be permitted to commit works of rebellion
against the second table.[5] I would be sorry by the sword to diminish their number, but I would be also loath that, by too great
connivance and oversight given unto them, their numbers
should so increase in that land as, by continual multiplication,
they might at last become masters, having already such a settled
monarchy amongst them as their archpriest with his twelve
apostles,[6] keeping their terms in London and judging all questions, as well civil as spiritual, amongst all Catholics. It is for the
preventing of their multiplying and new set-up empire that I
long to see the execution of the last edict against them, not that
thereby I wish to have their heads divided from their bodies but
that I would be glad to have both their heads and bodies separated from this whole island and safely transported beyond

204

seas, where they may freely glut themselves upon their imagined gods. No! I am so far from any intention of persecution as, I protest to God, I reverence their church as our mother church although clogged with many infirmities and corruptions, besides that I did ever hold persecution as one of the infallible notes of a false church. I only wish that such order might be taken as the land might be purged of such great flocks of them that daily diverts the souls of many from the sincerity of the gospel, and withal that some means might be found for debarring their entry again, at least in so great swarms. And as for the distinction of their ranks (I mean betwixt the Jesuits and the secular priests), although I deny not that the Jesuits, like venomed wasps and firebrands of sedition, are far more intolerable than the other sort that seem to profess loyalty, yet is their so plausible profession the more to be distrusted that, like married women or minors whose vows are ever subject to the controlment of their husbands and tutors, their consciences must ever be commanded and overruled by their Romish god as it pleases him to allow or revoke their conclusions.

Thus remitting all other matters to the letters of faithful 8 [Bruce], not being able to express my thankfulness for your so great care to furnish a guard unto me, and recommending me most heartily to my most faithful 40 [Nottingham?], I end with renewing unto you the assurance of the constant love of

Your most loving friend,

30

Cecil Papers   Holograph
135: 80

¹This letter is endorsed "R. Mars 30 to 10," apparently indicating that Cecil received the letter in March. The only March compatible with the contents of the letter is that of 1603. Of course, the King could have written the letter late in February 1603; too much faith should not be placed in this endorsed notation, which may be late and approximate.
²Letter 89.
³See Letter 89, n. 2.
⁴A reference to *Basilikon Doron* (see *The Political Works of James I,* ed. C. H. McIlwain, p. 17). Although *Basilikon Doron* was not entered into the

205

Stationers' Register until 28 March 1603, a Scottish edition appeared a little earlier. In mid-October 1602 John Chamberlain reported, "I hear that king is printing a little peece of worke christened with a Greeke name" (*Letters*, ed. N. E. McClure, I: 167.)

⁵"The two divisions of the decalogue, relating to religious and moral duties respectively, held to have occupied the two 'tables of stone'" (*O.E.D.*).

⁶The reference is to George Blackwell who, in March 1598, in the absence of a Roman Catholic episcopate in England, was appointed Archpriest with the jurisdiction of a bishop. He was assisted by a council of twelve priests, six chosen by himself and six by the Cardinal Protector of England.

Letter 92

To Henry Percy, Earl of Northumberland

For about a year Northumberland had heeded King James's injunction only to write to him "if some great occasion shall require it." On 17 March 1603, with Queen Elizabeth plainly approaching her end, Northumberland deemed that he had great occasion and wrote the letter that James answered in this of 24 March, unaware that early that morning Queen Elizabeth had died and he was now both King of Scotland and King of England.

24 March [1603]

Right trusty and well-beloved cousin,

The more I hear from you the more am I rejoiced and do think myself infinitely happy that one of your place, endued with such sincerity of love towards me and with all other parts of sufficiency, should be born one day to be a subject unto me. For I protest unto you that in your letter ye have comprised the very sum of all the true news of the state of things there, according as I was by divers hands advertised this month past.

And as to the form of my entry there whenever it shall please God to call your sovereign, as in my first letter I wrote unto you, so now by these presents do I confirm and renew the same: that is to say that, as God is my witness, it never was, is, nor shall be my intention to enter that kingdom in any other sort but as the son and righteous heir of England, with all peace and calmness, and without any kind of alteration in state or government as far as possible I can. All men that hath truly served their present sovereign shall be alike welcome to me as they are presently or were in time past unto her, claiming nothing in that turn as King of Scotland but hoping thereby to have the means to knit that whole island in a happy and perpetual unity.

As for the Catholics, I will neither persecute any that will be quiet and give but an outward obedience to the law, neither will I spare to advance any of them that will by good service worthily deserve it. And if this course will not serve to win every particular honest man, my privy dealing with any of them can avail but little.

And thus I end, praying [you] for your own part to rest fully assured that ye shall in the owne* time have proof in what high account ye are with

Your most loving friend,
JAMES R.

Holyroodhouse, the 24 of March

Cecil Papers
135: 100

Copy, apparently of a
lost holograph

[1]For Northumberland's letter, dated 17 March, see J. Bruce, *Letters of Queen Elizabeth and King James of Scotland*, pp. 72–75.

Letter 93

To Sir Robert Cecil

Late on the night of 26 March 1603, Sir Robert Carey completed his famous three-day ride from London to Edinburgh and gave King James his first news of the death of Queen Elizabeth and the proclamation of his own succession. The next day,

without waiting for an official communication from Cecil and
the Council, James despatched the following message.

27 March 1603

Most worthy and most trusty counsellor, we greet you
heartily well.

We received your last written with your own hand of the 22
of this instant a very short space after the coming of Sir Robert
Carey, who did first acquaint us with the Queen's death and that
God had called her to his mercy, as also that the whole state, by
the good advice and grave judgement of those that have voice in
council, had uniformly consented to proclaim us her lawful successor and to be their king, for the which we offer first our most
hearty thanks to God, craving that of his free grace and favour
he would vouchsafe us two things: the first, that it may please
his divine majesty to make us equal and answerable to that high
place your state hath called us unto; the second, that we never
suffer so inestimable benefits as hath been wrought unto us by
the wisdom, providence, and policy of our dearest friends to
slide out of our memory without condign remuneration. And as
no age hath yielded any example of such industry, care, and
devotion of councillors in the translation of a monarchy, so
shall you see us strain the uttermost of our wits and endeavours
to make you know that no prince in earth shall go before us in
justice, piety, policy, and all other parts which you expect of us.

And for the first "arres" [earnest] of our affection we send to
you in haste, by our servant Mr. Foulis, whom you will trust, a
ratification and approbation of your places in Council with all
your states, honours, offices and dignities in the same quality
and condition you did possess them heretofore, if so it shall
seem expedient to yourself, wherein we give you and to your
associates power to use your own discretion and judgement,
which shall be every way most agreeable unto us. We are to
second Mr. Foulis by our trusty counsellor my Lord Kinloss,[1] by
whom you shall understand more amply of our mind and intention in all we have acte[d].

208

Thus wishing you to persist in that honourable regard and earnest care you have begun and half accomplished of our good fortune and prosperity till we see you, which we gr[eatly] long for, we bid you in our most hearty manner farewell and wish you all happiness. At our palace of Holyroodhouse the 27 of March 1603.

JAMES R.

How happy I think myself by the conquest of so faithful and so wise a counsellor I reserve it to be expressed out of my own mouth unto you.

Cecil Papers   *Holograph signature and*
134: 28   *postscript*

[1]For David Foulis, see Letter 67, n. 1. For Kinloss, see Letter 74, headnote.

Letter 94

To "The Nobility and Late Council of Our Realm of England"

Immediately after the death of Elizabeth a great many courtiers and officeholders headed for Scotland, intent upon winning the favour of the new king. James was more pestered than flattered by their coming. As he was concerned that the necessary structure of authority be maintained in England during the slightly risky period preceding his own arrival in London, he despatched the following tactful letter in an effort to reduce the influx of English careerist officials and fortune-hunters.

2 April 1603

Right trusty and well-beloved cousins and councillors,
we greet you heartily well.

Although we have not long ago written answer to your
former letter yet, for that diverse occasions daily fall out minis-
tering matter to write unto you, we have thought good by these
presents to will you of the Council and so many of the nobility
as may conveniently stay at London to remain there together,
for taking order with all matters which may occur touching our
affairs and the quietness of the country. And that such of you of
the nobility as may best be spared be directed with convenient
speed, with the like care and diligence, every one to his own
charge. For although it be very agreeable to us and we receive no
small contentment by the officious [dutiful] disposition of so
many noble gentlemen, our subjects, daily coming to meet us,
yet it is no less acceptable to us to have a sufficient number of
you together attending at London with your accustomed care
upon our affairs, and the rest to be waiting upon their particular
charges lest, by your absence from them, anything should fall
out which might breed disorder, or be omitted which might any
way tend to the settling of the estate. And, at our approaching
nearer unto you, you shall be further advertised of our pleasure.

Thus we bid you all heartily farewell. From our palace of
Holyroodhouse, the second of April, in the first year of our reign.

JAMES R.

This noble gentleman, bearer hereof, will more particularly acquaint you with our mind in this purpose.

*Bodleian Library
Ashmol. 1729,
Item 27, f. 49*

*Holograph signature and
postscript*

210

Letter 95

To Prince Henry

On 5 April 1603 King James VI of Scotland and I of England set out from Edinburgh for London. Before leaving, unaccompanied by any of his immediate family, James wrote the following letter to his heir. (Henry left for England with his mother at the end of May).

[*Early April 1603*]

My son,

That I see you not before my parting, impute it to this great occasion wherein time is so precious, but that shall (by God's grace) shortly be recompensed by your coming to me shortly and continual residence with me ever after.

Let not this news make you proud or insolent, for a king's son and heir was ye before, and no more are ye yet. The augmentation that is hereby like to fall unto you is but in cares and heavy burdens. Be therefore merry but not insolent. Keep a greatness but *sine fastu*.[1] Be resolute but not wilful. Keep your kindness, but in honourable sort. Choose none to be your playfellows but them that are well born. And, above all things, give never good countenance to any but according as ye shall be informed that they are in estimation with me. Look upon all Englishmen that shall come to visit you as upon your loving subjects, not with that ceremony as towards strangers and yet with such heartiness as at this time they deserve.

This gentleman whom this bearer accompanies is worthy and of good rank, and now my familiar servitor. Use him therefore in a more homely loving sort nor others. I send you herewith my book lately printed;[2] study and profit in it as ye would deserve my blessing. And as there can nothing happen unto you whereof ye will not find the general ground therein (if not the very particular point touched), so maun* ye level every man's opinions or advices unto you as ye find them agree or discord with the rules there set down, allowing and following their

211

advices that agrees with the same, mistrusting and frowning upon them that advises you to the contrary. Be diligent and earnest in your studies, that at your meeting with me I may praise you for your progress in learning. Be obedient to your master for your own weal and to procure my thanks, for in reverencing him ye obey me and honour yourself. Farewell.

Your loving father,
JAMES R.

British Library   Holograph
Harl. 6986, f. 65

[1]"Without haughtiness."
[2]*Basilikon Doron* (see Letter 71). The first edition made available to the public appeared in March 1603.

Letter 96

To Lord Henry Howard

James thanks him for a sum of money and announces that he will enter York in state.

[9? *April* 1603][1]
Right trusty and well-beloved, we greet you heartily well.

We received at Berwick, by the hands of Roger Aston,[2] the money sent by you, wherein we allow of your discretion.

Meaning now to hasten forward, as much as we may conveniently, to our city of York, which place (because we account it the second city of our kingdom) we mean to enter in a manner more public, and therefore like it well that some of our servants and officers have authority to meet us, not being any of those

212

principals which may diminish part of that honour and dignity which belongs to our dearest sister as long as her body is above ground, to whom we are not only successor in her kingdom but so near of blood as we will not stand so much upon the ceremony of our own joy but that we would have all things observed which may testify the honour we bear to her memory.

As touching our guard, we do like it well that they do remain still entire as they were at her death, to attend her body and her funeral—our meaning being that none of the principal officers, either of our house or of our guards, do part from the body of the defunct without further direction from us.

Cecil Papers   *Copy*
187: 27

¹This letter is endorsed "12 April 1603," which is probably the date of its receipt. King James entered Berwick on 6 April and left on 8 April; he entered York on 16 April.
²On Aston, see Letter 42, headnote.

Letter 97

To Queen Anne

When King James set out for England, he left his wife and children to follow later. At the end of May, after a furious quarrel with the Earl of Mar, Anne extorted from James a warrant for Mar to hand Prince Henry over to her. The health of Prince Charles being deemed too precarious to permit the journey, he was not with his mother when, fulfilling the hope expressed at the end of this letter, she, accompanied by Prince Henry and Princess Elizabeth, rejoined the King at Easton Neston in Northamptonshire.

My heart,

   Immediately before the receipt of your letter I was purposed to have written unto you, and that without any great occasion except for freeing myself at your hands from the imputation of swearenes.* But now your letter has given me more matter to write, although I take small delight to meddle in so unpleasant a process.

   I wonder that neither your long knowledge of my naturall* nor my late earnest purgation unto you can cure you of that rooted error that any living dare speak or inform me in any ways to your prejudice or yet that ye can think them your un-friends that are true servants to me. I can say no more but pro-test, upon the peril of my salvation and damnation, that neither the Earl of Mar nor any flesh living ever informed me that ye was upon any papist or Spanish course, or that ye had any other thoughts but a wrong-conceived opinion that he claimed inter-est in your son or would not deliver him unto you. Neither does he farther charge the noblemen that was with you there but that he was informed that some of them thought by force to have assisted you in the taking of my son out of his friends' hands. But as for any other papist or foreign practice, by God, he doth not so much as allege it. And therefore he says he will never presume to accuse them, since it may import your offence.

   And therefore I say over again, leave these womanly appre-hensions, for I thank God I carry that love and respect unto you which, by the law of God and nature, I ought to do to my wife and mother of my children. But not for that ye are a king's daughter, for, whether ye were a king's or a cook's daughter, ye must be all alike to me being once my wife. For the respect of your honourable birth and descent I married you; but the love and respect I now bear you is for that ye are my married wife and so partaker of my honour, as of all my other fortunes.

   I beseech you excuse my rude plainness in this, for the casting up of your birth is a needless argument to me. God is my witness I ever preferred you to all my bairns, much more than to any sub-ject. But if ye will ever give place to the report of every flattering sycophant that will persuade you that when I account well of an honest servant for his true service to me, it is to compare or prefer him to you, then will neither ye or I be ever at rest. I have, according to my promise, copied so much of that plot whereof I wrote unto you in my last as did concern my son, which herein is enclosed that ye may see I wrote it not without cause. But I desire it not to have any other secretaries than yourself.

As for your doole weede,* wearing it is utterly impertinent at this time[1] for sic* reasons as the bearer will show unto you, whom I have likewise commanded to impart divers other points unto you, which, for fear of wearying your eyes with my ragged hand, I have herein omitted.

Praying God, my heart, to preserve you and all the bairns, and to send me a blithe meeting with you and a couple of them.

Your own,
JAMES R.

Historical Society of   *Holograph*
Pennsylvania, Ferdinand
Dreer Autograph
Collection, Vol. 173

[1]I.e., it is entirely unnecessary for her to wear mourning attire because of the death of Queen Elizabeth.

Letter 98

To John Whitgift, Archbishop of Canterbury

Queen Elizabeth's concerns with the national church seem to have been almost entirely political, but King James took religion more to heart. Reading the Millenary Petition, submitted to him when he travelled south from Scotland, and hearkening to other representations from his Puritan subjects, he became concerned about the alleged abuses in the Church of England and directed the following letter to the primate.

Most reverend father in God, our right trusty and
well-beloved counsellor, we greet you well.

As by our late proclamation you may perceive what our intent is in matters ecclesiastic of this realm, and what care we
have to preserve the same in such state as we found them established by your laws, and not to give way to unquiet persons, out
of private humours, to impugn them: so that we thought it convenient to let you understand that informations from many
places of our kingdom, and from persons of great sort, are so
continually and so credibly delivered unto us, as we cannot but
give you some word to hear that in many parts of the realm the
parishes are so ill-served with persons not able to instruct in
matters of their faith as is very scandalous to those of your degree and giveth much advantage to the adversary to seduce
them and, if it should continue, would be very heavy to our conscience in our account to God in case it be not amended.

Which informations notwithstanding, we are not so transported withal but that we would first hear from you how far
they be true or false. Wherefore, for satisfaction, we require you
to cause the several bishops of your provinces within some convenient time to make certificate to you in writing what number
of churches with cure of souls be under each of them; what the
incumbents are, of what degree in school, and how qualified to
preach, and what the several livings of each church. Which cer-
tificates you shall send unto us or bring them yourself, by view
whereof we shall be able to discern how the said churches are
provided for and which do suffer defect. For we would not have
you ignorant that although our purpose is not to constrain either colleges or private persons to depart with their impropriations, which we understand are now by the law of this realm in
many of them as their freehold, nor likewise to diminish our
own revenues so far as to divest ourselves of all such as we have
found our Crown possessed of, yet shall we be content in all
such vicarages whereof the tenths impropriated are in our
hands, if they be not able to maintain a sufficient minister, to

add some relief unto them by such convenient means as we may and as upon deliberation of our Council shall be thought fit.

Further we have thought good to signify unto you that we hear that some ministers in the celebration of divine service and sacraments do use new forms not prescribed by authority, which we take to proceed of humour and affecting of novelties. And having by our proclamation[1] made known our meaning in those things, we require you to cause those novelties to be severally repressed and all men to conform themselves to that which we have by open declaration published, so that if hereafter there be any omission in their services, seeing you cannot be ignorant of our pleasure, we will ask account of it only at your hands. Given under our signet at Wilton the 29 of October in the first year of our reign of England, France and Ireland and of Scotland the 37.

British Library   *Copy*
Harl. 677, f. 107

[1]This is the proclamation of 24 October 1603, "For Reformation of Church Matters" (No. 974 in Crawford, *Bibliography of Royal Proclamations of the Tudor and Stuart Sovereigns*).

Letter 99

To Sir Benjamin Tichbourne, Sheriff of Hampshire

The Bye Plot of mid-1603 brought together one of the most illassorted groups of conspirators in English history. Some were Catholics who felt frustrated because James had not granted them religious toleration. Others were Protestants with personal grievances. Together they plotted to seize King James, force a change of royal ministers, and extort religious toleration.

Chief among the conspirators, not all of whom may have known the full scope of the intended operation, were two Catholic priests (Watson and Clarke), a Catholic gentleman (Sir

Gervase Markham), and the left-wing Protestants, Lord Grey of Wilton and George Brooke. These with Brooke's brother, Lord Cobham, who had been planning other treasons, were arraigned in November, convicted, and condemned to death. On 29 November the two priests were executed, with Brooke joining them in death five days later. On 9 December Lords Grey and Cobham and Sir Gervase Markham were to undergo the like fate. However, just as the first of them, Markham, was on the scaffold and the headsman was making ready, a Scottish servant to the King arrived with the following letter, which James, reportedly, had written with his own hand the previous day.

[8 *December* 1603]

Although it be true that all well-governed and flourishing kingdoms and commonwealths are established by justice and that these two noblemen by birth that are now upon the point of execution are, for their treasonable practices, condemned by the law and adjudged worthy of execution thereof, to the example and terror of others (the one of them having filthily practised the overthrow of the whole kingdom, and the other for the surprise of our own person) yet, in regard that this is the first year of our reign in this kingdom, and that never king was so far obliged to his people as we have been to this, by our entry here with so hearty and general an applause of all sorts (among whom all the kin, friends, and allies of the said condemned persons were as forward and dutiful as any other our good subjects), as also that at the very time of their arraignment none did more freely and readily give their assent to their conviction and to deliver them into the hands of justice, than so many of their nearest kinsmen and allies (as being peers) were upon their jury; as likewise in regard that justice hath in some sort gotten course already by the execution of the two priests and George Brooke, that were the principal plotters and enticers of all the rest to the embracing of the said treasonable machinations, we therefore (being resolved to mix clemency with justice) are contented, and by these presents command you, our present Sheriff of Hampshire, to supersede the execution of the said two noble-

218

men and take them back to their prison again until our further pleasure be known.

And since we will not have our laws to have respect to persons, in sparing the great and striking the meaner sort, it is our pleasure that the like course be also taken with Markham, being sorry from our heart that such is not only the heinous nature of the said condemned persons' crime but even the corruption is so great of their natural disposition, as the care we have for the safety and quiet of our state and good subjects will not permit us to use that clemency towards them which in our own natural inclination we might very easily be persuaded unto.

John Stow, Annales or a
General Chronicle of England,
*continued by Edmund
Howes (London, 1631), sig.
Aaaa2ᵛ (p. 833)*

*Printed text, possibly of a
lost holograph*

Letter 100

To Prince Henry

A letter of fatherly advice.

[1603?]

My son,

I am glad that by your letter I may perceive that ye make some progress in learning, although I suspect ye have rather written than indited it. For I confess I long to receive a letter from you that may be wholly yours, as well matter as form, as well formed by your mind as drawn by your fingers. For ye may remember that in my book[1] to you, I warn you to be wary with that kind of wit that may fly out at the end of your fingers. Not that I commend not a fair handwriting, *sed hoc facito, illud non omittito,*[2] and the other is *multo magis praecipuum.*[3] But nothing will be impossible for you, if ye will only remember two rules: the one *aude*

219

semper[4] in all virtuous actions (trust a little more to your own strength, and away with childish bashfulness, *audaces fortuna iuvat timidosque repellit*);[5] the other is my old oft-repeated rule unto you, whatever ye are about, *hoc age.*[6]

I am also glad of the discovery of yon little counterfeit wench. I pray God ye may be my heir in such discoveries. Ye have oft heard me say that most miracles nowadays proves but illusions, and ye may see by this how wary judges should be in trusting accusations without an exact trial, and likewise how easily people are induced to trust wonders. Let her be kept fast till my coming. And thus God bless you, my son.

Your loving father,
JAMES R.

British Library   *Holograph*
Harl. 6986, f. 67

[1] *Basilikon Doron.*
[2] "But this being done, that is not to be omitted" (adapted from Luke 11:42: "These ought ye to have done, and not to leave the other undone").
[3] "Much more excellent."
[4] "Be audacious always."
[5] "Fortune helps the bold and rejects the timid" (perhaps a completing of a fragmentary line in Virgil's *Aeneid* 10.284: "audentes fortuna iuvat").
[6] "Attend to the matter in hand."

Letter 101

To Lord Henry Howard

After coming to the English throne, King James occasionally continued to use the code numbers which he had employed in his secret correspondence from Scotland. Thus, the "3" of this letter was Lord Henry Howard. Judging from the contents, one may reasonably assign it to the period of the Hampton Court Conference of 14–18 January, 1604.

[17? January 1604]

My honest black, I dare not say　　　faced,[1] 3,

The letter talking of "deambulatory councils"[2] and suchlike satiric tricks did a little chafe me; but ye may see I answered according to the old scholars' rule, *in quo casu quaeris in eodem respondere teneris*,[3] for I would be sorry not to be as constant indeed as she was that called herself *semper eadem*.[4] Indeed, ye may tell the beagle[5] that he hath best cause to complain of my being a peripatetic, for I will ofttimes walk so fast roundabout and about with him that he will be like to fall down dead upon the floor. I can give you no other thanks for your daily working and public railing upon me save only this: do what ye can, ye can give me no more arguments of your faithful affection towards me; and do what I can unto you, I can never increase a hair the devotion of your service towards me.

We have kept such a revel with the Puritans here these two days as was never heard the like, where I have peppered them as soundly as ye have done the Papists there. It were no reason that those that will refuse the airy sign of the cross after baptism should have their purses stuffed with any more solid and substantial crosses.[6] They fled me so from argument to argument without ever answering me directly, *ut est eorum moris*,[7] as I was forced at last to say unto them that if any of them had been in a college disputing with their scholars, if any of their disciples had answered them in that sort, they would have fetched him up in place of a reply, and so should the rod have plyed upon the poor boy's buttocks. I have such a book of theirs as may well convert infidels, but it shall never convert me except by turning me more earnestly against them.

And thus praying you to commend me to the honest chamberlain,[8] I bid you heartily farewell.

JAMES R.

British Library, Cotton MSS.,　　　　　　　*Holograph*
Vespasian F III, f. 76

[1]The King has left a large blank space before "faced," in place of an epithet

repugnant to Howard. The sense of this jesting opening is "Since you will not permit me to call you – – – – faced, I shall call you black-faced." We have various references to Lord Henry Howard's dark features. The word that the King dared not use was "evil." (See Letter 122.)

²King James had a curious mannerism of walking in circles while deep in conversation. Apparently, this had inspired Howard to coin the phrase "deambulatory councils," which did not entirely amuse His Majesty. For other mentions of the phrase see Letters 102 and 111.

³"In whatever case you inquire, you are bound to reply in the same."

⁴"Always the same" (the personal motto of Elizabeth I).

⁵The nickname which King James devised for Sir Robert Cecil, later Earl of Salisbury.

⁶A cross was originally a coin marked with a cross on one side; later the term was applied to any coin.

⁷"As is their custom."

⁸Thomas Howard, Earl of Suffolk, appointed Lord Chamberlain on 4 May 1603.

Letter 102

To the Council

At some point after the Hampton Court Conference, King James wrote the following letter to his Council, reassuring them on various points and giving the bishops freedom to deal with the Puritans. Apparently the opening portion of this letter has been lost.

[1604?]¹

First, I never changed the smallest jot of my conclusion in this point and therefore there needs no fear be had of my "deambulatory council,"² and if I had been upon any new resolution I would have directed some better warrant than the Dean's[3] letter in that errand.

Secondly, I never before conceived the difference between real obedience and promise by subscription to obey; and if I erred anything herein, it was upon this respect: that I thought if there was any degree of difference between real obedience (I mean in absolute obedience to all the church government) and promise by subscription to obey, I then thought that to wear the surplice indeed, to use cross after baptism, and do all the like in effect, was a greater obedience than to subscribe that they shall do it and, when the storm is past, never perform a word, and protest that their subscription was only *ex iusto metu*.[4] And therefore I thought that if they presently conformed themselves, and after that would refuse to subscribe to that which in deed they had already performed, it would be a means to make their vanities appear and every man to pity them the less. But, on the other part, I never meant that this should have been done as by a grace from me, and therefore my hand was never yet seen to such a motion; but only that the bishops (if so they had thought good) might have tried this trick upon them, as of their own heads, for their further confusion.

Thirdly, I am so far from yielding anything for fear of their popularity as I am heartily glad of your stoutness in this case that are councillors, for if I be grown so easy now to be threatened I am sure it is in my last days. And, therefore, since I am interpreted to have inclined this way for fear of their mutiny, my resolution is that the bishops go on now with their own course according to the proclamation,[5] and if my eye either spare or pity any of the disobedient, then let me incur both the shame and the harm in God's name.

And lastly, if my continual presence in London be so necessary as my absence for my health makes the councillors to be without authority or respect, one word shall bring me home and make me work till my breath work out, if that be the greatest weal for the kingdom. But I cannot think that course so needful if ye make not mountains of molehills, as in this case interpreting a conjectural motion to a royal decree, wherein, if ye had not

223

mistaken me, ye needed not to have troubled so far your own minds and my hand.

JAMES R.

Cecil Papers   *Holograph*
134: 52

[1]A difficult letter to date. It may have been written as late as January 1605.
[2]See Letter 101, n. 2.
[3]Apparently James Montagu, Dean of the Chapel Royal. He had been present at the Hampton Court Conference. In 1616, when Bishop of Winchester, he was to edit the *Works* of King James.
[4]"Out of justified fear."
[5]On 5 March 1604 a proclamation was issued ridiculing Puritan arguments and calling for conformity by Midsummer Day (24 June).

Letter 103

To Robert Cecil, Baron Essendon

On 16 April 1604 the House of Commons received a proposal that henceforth England and Scotland should be known as "Great Britain." The Commons, however, proved reluctant to support the project, it being alleged that a change in the title of the kingdom would abrogate the existing laws of England. King James responded by offering to refer the question to the judges for their opinion. Such, then, is the background to the following memorandum endorsed by Cecil, "The ks addition to his speach written with his own hand concerning Brittane."

In the sequel, the judges decided that Parliament's introduction of the new name would indeed entail "an utter extinction of all the laws now in force."[1]

[*18? April 1604*]

Forget not adjure the judges, upon their consciences to God
and their allegiances to me, to declare the truth if I may not at this
time use the name of Britain, warranted by Act of Parliament,
without the direct abrogation of all the laws, and that they
ground all their judgements upon reason, policy, and example of
other kingdoms and the solid law indeed, and not upon curious
wresting the letter of the common law of England against all
reason, and if the name, as I mean it, be so absolutely incompati-
ble with the present distinction of laws betwixt the realms.

Public Record Office   *Holograph*
SP 14/7/38

[1]Quoted by R. C. Murdin in *Faction and Parliament,* ed. K. Sharpe (Oxford,
1978), p. 65.

Letter 104

To the House of Commons

Frustrated by the continuing opposition of the English par-
liament both to his proposed title of "King of Great Britain"
and his scheme for a total merger of England and Scotland,
James addressed the following letter to the House of Commons.
It achieved little. Finally, on 24 October 1604, James had him-
self proclaimed King of Great Britain even though Parliament
had not approved the title.

1 May 1604

Ye see with what clearness and sincerity I have behaved myself in this errand even through all the progress thereof, though I
will not say too little regarded by you, but I may justly say not so

willingly embraced by you as the worthiness of the matter doth well deserve.

I protest to God, the fruit thereof will chiefly tend to your own weal, prosperity, and increase of strength and greatness. Nothing can stay you from harkening to it but jealousy and distrust, either of me the propounder or of the matter by me propounded. If of me, then do ye both me and yourselves an infinite wrong, my conscience bearing me record that I ever deserved the contrary at your hands. But if your distrust be of the matter itself, then distrust you nothing but your own wisdoms or honesties. For as I have given over wrangling upon words with you, so crave I no conclusion to be taken at this time herein but only a commission, that it may be disputed, considered upon, and reported unto you. And then will ye be your own cooks to dress it as ye list, so that (as I have already said) since the conclusion thereof can never be without your own assent, if you be true to yourselves, no man can deceive you in it. Let not yourselves therefore be transported with the curiosity of a few giddy heads, for it is in you now to make the choice: either, by yielding to the providence of God and embracing that which he hath cast in your mouths, to procure the prosperity and increase of greatness to me and mine, you and yours, and by the away-taking of that partition wall which already, by God's providence, in my blood is rent asunder, to establish my throne, and your body politic, in a perpetual and flourishing peace; or else, contemning God's benefits freely offered unto us, to spit and blaspheme in his face by preferring war to peace, trouble to quietness, hatred to love, weakness to greatness, and division to union, to sow the seeds of discord to all our posterities, to dishonour your king, to make both me and yourselves a proverb of reproach in the mouths of all strangers, and all enemies of this nation, and enviers of my greatness. And our next labour to be to take up new garrisons for the Borders, and to make new fortifications there. *Sed meliora spero.*[1] I hope that God in this choice and free will of yours will not suffer you, with old Adam, to choose the worst and so to procure the defacing of this earthly paradise, but by the contrary that he shall inspire you so, as with the second Adam, ye shall produce peace and so beautify this our earthly kingdom herewith, as it may represent and be an earnest penny unto us of eternal peace in that spiritual kingdom which is prepared for the perpetual residence of all his chosen children.

British Library   Copy
Harl. 1583, f. 156

[1]"But I hope for better things" (an echo of Cicero's *spero meliora* in his letters to Atticus, 14.16.3).

Letter 105

To Robert Cecil, Baron Essendon

The "wearisome work" mentioned by James in this letter is probably the extended wrangling with Parliament in 1604 as the King's ministers sought to win its approval for a complete union of England and Scotland. Apparently he wrote this sportive letter to hearten his Council in London while he enjoyed his recreation in the country.

[*Spring 1604?*]

My little beagle,

Although I be now in the midst of my paradise of pleasure yet will I not be forgetful of you and your fellows that are frying in the pains of purgatory for my service. I do so greedily expect good news from you anent your proceeding there as, I protest, I am but half a man till I hear of the good end of that wearisome work. Only your care must be to preserve things from extremities in case crosses do fall out, and to keep things from such conclusions as may be justly displeasing unto me, *sed melius ominor,*[1] and I do strengthen myself by the trust I have in so good servants whom to I hope no virtuous thing, how difficult soever, being undertaken *meis auspiciis*[2] shall be impossible. Although I have many other turns* to remember you of, yet will I not trouble you with any of them till ye have first well put off

227

that great errand which ye have now in hand. And so I make an end with my hearty commendations to all your honest society and hoping that 3 and 10[3] will pardon me for my overwatching them the last night and morning that I was amongst you.

JAMES R.

Cecil Papers   *Holograph*
134: 59

[1]"But I predict better." The phrase occurs in Cicero *Brutus* 329.
[2]"Under my auspices."
[3]Lord Henry Howard, now Earl of Northhampton, and Cecil himself.

Letter 106

To Richard Bancroft, Bishop of London

The most important result of the Hampton Court Confer-ence was the King James translation of the Bible. The following letter, apparently drafted by a secretary but sent out over the King's signature, specifies steps to be taken in securing and financing the translators.

22 July 1604

Right trusty and well-beloved, we greet you well.

Whereas we have appointed certain learned men, to the number of four and fifty, for the translating of the Bible, and that in this number divers of them have either no ecclesiastical preferment at all or else so very small as the same is far unmeet for men of their deserts, and yet we of ourself in any convenient time cannot well remedy it; therefore we do hereby require you that presently you write in our name as well to the Archbishop of York as to the rest of the bishops of the province of Canterbury,[1] signifying unto them that we do will and straitly charge every one of them, as also the other bishops in the province of York, as they tender our good favour towards them that (all excuses set apart) when any prebend or parsonage being vested in our Book of Taxations (the prebends to twenty pound at the least, and the parsonage to the like sum and upwards) shall next upon any occasion happen to be void and to be of the patronage and gift of any lay person whosoever, they do make stay thereof and admit none unto it until certifying us of the avoidance of it and of the name of the patron (if it be not of your own gift) [so that] we may commend for the same some such of the said learned men as we shall think fit to be preferred to it, and not doubting of the bishops' readiness to satisfy us herein, or that any of the laity, when we shall in time move them to so good and religious an act, will be unwilling to give us the like due contentment and satisfaction, we ourself having taken the same order for such prebends and benefices as shall fall void in our gift.

What we write to you of others you must apply it to yourself, as also not forget to move the said archbishop and the bishops with their deans and chapters of both provinces as touching the other point to be imparted otherwise by you unto them.

Furthermore, we require you to move all our bishops to inform themselves of all such learned men within their several dioceses as, having especial skill in the Hebrew and Greek tongues, have taken pains in their private studies of the Scriptures for the clearing of any obscurities either in the Hebrew or the Greek, or touching any difficulties or mistakings in the former English translation, which we have now commanded to be thoroughly viewed and amended, and thereupon to write unto them, earnestly charging them, and signifying our pleasure therein, that they send such their observations either to Mr. Lyvely our Hebrew Reader in Cambridge, or to Dr. Hardinge our Hebrew Reader in Oxford, or to Dr. Andrewes, Dean of Westminster, to be imparted to the rest of their several companies, that so our said intended translation may have the help and furtherance of all the principal learned men within this our kingdom.

Given under our signet, at our palace of Westminster, the two and twentieth of July in the second year of our reign of England, France, and Ireland, and of Scotland the seven and thirtieth.

Cambridge University Library   *Copy*
MS. Mm.1.43, p. 163

¹There was no Archbishop of Canterbury, Bancroft (to whom this letter is addressed) not having yet succeeded the recently deceased Archbishop Whitgift.

Letter 107

To the University, City, and County of Cambridge

James, who cherished learning, was naturally interested in the two great English universities. The following letter providing for the good order and discipline of the students at Cambridge was almost certainly drafted by one of the King's secretaries, but its sentiments were his.

23 July 1604

James by the Grace of God King etc.: To our Chancellor and Vice-Chancellor of our University of Cambridge in the County of Cambridge, and to all and singular our justices of peace, mayors, sheriffs, bailiffs, constables, gaolers, and to all other our ministers and officers within the said University and the Town of Cambridge and County aforesaid and to every of them, greeting.

For the better maintenance, safety, and quietness of that our said university, and all and every the students there, and to remove, take away, and prevent all occasions that may tend either to the infecting of their bodies or minds, or to the withdrawing or alienating the young sort from the courses of their studies there intended, we do by these presents authorize, will, and command you our said chancellor and vice-chancellor of our said university and either of you, and your successors, and the deputy or deputies of either of you and your successors, that you do from time to time forever hereafter, by virtue hereof, wholly and altogether restrain, inhibit, and forbid as well all and all manner of unprofitable or idle games, plays, or exercises to be used or made within our said university, and the town there, and within five miles' compass of and from the said university and town: especially bull baiting, bear baiting, common plays, public shows, interludes, comedies, and tragedies in the English tongue, games at loggets and nine holes, and all other sports and games whereby throngs, concourse, or multitudes are drawn together or whereby the younger sort are or may be drawn or provoked to vain expense, loss of time, or corruption of manners. As also all and all manner of persons that shall go about to publish, act, set out, or make any such unprofitable or idle games, public plays or exercises, within the said university or town, or within five miles' compass of or from the said university or town (any indulgence, liberty, privilege, or authority, by us granted or to be granted to any our officers or servants, or any other person or persons whomsoever to the contrary, in any wise notwithstanding), provided that it is not our pleasure and meaning hereby to abridge the students of their accustomed exercise (in any kind whatsoever) within their several colleges.[1] And if any person or persons, under colour, pretence, or virtue of any licence or authority by us, or any other whomsoever, granted or to be granted, or by any other means, colour, or pretence shall resist or refuse peaceably to obey your commands herein: then our will and pleasure is, and we do hereby authorize your said chancellor and vice-chancellor of our said university, and either of you and your successors, from time to time to apprehend all and every such offenders and them to commit to prison, either in the Castle of Cambridge or in any other gaol within the town of Cambridge, there to remain without bail or mainprize until they shall willingly submit themselves to your said commands, and abide such further order therein, as to you in your discretion shall be thought meet. Willing and by these presents commanding all you our said justices of peace, mayors, sheriffs, bailiffs, constables, and gaolers, and all other our said ministers and officers that upon intimation and show of this our will and command herein, you and every of you, being

own hunting. Yet ye have that advantage that I trust so much to your nose that when I hear you cry it I will halloo to you as freely as to the deepest-mouthed hound in all the kennel. And since ye have been so much used these three months past to hunt cold scents through the dry beaten ways of London, ye need not doubt but it will be easy for you to harbour a great stag amongst the sweet groves about your house. Only beware of drawing too greedily in the lyam,[2] for ye know how that trick hath already galled your neck. But in earnest, I lose all this year's progress if I begin not to hunt there upon Monday come eight days, for the season of the year will no more stay upon a king than a poor man, and I doubt if the Constable of Castile hath any power in his commission to stay the course of the sun. Commend me to that other hardill* of hounds that have so truly borne up the couples with you all this year, two of whom helped to hunt the Spanish game, but the third looks like one of my wife's country-men both in colour and quantity. I must not also forget honest Stanhope[3] that hath for our sins hunted all this year in inferno, that is, the lower regions. And so farewell and forget not to drink my health amongst you.

JAMES R.

Cecil Papers   *Holograph*
134: 130

[1]Cecil's magnificent country seat near London. In 1607 Cecil would present it to King James, receiving the manor of Hatfield in return.
[2]Leash.
[3]Sir John Stanhope, Vice-Chamberlain, and Treasurer of the Chamber.

Letter 109

To Robert Cecil, Baron Essendon

A letter of raillery, touching on how Cecil and the Earls of Suffolk and Northampton will govern England while King James is off on his summer progress.

My little beagle,

Ye and your fellows there are so proud now that ye have gotten the guiding again of a feminine court in the old fashion[1] as I know not how to deal with you. Ye sit at your ease and directs all. The news from all the parts of the world comes to you in your chamber. The King's own resolutions depends upon your posting despatches. And when ye list ye can (sitting on your bedsides) with one call or whistling in your fist make him to post night and day till he come to your presence.

Well I know Suffolk[2] is married and hath also his hands full now in harbouring that great little proud man[3] that comes in his chair. But for your part Master 10 [Cecil], who is wanton and wifeless, I cannot but be jealous of your greatness with my wife, but most of all am I suspicious of 3 [Northampton], who is so lately fallen in acquaintance with my wife. For besides that very number of "3" is well liked of by women, his face is so amiable[4] as it is able to entice, and his fortune has ever been to be great with she-saints. But his part is foul in this, that never having taken a wife to himself in his youth, he cannot now be content with his grey hairs to forbear another man's wife. But for expiation of this sin I hope that ye have all three with the rest of your society taken this day a Eucharistic cup of thankfulness for the occasion which fell out at a time when ye durst not avow me. And here hath been this day kept the feast of King James' delivery at Saint Johnstoun, in Saint John's house.[5] All other matters I refer to the old knave the bearer's report, and so fare ye well.

JAMES R.

British Library   *Holograph*
Harl. 6986, f. 69

[1]I.e., as in Queen Elizabeth's time. (During the absence of King James at his hunting, Queen Anne presided in London.)
[2]Thomas Howard, Earl of Suffolk, Lord Chamberlain of the Household.
[3]Cecil. What follows is probably a scurrilous pun, *chair* in French meaning "flesh".
[4]A jest; in Letter 122 James speaks of Northampton's features as black and grim.

apprehension in the hearts of all the people, who are more ruled with shadows than substance, that the Union is already made, as the occasion will thereby be extinguished of any future crosses which otherwise might have risen upon the other points which rests to be done for the performance of that great work. For being once made friends and homely together they will no more stick upon such punctilios which otherwise, as strangers, they might have stood upon. It only rests that, when ye end all other things, ye make such a pretty reference for the full accomplishment of all other points which fault of leisure could not now permit you to end as it may appear that working in this errand shall never be left off till it be fully accomplished—I mean specially by the uniting both of the laws and parliaments of both the nations. And for a fair *vale*[2] [at this?] time amongst you, I think it were not amiss that after your conclusion some one or two of the principals of your side should bestow a good dinner upon your northern neighbours and so end with a health to your common and indifferent [impartial] master.

I doubt not also but ere this time ye have received the Puritans' catholic petition,[3] for it neither names county, parish, nor pastor. What such a universal complaint deserves I need not to inform you, but I deceived their expectation by dismissing the multitude in fair terms. Only that knave that was the framer of the petition and drawer of them together deserves some correction. I would have been sorry that his three thousand should have boasted me, but he is so near of kin to Emmanuel[4] as I shall mistrust that race the more while I live. I heartily require you that with all convenient speed that knave may receive some public correction either in the Star Chamber or otherwise, since ye see I have daily more and more cause to hate and abhor all that sect: enemies to all kings and to me only because I am a king. But above all let him first be thoroughly well-examined.

Ye must also specially take heed that in this Act of Naturalization my promise be neither restricted till the full accomplishment of the Union or to any certain time, but only that I have declared my gracious pleasure and intention not to press too hastily to the preferring of Scottish men to such and such places which without a reasonable process of time they cannot be fit for, for many respects, but the words must be conceived alike for both the nations, and this ye know is according to my last conclusion with you in this errand, because I would have no *terminus ad quem*[5] in this reservation, but only that it should be left to the maturity of time, which must piece and piece take away distinction of nations as it hath already done here betwixt England and Wales.

But what should I weary myself by setting down particulars thus in writ, having employed herewith so sufficient a messenger as "my father," your fellow secretary,[6] whom I have directed to forewarn you that what for the pleasure I take of my recreation here, and what for the fear I stand in to offend the Puritans, I mind not to return to London till after that profane Christ's tide.[7] And therefore ye may for a two or three months send your niece to remain with your daughter in the country where she may be well brought up.

Let 3 [Henry Howard, Earl of Northampton] be your co-partner of this letter, as he was of many a one before I ever saw either of you. Commend me to your honest fellow labourers, and tell the Chamberlain[8] I would wish him here to be breathed before Christmas.

[Unsigned]

Cecil Papers   *Holograph*
134: 53

[1]This letter is endorsed "22 9bre His my." Since secretaries commonly endorsed communications with the date of their receipt, this letter may have been written a day or two before November 22.

[2]"Farewell."

[3]The Royston Petition, presented to James in a vain last attempt to save nonconforming clergymen from eviction from their livings after the end of November 1604.

[4]Richard Hildersham, cousin of the prominent Puritan divine Arthur Hildersham (*v.* B.W. Quintrell, "The Royal Hunt and the Puritans, 1604-1605," *Journal of Ecclesiastical History* XXXI (1980), 45). The allusion to Emmanuel relates to Emmanuel College, the Puritan stronghold at Cambridge.

[5]"Terminal date" (lit., "the limit to which").

[6]Sir John Herbert. See Letter 111, n. 3.

[7]James is sardonically using the language of the Puritans, who would not

speak of Christmas (Christ *mass*).

[8]The Earl of Suffolk.

Letter 111

To Robert Cecil, Viscount Cranborne

Mildly piqued by the way in which Cecil had replied to a letter from the Earl of Worcester, James amuses himself by playing the part of a secretary who would have referred the matter to the King. The letter seems to date from the period when English and Scottish commissioners were consulting in London on a possible union of their two kingdoms. These sessions commenced on 27 October 1604.

[*30 November? 1604*]

My little beagle,

Now that the Master Falconer[1] is bearer hereof I must inform you how welcome your grapes were unto me. But although I must confess I did eat more of them in shorter space than ever I did of any since I came in England, yet in truth ye was a prophet anent Herbert, for that monkey hath eaten five of them wherever I did eat one.[2] And I have also stranger news to tell you, that the number of letters that I have written since I came from home is equal to the number of hares that all this time I have killed. Therefore ye are in greater peril of me nor my "old father"[3] for your office since I am so prettily exercised in it already. And in proof thereof, if I had been secretary to Worcester's[4] letter anent the Puritans I would never have talked a word of deambulatory councils,[5] of their victory upon their petition, nor any such satiric phrases, but only that upon a sight we had of the Dean's letter and, being uncertain whether His Majesty's direction did proceed upon wrong information or that we had mistaken His Majesty's meaning therein, we thought good to represent the true state of the matter before His Majesty's eyes, that he might thereupon clear his meaning unto us, which we well knew to be ever one and alike

238

in all his royal resolutions. Look now how bravely I play the part
of a secretary! And as for the Union matter, make the best of it ye
can, as I have already written, either satisfy [me] in the form of
the preface, or conclude the articles and suspend the preface, or
let it go as it is. But then I will directly speak against it at the
presenting of it to the parliament. Or if the only impediment be
that the commissioners will not bide together an hour longer,
then spare me not. Upon the least word I shall post thither—they
cannot refuse to stay one day upon me—but upon condition that
I may go back, when that is at a point, for some few days further
recreation, for I swear I have been little less busy in affairs this
time past than ye have been; and thus I bid you farewell almost as
bleared as the beagle.

[Unsigned]

Cecil Papers   *Holograph*
134: 55

[1]Sir Roger Aston.
   [2]The Herbert is young Sir Philip Herbert, soon to be made Earl of Montgomery. Sir Thomas Lake mentions receipt of the grapes in his letter of 29 November 1604 to Cecil: "I delivered your letters this evening at his Majesty's return to
Sir Ph. Harbert, and the same instant also were presented your grapes brought
by your footman, which were very welcome to his Majesty" (HMC, *Salisbury
MSS.*, XVI: 371).
   [3]Old Sir John Herbert, second Secretary of State, according to the King's jest,
might want to supplant Cecil as Principal Secretary of State.
   [4]Edward Somerset, Earl of Worcester (c. 1550–1628).
   [5]For other mentions of "deambulatory councils," see Letters 101 and 102.

Letter 112

To Robert Cecil, Viscount Cranborne

*Early in December 1604 the English and Scottish commis-
sioners who were negotiating terms for a union of their kingdoms concluded their meetings. King James, elated by their
agreement upon common citizenship for English and Scots,*

239

*subsequently wrote this important letter to Cecil, promising
that under the existing conditions he would not promote Scots
to posts in England.*

[*December 1604*][1]

My little beagle,

Now that, God be praised, this session of the commissioners
hath had so happy a success, to the end that the commissioners
of England, and by them the whole people of England, may
discern the true difference between a crafty tyrant and a just
king, I will now, after the conclusion of this point of the naturalization, open my mind freelier therein than ever I would have
done before it had been agreed upon, whereas a tyrant would
but have given fair words till he had gotten his turn* done, and
then but have kept his promise as he had thought convenient.
First, therefore, I protest, in God's presence, never Scottishman
did either directly or indirectly make suit to me for any such
preferment as is reserved in your act. And whether they ever had
or not, God is my judge I was ever rooted in that firm resolution
never to have placed [a] Scottishman in any such room till, first,
time had begun to wear away that opinion of different nations
and, secondly, that this jealous apprehension of the Union had
been worn away and, thirdly, that Scottishmen had been
brought up here at the feet of Gamaliel.[2]

And when all this were done, I would ever all my life prefer an
Englishman to a Scottishman for any place, *cæteris paribus,*[3]
and would ever wish my successors after me to do the like, as my
book[4] to my son bears witness. Nay, though I knew a Scottishman, for a miracle, that were more capable for any such place
than any Englishman in England, yet shall I never be that greedy
of Scottishmen's preferment as to prefer any by whom occasion
might be given of the least discontentment to the people here. I
am not ignorant nor void of means "anew" [enough] to show
my thankfulness to my subjects of Scotland without any such
preferments. And therefore, after that in my name ye have given
my most hearty thanks to all your fellow commissioners for
their tender and reverend [*sic*] regard for the preservation of my

prerogative, and for the loving affection they have shown to that nation whom amongst I was born, whereof by their proceedings now they have given a most clear demonstration, let them hereby be informed that I was moved upon two regards to wish the act to be as generally and favourably conceived as I must confess now it is; first, that in my own nature I ever love to be as little bound by any conditions as can be, and loves ever to promise scarcely and perform fully, and next that Scotland may see that I ever reserve to myself that fullness of power to bestow such degrees of favour upon them as they shall be able from time to time to deserve.

And thus, having freely discharged my mind of the burden of my thoughts in this point, I am heartily contented that not only ye read this letter in the public audience of all the commissioners but that also it be reserved in the register of your actions for a perpetual memory as well of my honest sincerity as of my thankfulness towards you, as well for the expressing of your dutiful regards towards me as of your loving affections towards my Scottish subjects, now your countrymen. And thus I bid you heartily farewell.

JAMES R.

House of Lords Record Office   *Holograph*
Main Papers, [1607]

[1]This date is fairly secure. On 8 December 1604, Sir Henry Neville wrote to his friend Ralph Winwood reporting that the English and Scottish commissioners had completed their conference on the union of England and Scotland, and had presented to King James their "Instrument of Union" under their seals (*Memorials of Affairs of State . . . from the Original Papers of the Rt. Hon. Sir Ralph Winwood*, London, 1725, II: 37–38). Actually, the "Instrument" was not presented to the English parliament for ratification until 27 November 1606, a circumstance that led Professor Wallace Notestein (*The House of Commons 1604–1610*, New Haven, 1971, p. 214) to follow the editors of the HMC *Third Report* in assigning the present letter to 1607. The tone of the letter seems to show, however, that it was written earlier in the reign, almost certainly just after James received the "Instrument" from the commissioners.

[2]Gamaliel is mentioned in Acts 5: 34 as "a doctor of the law, had in reputation among all the people." St. Paul was proud that he had been "brought up . . . at the feet of Gamaliel" (Acts 22:3). King James saw himself as a latter-day Gamaliel.

[3]"Other things being equal."
[4]*Basilikon Doron* (Craigie ed., pp. 116–17).

Letter 113

To Robert Cecil, Viscount Cranborne

The following letter provides an interesting account of how James was beset by noblemen hungry for the royal largesse. The petitioner in this case was Lord Sheffield, a veteran soldier who held the very important position of Lord President of the Council of the North. Present in London during meetings of the commissioners for the union with Scotland, Sheffield seized the opportunity to press for a large gift of money. James here presents Cecil with a detailed account of the interview at which Sheffield persisted in his demands.

[*Late 1604*]

My little beagle,

The bearer[1] hath craved my determinate answer anent his suit, whereupon I first opened unto him the care which ye his auditors had to see him both quickly and reasonably satisfied, insofar as notwithstanding that my last journey to London was like a flash of lightning, both in going, stay there, and returning, yet did ye not pretermit that posted minute of time without the full and true informing of me of the whole success of that business and what was the determination of the judges therein. Whereupon I told him that because I had not will to make him linger any longer here to his greater charges, having already so willingly attended all the time of the commissioners' sitting, as also that the weal of my service did require his present attendance in the place of his employment, I would therefore deal frankly and plainly with him. First, I doubted not but he did discern of my goodwill to help him, by employing none in his errand but those, and only those, whom himself did name unto me. Next, I did refer it to his discretion to consider how fit a

(because I knew his weak estate) I was moved now to allow him this help, not for filling up all his wants but for the better enabling him to serve in that place. As for his merit he could claim none of me, for I protested that before the Queen's death I never knew that there was a Lord Sheffield living in England. At this he chafed, and said that those that I knew before this time knew well enough his mind to my service. I answered him that if at that time he had required any man to have acquainted me with his mind then surely he was evil dealt with by them; but if not, then can he blame none but himself, for as to his good mind there is never a man in England that claims not to the like. Oh, then he reckoned that I had repaired the ruins of every nobleman's estate in England except his, at least that had done any service to the preterite state. I told him he was far deceived in that count and that I was daily troubled with the poor Lord Cromwell's begging leave to sell the last pieces of his land, who had valiantly served the state in the wars as well as he. And as for the great profit that he said would come to me by the means of his overture, I said I was not so envious of his weal so it were not against mine, but that I was contented, if the judges would under their hands promise to make this matter worth ten thousand pounds a year unto me, he should with goodwill have two thousand of it, if fifteen he should have three, but the thing that I spoke of was a sure thing to him for all the days of his life, and I to bear the hazard of the other as it fell forth, and that, as I had already told him, never greater gift of that nature was given in England. Great Oxford when his state was whole ruined got no more of the late Queen.[3] I myself bestows no more upon Arbella my only near cousin. Nay, a foreign prince of Germany that was here the last year got not so much. But, most of all, myself being heir to this Crown got but thrice as much, and I was sure, I said, he would not deny but I had been thrice more steadful to the state than ever he had been. And since he took example by other men's gifts, I asked him what example would other men take of his gift being bestowed upon no greater person than a baron. To this there was no answer but if this was my resolution he behoved to quit his office and in retired life pray for me. And so we parted. But immediately he followed me and said that he would

244

accept my offer for a certainty, but he would only crave that if my profit of his overture did yearly amount to such a reasonable value as I would agree upon, that then I would give him another thousand pounds yearly out of that augmentation. I told him I knew not in what form that could be done, yet he humbly insisted with me that I might command you that heard his matter to advise upon it. But how this can be I know not, except it were by a private promise that if I get by this suit yearly ten thousand pounds, one thousand thereof shall be added to his pension.

Thus have ye laid before you the whole discourse of this flight and how many stoopings I made upon him, which I ordain you the beagle to impart only to those of your fellowship that heard his cause, and so farewell.

JAMES R.

My little beagle, my Lord of Berwick[4] hath something to speak to you alone which must be done with all secrecy.

Cecil Papers   *Holograph*
134: 56

[1]Edmund Sheffield, 3rd Baron Sheffield and subsequently 1st Earl of Mulgrave.

[2]A Scottish idiom signifying "in its proper nature."

[3]On 26 June 1586, the impoverished 17th Earl of Oxford was granted an annuity of £1000 by Queen Elizabeth.

[4]George Home was created Baron of Berwick on 7 July 1604 and Earl of Dunbar on 3 July 1605.

Letter 114

To the Privy Council

Claiming that his health required the exercise provided by hunting, King James spent a great amount of time enjoying this sport. In the following letter, written when he was about to return to his hunting after the Christmas revels at Whitehall,

James formalizes the arrangements for the government of England during his absences in pursuit of the stag and the hare.

In this letter James seems chiefly concerned to keep the Council from taking over the functions of the courts of justice, while permitting it to intervene in extraordinary cases.

9 *January* 1605

Right trusty and right well-beloved, and right trusty and well-beloved, etc., we greet you well.

Although it is so well known to all men, by common experience, that lack of open air and exercise bringeth with it present indisposition, even in strongest bodies which have used the same, as we make little doubt of your desires and cares to yield to us (who have found it so necessary for our health) the best means you can devise for enjoying both at convenient times. Yet we thought good, before we resolved to begin that course, to give some such directions for the execution of your places in our absence as may supply any lack or inconvenience likely to arise in the managing of our affairs during the short times which we shall think fit to spend abroad from those places which are most commodious for the ordinary residence of our Council and officers of estate, from whom (as our subordinate ministers) so many men are to receive rules and directions, as well concerning our own public and private services as for the universal satisfaction of our subjects, every man according to his particular occasions.

Not doubting but you, that have had the honour and trust to be of our Privy Council, have so well observed the course of our proceeding hitherto, whensoever our own presence was necessary, as you may remain assured that we will sooner undergo the peril (or rather the overthrow) of our own health than suffer this state, over which Almighty God hath made us supreme head, to feel any inconvenience in the constitution thereof by our long absence or by omission of those cares which any of our progenitors have taken either for the safety, the justice, or honour of the same in general or particular. The public wealth whereof is more precious unto us than our well-doing, in which consideration, having now resolved (as our business and the season of the year may permit us) to remove sometimes to places distant from this city and our houses nearest to it, with some small company to attend us in our sports and private journeys, only used for preservation of our health.

Forasmuch as those things are despatched which we left last in memorial with you, our Principal Secretary,[1] to be debated of by our Council, and that the state of our affairs at this time doth not require many particular directions from ourselves before our departure, yet, considering now that in such a kingdom as this there must both foreign and domestical occasions daily rise which are fit to be considered of and despatched, some by our Council in general, some by a fewer number of them, according to the quality of the occasions, we think it meet, as well for the present as for hereafter, to give you this provisional authority and commandment: that you shall assemble yourselves, in our absence, once every week, besides the Sunday after the sermon, in such places as our dearest wife shall keep her court, to the intent that all our subjects (according to their wonted custom) may know some certain place where they shall receive despatch in all those things which do depend upon our own directions to you or upon the provisional power which we have given you to assemble at times, either for suppressing of any sudden disorders or expediting the multiplicity of all other causes which appertain to you to despatch and direct, either as you are officers of estate or of our Privy Council.

In which course, although such is the laudable institution of the government of this our kingdom as no persons whatsoever shall need to crave remedy from you in matters of justice, if they will take the ordinary way which lieth open to every subject how mean soever (and not out of presumption to obscure truth [to] address themselves to you at the Council table because they would make you judges of actions between party and party, for whom it is not possible to be able to distinguish and discern particulars so well as they that hear all parties judicially), yet if, at any time, some special case shall come before you, either by our reference to you or by the party's own importunity, wherein you conceive that those who have the cause before them use any delay or would take other course with the petitioners if they were acquainted with some particular circumstances better known to you—in that case we take it to stand with the rule of honour and charity for you to make some reference by your letters, or otherwise, in the favour of the party (remitting still the cause to the ordinary place where it dependeth, without judging the proceeding, whereby to draw to you the censure of such things as are proper for determination in other places).

And where experience hath taught us, since our coming, that many men who know their causes to be most unjust are so far from contentation* with any order or end therein as, when they have passed up and down through all the courts of Westminster Hall, they cease not still to importune us to interpose ourselves immediately, or by you, into the same, taking exception implicit to the judgements passed elsewhere. We have thought good hereby to admonish you (in case their complaints contain any matter of slander to the place of justice where they have been heard) that you shall cause the parties to be forthcoming to make proof of their complaint. Because our meaning is that all our magistrates and officers may know, on the one side, that we intend not to stop our ears to the just complaints of our people; and all other persons may know, on the other side, that whensoever their own passion or partiality doth so far possess them as to suffer them slanderously or causelessly to forget the duties they owe to lawful authority, that all such insolencies shall be corrected with due severity.

For all other causes daily occurring, seeing we do repose so great confidence in you as to qualify you with a representative power in our absence, and to be pleased not only to assist ourselves with your advice when we see cause but to commit to you the trust and power (wheresoever we are) to prevent by your care and providence all those things which come to your knowledge with any appearance of prejudice to us and our state, whomsoever it doth concern; we do hereby command you all (except your health or some other extraordinary cause withhold you) so to dispose yourselves as not only to hold your assemblies as aforesaid although no extraordinary cause be made known to you beforehand, but also to be ready to do the like as often as you shall be advertised by our Principal Secretaries that they have received directions from us to acquaint you with our pleasure or that any matter worthy your meeting is come to their knowledge, to whom particular advertisements are usually addressed in respect of their place and offices in the Council. In all which, remitting unto you the consideration whether it doth not as properly belong unto you, whom we have graced and trusted so far beyond others, to be careful of this to which we enjoin you, both for the honour of that board in our absence and for the contentation of our people, as it shall be for us to respect you according to our observation of every man's care and diligence in his peculiar duty.

We end with this further assurance, that whensoever you shall advertise us of any cause which doth require our presence (how far soever we be removed from your residence or howsoever our journeys were before resolved), we shall presently make it appear, by our return, how much we prefer the care of such occasions beyond our own private contentation, for which purpose we expect that you, our Principal Secretary, as time shall breed any matter worthy our knowledge, do use diligence to acquaint us how all things pass among you, whereby we may either send you our approbation or give you some further directions.

Given under our signet, at our palace of Westminster, the 9 day of January in the second year of our reign of Great Britain, France, and Ireland.

Public Record Office   *Copy*
SP 14/12/13

¹Robert Cecil, Viscount Cranborne, shortly to be created Earl of Salisbury.

Letter 115

To Robert Cecil, Viscount Cranborne

King James, it has been observed, was an "inveterate scribbler." Inconsequential though much of this jocular note to Cecil is, some special interest attaches to the part relating to "3," the Earl of Northampton. Whether the somewhat ambiguous denunciations of the latter here and in Letters 116 and 117 are part of an elaborate game or whether James was having serious doubts about Northampton's loyalty, it is difficult to say.

[*Early 1605?*]

My little beagle,

Although I have been out of privy intelligence with you since my last parting for having been ever kept so busy with hunting of witches, prophets,[1] Puritans, dead cats, and hares, yet will I not suffer this bearer, your fellow secretary, to go unaccompanied with this present—who should have carried the witches with him as ye desired, had it not been that he rides post and witches rides never post but to the devil. He hath conjured all the devils here with his Welsh tongue, for the devil himself (I trow) dare not speak Welsh. Haste him back, I pray you, for our match again Sunday at night, for he is secretary of our corporation that is of fools, horses and dogs, and I dare swear he is more qualified for that office than either ye or old Secretary Herbert.[2]

If your niece[3] be angry at me for his short abode at this time, tell her I shall make her satisfaction at my return with a tribute of kisses. But this must be kept counsel of, both from the bearer and my wife. Commend me to honest big Suffolk[4]—and the greater an honest thing be, it is the better.

Commend me also to my envious enemy "3" [Northampton], and tell him that since it grieves him to see my two sons there prosper so well, I hope with God's grace within few years to multiply his griefs by some more such pricks in his eyes and thorns in his sides. But be he sure I will immediately upon my return have his head for this labour in as great haste as King Henry, my noble predecessor, got his father's,[5] who could not go *ad centrum terr[a]e*[6] without it. But in one point I am greedier than he was, for whereas the head alone served him, I will have body and all together. Otherwise I disdain his head alone, so far as I protest I had rather have a kid or a lamb's head this time of the year. And so farewell.

JAMES R.

Cecil Papers   *Holograph*
134: 71

[1]Probably the same "prophets here and witches" mentioned in a letter by Sir Thomas Lake when the Court was at Hinchingbrooke, 18 January 1605 (HMC, *Salisbury MSS.,* XVII:19).

[2]Sir John Herbert, the second Secretary of State.

[3]On 27 December 1604, one of Cecil's nieces, Lady Susan Vere, had married Sir Philip Herbert, soon to become Earl of Montgomery. James apparently is jesting about the way he is calling the bridegroom away from the bride, to attend on him again at his hunting lodge, after only a brief visit to London.

[4]Thomas Howard, Earl of Suffolk, the Lord Chamberlain. His fatness is mentioned in Letter 119.

[5]Northampton's father, the poet Henry Howard, Earl of Surrey, was beheaded by Henry VIII in 1547.

[6]"To the centre of the earth."

Letter 116

To Robert Cecil, Viscount Cranborne

The following, one of many familiar letters in which King James greeted Cecil as "my little beagle," bears also the outside address, "To my littill wiffe waffe." The letter itself is a good example of the semi-jocular vein in which James, engaged in his hunting at Royston or Newmarket, conducted much of his correspondence with his Principal Secretary of State.

[*Early 1605?*]

My little beagle,

Now that the Master Falconer[1] doth return, I cannot but accompany him with these few lines, although indeed I might very evil have spared him at this time, as well for ruling of the hawks as for being so fit a man for trying of our hounds. Yet, since he will needs be gone, I pray you let him be saluted with a good pipe of tobacco. And I pray you put out him of his new custom, which is to drink nothing but ale after supper.

Surely ye made a brave choice of him for presenting your ciphered letters unto me, for he himself can write nothing but ciphers. But in good faith he had almost put me in a fray at the receipt of them, for he came very grandie* unto me while I was sitting at supper and whispered in my ear very quietly that he had letters from you unto me but he durst not give me them till I were all alone in my chamber, and left me to guess what kind of matter it could be.

But I pray you commend me heartily to good Master Intelligencer[2] and wish him to be plain in two things: first, what moved him to envy my doing honour to my poor young baby Charles;[3] and next, what ails him at Scotland, for in truth I know not what he can mean by quarreling their continuance in their form of government. But it is well ye have him now to be Oedipus of his own riddles.

And thus praying you to commend me to the two mentioned in my former letter, not omitting all the rest of your honest society, I bid you heartily farewell, having now so much mind of good large hounds in this rainy deep weather as I have forgotten all beagles till I come back to the chimney corner again to hunt a mouse.

JAMES R.

Norfolk Archaeology,
Vol. III (1852), pp. 78–79

*The editor has been unable
to find the original,
undoubtedly holograph, of
this letter.*

[1]Sir Roger Aston.

[2]Henry Howard, Earl of Northampton?

[3]A possible reference to Prince Charles having been created Duke of York on 6 January 1605. In Letter 115 James accuses Northampton of grieving to see Prince Henry and Prince Charles prosper, and in Letter 117 he asks him why he makes "cruel and malicious speeches against Baby Charles."

Letter 117

To Henry Howard, Earl of Northampton

A very curious cat-and-mouse letter. In the first half, James thanks Northampton for being a diligent and faithful servant during some secret mission (possibly to Scotland) and assures him that he has burned his confidential letters and will give no sign of the information that he has received in them. In the second half of the letter, the King suddenly accuses Northampton of hypocrisy and of hatred towards himself, Prince Charles, and the Scots. He leaves Northampton to let his own conscience dictate which part of the letter he will believe. One can only wonder what tumultuous feelings filled Northampton's breast as he approached the meeting with the King promised in the conclusion of the letter.

[*Early 1605?*]

My faithful 3,

If I had had any particular occasion worthy the troubling you with to have recommended unto you all this time of my absence, your letters should not have been answerless. But if for fault of other matter I had desired you to have been diligent and careful in my affairs there, it had been but to bid a running man go faster, which is both unnecessary and injurious, for I may easily judge of your diligence by your account. For if the unjust steward in the Gospel could have given as good a *reddere rationem*[1] for his diligence as ye have given to the chief of the Stewards,[2] he had never been cast in utter darkness. And yet my eyes saw all your letters consumed with fire, though without weeping or gnashing of

253

teeth. My reading of them carrying likewise that other Acheron-tide quality with it that, like as I had drunken of Lethe flood, when any point contained in any of them is told me by any other person, I can never remember to have heard of it before.

But now I must turn my pen to a far contrary style, repenting me of that epithet I give you in the first words hereof. For what can I think of your affection to me and the Union whenas your works declare the contrary? I must judge of your mind by your actions and not by your words. Your orations in Parliament in advancement of the Union are but words, but your officers' sever-ity in Dover[3] are actions. A strange thing, that your natural ava-rice, and innate hatred to me and all Scotland for my cause, should make you to cause your officers at such a time pick shil-lings from poor Scotsmen. Well, I protest to God, I thought you at my parting from you as honest a servant as ever king had, but what now I think of you since the discovery of this your great hypocrisy, judge ye and, according to your faith, so be it unto you, as ever it be. I am glad that I have gotten this ground to pay you home upon for your often cruel and malicious speeches against Baby Charles[4] and his honest father. But I know ye are now so proud of your new patron[5] as ye little care [for] your old friends.

I know this letter will be the more welcome that it is my pre-cursor, being shortly to follow who, like the sun in this season, am mounting in my sphere and approaching to shine upon your horizon. And so, praying you to believe the contrary either of the first or last part of this letter, I bid you heartily farewell for all this great quarrel.

JAMES R.

British Library, Cotton MSS.,   *Holograph*
Titus C VI, f. 178

[1] An echo of Luke 16:2, where the steward's master commands him to give an account of his stewardship (*redde rationem villicationis tuae*).

[2] James's pun on his family name.

[3] In January 1604, Northampton had been appointed Constable of Dover Cas-tle and Warden of the Cinque Ports. Obviously, his officers there had been deal-ing rigorously with Scots.

⁴It is hard to know what to make of these allusions, here and in Letters 115 and 116, to Northampton's hostility towards Prince Charles, a boy aged about five. Northampton may have argued against the prince being made Duke of York in January 1605.

⁵Possibly a gibe at the pension that Northampton received from the King of Spain in 1604.

Letter 118

To Robert Cecil, Viscount Cranborne

After the Hampton Court Conference failed to reconcile the Puritans to the discipline of the Church of England, James set about making good his threat to have them conform or to harry them out of his kingdom. In the following letter he congratulates Cecil and the Council on the way they have carried out his policy. The letter not only opens with the King's usual salutation to Cecil as "My little beagle" but has been addressed on the outside, in the royal hand, "To my little cankered beagle."

[*February 1605*]

My little beagle,

I am wonderfully well-satisfied with the Council's proceeding anent the Puritans since my departure. They have used justice upon the obstinate, shown grace to the penitent, and enlarge them that seem to be a little schooled by the rod of affliction. In this action they have, according to the 101 Psalm, sung of mercy and of judgement both;¹ and therefore thank them in my name for their pains and uniform concurrence in my service, and tell them that there is not a king in the world so proud of his council as I am of mine. And assure them that I shall never take longer vacancy from them for the necessary maintenance of my health than other kings will consume upon their physical diets and going to their whores. Now that I have seen the Bishop of York's letter,² so much talked of, I can truly say *minuit praesentia famam.*³ But I am thoroughly pleased with your answer; and specially concerning my hunting ye have answered it according to my heart's desire, for a scornful answerless answer became best such a senseless proposition.

I thank my patient beagle for stopping the suit of Gray's Inn. I am glad that my son hath so far outshot me in schoolcraft as he should praeveine* me in the fellowship of any house of learning.[4] But in truth that matter had a greater consequence than I will think the propounders thereof had in their mind. I am also glad of the miracles wrought amongst you in satisfying both the French and Spanish ambassadors. For all those services I have only this reward to bestow upon you and your fellows, that ye shall not be much troubled with suits recommended by me unto you during my absence.

All news here I remit to the Master Falconer's[5] report, who is now become alike keen and skilful both of hunting and hawking. And thus commending me to Suffolk and you in particular, and to all your honest society in general, I bid you heartily farewell, having enjoined the bearer to drink good pipes of tobacco to all your company.

JAMES R.

Cecil Papers   *Holograph*
134: 48

[1]Psalm 101 opens, "My song shall be of mercy and of judgement."

[2]Archbishop Matthew Hutton, writing to Cecil on 18 December 1604, had criticized the King's extravagance and his addiction to hunting. When he learned that transcripts of this letter were being passed around, Cecil wrote rebuking the old prelate. On 25 February 1605 the Earl of Worcester informed Cecil that the King, having seen both Hutton's letter and Cecil's reply, "said it was the foolishest letter that ever he read and Cranborne's an excellent answer." (HMC, *Salisbury MSS.,* XVII:70.

[3]The sense of this Latin tag is that now that the King has this letter in front of him he attaches less importance to it and its author.

[4]The King had been piqued to learn that Prince Henry was being proposed for honorary membership in Gray's Inn when no one had thought to nominate James himself.

[5]Sir Roger Aston.

Letter 119

To Viscount Cranborne and the Earls of Suffolk
and Northampton[?]

On 9 April 1605, Queen Anne gave birth at Greenwich to
the first royal child to be born in England in seventy years. King
James, in this buoyant letter written before he came to
Greenwich for his wife's accouchement, clearly hopes for a son.
Instead he received the Princess Mary, who died in infancy.

[*March? 1605*]

A cartel or challenge to a trinity of knaves.

If I find not at my coming to Greenwich that the big Chamberlain have ordered well all my lodging, that the little saucy Constable have made the house sweet and built a coke pit, and that the fast-walking Keeper of the Park have the park in good order and the does all with fawn although he have never been a good breeder himself, then shall I at my return, finding those things out of order, make the fat Chamberlain[1] to puff, the little cankered beagle[2] to whine, and the tall black and co[a]l-faced Keeper[3] to glower. As Sir Roger Aston said, if my wife shall not produce a fair young lion at this time, the Constable shall bear the blame; if I have not good fortune at the beginning of my hunting there the Keeper shall have the shame, and never be thought a good huntsman after; and if I get not good rest all night, the big Chamberlain's fat back shall bear the burthen of all. And so farewell as ye deserve. And as for the bearer, I have made choice of this worshipful Knight of the Bath to carry this cartel, who swears he will venture all the hairs of his beard in my quarrel.

JAMES R.

If the Master of Gray were here he would say it might be thought when Councillors goes to the Tower to visit the lion's whelp that hath so fair a nurse that the old Scottish proverb is true in them, that many a man courts the child for love of the nurse, especially some of them with whose chastity he was so well-acquainted. To conclude, I end with a miracle. What a luck it is that, notwithstanding that the ancient, reverend father of York hath reprehended the King's hunting,[4] yet hath the King lately received out of York House[5] the allowance of his hunting by very many hands. And so it is like the miracle of Balaam's ass,[6] that the house is wiser than the great prophet that is owner thereof.

Cecil Papers   *Holograph*
134: 66

[1]Thomas Howard, Earl of Suffolk. His bulk is the subject of a jest in Letter 115.
[2]Robert Cecil, Viscount Cranborne, who became Earl of Salisbury in May 1605.
[3]Henry Howard, Earl of Northampton. James refers to him as "a black grim-faced gentleman" in Letter 122.
[4]See Letter 118, n. 2.
[5]The occupant of York House was Thomas Egerton, Baron Ellesmere, the Lord Keeper of the Great Seal.
[6]Numbers 22–23.

Letter 120

To Robert Cecil, Earl of Salisbury

In 1605, King James sent the Lord Admiral of England (the Earl of Nottingham) on an embassy to Madrid to secure the Spanish ratification of the peace negotiated with England the previous year. He arrived back in England on 29 June 1605. In the following letter James speaks of a pair of talking parrots that Nottingham had presented to Queen Anne.

This letter is interesting chiefly because of the account that King James gives of a theological work which he had written around 1584, when he was aged about eighteen. This was not included in the King's Works *published in 1617 and has apparently been lost.*

[*July 1605*]

My little beagle,

It were high time that the Council's request were sent unto me for staying the current of suits, for I cannot yet be quit of begging, and even yesternight did Alan Percy[1] make a suit to me for a fee farm of a hundred pound land of impropriations, but with a present *nolimus*[2] he was quiet.

As for my book which ye praise so much, it is in truth an old book whereof there is nothing new but the covering. The language is extremely bad for, although it was first written all with my own hand, it was first marred in the orthography by Geddes copying it (the knave whom ye knew) in very rude Scottish spelling, and next was it copied by Sir Peter Young's son,[3] who pressing to English it, hath marred it quite and made it neither. And so it is now good Britain language, or rather Welsh, much like Sir Roger's style. It was my *puerilia*,[4] written by me in Dalkeith a five or six years at least before I was married. I think ye may remember to have seen that gentleman's hand that interlines it in divers places. It contains a short compend of the history of the Church, the grounds and antiquity of our religion, and the special times when the grossest Popish errors were introduced, which last ye will see specially collected in the table at the end of the book.

If one of the letters (I mean the shortest) that the Admiral[5] carried was written by his own knowledge, he is an old coxswain, for if I were the King's subject I would not desire another King's subject to make suit for me. But ye may tell my wife that what I wrote unto her anent the parrots was plain prophecy, for I saw not the Admiral three or four hours after that, who no sooner told me that he had sent two parrots to the Queen that spake good Spanish. But ye may judge what pain I was in to keep me from laughing. But for satisfying the King of Spain's request I think good to make him a grande[e]. And so praying you to commend me to Suffolk and 3 [Northampton], I bid you all three heartily farewell.

JAMES R.

Cecil Papers
134: 132

Holograph

¹Sir Allan Percy, brother of the Earl of Northumberland, was Lieutenant of the Band of Gentlemen Pensioners.

²"We should be unwilling."

³Patrick Young. His father had been King James's tutor.

⁴"Boyhood writing." This early work is mentioned by Sir Thomas Lake in a letter of 2 July 1605 addressed to Cecil: "This morning after his Majesty was ready, he called for me to command me to signify to you that yesterday he did not answer one part of your letter, which was your suit for his *Collections*, which now he has sent to you, with this remembrance, that the same were made when he was very young, and therefore to be judged of thereafter by you. . . . The language his Majesty doth also excuse, being neither good Scottish nor English, but lays that to the transcriber's fault" (HMC, *Salisbury MSS.*, XVII: 298).

⁵The Earl of Nottingham. (See headnote.)

Letter 121

To Robert Cecil, Earl of Salisbury

During his first months in England, James had a somewhat euphoric sense of the wealth of his new kingdom. However, as this letter indicates, he soon discovered that in England, as in Scotland, he would be constantly harassed by problems with the royal finances.

Besides opening this letter with his customary salutation to Cecil, "My little beagle," James has jocularly addressed it on the outside, "To the little beagle that lyes at hoame by the fyre quhen all the goode houndis are daylie running on the feildis."

[*October 1605*]

My little beagle,

Ye cannot think how great a pleasure ye did me in your discreet dealing with Cumberland,¹ whereby ye relieved me out of a strait that could not but have fashit* me, and I protest to God I know none living I could have employed in such an errand but you. As for his suit anent the debatable lands, ye know how that matter was left and what was last offered for them, being a far greater rent than ever he would speak of. And therefore, since it is to be an imp[roved?] rent, I look that he will perform as much as others would if he will have it, since he never craved it upon any other condition but for the uttermost value. I am heartily glad that he hath at this time so worthily behaved himself in all respects, and I shall be much more glad if God will yet restore him again unto us after so good an estimation as he hath now conquered unto himself. As for his place of Council, in case it should be void,[2] ye need never doubt of my resolution not only to make them fewer, according to the Act, but also never to make a Councillor for the request or suit of any living, but only out of my own judgement and conscience to make choice of him whom I think fittest for that place, as I do with the bishops. And therefore the only intercessors that I will admit for a Councillor must be his own piety, good fame, wisdom, sincerity, discretion, experience, and diligence; and if those seven good fellows concur in soliciting me for a Councillor's place they shall be sure to have more credit with me than any fourteen persons living.

Now, as for that point in your own letter wherein ye desire to be satisfied, I cannot but confess that it is a horror to me to think upon the height of my place, the greatness of my debts, and the smallness of my means. It is true my heart is greater than my rent, and my care to preserve my honour and credit by payment of my debts far greater than my possibility. This cannot but trouble me at home and torture me abroad, for I confess though I have more exercise of body here, I have less contentment of spirit than at home, for there by conference I get some relief and here I do only dream upon it with myself. And therefore as ye have perfectly used the first part of a physician's office in rightly describing the nature of the humour that troubles me, so lies it only in your hands and your fellows' by using also the other part of that office, perfectly to cure me—which is, by your pains and labours, to take away the cause of my care in letting me see how my state may be made able to subsist with honour and credit,

261

which if I might be persuaded were possible I would be relieved of a greater burden than ye can imagine. And you that are Councillors must I only use and trust in this. Your resolution will comfort me absent, and your honest account at my return will make me happy at home. I know great in weight and infinite in number are my affairs that your fellows and ye are now in hand with, and yet urgent is the necessity that they be done before the sitting down of the Parliament,[3] but your zeal and diligence is so great as I will cheer myself in your faithfulness and assure myself that God hath ordained to make me happy in sending me so good servants, for whose sake I protest to God I shall have a greater desire to live than for my own.

And as for the beagle[4] in special, I have had from Dunbar[5] a long discourse of your pains the last day. I can say no more, but what ye promise for me I shall be loath to break to him whom, before God, I account the best servant that ever I had, albeit he be but a beagle. For I know that what ye do in this errand of my profit, ye do it not out of the duty of your office but only for your love to my person. But I suspect Dunbar's report of you, lest ye as two knaves do recommend one another for cozening of me.

And so, recommending the Master Falconer[6] unto you that every one of your society may bestow a pipe of tobacco upon him, I bid you and them all heartily farewell.

JAMES R.

In the matter of the house,[7] because ye seem to write slightly that ye have been thinking upon some projects in it, I have only to recommend unto you such an honourable and reasonable order is fit to be taken with it now that it may never be altered again but stand like a Persian law[8] during my life.

Cecil Papers   *Holograph*
134: 49

[1]George Clifford, Earl of Cumberland. The King is replying to Cecil's long letter of 21 October 1605 (HMC, *Salisbury MSS.*, XVII: 459–61) reporting on his interview with the dying Cumberland. Cecil had had to intimate that James

was not ready to let Cumberland's brother receive the hunting lodge at Grafton which the Earl had held from the Crown, but meant to give it to the Duke of Lennox.

²Cumberland died on 29 October.

³Parliament, in recess since July 1604, reconvened on 5 November 1605.

⁴Cecil himself.

⁵George Home was created Earl of Dunbar on 3 July of this year.

⁶Sir Roger Aston.

⁷The royal household.

⁸For the immutability of the laws of the Medes and the Persians see Daniel 6: 12.

Letter 122

To Henry Howard, Earl of Northampton

After King James's first English parliament convened on 19 March 1604, it attacked the right of the royal purveyors to buy goods far below their market price. Everybody knew that many of the goods so purchased were never used by the royal household but were resold to the considerable profit of the purveyors. In the following letter, James is concerned that action be taken against the purveyors in order to prevent more trouble with Parliament after it meets for its second session in November 1605.

[*October? 1605*]

My honest 3,

By your last letter I have cause to suspect that I may thank Friday for your writing unto me that time of the day, and yet ye can have no merit in that day's fast, for ye bestowed the time thereof upon me and not upon God. I know now ye will say that nothing escapes me; I answer, no more than the poor purveyors escapes you and your fellows. Well, I dare not say that that traitor that made that public invective oration upon me is evil-faced, but sure I am he is a black grim-faced gentleman,[1] how well-shapen soever all the features of his face be. I think that purveyor's double name is unfortunate, for Jean Jean is a cuckold in French. In earnest, as I am glad of his handling so do I wish that all the rest whom he hath discovered were with all

263

speed tried and rewarded according to their deserving, for turns* of this nature would be *in esse*, and not *in fieri*,[2] against the sitting down of the parliament, that Cerberus' mouth may so be stopped *cum offa*[3] and Momus stilled. But it is in vain to spur running men, and therefore I end with this wish, that ye and your fellows may have as good success in the concluding of my affairs as ye have and still do use care and diligence in the working of them, and so farewell.

JAMES R.

Tell the King's beagle that the cause of his seldom writing to me now with his own hand is his old fear that some of his letters should miscarry and fall in the old queen's hand, but I know ye will maliciously say he needs not, for Pluto is no good secretary he dwells in so dark a dungeon.

British Library, Cotton MSS.,   *Holograph*
Vespasion F III, f. 32

---

[1]The gentleman is Northampton himself. For his black countenance which the King dared not call "evil," see the salutation that opens Letter 101. Ponderous royal humour lies behind the reference to Northampton as a traitor who spoke invectively against the King.

[2]"An accomplished deed, not something in the process of becoming."

[3]"With a morsel." For this "sop to Cerberus," cf. Virgil *Aeneid* 6.420–21, where the Sibyl *melle soporatim et medicatis fingis offam obicit.* The King here follows English syntax, not Latin, when he allows *cum* to be used with an ablative of means or instrument.

Letter 123

To Robert Cecil, Earl of Salisbury

After giving Cecil some instructions about steps to be taken before Parliament reconvenes, King James turns to the eclipse of 2 October 1605 and amuses himself by burlesquing the interpretations of the astrologers. (Cf. King Lear, *I, ii, 112–17.)*

My little beagle,

Though it be superfluous to heap coals on a burning fire, to throw water in the sea, to spur a free-running horse, or to furnish more matter to the Council to deliberate upon now when ye have all so heavy a task of weighty affairs laid upon your shoulders, yet such is the shortness and necessity of the time before the parliament² as I must add one point more to be at this time deliberated upon amongst you, and that is the matter anent the Marches of Wales.³ For it will be both a great dishonour and inconvenient unto me that the parliament should bandy that matter amongst them before I be first at my wit's end into it. This far only I recommend to your considerations, that a king's old prerogative in continual possession may be in as great security as a private subject's old possession, that the common law be not made to fight against the king's authority, that the abuse of a king's predecessor be not a ground to deprive his successor of his lawful and rightly used privilege, and that the country of Wales be not too justly grieved by dismembering from them their ancient neighbours. All other matters I remit to your care and diligence. But, above all, be earnest in trying and severe in punishing the thievish purveyors,⁴ and take all the pains ye can to inform and tune well the parliament men.

But now will I go to higher matters and tell you what I have observed anent the effects of this late eclipse, for as the troglodytes of the Nile that dwelt in caverns, the shepherds of Arcadia dwelling in little cabins, the Tartars harbouring in their tents like the old patriarchs, so I, having now remained a while in this hunting cottage, am abler to judge of astronomical motions than ye that lives in the delicious courts of princes. The effects then of this eclipse for this year are very many and wondrous. It shall make divers noblemen at the Court loathe their wives and wish they were better married, such as Lennox, Pembroke, and Roxburghe.⁵ It shall make some widowers loath to marry again. (The beagle knows who this is.)⁶ Yea, it shall make some that never were married loath to begin now. (This riddle 3 can solve.)⁷ And all those anti-conjugal qualities do proceed from the malign influence of Phoebus, wroth with his sister Cynthia for defrauding his spouse Rhea of the comfort of his beams, by her unmannerly interposition. And the disdain also that Apollo hath taken to have been so violently obscured hath made him strain himself to shine so much the brighter and thereby, he being also the god of all prophecy, divers great mysteries and secrets are discovered and brought to light this year. First, a great dreaming divine[8] hath closed his prophetical mouth and taken up his clyster spout again. And now very lately a strangely possessed maid,[9] whose breast was nothing but a pillow for pins, is by the strength of love and virtue of physic dispossessed of all her pins and spoiled of all the rest of her tricks, but especially by the virtue of a perfumed tablet hanged about her neck, which is as powerful to banish the devil by the strong scent it hath as ever the smoke of Tobias' fish liver was.[10] Now if my Lord Knollys be yet a Saint Thomas, as the apostle would not believe till he touched, so let him taste, if he please, of the tablet and he will easily guess at the chief ingredient, called *Album Graecum*.[11] And therefore if any man knows any lawful impediment why this dreaming prophet and possessed maid may not be joined together in the bonds of matrimony let him declare in time. Sure I am that these revelations were better bestowed on Stow's chronicle[12] than to tell how many dishes of wild meat were served at the mayor's feast. Many other prodigious events are flowed from this eclipse, *sed me plura effari vetat Apollo.*[13] If Doctor Bruce have lied no more in all his prophecies he deserves a prophetic crown, *an secus*[14] on my conscience he merits to be hanged.

Thus thanking the beagle for his fine peaches and grapes, I pray him to make my commendations to Suffolk, 3 and all the rest of his honest society.

JAMES R.

Cecil Papers   Holograph
134: 79

[1]The "7 October" endorsed in a contemporary hand is presumably Cecil's

clerk's date of receipt.

[2]Parliament was to reconvene on 5 November 1605.

[3]The King in what follows refers to the efforts of the counties of Gloucestershire, Worcestershire, Herefordshire, and Shropshire to free themselves from the jurisdiction of the Council for the Marches of Wales and so to obtain the same measure of local self-government as the other English counties.

[4]See Letter 122, headnote.

[5]The Duke of Lennox had married Jane Montgomery in 1598; the Earl of Pembroke had married Lady Mary Talbot, co-heiress of the Earl of Shrewsbury, in 1604; Lord Roxburghe had married Margaret Maitland, only daughter and heiress of Maitland of Lethington, in 1587. Of Pembroke's marriage Clarendon quipped, "he was most unhappy, for he paid much too dear for his wife's fortune by taking her person into the bargain" (*History of the Rebellion*, Oxford [1888], I: 72).

[6]Cecil never remarried after the death of his wife in 1597.

[7]Northampton never married.

[8]Richard Haydock (or Haddock), the famous "Sleeping Preacher," who in April 1605 had confessed his imposture after the King had heard him preach, supposedly while in a deep sleep.

[9]Anne Gunter (see Letter 124).

[10]See the apocryphal Book of Tobit 6:7.

[11]Leucorrhea.

[12]John Stow's *Chronicles of England* was first published in 1580. Numerous later editions were updated.

[13]"But Apollo forbids me to declare more."

[14]"Otherwise."

Letter 124

To Robert Cecil, Earl of Salisbury

A personal link had been forged between James and Cecil, with the two corresponding in their own handwriting. The King, with plenty of leisure at his hunting lodge, had time enough to pen his long, discursive, and jocular missives to his Principal Secretary of State. Cecil, attending to the daily operation of the government, had not the same leisure. When he found himself charged with the additional labour of preparing to deal with the parliament shortly to be reconvened, he sought the King's permission to dictate his letters to a secretary. The

King gives his consent in this letter but retaliates by having a secretary pen it for him and merely authenticating it, like any piece of routine business, with his sign manual at the head.

JAMES R.

Right trusty and well-beloved cousin and counsellor,
we greet you well.

For your better satisfaction touching Anne Gunter,[1] we let you wit (according to our promise) that whereas not long since she was a creature in outward show most weak and impotent, yet she did yesterday in our own view dance with that strength and comeliness, and leap with such agility and dexterity of body that we, marvelling thereat to see the full and great change, spent some time this day in the examination of her concerning the same. And we find by her confession that she holdeth herself perfectly cured from her former weakness by a potion given unto her by a physician, and a tablet hanged about her neck; that she was never possessed with any devil nor bewitched; that the practice of the pins grew at the first from a pin that she put into her mouth, affirmed by her father to be cast therein by the devil; and afterwards that and some other such pin-pranks which she used, together with the swelling of her belly occasioned by the disease called "the mother,"[2] wherewith she was oftentimes vehemently afflicted, she did of long time by daily use and practice make show to be matters of truth to the beholders thereof; and lastly that she hath been very far in love with one Ashley, servant to the Lord of Canterbury, and is still, hath sought his love long most importunately and immodestly (in manner unfit to be written) and now she doth most humbly and earnestly crave our furtherance that she may marry him; and this last is confessed also by himself, whereof ye shall hear more by the next messenger. In the meantime we have sent you this letter enclosed for the better satisfaction of my lords and yourself.

And whereas we know that you cannot so conveniently, by reason of the parliament and other weighty business, write much unto us with your own hand, we shall be well contented, according to your desire (unless it be in causes of very great importance) that you shall use your secretaries' labour therein to ease both yourself of writing and us of reading thereof. And so we bid you farewell.

Finchingbrooke³ 10 October 1605

Cecil Papers   *Letter under the sign manual*
134: 70

¹The "strangely possessed maid" of Letter 123.
²A type of hysteria. The description appears to be of false (hysterical) pregnancy.
³I.e., Hinchingbrooke, Hunts., the home of Sir Oliver Cromwell.

Letter 125

To Robert Cecil, Earl of Salisbury

An unhappy monarch, mired in financial difficulties and depressed by the way foreign ambassadors cadge expensive gifts, James can hardly bring himself to his old jocular playing of the role of astrologer.(Cf. Letter 123).

[18? October 1605]¹

My little beagle,

That I have been so long unwriting unto you, ye may only impute it to lack of matter, for I daily hear of so great diligence and carefulness in all the Council, and of your so continual consultations upon all my affairs, as I protest I was never so void of care for all my great turns. * But on the other part I cannot but be sensible of that needless and unseasonable profusion of expenses whereof ye wrote in your last to Lake.² Ye best know both my part and mind in all the unnecessary waste that comes that way. That anent the Spanish ambassador I never heard it nor can yet understand it. As for the other, he is such an insatiable epitome of avarice as I doubt not but he hath found out a new art of begging, whereupon he may add a book to the bibliothèque of his countryman Rabelais.[3]

But when I consider the extremity of my state at this time, my only hap and hope that upholds me is in my good servants that will sweat and labour for my relief upon such grounds as I laid at my parting. Otherwise I could rather have wished with Job never to have been,[4] than that the glorious sunshine of my entry here should be so soon overcast with the dark clouds of irreparable misery. I have promised, and I will perform it, that there shall be no default in me. My only comfort will be to know it is mendable, for my apprehension of this strait (however I disguise it outwardly) hath done me more harm already than ye would be glad of. As I cannot but highly commend the Council's care in all their consultations, so can I not forbear to express my good liking in special of that letter written by them to the judges anent the reformation of abuses in and about London, the execution whereof will produce many great good effects. The Duke of Lennox importunes me daily to put an end to his turn, wherein I can say nothing till I hear your advices that I employed in that errand.

I am not now in humour to write in my former style unto you for, except that thing I write of be helped, I can sing no other song but *ad vada Mæandri concinit albus olor*,[5] and swanlike shall I live and die, both in purity and innocence. Only this word of mirth: that I envy your nephew that hath observed that strange alteration in the Earl of Lincoln which I could not foretell by all my astrology.[6] But the reason is that that now noble lord lives by the influence of Dis that domines* over him, and therefore is not under the climate of Phoebus nor subject to any celestial influences. And to the purpose of this Plutonical subject, I am glad to hear how 3 [Northampton] hath coursed the priest and his devil. And now ye may see for how many bad purposes this counterfeit deviltry would serve for if it were not prevented. But ask of 3 how he thinks a priest can both make a god, and eat a god, and lodge both God and the Devil within him *simul et semel*.[7] But sure I am that 3 loves so dearly his old 30 [King James] as he spares not to conjure both priests and devils for his master's service. And thus, with my kindest commendations to him and Suffolk and Worcester, and all the rest of your honest society, I bid you heartily farewell.

JAMES R.

Cecil Papers
134: 72

Holograph

[1]Endorsed "18.8^bris 1605 His M^ty to me."
[2]Sir Thomas Lake, the Clerk of the Signet who helped the King with matters of state when he was away from London.
[3]The greedy French ambassador is Christopher de Harlay, Comte de Beaumont. For the scandal he caused at his departure by his requests for gifts, see John Chamberlain's letter of 7 November 1605 (*Letters*, ed. McClure, I: 214).
[4]Job 3:3–11 and passim.
[5]"By the shallows of Mæander sings the white swan" (Ovid *Heroides* 7.2).
[6]A reference to Letter 123. The domineering and erratic character of old Henry Clinton, Earl of Lincoln, has been described as "strongly tinctured with insanity."
[7]"At one and the same time." The reference is, of course, to the doctrine of transubstantiation, and it indicates that King James knew that Northampton was a Catholic.

Letter 126

To George Clifford, Earl of Cumberland

A friendly letter to the Earl in his sickness. He died "of the bloody flux" five days after the King sent this message of encouragement.

24 October 1605

JAMES R.

Right trusty and right well-beloved cousin and counsellor, we greet you well.

If we were not at this instant in haste to that sport which you love as well as we, with our hand we would have signified to you how glad we were, first by letters of our cousin the Earl of Salisbury, to receive hope, and then by this gentleman a confirmation, of the great likelihood of your recovery, and of the message you sent by him that you did not despair to attend us again at our pastimes. Whereof, if we be glad to have the hope, yourself may judge what we shall be to have the fruition. And so, out of your hope conceiving another hope, that once again we shall hear the wild hallow, we have thought best to return the old messenger to you to assure you that nothing can be more pleasing to us than if it shall please God to perform what we both hope for, that is, your recovery.

Given under our hand at Royston the four and twentieth day of October in the third year of our reign of Great Britain, France, and Ireland.

Cumbria Record Office
(Kendal), Hothfield MSS.,
Box 44

Letter under the
sign manual

Letter 127

To Robert Cecil, Earl of Salisbury

A note concerning ambassadors.

[*Late October 1605*][1]

My little beagle,

Because French Monsieur[2] is to take his leave of me upon Tuesday next, I thought good to remember you, if he have gotten word that old Don Diego[3] got a ring from me besides his present, he will think evil if he get not the like. Therefore I leave to your discretion to try if it be comed* to his knowledge or not, that in case it be ye may have a ring hasted to me before his coming, for I doubt if he be as honest as the other was, but I am sure he is as greedy as the best of them.

I doubt not but ye have remembered to put the Spanish ambassador[4] to a point anent his complaints upon the States. It were also good time now, if it were possible, to put the Archduke's ambassador[5] to a point anent my people's commerce with his master. And thus hunt ye well there, for I am going to hunt here.

JAMES R.

Cecil Papers   *Holograph*
134: 133

[1]Erroneously assigned to August 1609 in HMC, *Salisbury MSS.,* IX:124.
[2]Christopher de Harlay, Comte de Beaumont (see Letter 125, n.3).
[3]"Diego" as a generic nickname for any Spaniard became slurred into "dago." H. L. Mencken in *The American Language, Supplement One* (p. 606) noted 1832 for the first recorded mention of "dago" in the United States and thought that the word was probably extended to the Italians about the 1880s.
     The HMC editor (*Salisbury MSS.,* XVIII:vi–vii), unable to find an actual Don Diego in England at this time, hazards the guess that the "Diego" was Zuñiga (see n.4 below).
[4]Pedro de Zuñiga, the Spanish ambassador, who had first been received by the King on 21 July 1605.
[5]Baron Hobach, ambassador of Albert, Archduke of Austria, the ruler of the Spanish Netherlands.

Letter 128

To the Privy Council [?]

About eleven o'clock in the evening of 4 November 1605, one "John Johnson" was apprehended while standing guard over thirty-six barrels of gunpowder concealed under the Parliament House. Johnson's real name was Guy Fawkes, and the gunpowder was to have been exploded the following day, November 5, when King James came to open a new session of Parliament. The King followed very closely the investigation, which was begun at once, and he drafted the following interrogatory to be put to "Johnson."

This examinate would now be made to answer to formal interrogators:

1. As what he is (for I can never yet hear of any man that knows him)?
2. Where he was born?
3. What were his parents' names?
4. What age he is of?
5. Where he hath lived?
6. How he hath lived and by what trade of life?
7. How he received those wounds in his breast?
8. If he was ever in service with any other before Percy,[1] and what they were, and how long?
9. How came he in Percy's service, by what means and at what time?
10. What time was this house hired by his master?
11. And how soon after the possessing of it did he begin to his devilish preparations?
12. When and where learned he to speak French?
13. What gentlewoman's letter it was that was found upon him?
14. And wherefor doth she give him another name in it than he gives to himself?
15. If he was ever a papist, and if so who brought him up in it?
16. If otherwise, how was he converted, where, when, and by whom?

This course of his life I am the more desirous to know because I have divers motives leading me to suspect that he hath remained long beyond the seas and either is a priest or hath long served some priest or fugitive abroad, for I can yet (as I said in the beginning hereof) meet with no man that knows him. The letter found upon him gives him another name, and those that best knows his master can never remember to have seen him in his company, whereupon it should seem that he hath been recommended by some persons to his master's service only for this use, wherein only he hath served him. And therefore he would also be asked in what company and ship he went out of England, and the port he shipped at, and the like questions would be asked anent the form of his return. As for these trumpery wares found upon him, the signification and use of every one of them would be known. And what I have observed in them the bearer will show you. Now last, ye remember of the cruelly villainous pasquil that railed upon me for the name of Britain.[2] If I remember right, it spake something of harvest and prophesied my destruction about that time. Ye may think of this for it is like to be the labour of such a desperate fellow as this is.

If he will not otherwise confess, the gentler tortures are to be first used unto him, *et sic per gradus ad ima tenditur.*[3] And so God speed your good work.

JAMES R.

Public Record Office   *Holograph*
SP 14/216/17

[1]Thomas Percy, one of the Gunpowder Plot conspirators. A cousin of the Earl of Northumberland, he was a royal Gentleman Pensioner and the Constable of Alnwick Castle.

[2]On 24 October 1604, James was proclaimed "King of Great Britain." The new title, not approved by Parliament, caused some offence.

[3]"And so by degrees until the ultimate is reached."

Letter 129

To Christian IV, King of Denmark

After most of Guy Fawkes's fellow conspirators had been either killed or captured following the attack on Holbeach

House by the High Sheriff of Worcestershire and his levies, King James sent an account of the Gunpowder Plot to his brother-in-law. With it he despatched the following personal letter.

TRANSLATED FROM THE LATIN

11 November 1605

Most serene prince, brother in blood, and our
most dear associate,

There is nothing in our affairs, whether prosperous or adverse, joyful or sorrowful, which greatly concerns us but the same touches Your Serenity through brotherly kinship and the very great bonds of goodwill between us. Accordingly just as, long before this, when by the favour of the divine power we on the fifth day of August in the year 1599[1] escaped the impious and wicked hands of traitors bent on our destruction, we at once caused report of this matter to be borne to Your Serenity, so now we cannot refrain from informing you of a far more atrocious crime, the most horrid and detestable of all treasons either undertaken anywhere in the world within the memory of man or conceived in thought and mind. It is all the more atrocious since it was to be undertaken by men professing themselves to be adherents and avengers of the Roman and papist religion (or rather of a most impure superstition). And since among all kings we two have now been left as the ones against whom the counsels and attempts of the papists are chiefly directed, it is meet, not only because of these bonds and kinship which we have mentioned but because of the common cause of religion by which we are joined, that this matter be understood by Your Serenity.

Although many proofs (and those exceptional) of divine kindness and clemency towards us have stood out, nevertheless none could be more notable or marvelous than that the same has freed us from so imminent (or rather present) danger and has turned so horrid a crime into its own glory and into the happiness of ourselves and our subjects.

And this plot was so disclosed and revealed that (with all our subjects abominating with general hatred so execrable a crime) it was not necessary for a soldier to be enlisted, for arms to be taken up, for any force (almost) to be applied—and the authors of the crime, with almost no uproar or disturbance, have been slain or seized. Such are wont to be the wonderful works of God, who sometimes shows dangers all the greater in order that he may display greater power and grace; and the more frequently we have experienced this, the more we trust that we are beloved by him and fortified by him with a stronger defence. But in order that Your Serenity may understand the course of the entire business in its particulars (which would be rather too long were we to desire it to fall within the compass of this present letter), we have had a short but very accurate separate account added,[2] and this will be borne to Your Serenity along with this present letter. When you have read this account you will understand that we have had a marvelous deliverance and you will rejoice; and along with us you will give special thanks to God, the most mighty champion of our safety, to whose guard, with the most ardent prayers, we commend you and all yours.

Given from our palace of Westminster, the eleventh day of the month of November in the year of our Lord 1605.

Your Serenity's most
loving brother,
JACOBUS R.

Copenhagen, Rigsarkivet   *Last five words and*
England, AI2   *signature holograph*
1605 11/11

[1] Amazingly, the date of the Gowrie Plot is given incorrectly: it took place on 5 August 1600, not 1599!
[2] This does not survive with the letter.

277

Letter 130

To Robert Cecil, Earl of Salisbury

James "plays the truant" and recounts the results of his hunting while Cecil and his associates labour in London preparing for the coming session of Parliament.

[*1605–1606?*]

My little beagle,

I received your letter the day [today]at the end of the second chase. It was a strange constellation of concurring accidents between the fairness of the weather, the pleasure of the sport, and the substance of your letter. I confess I am happy in such servants that watch for me when I sleep and in my absence are careful so to sweep and trim the house against my return as I may, in the meantime, *dormire securus in utramque aurem.*[1] Those concurring accidents have made me resolve to play the truant for a day or two longer. And for your part, to teach you to be so busy, I enjoin you for penance to make my excuse to the fairest and comeliest lady[2] at that court, whom only I wrong by my absence, and to tell her that she shall certainly be advertised of my coming the night before.

In the meantime I can but wish that the master's care and the servant's diligence may have success accordingly. And now only when the day of the Lord draws near I am to remember your fellows and you to be extremely careful in two main grounds: the one, to sound and prevent all occasions of scandal or grudge that may trouble the parliament and that before their meeting, which is the ground of all your consultations at this time, to the effect that they may sit down as well prepared for good and purged of evil as may be; the other is that ye may sound and try the bottoms of their minds and intentions before the hand as deeply as is possible, that at the least nothing "uprouysed"[3] may befall unto us.

And so, going to bed after the death of six hares, a pair of

278

fowls, and a heron, I bid you and all your honest society heartily farewell.

JAMES R.

I wonder what truce ye have lately taken with your nephew[4] that I have heard no new accusations of his knavery from you these five or six days.

Cecil Papers   *Holograph*
134: 145

[1]"To sleep without anxiety." (The King uses the same Terentian tag in Letter 80.)

[2]There is no reason for suspecting that the King is referring to anyone other than the Queen. Although their marriage was not a very happy one, at this period their relationship was unusually cordial (see Letter 134).

[3]*Sic.* HMC, *Salisbury MSS.,* XXI: 274, reads "improvised," but according to the *O.E.D.* that word did not enter the language until the nineteenth century. The sense is "unprovided for."

[4]The depraved young William Cecil, Lord Roos or Ros. Actually a grandson of Salisbury's older brother, the Earl of Exeter, Roos was commonly referred to as Salisbury's nephew (cf. HMC, *Salisbury MSS.,* XVIII: 71, 130).

Letter 131

To Robert Cecil, Earl of Salisbury

A jocular letter in which James expresses a poor opinion of Henri IV, King of France.

[23? January[1] 1606]

My little beagle,

Because ye are lying idle there in mew, I have found you an errand to deliver a letter of mine to the fairest unpainted lady in all the Court.[2] And because Tom Pott[3] hath a fine kennel of very little beagles ready to carry to France, I would know in time if ye mind to be one of that number, for that king[4] would be a fine huntsman for you, except that ye could never trust his hallow. I think the Rochelle[5] needs to give him no other answer but if that His Majesty would with his tongue feel the want of his tooth, they are sure he would never press them to admit the Jesuits amongst them.

For news here we have none but that we fear ye shall think us all turned Puritans for such a feasting night as was made upon Friday last in this town, wherein I assure you it chanced well that the Act of Parliament against drunkenness is not yet passed,[6] otherwise the Justices of Peace had had much work ado here at that time. As for your last letter I need not answer it, for in my former I sent you the true image of my mind. If Tom Lake[7] did in my name desire to be informed for whom that bill of recusants was made, it was merely out of his own curiosity, for I verily thought that they were for the matter of the chain and therefore gave him no direction for any such question. And so farewell.

JAMES R.

Cecil Papers   *Holograph*
134: 140

[1]Endorsed "23 Jan" without any year. Perhaps the day is that of receipt. For the year see n. 6.

[2]Almost certainly Queen Anne (see Letter 130, n.2).

[3]Keeper of Prince Henry's dogs.

[4]Henri IV.

[5]La Rochelle, one of France's chief ports, was controlled by the Huguenots.

[6]The Bill Against the Loathsome Sin of Drunkenness received its first reading on 7 March 1606, its second reading on 19 March, and its third reading on 17 April, when it was passed (*Journals of the House of Commons,* I:279, 286, 299).

[7]Sir Thomas Lake, Clerk of the Signet and a future Secretary of State.

Letter 132

To Christian IV, King of Denmark

From mid-July to mid-August 1606, King James and his queen were visited by Anne's brother, the King of Denmark. The Danes were notorious for their heavy drinking, and the English and Scots tried hard to keep up with them. At one of the drunken revels, King Christian made the sign of a cuckold at the seventy-year-old Earl of Nottingham, Lord High Admiral of England, who several years earlier had married the youthful Lady Margaret Stewart. The Countess, when she was informed of the incident, was furious at the insult. King Christian became sensitive about the affair, and after he left for home King James wrote the following letter to try to put the best appearance possible on the whole embarrassing episode.

TRANSLATED FROM THE LATIN

20 August [1606]

Most excellent king and dearest brother,

Although I have not as yet any certain notice of your arrival in your kingdom, yet I was very glad to understand by some of my servants lately come from you in your passage that you were gone beyond the sands[1] in our Narrow Seas. And withal, the wind holding fair and good so long as it hath done, maketh me presume (with apprehension of no little joy for it beforehand) that you are long ere this safely arrived.

But whereas you yield me many thanks by your letters, how much rather are they due from myself to you unto whom all things from us (through your great gentleness and courtesy) were acceptable and well pleasing during your abode here, which to remember is a great contentment to me. So, doubtless, neither at nor after your departure should you have found cause of any the least offence or distaste if that indiscreet and foolish woman[2] had not played such a fond part as she hath done. But what remedy when even in Paradise itself the first man could not

281

avoid this rashness and light credulity of a woman? And whereas it is a grief unto you that any such matter hath happened,[3] truly it ought to be, and indeed so is, much more displeasing unto me that any such occasion should be given to trouble and disquiet your mind. Howbeit, I cannot but in this respect also take great comfort and joy that your excellent and truly royal letters do show your noble mind to be so affected herein and the matter itself to be conceived by you as becometh a most worthy and wise prince.

The authors whereof and devisors whereas you desire to know (supposing it to be the practice of some envious and malicious sycophants) although your own sister hath taken much care and pains to sift out the truth thereof, yet myself, not contented therewith but causing it more thoroughly to be examined, do find no other ground of it but that, by way of sport and merriment at the table and time of banquet, you did (as the fashion is almost of all men without offence) familiarly and pleasantly jest with my Admiral, not doubting anything nor peradventure minding it afterwards as a matter of no reckoning. Whereat (as myself can truly testify) the Admiral was so far from taking any offence as that he did both by countenance and words plainly acknowledge and profess himself to be most graciously and kindly used by you, which nevertheless being reported to his wife not of any malice but (as it is usual in such matters) by certain idle babblers and talebearers, she, being overmuch suspicious (as she now acknowledgeth) and of a weak mind, took it in evil sense, and yet is so obstinate as she doth profess that she will rather endure all extremities than tell the authors[4] of this foolish fable. But of all this matter and the circumstances of it I doubt not Sinclair[5] hath put you in remembrance. At what time, very many being present, it was so far from any man's thought to apprehend the least conceit of any contumelious words or deed offered by you, as on the other side you may hold yourself assured that all men did much observe and do rightly commend that noble and fair condition in you that all the time that you were here present (alas, too short a time) none never heard the reputation of any, either man or woman, so much as by one word impeached by you. And therefore for this matter never trouble your mind more, wherein for mine own part, as it is no small contentment unto me that you do so nobly declare what reckoning you make of the matter itself, so it would please me much more if I could satisfy mine own mind, being exceedingly offended that this offence hath been offered you, unto whom, as unto my most dear brother and singular friend linked in perpetual and inviolable love and amity, I do and ever will bear most entire affection and wish all happiness.

These will be transmitted immediately, from our hunting, August 20.

Your brother, sincerely and
faithfully most loving
while life lasts,

Somerset Record Office   Copy of a lost holograph[6]
Phelips MSS., DD/PH 218
(Latin text and
contemporary English
translation)

[1]The Goodwin Sands.
[2]The Countess of Nottingham.
[3]The Countess had written a stinging letter to King Christian's secretary after she had been informed that the visiting sovereign had waggled his fingers at her husband, making the sign of a cuckold's horns.
[4]Those who reported the insult to her.
[5]Presumably the "Andreas Sinklar, cubicularius [Gentleman of the Bedchamber]," who was one of King Christian's attendants during his visit to England (HMC, *Salisbury MSS.*, XVIII: 269).
[6]The Phelips copy is headed "To the King of Denmarke written wth the Kings owne hand."

Letter 133

To Robert Cecil, Earl of Salisbury

Although peace had been made between England and Spain in 1604, war continued between Spain and England's former

ally, Holland. This letter deals with the repercussions after
some Spanish ships put into English waters in order to escape
capture by the Dutch.

[1606?]

My little beagle,

I have now talked at length with Caron,[1] in whom I find that
his English education cannot amend his native German prolix-
ity; for, if I had not interrupted him, it had been tomorrow
morning before I had begun to speak. God preserve me from
hearing a cause debated between Don Diego[2] and him.

Always he and I are very well agreed in all things. He will
inform his masters of my inclination in general and of this request of mine in special, that I do it not as won by the importunity of Spain or as blind of Spain's encroachments upon my
favour, but upon a "seene" [?] well for me and the States both in
times to come, upon Spain's promise never to play any more
such tricks in my harbours, and if they do that I will allow the
States to pursue them to my very shore. I have ingenuously told
him that I will think myself much obliged to the States if they
grant it, but will not quarrel them for refusal thereof if upon a
sound reason. And he hath faithfully promised to persuade
them to it all he can, and in his own opinion he thinks it reasonable. And therefore the sooner ye make ready the despatch for
Winwood[3] the better it is.

Thus have I walked *in via regia*[4] with both the parties, and I
protest to God I care not although everyone told what I said to
the other. *Qui vadit plane, vadit sane.*[5] All the particular arguments I remit to the bearer's relation. I have also spoken unto
him anent the trade that some middes* might be found out in
that matter, which although he confesses is a very tender point,
yet he says it is not only a thing reasonable but necessary that
some means may be agreed upon whereby the Archduke[6] may
receive some measure of satisfaction in that point.

In truth it is good dealing with so wise and honest a man,
although he be somewhat longsome.* Ye may upon Sunday let
me see the draft of the letter to Winwood, and the less that

284

Caron make the French ambassador acquainted with this matter till it be at a point, it will work the better. Farewell.

JAMES R.

I have also spoken with the French ambassador anent the matter of the merchants. He is willingly contented to speak with you in that matter before the meeting in France and to end it in substance between you before it go there.

Cecil Papers   *Holograph*
134: 102

[1] Noel de Caron, the Dutch agent in London.
[2] See Letter 127, n.3 and n.4.
[3] Sir Ralph Winwood, the English agent in The Hague.
[4] "In the kingly way."
[5] "Who walks openly walks safely."
[6] Albert, Archduke of Austria, the ruler of the Spanish Netherlands.

Letter 134

To Robert Cecil, Earl of Salisbury

The situation set forth in this letter is clear enough. One person has accused another of being Queen Anne's lover. James is aware that, if he makes a charge of slander and refers the matter to the courts, he will only give most objectionable publicity to what he regards as a malicious lie. The solution is to put the slanderer on trial for other libels spoken against the King.

Because of the extreme discretion with which this episode was handled, no mention of it has been preserved in any other documents. Thus a modern editor is left with no clue to the date of this letter other than that it was written after James had been long enough in England for Cecil (as the King notes) frequently to have kept disturbing libels from coming to the King's notice.

My little beagle,

I am glad that your opinion jumps so right with mine in this, as I have already (in a part) done the same which ye now wish to be done. For upon the first relation of this knave's talk I considered with myself that this malicious scandal of his was not of that nature as was possible to be buried, whereupon I thought fit to acquaint her [Queen Anne] a little with it,[1] lest other reports might have been made of it unto her. And therefore, amongst other of his villainous speeches concerning me, I told her that amongst the rest (but in such a fashion as she might easily discern what account I made of it). But now that this process is comed* to a greater maturity, I think it very fit that either both ye and Dunbar,[2] or any one of you, acquaint her with the whole proceeding, and show that as if it had been of the nature of a pasquil it should have been buried from her ears and all the world's, as yourself hath done with divers of them that concerned me. So soon this hath passed the ears of two or three I thought good she should be acquainted with my behaviour in it and how order shall be taken for the punishment of the villain, without either accusing him or acquainting any of my learned counsel with this malicious lie. For as his tale is but a feckless scorn, merely proceeding from the malice that he bears at me, so am I not so simple as to doubt that her reproach can ever be separated from the dishonour of me and all my posterity. (And through the misknowledge of this maxim many unwise husbands have, by curious and unjust searching to discover their wife's shame, procured their own eternal infamy.) But God be thanked, this tale doth clearly appear to be groundless and only hatched by his own malice, since the party whom he accuses of it doth avow the contrary to his face, being known to be an honester man than himself. And I had been far to blame if I had had any such intention against her, especially at this time when, as I must confess, she uses me so kindly in all things that if it were possible for me to love her better than ever I did before it were my part to do it.

And thus, going to sup my hawks, I bid you heartily farewell, and recommends the knave to the gallows for the points of my

286

to beware. For in general I never saw any man so freely and so oft resist his dearest friends; humours in unreasonable things as I have seen you do. In which service, I do freely confess, ye have more eased and contented my mind than any other living could ever do. And as for this dead man in particular, I can neither forget how the first ground of your friendship with him came only from me while I was yet in Scotland and the nobleman himself in the late Queen's disgrace, nor yet am I unmindful how, in the time of your greatest friendship with him, ye carefully diverted an occasion which he thought to have taken hold of for his preferment to a place for which he was not very fit.

Having then first told you what I never meant to apply unto you, I am next to tell you what was my true meaning in those words, which is shortly this: all the sons of men are without exception of this nature, that they do make great or less account of any action according as the person of the actor is liked or disliked of them. And therefore it is that the person of the preacher must be acceptable to the auditor or otherwise his doctrine will never edify them. If ye see your son will contend in any exercise with another youth, in case he do it indeed but as well as the other, ye will think, I warrant you, that he performs it something better, for Nature teaches us all with the raven ever to think our own birds whitest. Set another leg as well made beside mine, I warrant you 3 [Northampton] will swear the King's sweet leg is the far finest. And as the best of us all doth a little thus overvalue our friends' good qualities, so do we a little diminish their slips and errors. No, oftentimes this sickness most prevails upon best natures that are full of charity. Nay, in some sort we are commanded so to do by the word of God: charity, saith Saint Paul, "burries" [sic: bears?] all things, interprets all to the best, and is not suspicious.[2] And therefore a man will be loather to trust an ill report of his friend than of another. And although in any matter that may touch a king's person or state in any high degree, a faithful minister will be as curious and earnest against his dearest friend as against his greatest enemy, yet in a matter of no great importance he may either carelessly not trust that his friend hath committed any error in such a matter or else think the error to be more aggravated than

288

it ought to be. To this natural disease I confess myself to be as much subject as some other men, as the sickness that oft abuses best natures. What large and eternal proof I have of 3 his fidelity ye best know, and yet I would no more trust him than one of the corruptest lawyers in the trial of a mean error upon one of his dearest friends, and therefore thinking no worse of you than of myself, or of any of my faithfulest servants, did I use that word of caution unto you: that in this or the like cases concerning me, ye might bury trust, waken up a sort of suspicious curiosity and, putting on the person as it were of an enemy at that instant, try what could be the worst that might be proved in that matter.

Now I know ye will think that I use a needless long discourse unto you for interpretation of my meaning, but let me plainly tell you that, as ye was wont to guess by the old Queen's eyes, if I had not found by your facon* divers times since I spake with you upon this matter what time ye apprehended that I was not well pleased with you, that ye had ever some conceit sticking in your mind that I was a little colder to you than before, notwithstanding that I resolved you largely of the contrary out of my own mouth; if, I say, I had not found this opinion yet sticking in you by divers conjecturals, besides the letter which ye wrote in answer of that of mine, I would never otherwise have troubled you with so long and idle a discourse. But that ye may never more misjudge me in any such case, let this one sentence serve for all: I think as well of you and trust as much in you as of any servant that ever did, does, or shall serve me, *in sæcula sæculorum,*[3] amen. And therefore if ye deserve it not, the more is your blame.

Now I confess I am the more encouraged to utter this conclusion out of the abundance of my heart for the message ye sent with Aston.[4] For if ye would have been partial to any friends ye would have been partial to them. But the best is that the matter was a mere mistaking or else a wilful gross addition in Lake,[5] for I only spake it by comparison, that such a power could not well be refused to Dunbar,[6] whenas I could have wished that that garrison should be so diligent as not only to ride upon any purpose of Dunbar's making unto them, but even if Lord William Howard[7] or any gentleman of the country could inform them where any of the outlaws were, they should not spare their pains in riding to make a search for them. And in good faith it was a strange fortune that speaking since that time anent the said Lord William, in the presence of two or three of the Chamber whereof Hay[8] was one, I chanced to say that the said gentleman's religion did him great harm at my hands for, notwithstanding of the infinite trust I had in the faithfulness of his brother and uncle, yet I durst never bestow any preferment upon him in my days only because of his religion and devotion to the Jesuits. How this now agrees with Lake's recommendation of him judge ye. Always ye may be sure of my counsel-keeping from all flesh, for I were unworthy to be a king if ever I wronged you in that sort. And as for the matter itself, it falls of will as a mistaking, and so there needeth never any more mention to be made of it.

And thus praying you to recommend me to all your fellow labourers and to prepare for me a good account of all your memorial against my return, I bid you heartily farewell.

JAMES R.

Cecil Papers   *Holograph*
134: 91

[1]Endorsed "22 Febr. 1606." On endorsed dates see Introduction p. 38.
[2]Cf. I Cor. 13:4–7.
[3]Rendered as "world without end" in the Anglican liturgy.
[4]Sir Roger Aston (*v.* Letter 42, headnote).
[5]Sir Thomas Lake.
[6]The Earl of Dunbar had been sent to impose peace upon the Anglo–Scottish border.
[7]Associated with Dunbar in the pacification of the borderers was Lord Howard of Effingham, son of the Earl of Nottingham.
[8]Lord Hay, one of the King's Scottish favourites, who subsequently became Viscount Doncaster and Earl of Carlisle.

Letter 136

To the Council

Likening himself to a patient and the members of his Council to physicians, James calls on them to cure the financial cancer that is ruining his life.

[*19? October 1607*]¹

My lords,

The only disease and consumption which I can ever apprehend as likeliest to endanger me is this eating canker of want, which being removed, I could think myself as happy in all other respects as any other king or monarch that ever was since the birth of Christ. In this disease I am the patient, and ye have promised to be the physicians and to use the best cure upon me that your wits, faithfulness, and diligence can reach unto. As for my part, ye may assure yourselves that I shall facilitate your cure by all the means possible for a poor patient, both by observing as strait a diet as ye can in honour and reason prescribe unto me, as also by using seasonably and in the right form such remedies and antidotes as ye are to apply unto my disease. And as for your parts, I know it is the chief and, in a manner, the only subject whereupon ye break your brains all this time of my absence.² And first, for your labour of borrowing money, to remember you thereof were to spur a running horse. I only wish you better success therein than I dare hope for till I hear of the conclusion. In the meantime I doubt not ye will not omit to think upon all means of addition and increase of rent, as well by some new and lawful inventions (without the unjust burthen of the people) as also by your frequent sitting upon your ordinary commissions of assertis,* leases, concealments, and such like. And on the other part that ye will also be thinking upon the best means for subtraction and decrease of charges, as well by reformation of corruptions and abuses as by cutting of needless superfluities (the honour, greatness, and safety of the king and kingdom being always respected).

Some more general rules will I also remember you of, in addition to those which at my parting I recommended unto you concerning this errand. First, that none of you either jointly or in particular shall either recommend to me or allow of any such indefinite or vast suit whereof none of yourselves can guess what the value may prove, which is the most thankless and ignorant prodigality that any prince can use; but, that whatsomever nature the suit be of, I may first be informed of the true value, and then is it my part only to consider what out of the measure of my liberality I will bestow upon the suitor. (I mean either of any new invention found out by a suitor, or of any concealed unknown debt as was the nature of Sir James Sandiland's suit anent that recusant's unknown debt.)[3] So shall I never need to repent me of my liberality, nor the suitors have cause to thank their own wits but my free favour only. Secondly, I would have you to help my memory when men come with new suits that have already been largely rewarded, for since there are so many gapers and so little to be spared, I must needs answer those that are so diseased with the *boulimie*[4] or *caninus appetitus*[5] as a king of France did long ago answer one, *ceci sera pour un autre*.[6] Thirdly, if any suits come for unseasonable renewing of leases or farms of customs or imposts, ye know how greatly that concerns my profit, and that that is almost the only sure hope that is left for increase of my rent.

Now having touched three points as helps to stay this continual haemorrhage of outletting, I will only remember you of two restoratives again for nourishment whereof I have oftentimes spoken unto you: the one, that it be no longer forgotten to make my profit as well of the lands of those that are attainted for treason as of the fines of these noblemen that were fined for little better deserts (I mean with that moderation as I ever intended it and wherein ye are already sufficiently acquainted with my mind); the other thing is that there be some strait and diligent order taken as well for the timous* recovery of my sperable* debts as for the seasonable payment and inbringing as well of my ordinary rents as subsidies.

And thus assuring you of as counsellable and pliable a patient, as I assure myself ye will prove faithful, diligent, (and I

hope) fortunate physicians, I bid you heartily farewell, praying
God to bless you with a happy success.

JAMES R.

Cecil Papers   *Holograph*
134: 113

¹Endorsed "19 of october 1607." The year, 1607, may be a later addition.
²The King was at Royston enjoying his hunting.
³For a document, undated, concerning some £3000 that Sandiland stood to
recover from recusants in arrears, partly due to concealment in Elizabeth's
time, see HMC, *Salisbury MSS.*, XXIII: 123. Nichols (*Progresses of James I*, II:
123) notes that in 1606–1607, Sandiland received £1500 "out of the Recusants" and a further £150.
⁴Greek: "ox famine" (a great and paralyzing hunger).
⁵"Canine hunger" (a morbid or pathological hunger).
⁶"This will be for another."

Letter 137

To Robert Cecil, Earl of Salisbury

*The bantering tone that marked earlier letters to the Secretary
is here less in evidence. James can see no justification for intervening at this point in the peace negotiations between the Dutch and
the Spanish. He is concerned to know how far the loan arranged
by the Council will aid him, and he affirms his support for the
Church of England as a bulwark of the monarchy.*

[19? October 1607]¹

My little beagle,

I have considered upon your despatch from the Low Countries, and as for that matter as it now stands, I can assure you
that, although I had been present and sitting amongst you, I
could have given it no other answer than ye have done in that
draft of a letter that ye sent me to see, for as long as Verreyken²
or the friar³ holds them in hope by their letters of a further
agreation* to come, and till the States have made manifest their

resolution whether they will harken to any less than the uttermost that they have craved, and also till the French deputies have plainly discovered their master's resolution, it were no purpose nor wisdom in me to discover myself in so perplex and thankless an errand.

And now for the other news ye sent me anent the success that your fellow councillors and ye have had for the borrowing of money. I can no more thank you for your part in sending the news thereof than I would thank a parrot for prattling what she hears talked of others. But this metaphor must I use out of this hunting place that, although I cannot deny but the beagle hath tried well and stuck well by the scent, yet I cannot properly say that it was this hound or that that made so good a chase, but it was a good kennel that all run well, and therefore I can give no other thanks to the Council but this: that never king thought himself more happy in his council than I do, and that herein I may truly glory that no king in our age is so well served by his council as I am.

Only three points I must now desire to be cleared in anent the use of this borrowed money: first, whether I may hereby have means or not to buy in a number of these idle pensions, the continuance whereof exhausts my state, and yet a number would be gladly rid of them by reason of their long evil payment; next, if by this means I shall not now be able to do my turns* hereafter with ready money and not to do all upon credit as I did before, which was the only main eating canker of my state, keeping me still in a consumption and making me still disburse the third penny more than need, for if this be not now remedied, this will prove but a year's off-putting, and then must I fall in a new dangerous relapse again of my *morbus recidivus;*[4] and lastly, ye have made mention in your letter of the first payment and the time thereof but not when the rest shall be paid, which I could wish as was thought by you all at my parting from you, to be betwixt [word omitted] and the end of December.

To conclude now, I pray you forget not Fuller's matter,[5] that the ecclesiastical commission may not be suffered to sink, besides the evil deserts of the villain; for this far dare I prophesy unto you, that whensoever the ecclesiastical dignity together with the king's government thereof shall be turned in contempt and begin to vanish in this kingdom, the kings hereof shall not long after prosper in their government, and the monarchy shall fall to ruin, which I pray God I may never live to see. And so farewell.

JAMES R.

I can do no more but I shall wish you here every night after supper, but more for your folly nor your wisdom.

Cecil Papers   *Holograph*
134:126

[1] Endorsed "19th of october."
[2] Louis Verreyken, Secretary to the Archduke Albert.
[3] One of the emissaries of the Archduke Albert was a Franciscan friar who, disguised as a captain, went to The Hague to negotiate a truce with the Dutch.
[4] "Returning sickness."
[5] Nicholas Fuller, a Puritan barrister, had argued that the ecclesiastical Court of High Commission had no power to imprison, put to oath, or fine any of His Majesty's subjects. Enraged, the High Commission imprisoned Fuller and fined him £200. Appealing to the judges, Fuller obtained an order requiring the High Commission to desist, but under pressure the judges rescinded their "prohibition."

Letter 138

To Robert Cecil, Earl of Salisbury

James takes up matters which he admits he should have mentioned in an earlier letter: his concern about his rents, legal negotiations with the Scots, treatment of hostile Members of Parliament, punishment of enclosers whose illegal actions had provoked unrest in the countryside, and the vexatious question of "prohibitions."

My little beagle,

In my last the paper failed me before the matter, [I] being infected with a longsome* style by the sympathy of these long-some phlegmatic people which were my subject[s],² where-through I am now constrained to remember by a second letter such things as my former could not contain, but with the renewing of my former excuse that ye nor your fellows should not think that I am therefore in any doubt of your continual and unceasing diligence, not only in all that is committed unto you but even in whatsomever other thing shall occur or shall by you be thought fit for the furtherance of my service.

As for the matter of my rents, which I cannot deny sticks much in my mind till I see it come to some good and certain end, for that matter I say I have said enough (though but in two words) in my last; for when I name it generally, I mean by all the parts thereof as well addition and multiplication of means as by reformation of abuses and subtraction of unnecessary and not honourable charges.

I am likewise to advertise you that I have heard word out of Scotland of a good beginning they have made there anent the advising upon a union of the laws. And because the Secretary and the Advocate³ are to be shortly up, I would have you to warn our lawyers here that they may be ready every one to give an account and confer with others upon their labours at meeting. By Fuller's so humble submission⁴ that sentence of Solomon is verified, *Qui parcit virgae odit puerum*,⁵ which should likewise put us in memory of Yelverton⁶ that he be not forgotten *ad correctionem*.⁷ I mean young Yelverton, though for your distinction between the father and the son I care not much, thinking neither barrel better herring. Ye remember to which three of you I gave this charge before my parting; for, if one way or other be not found to make him a little feel the weight of my displeasure, I can never be disburdened of the weight he laid upon my heart. And now I hope that both 3 [Northampton] and 10 [Cecil] will begin to reform the opinion ye both had of my nature when ye would often tell me that, if the Lower House men that most offended looked not to be as welcome to me the next day as the honestest man would be, they durst not presume to do as they did, [the two of you] praising that virtue in the late queen that she would be loath ever to be reconciled in her countenance to them who had wilfully offended her. And 3 used ever to say, if my *manus Christi*[8] whereof I was wholly compounded were mixed with a little "verdius" [verjuice] it would mend all this matter.

I must also remember you that something may be done upon the unlawful depopulators[9] lest the Diggers[10] call us fair counters but evil payers, having made a fair popular show without substance. Let therefore some symmetry be used between my justice upon the Diggers and them that furnished them the cause to offend that, as a great number was put in fear and but a very few punished of the one sort, so there may be some one or two at least of the other sort punished exemplarily, being of the principal offenders and of worst fame, so as *poena ad pauces, metus ad plures*[11] may thereby be extended.

And for conclusion of all, I heartily pray you to do the best ye can in settling and putting to a good end yon fashouse* jars between the Church and the judges anent the prohibitions. I know your tempers in handling it cannot but work good effects, and so ending with so godly an errand, I bid you heartily farewell, assuring you that every night after supper I have as good mind of Tom Durie[12] and "the beagle" as I have mind of my affairs in the morning and despatches to my Principal Secretary, praying you not to forget to commend me to all your fellow labourers.

JAMES R.

Cecil Papers   Holograph
134: 84

[1]Endorsed "3 of xbre."
[2]The Scots.
[3]Lord Balmerino and Sir Thomas Hamilton.
[4]For Fuller, see Letter 137, n. 5.
[5]"Who spares the rod hates the child" (Proverbs 13:24).
[6]Henry, son of Sir Christopher Yelverton, Justice of King's Bench. He had offended the King by speaking freely in Parliament.
[7]"With a view to his correction."

⁸Literally, "the hand of Christ." The name of a cordial made by boiling a mixture of sugar and rosewater.

⁹The enclosers of common land.

¹⁰James is referring to the agricultural labourers involved in the Midland Insurrection of 1607. These "Diggers" (the King's use of the term is interesting) are not to be confused with the Diggers of 1649, the rural communists led by William Everard and Gerrard Winstanley. These later Diggers were said to have received their name from their demonstration of 8 April of that year, when they began to dig up uncultivated land near Cobham.

¹¹"Punishment to few, fear to more."

¹²The HMC's editors of the *Salisbury MSS.* identify "Tom Durie" or "Durey" as, like "the beagle," one of the King's nicknames for Cecil (XIX: 555).

Letter 139

To Robert Cecil, Earl of Salisbury

James is concerned that before Balmerino, the Scottish Secretary, returns home the latter have a conference with Ellesmere, the English Lord Chancellor, about reconciling the legal systems of the two kingdoms.

[*December? 1607*]¹

My little beagle,

I am forced to write unto you sooner than I thought to have done, for fear of losing the occasion of the Scottish Secretary's being there, who is shortly to return. I would therefore have you to desire him to speak with the Chancellor and my learned counsel anent the matter of the Union, that there may be a concurrence betwixt them of England and them of Scotland whom I have appointed to study the uniformity of the laws² and that there may be such a correspondent course holden betwixt them as each of them may supply others in that errand as shall be requisite. I pray you likewise not to forget Mr. Fuller's process,³ as also the framing of a plea for the post-nati;⁴ thus ye may see how the confusion of businesses before my parting made me to forget those principal things whereof I should then have put you in remembrance.

And so I bid you heartily farewell, assuring you that I will every night wish for young Tom Durie's company[5] to make me merry with when I am going to bed.

JAMES R.

Cecil Papers
134:116

Holograph

[1]Endorsed "1607 His Ma^{ty} to me." The year may be a later addition.

[2]James appointed this committee in October 1607. See Brian P. Levack, "The Proposed Union of English Law and Scots Law in the Seventeenth Century," *Juridical Review* N.S. XX (1975), 108.

[3]See Letters 137 and 138.

[4]The *post-nati* were those born after James had come to the English throne. The point at issue was whether or not post-nati Scots should be regarded as naturalized English citizens. The matter was settled by the ruling of the judges in Calvin's Case (1608) that the post-nati were de facto naturalized. Sir Edward Coke made the point that post-nati Scots who owned land in England would be subject to the same legal liabilities as native-born Englishmen (see Levack, "Proposed Union," p. 111).

[5]See Letter 138, n. 12.

Letter 140

To Robert Cecil, Earl of Salisbury

One of the many monopolies by which parasitic courtiers drained wealth from the Jacobean economy was a very lucrative one on the import of logwood, brought from the New World to make cheap but inferior dyes. This monopoly was given in August 1604 to a syndicate headed by Sir Arthur Aston. The next year one of James's cronies, very soon to be made Earl of Dunbar, decided that he would like to get in on the profits, so he surrendered to James the manor of Hartington and in return was given a grant charged against the logwood receipts. Unfortunately, the exactions of the officers in charge of the logwood monopoly became a national scandal. Parliament listed it by name in a Petition of Grievances, and King James found it advisable to "resume" (cancel) the letters patent. The following letter about providing compensation for Dunbar had a result

*that should have been highly satisfactory for the latter—in June
1608 he was granted a pension of £4000, a tremendous sum in
those days, in lieu of his logwood income.*

[April? 1608]

My little beagle,

Although I sent you divers messages with the last fat post out
of Newmarket,[1] yet I spared him in carrying of one message
that concerned his own errand, according to that rule that I
have oft given you and the Treasurer[2] both, never to trust a man
that carries a message from me in his own errand. And therefore I thought this point fitter to be reserved for my pen than his
own report. Ye know what land I took from him again upon the
deceitful hope of the log wood, so as now he lies void of any
recompense for his land. Now that I, that have been so liberal or
rather prodigal to so many whomto I owed nothing nor could
claim no deserts, should be not sparing but unjust to so well a
deserving servant, it were a strange change in me to the other
extremity, and an evil example for the rest of you that are his
fellows in honest and painful service, especially since ye know
him to be far from aiming at anything that may impair my rent.
And therefore I only desire that ye assist him in the finding out
of some such thing as may rather better my estate and yet in
some sort satisfy his loss.[3] And ye are sure, I hope, that he will
not importune you at unfit times, for ye know that the man
whom of ye and I spake at our parting, and this man, are otherwise to be respected than many others. And so farewell, with
my commendations to the said old 3 [Northampton], your fellow hound.

JAMES R.

Cecil Papers   *Holograph*
134:154

[1]The King left his hunting at Newmarket in late April this year.
[2]The Earl of Dorset.
[3]On 13 June 1608, a warrant authorized payment of £4000 as compensation

Letter 141

To the Council

*In 1608, in a work written by Cardinal Bellarmine but pub-
lished under the name of his chaplain, the world was informed
that in 1599 James had sent Pope Clement VIII a letter suggesting that the King might become a convert to Catholicism. This
revelation was a great shock to James, who saw himself as the
leader of Protestant Europe. In the following letter he commissions the Council of England to investigate the matter, with particular attention to the role played by James Elphinstone (created Lord Balmerino or Balmerinoch in 1606). Balmerino had
been Secretary in Scotland at the time of the despatch of the
letter and still held that post.*

*The official finding was that Balmerino had treacherously
slipped the letter into a sheaf of documents requiring the for-
mality of the King's signature, and accordingly James had been
tricked into signing the letter without reading it. This explanation was fairly widely accepted until the present century, when a
more sceptical breed of historian has taken the view that James
knowingly sent the letter as one of his moves to remove Catholic opposition to his succession to the English throne and that
Balmerino was simply made the scapegoat in order to keep un-
blemished the King's reputation as a Protestant.*

*Balmerino was sentenced to death and attainted in March
1609. His life was spared, however, after he exculpated the King
and accepted responsibility for the notorious letter. Balmerino's
subsequent imprisonment was commuted. After his death in
1612 his son and heir was restored in blood and given the peerage lost by the father—all of which rather indicates that James
knew that he had sacrificed an innocent man.*

JAMES R.

Right trusty and right well-beloved cousins and councillors, we greet you well.

If we were not persuaded that your affection towards us were not only grounded upon the duty you owe us as your king but also upon an entire love of our person, we should not take so great comfort as we do in the use of your service in all things which do concern either the good of our estate or our own honour. But because we are thereof confident and do withal assure ourself that whosoever loveth our person or our honour now as King of England will hold no less dear anything that doth or did concern our reputation as King of Scotland at any time since we bore a crown and before we came into this kingdom than he would a matter of that nature that should or may befall us as king of this realm (seeing no stain can be found in the honour or honesty of the King of Scotland that doth not cast a blemish upon the King of England's brow).

We have, out of that assurance, in a late accident happened which doth as nearly touch us in reputation as any one that ever happened unto us in all our life, reposed ourself upon your faith and loves to us; both by your diligence to discover the very truth, and out of your affections to advise what course is meetest for us to hold to clear our reputation in so public a note cast upon us. The matter is concerning the defamation wherewith we are charged in a book lately published in the name of a chaplain[1] of the Cardinal Bellarmine, that we should have written letters to the Pope and to certain cardinals of the tenor mentioned in the said book, which many of you have seen, a matter which doth concern us to clear ourself of, not only in regard of ourself but of the expectation of all Christendom howsoever in religion divided, the part that is adverse to us hoping, no doubt with gladness, to see us fouled, the other, concurring with us in the same profession of religion and holding us, wheresoever dispersed, as the chief and head of their profession, being no less attentive to hear what our purgation will be; whereof though from the beginning we know ourself innocent, yet because that sufficed not for our justification against a charge so confidently and so openly laid to us, we were forced to bethink ourself how we might make our innocency manifest. And, by the help of our own memory having called to mind such circumstances as might serve to that end, in our late speech with our Secretary of Scotland we have drawn from him a confession that the said letters were written by him or by his privity. But how our hand was gotten to them it is not yet clearly discovered.

Wherefore, for the further manifestation thereof, as a matter necessary for our justification, we have thought good to use your service in a diligent examination of him. And, for some light to you therein, we have conceived certain necessary interrogatories to be ministered unto him and sent the same to you herewith in writing, by which and by your own wisdoms and such diligence as we doubt not you will bestow in a matter so nearly touching our honour, we assure ourself the very truth will be brought to light. Wherefore, our pleasure is that you call before you the Lord Balmerinoth [Balmerino], our Secretary of Scotland, and first admonish him of his breach of duty committed in that, being at his departure from us at Royston commanded to keep his chamber, he hath notwithstanding presumed to show himself abroad as well in our palace at Westminster as in other places, then to proceed to examine him as well upon these articles now sent unto you as upon any other circumstance that shall occur to you to be meet to be known for the finding out of the truth. In the handling whereof as we doubt not but we shall have like trial of your love and discretions as in other matters we have proved, so do we expect that, with as much expedition as may be, ye do advertise us of your proceeding therein. Assuring you that in no one thing you can yield us a more acceptable trial of your affections to us and of your judgement than in this which concerneth so nearly our honour which to us is dearer than our life, especially being in the point of our religion, wherein our care hath ever been to go with clear and upright steps.

Given under our signet, at Newmarket, the seventeenth day of October in the sixth year of our reign of Great Britain, France, and Ireland.

Though ye were born strangers to the country where this was done, yet are ye no strangers to the king thereof. And ye know if the King of Scotland prove a knave, the King of England can never be an honest man. Work so therefore in this as having interest in your king's reputation.

Cecil Papers   *Letter under the sign*
134:123   *manual, with holograph*
                                                            postscript

¹Matthew Tortus. Actually, Cardinal Bellarmine was the author of *Responsio ad Librum Inscriptum Triplici Nodo, Triplex Cuneus, sive Apologia,* the Catholic reply to King James's *An Apologie for the Oath of Allegiance,* which had been published anonymously.

Letter 142

To the Earl of Salisbury, and others

Judging from the tenor of the following letter, the Council had no enthusiasm for the part King James had assigned it in proclaiming himself the innocent victim of the Balmerino affair. Indeed, the vehement insistence with which the King refers to Hay's testimony suggests that the councillors, like a number of other persons, may have had some doubts about Balmerino's guilt.

[19? October 1608]¹

I have received your joint letter, at two points whereof I am so amazed as I am forced to seek from you a further resolution in them by these few lines. First ye write a riddle, for after that by a large preface ye have promised first to inform me of the truth, next to let me know a way how to effect my just desire, and last how to free myself from importunity; yet when ye come to the matter, ye say nothing in that second point which is most material of all, save that it is necessary that I be thought earnest out of my own sense and not out of the infusion of others. How I should work this ye make no mention, neither know I how I could have done more in that than I have done as yet, for trial must precede any thinking of punishment, and by this time every man knows how earnest I am in that. And the more I wonder that ye make no mention of the receipt of my letter to the Council anent that, so as ye may be sure that I will leave no means (if I know them) that may satisfy the world of the truth of my part. The other point is that I cannot wonder enough how those false reports can be spread; for Hay[2] himself was a witness, with other two or three more, that at my first entering with him [Balmerino] in that purpose he made no sticks to confess at the first that he himself was the maker of that despatch to the Pope and his cardinals, that he had oft solicited me in it for the weal of my service, and that I had oft refused him. Indeed he would fain have bound it upon me that at the last, through his importunity, I had granted unto it, but there we differed. This was in my withdrawing chamber in Royston when, I confess, I purposely left my bedchamber door open that two or three there might hear what passed betwixt us, whereof Hay, as I said, was one but how far after noon he confessed his own guilt in the presence of his fellow secretary, how on his knees he craved pardon, wishing he had never been born, and how I told him that I could not resolve what pardon to bestow upon him till first I had clearly tried all, and then would advise how far my own honour would permit me to pardon him. Of all this, I say, I am sure ye are long ago informed by him that was the only witness at our afternoon's meeting, so as his false suggestions shall, I hope, produce no other effects but the just aggravating of his own punishment.

As for my behaviour towards Hay, I could say no otherwise to him nor no man except I were not true nor honest to myself. And the better I may say it unto him since he himself hath already taught me that lesson for, not a day before his parting out of this, he begun purpose with me anent that man, protesting unto me that he never saw man look as he did that Sunday, and of himself concluded that, if any rigour were spared in that man's punishment, my honour could never be cleared. For, he said, the least sparing of him would ever be thought collusion betwixt me and him but, since it goes so, the publicer my actions be in this, the better it is.

To conclude now, I remit to you and all honest men to think upon all the ways that may be for clearing of my honesty in it, which I had the more need to do considering his treachery. I only pray you to think that never thing in this world touched me "neerelier" [more nearly] than this doth. God knows I am and ever was upright and innocent. But how the world may know it, that must chiefly be done by some public course of his punishment, wherein I look to hear your advice after his examination, and so farewell.

JAMES R.

Cecil Papers   *Holograph*
134: 104

[1] The endorsed date, partly obscured by binding, is 19 October.
[2] Lord Hay, later Earl of Carlisle, one of the most prodigal of the King's Scottish favourites.

Letter 143

To Robert Cecil, Earl of Salisbury

Perhaps no other letter more clearly reveals the nature of Jacobean court intrigue. Lord Hay, in the midst of being very useful to His Majesty with his testimony against Balmerino, began to press for favours. Meanwhile a manœuvre was devised to keep Jane Drummond, the Queen's favourite, from persuading Her Majesty to come to Balmerino's aid.

My little beagle,

I have now reason to long to be advertised what is done in the examination of that person [Balmerino] that was before the Council, being three days since he was examined, which (by your letter even now received since I began to write) I perceive is acoming. But in the meantime that ye and your fat fellow Treasurer² may know what we are doing here, Hay is returned with open mouth against the examinate. He told me of his being at Hampton Court, whereof I seemed to have been ignorant. He assured me that she [Queen Anne] spake as far against that man and condemned him as far of dishonest dealing as I could have wished. He assured me that she would never open her mouth for him if it were not by Mistress Drummond's³ persuasion, which he says he told to Drummond, who answered him only with a blush; and therefore he advised me to seem angry at the Chancellor⁴ for another cause for which they already feared my wrath, and he said that would move Drummond, who loved the Chancellor much better than the other, to be so careful for appeasing me towards him as she would gladly let the other run his destiny. He swears no creature pities him as being, besides this offence, a dishonest, partial, bribing man of his own nature. He says whatsomever punishment I spare towards him I lay it upon my own honour. But at one thing ye will smile: he advised me not to sell the bear's skin before he were slain; for, said he, that would be thought men's particular, and immediately thereafter made suit for Sir George Hay to be Secretary,⁵ and for Roper's office⁶ to Robin Carr,⁷ and made Carr suit for a Scottish register which the party hath for the Controller⁸ his father. All my answer was short after much hearing: that I would proceed in the course of his trial and punishment with a cold dry resolution only to seek the clearing of my honour to the uttermost; that it was true my honour bound me to it not to spare any punishment towards him that the rigour of law would allow; if my wife would forbear to mediate, I would be the more glad; if otherwise, I would constantly go on my own course without the least alteration for her or any flesh, for, if she did meddle in a thing thus belonging to my honour, it might well harm herself but it would never move me. As for other suits, I told him it was not yet time to talk of them.

To conclude now, since he is examined I would be glad to be well resolved what is my best course for clearing of my innocency. I am able to prove that he hath spread two or three sorts of false and contrary reports in this errand, for which he merits less favour. I must now likewise resolve how and in what manner he is to be tried. And in my conscience I cannot see how my honour can permit me to mitigate any punishment that the severity of law can lay upon him, especially in regard of the false rumours he hath spread. And yet so fully must I satisfy the world in the trial of this that my greatness must never colour my goodness, nor my authority my honesty, for I shall never desire to be thought a great king if the reputation of an honest man be not joined thereunto. And so farewell.

JAMES R.

Cecil Papers   *Holograph*
134: 147

[1]Endorsed date is a minimal "xx[th]."

[2]Cecil became Treasurer of England on 4 May 1608. His "fat fellow Treasurer" was probably the Earl of Dunbar, Treasurer of Scotland.

[3]Jane Drummond, First Lady of the Queen's Bedchamber, was one of Anne's trusted confidantes. She married Lord Roxburghe in 1614.

[4]The English chancellor was Thomas Egerton, Lord Ellesmere; the Scottish chancellor was Alexander Seton, Earl of Dunfermline. James is probably referring to the latter.

[5]I.e., Balmerino's successor. The secretaryship went to Sir Alexander Hay, who was already joint secretary.

[6]The office of Chief Clerk of the Court of King's Bench had come to be known informally as "Roper's Office" since the Roper family had held it for over a century. G. E. Aylmer has pointed out (*The King's Servants,* London, 1961, p. 135) that its rewards, about £3500 annually, made it "probably the most valuable post in the entire administration below the top half-dozen or so great offices."

[7]Sir Robert Carr, already a prime favourite of the King.

[8]On 18 February of this year, Hay's father, Sir James Hay of Fingask, had been appointed Comptroller of Scotland.

Letter 144

To Robert Cecil, Earl of Salisbury

In high good humour now that the Council had concurred in finding Balmerino guilty, James writes to Cecil in his old jocular vein, heaping praises on the councillors who had brought in the verdict that he wanted.

[*October 1608*]

My little beagle,

Although I am not now to be long absent, yet can I not delay that piece of time before that your fellow councillors should be acquainted with my thankfulness for their honest endeavours in this trial so nearly concerning me. Ye shall therefore tell them that there could not have been a more proper and pleasing antidote ministered unto me against the just grief I had conceived of the slandering my reputation in a case of this nature than when I heard with what a full cry ye, all and every one of you, went against that man in the defence of my innocency, and how every man strove to show his zeal and affection above his fellows, if he could, for the clearing of his master; and how God hath now blest their pains and honest intentions they may likewise see.

For my part, I may justly say that the name given me of James included a prophetical mystery of my fortune, for as a Jacob[1] I wrestled with my arms upon the 5 of August for my life, and overcame;[2] upon the 5 of November I wrestled and overcame with my wit;[3] and now, in a case ten times dearer to me than my life (I mean my reputation), I have wrestled and overcome with my memory. I cannot also conceal your happiness to be the Treasurer in such a time when as the office of Secretary is so unlucky.[4] Two years ago, in France, a Secretary betrayed his master's trust, and by drowning escaped hanging. The last year the Principal Secretary of Spain was tried a knave, and made invisible. This year now the Scottish Secretary is like to speed little better. Well, ye are happy that are more than a Secretary,

309

but if the Secretary here prove a knave, what will come of the Treasurer? Show this part of my letter if ye dare now to your fellows. To end now I remit to the bearer to show you what course I would have taken now both anent the party and for my honour's clearing. Farewell.

JAMES R.

Cecil Papers   *Holograph*
134: 98

[1]The Latin for James is *Jacobus*.
[2]Alluding to the Gowrie Plot, 5 August 1600. James had grappled physically with the Master of Ruthven.
[3]Alluding to the Gunpowder Plot, 5 November 1605. James claimed credit for realizing that the veiled language in the Mounteagle letter referred to a gunpowder plot.
[4]Actually, Cecil had continued as Principal Secretary of State after he had become Treasurer on 4 May 1608.

Letter 145

To Robert Cecil, Earl of Salisbury

Partly in consequence of Cecil's enmity, Sir Walter Raleigh, on the weakest of evidence, was convicted of treason on 17 November 1603. King James commuted his death sentence to one of life imprisonment, and Raleigh began his long years in the Tower. One possession that Raleigh had been able to save from his ruin was his estate of Sherborne in Dorset. In January 1609, King James, taking advantage of a scribal error in a key document relating to Sherborne, deprived Raleigh of the manor and gave it to young Robert Carr, who was rapidly emerging as the King's

*prime favourite. The following letter shows some of the by-play
that preceded James's transfer of the property to Carr.*

My little beagle,
    Now that I have a little more respiration than I had at London, although God knows I am guiltless of the sin of idleness, I must not forget to tell you that, the more I think of your remembrance of Robert Carr for yon manor of Sherborne, the more cause have I to conclude that your mind ever watcheth to seek out all advantages for my honour and contentment; for as it is only your duty and affection to me that makes you careful for them that serve me, so must I confess that he is the only young man whom as I brought with me, and brought up of a child, that was now left unprovided for, I mean according to that rank whereunto I have promouid* him. Besides that the thing itself, when I have now considered it, will prove excellent fit for him, and withal that 3 [Northampton] before my parting requested me for him in it, who as I told you was ever before otherwise minded in that matter, whom unto I seemed not to take knowledge that any other had moved me in that matter before. Always as ye have been the beginner of it, so shall ye be the only director of his course therein, who as he is more thankful in his heart to you than he can express so will Dunbar answer to you for the honesty of his nature. Thus I hope all Scottishmen shall not prove unthankful.
    As for your last letter, I only dislike that sentence in it *sic soles beare servos*² because ye told me in what sense Essex used it to the old queen. And as for your request, I hope ye shall never have need to make it; for yon unhappy man³ is the first and last that ever I heard complain of you since ye had this office, and God is my judge I daily hear the contrary by Scottishmen. If any shall do, ye may be sure I shall never conceal them nor spare their punishment; only I wish an Englishman rather to commit that error than a Scottishman.
    I will now conclude this letter with a congratulation unto you of your renewed grace there, whereof ye may be glad in that

measure when ye have it, as ye need not break your heart upon the next causeless change. And so farewell, and help all ye can to make this long drunken bearer a girdler.

JAMES R.

Cecil Papers   *Holograph*
134: 149

[1] Endorsed "23 Novemb."
[2] "So thou art wont to bless thy servants."
[3] Raleigh.

Letter 146

To Robert Cecil, Earl of Salisbury

In 1609 King James published his Premonition to all Christian Monarchies, Free Princes, and States, *warning against the temporal encroachments of the popes. The work was received with marked hostility in Catholic countries. In this letter James comments on its reception in Venice and on the reaction of Sir Henry Wotton, his ambassador there.*

[*12? September 1609*][1]

My little beagle,

I have been this night surprised by the Venetian ambassador,[2] who, for all my hunting, hath not spared to hunt me out here. To be short, his chief errand was to tell me of a great fray in Venice betwixt my ambassador there and that state anent a prohibition that the Inquisition of Venice hath set forth against the publishing of my book there. He hath complained that my ambassador takes this so hotly as passeth on disorder. He hath bestowed an hour's vehement oration upon me for this purpose. My answer was that I could never dream that either the state of Venice would ever give me any just cause of offence or yet that ever my ambassador there would do them any evil office; but as to give him any particular answer, I told him I must first hear from my own ambassador, for he knew well enough that every prince or state must have a great trust in their own ministers.

I only write this unto you now that, in case this pantaloon come unto you, ye may give him the like deferring answer. Albeit, if I should tell you my conscience, if all this man's tale be true, my ambassador hath used this matter with a little more fervent zeal than temperate wisdom. I now hope to hear from you the assurance that your son is well. And so farewell.

JAMES R.

A. *Collins*, Letters and
Memorials of State
(London, 1746), II: 325

*Copy, apparently of a lost
holograph*

[1]Collins notes, "Without Date, but indorsed in the Hand-writing of *Robert* Cecil Earl of Salisbury His Majestye to me, 12 7ber, 1609."
[2]Marc Antonio Correr.

Letter 147

To a Committee of the House of Lords

King James's government was financed to a major extent out of the proceeds from a whole series of ancient and much abused royal rights. This "fiscal feudalism" was the source of many grievances. When Parliament convened in February 1610, Cecil, as Lord Treasurer, advanced a plan whereby the King, in return for having the sporadic votes of supply from Parliament supplemented by a fixed annual vote for his support, would surrender or limit a number of these traditional rights, including purveyance, wardship, and the terms of tenure from the Crown. In the following letter concerning the offering of the "Great Contract" to Parliament, James sets his price at £140,000. As the negotiating continued with the stakes being raised, James increased his demand to £300,000 per annum. When Parliament

*recessed in July, agreement had apparently been reached, with
the price for the surrendered rights set at £200,000.*

*During the recess both sides had second thoughts, and each
came back looking for a better bargain. The upshot was that in
mid-November the Commons decided to abandon the Great
Contract, and the King promptly accepted their decision.*

[*March? 1610*]

My Lords,

According to my promise unto you yesternight, I do by these
presents let you know that I crave seven score thousand pounds
by year in retribution of such things as I am to bargain for with
the parliament at this time. I mean this sum to be of clear addition to that which formerly I did spend by the natures of those
things that are now to be bargained for. And with this my demand ye are now to acquaint the committees of the lower house.

JAMES R.

Bodleian Library   *Holograph*
Clarendon State Papers,
Vol. 91, f. 1

Letter 148

To Robert Cecil, Earl of Salisbury

*A note about amendments to a proposed general pardon. In
view of the evidence identifying James as a homosexual, it
is worth noting that he explicitly excludes sodomy from the
pardon.*

[*July 1610*]

My little beagle,

I have thought by these few lines to remember you of three
things. First, I desire to have a roll sent me, or at least delivered

me when I come there, of all my servants' names that sat against me for the poor fifteen,[1] for I cannot know them by the scent. Secondly, I desire three exceptions to be cleared in the general pardon:[2] first, that sodomy be *nominatim* excepted in it that no more colour may be left to the judges to work upon their wits in that point; secondly, that in the point of piracy where the abettors of piracy are mentioned that it may be thus cleared, "and all abettors of piracy or pirates, whether before or after the committing of the crime," and this is likewise for avoiding of a witty distinction of the judges; and thirdly, that since I have in my late proclamation against deer-stealing[3] promised that all deer-stealers shall be excepted out of the next general pardon, that therefore for my honour's sake all deer-stealers since the publication of my said proclamation may be excepted. And my last desire is that, according to the order I gave before my parting, the Council would now in my absence meet and maturely deliberate upon my answer to the grievances, and that they may be ready to give me their advices therein against my return there, and specially that my Lords Canterbury and Chancellor be remembered to contribute their labour in this errand. To conclude now, I hope the bill of remanding[4] be not forgotten. And so farewell.

JAMES R.

Cecil Papers   *Holograph*
134: 146

[1] On 11 July 1610, by a vote of 145 to 130, Parliament limited the King to a single fifteenth (*Journals of the House of Commons 1547–1628*, p. 448).

[2] It was customary for the King to issue a general pardon at the end of a parliamentary session.

[3] The proclamation of 9 September 1609 (Crawford, *Tudor and Stuart Proclamations*, No. 1084).

[4] V. *Commons Journal*, p. 446.

Letter 149

To Robert Cecil, Earl of Salisbury

*Although the King explicitly denies the fact in this letter, af-
ter the failure of the Great Contract he became cooler towards
Cecil, the begetter of that project. During the eighteen months
of life which remained for Cecil, he would not enjoy the old
cordial friendship with the King.*

[6? December 1610][1]

My little beagle,

I wonder what should make you to conceit so the alteration
or diminishing of my favour towards you, as I find ye do by divers passages of your letter, for I am sure I never gave you any
such occasion, and all that know me do know that I never use to
change my affection from any man except the cause be printed
on his forehead. It is true that I have found that by the perturbations of your mind, ye have broken forth in more passionate and
strange discourses these two last sessions of Parliament than
ever ye were wont to do; wherein for pity of your great burden I
forbore to admonish you, being so far ashamed as, I confess, I
had rather write than speak it unto you, *nam lit[t]erae non
erubescunt.*[2] But ye may be sure if ever I had found any ground
of jealousy of your faith and honesty, I would never have concealed it from you.

As for this particular that troubleth you, it is true that the
first night of Lake's[3] coming to Royston, he did broadly and
roundly inform me that ye had told him that there was a worse
thing in head than anything whereof ye had advertised me,
which was that ye had intelligence that, if the Lower House had
met again, one had made a motion for a petition to be made
unto me that I would be pleased to send home the Scots if I
looked for any supply from them. But the next morning, when I
urged him to repeat the words again, he minced it in those
terms as ye now have it under his hand, which yet is directly

contrary to that which ye affirm in your letter. Judge ye then if I have not reason to hunt such tales, for that nation cannot be hated by any that loves me. And as I would be sorry that this people should be so unthankfully malicious as to bear grudge at them, so can I not but be more sensible that any, either of high or low degree in the Court, should falsely father upon the people their own partialities. And if whenever the tenor of bounty is touched, the Scots must ever be tacitly understood, I will be forced to disabuse the world in that point and publish the truth that the English have tasted as much and more of my liberality than the Scots have done. To conclude now ye need trouble you no more with this purpose since all is tried in it that can be. And all cometh to this: that Lake in his report hath made of a mote a mountain. The worst is that he spread this mistaking of his to three or four of the Lower House before his coming to Royston, as ye may perceive by his letter unto you.

Well, it is now time for you to cast your care upon the next best means how to help my state, since ye see there is no more trust to be laid upon this rotten reed of Egypt, for your greatest error hath been that ye ever expected to draw honey out of gall, being a little blinded with the self-love of your own counsel in holding together of this parliament[4] whereof all men were despaired (as I have oft told you) but yourself alone. But God send us some better comfort after this misery, and so farewell.

JAMES R.

Cecil Papers
134: 143

Holograph

[1]Endorsed "6 xbris 1610."

[2]"For letters do not blush." The King appears to be misquoting Cicero (*Ep. ad Fam.* 5.12.1): *Epistola enim non erubescit.*

[3]Sir Thomas Lake.

[4]The King dissolved Parliament on 31 December, obviously against Cecil's advice.

Letter 150

To the Council

Just a few weeks before his proclamation of 31 December 1610, dissolving Parliament, King James, furious both at its refusal to conclude the Great Contract upon the terms that he desired and at its expressions of anti-Scottish sentiments, relieved his feelings in the following letter.

7 December 1610

JAMES [R.]

Right trusty and right well-beloved cousins and counsellors, we greet you well.

We have seen and considered your long letter though written upon a short and naughty subject, to which we can give none other answer than this: that from you we received first the information of this lewd [base] fellow's speech, aggravated with these words, that he made his allusion of Joram[1] a king not to be desired *conceptis verbis.*[2] And now from you again we have received a new repetition of it, though qualified and moderated as much as may be.

As for our resolution what we will have to be done in this case, we will ourself tell you our pleasure at meeting. Only thus far we thought good in the meantime to signify unto you, that we would have wished that our councillors and servants in the Lower House had taken more heed to any speech that concerned our honour than to keep of the refusal of a subsidy; for such bold and villainous speeches ought ever to be crushed in the cradle. And as for the fear they had that that might have moved more bitterness in the House, not only against themselves but also to have made the House descend into some further complaints to our greater disliking, we must to that point say thus far: that we could not but have wondered greatly what more unjust complaints they could have found out than they have already, since we are sure no House save the House of Hell

318

could have found so many as they have already done. But for our part we should never have cared what they could have complained against us; for we hope never to live to see the day that we shall need to care what may be justly said against us, so that lies and counterfeit inventions be barred. Only we are sorry of our ill fortune in this country, that having lived so long as we did in the kingdom where we were born, we came out of it with an unstained reputation and without any grudge in the people's hearts but for wanting of us. Wherein we have misbehaved ourself here we know not, nor we can never yet learn. But sure we are we may say with Bellarmine in his book, that in all the Lower Houses these seven years past, especially these two last sessions, *ego pungor, ego carpor*.[3] Our fame and actions have been daily tossed like tennis balls amongst them, and all that spite and malice durst do to disgrace and infame* us hath been used. To be short, this Lower House by their behaviour have perilled and annoyed our health, wounded our reputation, emboldened all ill-natured people, encroached upon many of our privileges, and plagued our purse with their delays. It only resteth now that you labour all you can to do that you think best to the repairing of our estate. And as for the repairing and clearing of our honour, we will ourself think specially thereupon and at our return acquaint you with our thoughts therein.

Given under our signet, at Hinchingbrooke, the 7 December in the year of our reign of Great Britain the eighth.

Cecil Papers
147: 162

*Letter under
the sign manual*

[1]The King had been angered by an implied parallel between himself and Joram (or Jehoram), an evil king. See II Chronicles 21 and II Kings 8.
[2]"With express mention."
[3]"It is I who am stung, I who am harassed."

Letter 151

To William James, Bishop of Durham

The following letter concerns a sad little episode. When James came down to England, his nearest kin there was Lady Arabella (Arbella) Stuart, whom he proceeded to make one of his family. Although James was prepared to let his cousin marry any faithful subject of his whom she might choose, there was one exception. Young William Seymour, grandson of the Earl of Hertford, shared in the royal blood also, and James wanted no union of Arabella and Seymour from which might spring a future claimant to the throne. Some fatality drove Arabella and Seymour to love. King James, aware of the fact, briefly imprisoned them and forbade any match between them. On 21 June 1610, in defiance of the King, the two were secretly married, but their secret was soon discovered. They were arrested and imprisoned, but under such lenient terms that they had little difficulty in arranging meetings. To remove the possibility of the begetting of a child during some surreptitious encounter, James decided to transfer Arabella to the north of England while keeping Seymour in London. The following letter hands Arabella over to the custody of the Bishop of Durham.

The sequel was tragic. The lovers, before Arabella's transfer could be effected, contrived to escape. Setting forth in different ships, the two made for the Continent. Seymour was successful, but Arabella was intercepted by a ship of the Royal Navy and committed to the Tower, where she died in 1615.

13 March 1611

JAMES R.

Right reverend father in God, and trusty and well-beloved, we greet you well.

Whereas our cousin the Lady Arbella hath highly offended us in seeking to match herself without our knowledge (to whom she had the honour to be so near in blood) and in proceeding afterwards to a full conclusion of a marriage with the selfsame person whom, for many just causes, we had expressly forbidden to marry (after he had in our presence and before our Council forsworn all interest as concerning her either past or present, with solemn protestations upon his allegiance, in her own hearing, never to renew any such motion again); forasmuch as it is more necessary for us to make some such demonstration now of the just sense and feeling we have of so great an indignity offered unto us as may make others know, by her example, that no respect of personal affection can make us neglect those considerations wherein both the honour and order of our government is interested.

We have therefore thought good, out of our trust in your fidelity and discretion, to commit to your care and custody the person of our said cousin; requiring and authorizing you hereby to carry her down in your company to such houses of yours as unto you shall seem best and most convenient, there to remain in such sort as shall be set down to you by directions from our Council, or any six of them, to whom we have both declared our pleasure for the manner of her restraint and have also given in charge (upon conference with you) to take order for all things necessary either for her health or otherwise; this being the difference (as you see) between us and her, that whereas she hath abounded towards us in disobedience and ingratitude, we are, on the contrary, still apt to temper the severity of our justice with grace and favour towards her, as may well appear by the course we have taken to commit her only to your custody, in whose house she may be so well assured to receive all good usage and see more fruit and exercise of religion and virtue than in many other places. For all which this shall be your sufficient warrant.

From Royston this 13th of March 1610.

British Library
Harl. 7003, f. 94

Copy of a letter under
the sign manual

Letter 152

To the Emperor of Japan

Although it is highly unlikely that James did anything more than put his signature to this letter, presumably prepared by a secretary, it is printed here as an example of the range of the King's correspondence.

The original is so emblazoned and set forth in such superb calligraphy as to make it a work of art.

10 January 1612

To the High and Mighty, the Emperor of Japan etc.
Greeting.

Although we have already at sundry times by our especial letters made offer unto you of our amity and friendship, inasmuch as the same may tend to the settling and establishing of an intercourse of commerce and trade for the mutual good of each other's subjects; and that hitherto we have not received any answer from you, which we attribute to the remoteness and distance of the places of our dominions and not to any backwardness in you, of whose willing and favourable disposition to entertain all sorts of strangers that do resort unto your countries we have received many testimonies as well by our own subjects as by others; yet the love and desire which we have to the advancement of our subjects' good maketh us again to reiterate the same offices of friendship towards you, as an encouragement that thereby our people may receive of their better usage and entertainment of you. Wherein as we have that confidence that our people will so demean themselves with all due respects of courtesy and friendship towards yours, so we doubt not but they will be the better acceptable unto you and receive that just protection at your hands as may be expected of a prince and people that are sensible of their renown and glory and desirous to advance their profit and utility. And upon this ground we recommend these our subjects to your safeguard and protection, that both they may with security and safety settle their trade within your dominions and be defended from the malice and wrong of any others that should go about to interrupt or hinder them.

And so we pray Almighty God to preserve and prosper you, and to make you victorious over your enemies. From our royal palace at Westminster, this tenth of January in the ninth year of our reign of Great Britain, France and Ireland, etc.

JAMES R.

Letter 153

To Sir Thomas Edmondes

When the nine-year-old Louis XIII succeeded to the French throne, his mother, Marie de Medici, as Queen Regent took over the government of France. Marie, to quote S. R. Gardiner, "had learned from her childhood to look with awe and admiration upon the grandeur of the Spanish monarchy." Reversing the policy of Henri IV, she negotiated the double match that resulted in Louis XIII and the future Philip IV marrying sisters of each other. A mission to England by the Huguenot Duc de Bouillon failed to reassure an increasingly apprehensive James I, who that summer wrote the following letter to his ambassador in Paris, urging him to rally a party of French noblemen, chiefly Protestant, to counter the growing influence of Spain.

27 August 1612

JAMES R.

Trusty and well-beloved,

We have received your letter of the 18th of August, which came here with very great celerity, for we had it here at Grafton[1] upon the 24th of this month and before six in the morning.

One thing we observed—that we received your letter upon a St. Bartholomey Day in the morning, which made mention of a St. Bartholomey business and surely we have too great cause to fear that that bloody saint will once again bestir himself in France,[2] if it be not timously* prevented; therefore it is now high time that nothing be omitted by us which both our conscience and the security of our own state requires at our hands, and we assure ourselves that you will omit no pains nor industry to be a happy labourer for us in that place where now you reside. For although I ever suspect the inconstancy of the princes of the blood and holds their signing of the contract[3] at this time a very great sign of their weakness, yet you shall do well to work by all the means you can to hold them forward in this good resolution. They cannot but see themselves made fools and shadows of by the ministers of that state, especially in their alliance with Spain, wherein no less is intended than that the King of Spain shall be absolute governor of France during the king's minority, and so shall the wolf have the wether to keep. And it is the proper office of the princes of the blood in their king's minority to take care *ne quid detrimenti res publica capiat.*[4]

As for the Duke of Bouillon, you have done very well that have made him engage himself in this business by his letter unto us. And you may show him into our name that no man hath so much interest as he to be active in this errand, for he it was that was employed to us thereby to lay us on sleep, yea even to en-paunde* his particular credit with us that no Spanish nor popish plot did lurk under this alliance. And you may put him in mind, that at his first private audience (even in his fellow ambassador's[5] hearing) we told him merely that it was the fashion of princes when they deceive their neighbours first to deceive their own ambassadors. You shall also show him how happy a thing it is that the body of the religion there is reunited before the falling out of this business, and therefore you shall labour with all earnestness to hasten also, as soon as can be, a sound and perfect reconciliation betwixt the persons of Bouillon and Rohan.[6] You shall also use all the indirect means you can to win Monsieur de Guise[7] to be of this party and you may let it come to his ears that you hear that we wonder much that, notwith-standing of the message we sent him at Monsieur de Bouillon's departure by the Vicomte de Sardinie, we have never yet heard from him since.

To conclude then this purpose, we think ourself happy that have so faithful and well-experienced a minister there at this time when such a business is like to break out, and we expect from you all active and discreet diligence in furthering this in-tended purpose, but with that caution and wariness that you engage not or discover either us or yourself to any but to such as you may securely trust. The success that we expect is that, by the means of the princes of the blood, with the assistance of Bouil-lon, Desdiquiers, and all the body of the religion if need be, together with the House of Guise if they can be won, that perni-cious statesman[8] may be first removed, and then this alliance and popish cabal betwixt France and Spain to be quite broken off. A work which will be acceptable to God, will procure the preservation of his Church and the true peace, security, and qui-etness of that kingdom.

Thus praying God to bless it in your hands, we bid you fare-well from our Court at Woodstock this 27th of August 1612.

British Library   *Letter in the hand of Robert*
Stowe 173, f. 79   *Carr, Viscount Rochester,*
                                    under the sign manual

[1]Concerning Grafton, see Letter 121, n. 1. Apparently an arrangement had been made by which the Earl of Cumberland obtained from the Duke of Len-nox the lodge at Grafton.

[2]The reference is, of course, to the St. Bartholomew's Day Massacre of 24 August 1572.

[3]I.e., the contract for the double match.

[4]"Lest the state suffer any harm."

[5]Samuel Spifame, Sieur de Bisseaux, the "lieger" or ordinary ambassador, at the English court.

[6]The Duc de Rohan, like the Duc de Bouillon, was a principal leader of the Huguenots. Rohan had visited Scotland late in 1600, when he had been a god-father at the formal christening of Prince Charles.

[7]Charles de Lorraine, Duc de Guise, leader of the French Catholics.

[8]Concini, the favourite of Marie de Medici.

Letter 154

To the Dean and Chapter of Peterborough Cathedral

After the execution of Mary Queen of Scots, in Fotheringhay Castle in 1587, her remains were quietly buried in Peterborough Cathedral. After James became King of England, he decided that his mother should be buried in Westminster Abbey, with a tomb as elaborate as that of Queen Elizabeth. The following letter instructs the dean and chapter of Peterborough to cooperate in the translation of Mary's remains to Westminster, where they now lie.

28 September 1612

JAMES R.

Trusty and well-beloved, we greet you well.

For that we remember it appertains to the duty we owe to our dearest mother that like honour should be done to her body and like monument be extant of her as to others her and our progenitors have been used to be done, and ourselves have already performed to our dear sister, the late Queen Elizabeth, we commanded a memorial of her to be made in our Church of Westminster, the place where the kings and queens of this realm are usually interred. And for that we think it inconvenient that the monument and her body should be in several places, we have ordered that her said body, remaining now interred in that our Cathedral Church of Peterborough, shall be removed to Westminster to her said monument, and have committed the care and charge of the said translation of her body from Peterborough to Westminster to the reverend father in God, our right trusty and well-beloved servant, the Bishop of Coventry and Lichfield, bearer hereof, to whom we require you, or such as ye shall assign, to deliver the corpse of our said dearest mother, the same being taken up in as decent and respectful manner as is fitting. And for that there is a pall now upon the hearse over her grave, which will be requisite to be used to cover her said body in the removing thereof, which may perhaps be deemed as a fee that should belong to the church, we have appointed the said reverend father to pay you a reasonable redemption for the same, which being done by him we require you that he may have the pall to be used for the purpose aforesaid.

Given under our signet, at our honour of Hampton Court, the eight and twentieth day of September in the tenth year of our reign of England, France, and Ireland, and of Scotland the six and fortieth.

<table>
<tr><td>Peterborough Cathedral</td><td>Letter under the</td></tr>
<tr><td>Archives MS. 11a</td><td>sign manual</td></tr>
</table>

Letter 155

To Thomas Egerton, Lord Ellesmere

A somewhat mysterious note to the Lord Chancellor, Keeper of the Great Seal, relating to the King's prime favourite, Robert Carr (whom he created Viscount Rochester on 25 March 1611). The letter must antedate 3 November 1613, when Carr became Earl of Somerset.

[*November 1612?*]

My lord,

I pray you fail not to send me presently, by the bearer hereof, Rochester's two patents how soon ye have put the seal unto them; and if they be already past your hands, you may send for them again as if ye were in doubt of some word in them, and thereupon send them unto me. In the meantime ye shall keep this ticket for your warrant till ye speak with me.

JAMES R.

Close them up in a paper and send them sealed unto me, I mean the patents both of Winnike and Darcy's[1] lands, and let none alive know of this direction.

Huntington Library   *Holograph*
El. 1479

[1]For the struggle of Lord Darcy of Chiche late in 1612 to prevent loss of his lands because of recusancy, and a warrant enabling Carr to take possession of Darcy land in Essex, see *CSP Dom., 1611–18*, pp. 160, 162.

Letter 156

To Sir Thomas Edmondes

On 6 November 1612, Henry, Prince of Wales, died at the age of eighteen. At the time a marriage was being negotiated between him and Princess Christine, the six-year-old second sister of Louis XIII of France. With a singular lack of sensitivity, James almost at once suggested that, Prince Henry being dead, Princess Christine should marry Prince Charles instead. In the following letter to his ambassador to France, who had withheld the message, James concedes that his timing had been somewhat "blunt" but authorizes him to negotiate when the French once more bring up the subject of marriage to King James's heir.

14 December [1612]

JAMES R.

Trusty and well-beloved, we greet you well.

In regard of the multiplicity of our affairs at this time, we are enforced to make you the shorter answer at this time to your last letters, dated the 26 of November, wherein notwithstanding we will omit no essential points which shall be fit for you to labour in at this time.

And first, whereas you excuse yourself of not fulfilling the direction of our last despatch, in renewing again the motion of the match betwixt our dearest son Charles and Madame Christine, we do very well allow of your carriage therein, as fully agreeing with our meaning in our former direction, though peradventure some words therein might cause it to be mistaken. For it had been a very blunt thing in us that you, our minister, should so soon after such an irreparable loss received by us have begun to talk of marriage, the most contrary thing that could be to death and funerals. But because we doubted not that that motion would be renewed again unto you, if not by Villeroy[1] at least by the Duke of Bouillon,[2] our meaning was therefore that you should entertain the motion and that with so much the greater hope that that great and irremediable inequality of years is now taken away.

And next, as to that main question whether we should now stand upon these very terms we did before, that as soon as the eldest daughter of France should be sent to Spain the second should be sent hither, we do not indeed now see why we should so much stick upon this point, as things are now fallen out, as we did before. For since our son is not marriageable by the very civil law till he be full fourteen years of age, neither can the woman be so before she be twelve, we had rather trust to such other security as may be agreed on betwixt us for the confirmation of the marriage in the due time for supplying of that inequality betwixt our power of disposing of our children and the minority of that king than, by pressing the hastening thereof, to give them occasion to stand upon such strict points of religion which neither in conscience nor honour we can ever endure.

To conclude therefore this our letter, we wish you so to behave yourself in harkening to this their motion as they may neither apprehend that we are become greedy in urging it, nor yet upon the other side to give them any sense of distaste upon apprehension of our slowness and averseness in it; and especially to try both by Monsieur de Bouillon's means and all the other best ways you can how reasonable and moderate they will become in their conditions of religion if we may be moved to be content to spare her coming hither for two or three years; and in all the other conditions whereof you advertise in your former letters to go on with them in making it as clear as you can.

So we bid you farewell from our court at Royston this 14th of December.

British Library   Letter, under the sign
Stowe 173, f. 252   manual, in the hand of
                                         Robert Carr, Viscount
                                         Rochester

[1]Nicholas de Neufville, Seigneur de Villeroy, was appointed secretary of state for foreign affairs by Henri IV and continued in office by the Regent, Marie de Medici. Richelieu called him a "petrified colossus."

[2]Henri de la Tour d'Auvergne, Duc de Bouillon, leader of the Huguenots. He championed a close relationship between France and Britain but lacked political power.

Letter 157

To Sir Thomas Edmondes

When, late in 1614, a ship belonging to the governor of Dieppe was detained in England by the Court of Admiralty, the said governor began seizing the goods of the London merchants trading at Dieppe and declared he would continue to do so until his ship was released. When Louis XIII supported the governor, King James sent the following spirited letter.

7 November 1614

JAMES R.

Right trusty and well-beloved, we greet you well.

The French ambassador in a late audience hath imparted unto us a letter addressed to him from the king his master, written in a high and haughty style, wherein he willeth him to tell us that, if speedy justice be not done for the wrongs which the governor of Dieppe pretendeth to have received and other his subjects, he shall be forced to give letters of reprisal for their better satisfaction. Our purpose is come to that end we have given order that the ambassador shall deliver in writing a catalogue of his pretended grievances, which our Council hath charge presently to peruse and to return to him a particular answer.[1] Whereby it shall appear how justifiable our proceedings are in honour and justice and how scandalous their exclamations are against our ministers.

From our Secretary you shall receive a particular relation of the complaints of our subjects, which we require you to present to the hands of them who manage the affairs of that state and thereof to demand speedy reparation. And our pleasure is that in our name, you make the queen[2] know, and the principal officers of that crown, that no persuasions of what nature soever are so forcible to induce us to do justice as the love we bear to the execution of justice. And therefore we find it strange to hear such language from a king which but yesterday did issue out of his minority,[3] whenas during the time of the king his father, of happy memory, we never were acquainted with words of this strain. Our further pleasure is that in our name you demand speedy and severe justice for the insolency of the governor of Dieppe, who hath had the presumption to be his own executioner upon our subjects contrary to the laws of human reason. And therefore, if you find this his presumptuous boldness upon what colourable pretext soever to be excused and not (as it deserveth) exemplarily to be chastised, you may let the king and queen know our purpose is for the honour of the alliance between our crowns, not to suffer this audacious presumption to pass unpunished.

Given under our signet, at our palace of Westminster, the 7th of November 1614.

British Library
Stowe 175, f. 95

Letter under the sign
manual

[1]See *Acts of the Privy Council of England, 1613–1614* (London, HMSO, 1921), pp. 613–14.
[2]Marie de Medici, the Queen Mother.
[3]On 27 September of this year, when he turned thirteen.

Letter 158

To Arthur Chichester, Baron Chichester

During the Irish rebellions of the late sixteenth century the heart of resistance to the English had lain in Ulster. After the final subjugation of the rebels at the beginning of James's reign, much confiscated northern rebel land came into the possession of the Crown. James and his ministers decided to solve the Ulster problem by evicting the native Irish and replacing them with Scottish and English settlers, the forebears of the Protestant Ulstermen of today. In the following letter, the Lord Deputy of Ireland is informed of his home government's dissatisfaction with the way in which the "plantation" of Ulster is proceeding. A note in the King's own hand, added at the end, emphasizes the importance of the message.

25 March 1615

JAMES R.

Right trusty and well-beloved, we greet you well.

We received lately from you a relation of the present state of the plantation in Ulster, set down with so much clearness and order by the pen of Sir Josias Bodley,[1] according to the exactness of the survey hereof taken lately by himself by our commandment, that we do acknowledge his care and industry in performance of that service and do require you to give him thanks in our name for it. We have examined, viewed, and reviewed with our own eye every part hereof and find, greatly to our discontentment, the slow progression of that plantation, some few only of the British undertakers, servitors, and natives having as yet proceeded effectually to the accomplishing of such things in all points as are required of them by the Articles of the Plantation. The rest, and by much the greater part, having either done nothing at all, or so little or, by reason of the slightness hereof, to so little purpose that the work seems rather to us to be forgotten by them and to perish under their hand than any whit to be advanced by them: some having begun to build and not planted, others begun to plant and not build, and all of them in general retaining the Irish still upon their lands, the avoiding of which was with us the fundamental reason of that plantation. We have made a collection of their names as we find their endeavours or negligences noted in this service, which we will retain as a memorial with us, and they shall be sure to feel accordingly the effects of our favour and disfavour as there shall be occasion.

It is well known to you that if we had intended only our present profit, as it seems most of them overgreedily have done, we might have converted those large territories of our escheated lands to the great improvement of the revenues of our Crown here. But we chose rather, for the safety of that country and the civilizing of that people, to depart with the inheritance of them at extreme undervalues and to make a plantation of them. And since we were merely induced hereunto out of reason of state, we think we may without any breach of justice make bold with their rights who have neglected their duties in a service of so much importance unto us; and by the same law and reason of state resume their lands who have failed to perform according to our original intention the Articles of the Plantation, and to bestow them upon other men, more active and worthy of them than themselves. And though the time is long since expired within which they were bound to have finished to all purposes their plantation, so that we want not a just provocation to proceed presently with all [rigour?] against them, yet we are pleased in grace, and that they may be the more inexcusable if they fail in their duties hereafter, to assign them a further time, which shall be to the last day of August come twelvemonth, which will be in the year of our Lord one thousand six hundred and sixteen, which we are resolved shall be final and peremptory unto them; and at which time we are determined to seize into our hands the lands of any man whatsoever, without respect of persons, whether he be a British undertaker, servitor, or native, that shall be found idle in performing any of the Articles of the Plantation to which he was enjoined.

Our express pleasure therefore is that, as soon as this limited time of favour shall expire, that Sir Josias Bodley shall presently take a particular survey of the plantation as it then stands, and

of a kingdom which this plantation being well accomplished
will procure.

Bodleian Library   *Letter under the sign*
Carte Papers, Vol. 30, f. 88   *manual, with holograph*
                                                postscript

¹Sir Josias Bodley (1550?–1618), brother of Sir Thomas Bodley of library
fame, was an expert military engineer who became director of fortifications in
Ireland.

Letter 159

To Robert Carr, Earl of Somerset

After seven years of the rewards heaped upon a royal fa-
vourite, Carr became so spoilt and presumptuous that the King
could no longer endure his conduct. In this very long letter,
written "from the infinite grief of a deeply wounded heart,"
James reasons with Carr and urges him to seek his favours
through love, not intimidation.

[*Early 1615*]

First I take God, the searcher of all hearts, to record that in
all this time past of idle talk I never knew nor could out of any
observation of mine find any appearance of any such court faction as ye have apprehended; and so far was I ever from oversee-
ing or indirectly feeding of it (if I had apprehended it) as I protest to God I would have run upon it with my feet, as upon fire,
to have extinguished it if I could have seen any sparkle of it. As
for your informations, ye daily told me so many lies of myself
that were reported unto you as I confess I gave the less credit to
your reporters in other things since ye could not be an eyewit-
ness of it yourself. Next I take the same God to record that never
man of any degree did directly or indirectly let fall unto me
anything that might be interpreted for the lessening of your

credit with me—or that one man should not rule all, or that no man's dependence should be but upon the King, or any such like phrase, which if I had ever found, then would I have bestirred myself as became both so great a king and so infinitely loving a master. Thirdly, as God shall save me, I meant not in the letter I wrote unto you to be sparing in the least jot of uttering my affection towards you as far as yourself could require, my differing from your form in that point being only to follow my own style, which I thought the comeliest: so as, then, having delivered my mind as fully to May[1] as ye could have wished, having written this letter, having quite turned my countenance from "Grahme"[2] (the like whereof I never did to any man without a known offence), I having received your nephew in my bedchamber,[3] the fashion thereof being done in a needless bravery of the Queen, I did surely expect that this idle talk would wear out like the Pope's cursing, especially seeing my own heart knew it to be without a ground.

For I am far from thinking of any possibility of any man ever to come within many degrees of your trust with me, as I must ingenuously confess ye have deserved more trust and confidence of me than ever man did: in secrecy above all flesh, in feeling and unpartial respect, as well to my honour in every degree as to my profit. And all this without respect either to kin or ally or your nearest or dearest friend whatsomever, nay immovable in one hair that might concern me against the whole world. And in those points I confess I never saw any come towards your merit: I mean in the points of an inwardly trusty friend and servant.

But as a piece of ground cannot be so fertile but if, either by the own natural rankness or evil manuring thereof, it become also fertile of strong and noisome weeds, it then proves useless and altogether unprofitable: even so these before rehearsed worthy and rare parts and merits of yours have been of long time, but especially of late since this strange frenzy took you, so powdered and mixed with strange streams of unquietness, passion, fury, and insolent pride, and (which is worst of all) with a settled kind of induced obstinacy as it chokes and obscures all these excellent and good parts that God hath bestowed upon you. For although I confess the greatness of that trust and privacy betwixt us will very well allow unto you an infinitely great liberty and freedom of speech unto me, yea even to rebuke me more sharply and bitterly than ever my master[4] durst do, yet to invent a new art of railing upon me, nay to borrow the tongue of the devil, in comparison whereof all Peacham's book[5] is but a gentle admonition, that cannot come within the compass of any liberty of friendship.

And do not deceive yourself with that conceit that I allowed you that sort of licentious freedom till of late. For, as upon the one part it is true ye never passed all limits therein till of late, so, upon the other, I bore (God Almighty knows) with these passions of yours of old, dissembling my grief thereat only in hope that time and experience would reclaim and abate that heat which I thought to wear you out of by a long-suffering patience and many gentle admonitions. But the circumstances joined to the [same?] made them relish ten times worse to my taste than otherwise they would have done if they had only remained *in puris naturalibus*[6] of passions. For first, being uttered at unseasonable hours and so bereaving me of my rest, ye was so far from condemning your own indiscretion therein as, by the contrary, it seemed ye did it of purpose to grieve and vex me. Next, your fiery boutades[7] were coupled with a continual dogged sullen behaviour towards me; especially shortly after my fall,[8] though I gave you a far contrary proof after your fall[9] and in all the times of your other diseases. Thirdly, in all your dealing with me ye have many times uttered a kind of distrust of the honesty of my friendship towards you. And fourthly, which is worst of all and worse than any other thing that can be imagined, ye have in many of your mad fits done what you can [to?] persuade me that ye mean not so much to hold me by love hereafter as by awe, and that ye have me so far in your reverence as that I dare not offend you or resist your appetites. I leave out of this reckoning your long creeping back and withdrawing yourself from lying in my chamber, notwithstanding my many hundred times earnest soliciting you to the contrary, accounting that but as a point of unkindness. Now whether all your great parts and merits be not accompanied with a sour and distasteful sauce, yourself shall be judge.

337

Consider likewise of the difference of the things that ye lay to my charge and that I lay to yours. Here is not "he said" and "she said," no conjectural presumptions, nor things gathered out of outward appearance. I charge you with nothing but things directly acted or spoken to myself. I wish at [*sic*] God therefore, and I shall both pray for it and hope it, that ye may make good use of this little mirror of yourself which herein I present unto you. It is not like Sir Walter Raleigh's description of the kings that he hates, whomof he speaketh nothing but evil,[10] for this lays plainly and honestly before you both your best and worst parts.

To conclude then this discourse, proceeding from the infinite grief of a deeply wounded heart, I protest in the presence of the Almighty God that I have borne this grief within me to the uttermost of my ability; and as never grief since my birth seized so heavily upon me, so have I borne it as long as possibly I can. Neither can I bear it longer without committing an unpardonable sin against God in consuming myself wilfully, and not only myself but in perilling thereby not only the good estate of my own people but even the estate of religion through all Christendom, which almost wholly under God lies now upon my shoulders. Be not the occasion of the hastening of his death, through grief, who was not only your creator under God but hath many a time prayed for you, which I never did for no subject alive but for you. But the lightening my heart of this burden is not now the only cause that makes me press you indelayedly to ease my grief, for your own furious assaults of me at unseasonable hours hath now made it known to so many that ye have been in some cross discourse with me as there must be some exterior signs of the amendment of your behaviour towards me. These observations have been made and collected upon your long being with me at unseasonable hours, loud speaking on both parts, and their observation of my sadness after your parting, and want of rest.

What shall be the best remedy for this I will tell you by tongue. But for the easing of my inward and consuming grief, all I crave is that in all the words and actions of your life ye may ever make it appear to me that ye never think to hold grip of me but out of my mere love, and not one hair by fear. Consider that I am a freeman, if I were not a king. Remember that all your being, except your breathing and soul, is from me. I told you twice or thrice that ye might lead me by the heart and not by the nose. I cannot deal honestly if I deal not plainly with you. If ever I find that ye think to retain me by one sparkle of fear, all the violence of my love will in that instant be changed in[to] as violent a hatred. God is my judge my love hath been infinite towards you; and the only strength of my affection towards you hath made me bear with these things in you and bridle my passions to the uttermost of my ability. Let me be met then with your entire heart, but softened with humility. Let me never apprehend that ye disdain my person and undervalue my qualities (nor let it not appear that any part of your former affection is cooled towards me). A king may slack a part of his affection towards his servant upon the party's default and yet love him; but a servant cannot do so to his master but his master must hate him. Hold me thus by the heart, ye may build upon my favour as upon a rock that never shall fail you, that never shall weary to give new demonstrations of my affection towards you; nay, that shall never suffer any to rise in any degree of my favour except they may acknowledge and thank you as a furtherer of it and that I may be persuaded in my heart that they love and honour you for my sake, not that any living ever shall come to the twentie[th] degree of your favour. For although your good and heartily humble behaviour may wash quite out of my heart your bypast errors, yet shall I never pardon myself but shall carry that cross to the grave with me, for raising a man so high as might make one to presume to pierce my ears with such speeches.

To make an end then of this unpleasing discourse, think never to value yourself to me of any other merits so much as by love and heartily humble obedience. It hath ever been my common answer to any that would plead for favour to a Puritan minister by reason of his rare gifts, that I had rather have a conformable man with but ordinary parts than the rarest men in the world that will not be obedient, for that leaven of pride sours the whole loaf. What can or ever could thus trouble your mind? For the exterior to the world, what can any servants expect of their prince but countenance or reward? Do not all court graces and place come through your office as Chamberlain, and rewards through your father-in-law's that is Treasurer?[11] Do not ye two, as it were, hedge in all the court with a manner of necessity to depend upon you? And have ye not besides your own infinite privacy with me, together with the main offices you possess, your nephew in my bedchamber besides another far more active than he in court practices? And have ye not one of your newest kinsmen, that loves not to be idle, in my son's bed-chamber? With this should ye have silenced these news-bringers and makers of frays. For no other thing is left behind but my heart, which ye have neither cause to doubt nor, if it did need, could they counsel or advise you how to help.

Thus have I now set down unto you what I would say if I were to make my testament. It lies in your hand to make of me what you please, either the best master and truest friend or, if you force me once to call you ingrate, which the God of Heaven forbid, no so great earthly plague can light upon you. In a word, ye may procure me to delight to give daily more and more demonstrations of my favours towards you, if the fault be not in yourself.

Lambeth Palace Library   *Copy, apparently of*
MS. 930 (Gibson Papers,   *a lost holograph*
Vol. II), Item 90

[1]For testimony concerning Sir Humphrey May's influence with the King at this time, see *CSP Dom.*, *1611–18*, p. 327.

[2]Sir John Graham, Gentleman of the Privy Chamber, ally and adviser of George Villiers, who was already beginning to emerge as a new royal favourite.

[3]"... when yt was expected he [Villiers] shold be made of the bed-chamber, one Carre a bastard kinsman of the Lord Chamberlain is stept in and admitted to the place" (Chamberlain to Carleton, 24 November 1614, in *Letters*, I: 559).

[4]George Buchanan, his teacher in youth.

[5]Libellous papers found in the possession of the Rev. Edmond Peacham in December 1604.

[6]"In stark nudity."

[7]"Sudden outbursts" (*O.E.D.*).

[8]James had a bad fall in mid-November 1614, his horse coming down on top of him.

[9]Carr's emergence as a royal favourite dated from the King's visits to him after he had broken his leg when thrown by his horse in the royal presence in 1607.

[10]Raleigh's demonstration, in the opening of his *History of the World*, of Divine Providence in the misfortunes of various erring English kings so angered James that he suppressed the book after its publication in 1614.

Carr became Lord Chamberlain on 10 July 1614, the same day that the Earl of Suffolk became Lord Treasurer.

Letter 160

To Robert Carr, Earl of Somerset

A growing acerbity marks this letter, but James still professes his readiness to re-establish the old intimacy if Carr will show love and respect.

[*June? 1615*]

I have been needlessly troubled this day with your desperate letters. Ye may take the right way if ye list and neither grieve me nor yourself. No man nor woman's credit is able to cross you at my hands if ye pay me a part of that ye owe me. But how ye can give over that inward affection and yet be a dutiful servant, I cannot understand that distinction. Heaven and earth shall bear me witness that, if ye do but the half of your duty unto me, ye may be with me in the old manner only by expressing that love to my person and respect to your master that God and man craves of you, with a hearty and feeling penitence of your by-past errors.

As for the bishop,[1] if either his health may not permit him or that he is otherwise resolved not to go home, let him stay in God's name; albeit that I could rather wish that he were gone. If the Treasurer[2] have business to be with me on Sunday, he shall be very welcome; but that the bishop should also come it were extremely absurd. For as for his speaking with me, it will have a far better grace to be at London, whatever my resolution be; and in the meantime the Treasurer and ye shall be acquainted with my mind. But in this interim of your perturbations ye must not forget to talk at length the morrow with Argyll[3] anent the Isles business,[4] for he had need to be quickened and hastened for his journey to Scotland.

341

God move your heart to take the right course, for the fault shall only be in yourself; and so farewell. I can never believe that you meant in earnest the bishop's coming to Theobalds, for whether I were to grant, or deny, or delay his suit, his coming there could never but brand him with a disgrace.

JAMES R.

Lambeth Palace Library   *Copy, apparently*
MS. 930 (Gibson Papers,   *of a lost holograph*
Vol. II), Item 92

[1]Presumably Thomas Bilson, Bishop of Winchester, who was seeking to become Lord Privy Seal. He had close ties with Somerset and the latter's allies the Howards. His death in 1616 may be foreshadowed by the reference to ill health.
[2]Thomas Howard, Earl of Suffolk.
[3]Archibald Campbell, Earl of Argyll.
[4]For the rebellion in the Isles and Argyll's part in putting it down, see D. Gregory, *The History of the Western Highlands and Isles of Scotland from A. D. 1493 to A. D. 1625* (London, 1881), pp. 349–90.

Letter 161

To Robert Carr, Earl of Somerset

The greatest scandal in the English court during the reign of King James led to the downfall of Somerset. For long the favourite's favourite had been Sir Thomas Overbury, but the two had had a falling out when Overbury strongly opposed his patron's proposed marriage to Lady Frances Howard, daughter of the Earl of Suffolk. To get Overbury out of the way, the Howards secured his committal to the Tower in April 1613, ostensibly because he had refused to go abroad as an ambassador. On 15 September while still a prisoner, Overbury died. On 26 December Lady Frances was married to Carr, who had been newly promoted to the dignity of Earl of Somerset.

In the summer of 1615 a young Englishman confessed to the English ambassador at Brussels that he had been one of a group set to work by Lady Frances to procure Overbury's death through poisoning, a venture which, after much bungling and misadventure, had proved successful. King James was profoundly shocked when he learned that Overbury's death had almost certainly been murder. His own honour was directly involved since Overbury as a prisoner in the Tower had, in the parlance of the law, passed out of his own protection into that of the King. Accordingly, in October 1615 James appointed Lord Chancellor Ellesmere, the Duke of Lennox, and Lord Zouche as a commission to investigate the charges. In an attempt to protect his wife and possibly himself, Somerset sought to have the investigation called off. James's response is set forth in the following letter.

[October 1615]

I need not to answer your letter since Lennox[1] hath long before this time told you my resolution in that point whereupon you have bestowed so much scribbling and railing covertly against me and avowedly against the Chancellor.[2] Yet can I not abstain, partly for satisfaction of my own heart and partly for satisfying you and your ally with reason (if reasons can satisfy you), to send you these few observations upon your letter.

In a business of this nature I have nothing to look unto but first my conscience before God, and next my reputation in the eyes of the whole world. If I can find one man stricter than another in point of examination, I am bound in conscience to employ him in it; and when in my conscience I have set down a course, to change it at the instance of the party, without any other reason but because they will have it, it were little for my honour that I was too faint in not resisting the superb judges' wilfulness [sic]. I confess I ever was and will be faint in resisting to the trial of murder, and as bold and earnest in prosecuting the trial thereof. And as my proceedings from the beginning of this business have been only governed by the rule of my conscience, as the Searcher of all hearts knows, so must I to my great regret confess and avow that, from the beginning of this business, both your father-in-law[3] and ye have ever and at all times behaved yourselves quite contrary to the form that men that wish the trial of the verity ever did in such a case.

And how far it is now out of time, after that the Chancellor hath served me more than thirteen years with all honour and faithfulness, having ever been a regalist, to rake up from the bottomless pit the tragedy of my poor mother, I appeal to your own judgement. Then why should I be thus needlessly vexed? This warrant stretches only to examination, wherein no innocent persons can get wrong; and since the Chancellor sees himself so suspected, is it to be thought that he dare utter any partiality? And if ye will need suspect the worst, which is neither likely nor possible, were it not a more handsome way for my reputation that he might be privately advised to be silent when he were there except in yeas or noes; or else, in regard of his age and infirmities and his many businesses in the term time, to make his appearance but very seldom and so forbear to give any opinion, as not acquainted with the course of the business? And as for the external show of my election of him in disfavour of you: first, I am sorry that the world should see you except against so grave a man; and next, the more severe choice I make of persons for examination the more it is in your favour, if honour and trial of innocence be your end.

Now, as to your motion in putting all the judges in this warrant, if ye mean for trial in law, I never meant it otherwise; but if ye mean for examination, it is more than absurd. And whereas ye allege that great Councillors were never employed in the examination of a thing of this nature, I say the quite contrary is true whenas the circumstances or articles of the trial may reflect upon any great personages; in which case the judges dare never presume to meddle without better assistance. To conclude then, I never had the occasion to show the uprightness and sincerity that is required in a supreme judge as I have in this. If the delation prove false, God so deal with my soul as no man among you shall so much rejoice at it as I, nor never shall spare, I vow to God, one grain of rigour that can be stretched against the conspirators. If otherwise (as God forbid), none of you shall more heartily sorrow for it; and never king used that clemency as I

344

will do in such a case. But that I should suffer a murder (if it be so) to be suppressed and plastered over to the destruction both of my soul and reputation, I am no Christian. I never mean wittingly and willingly to bear any man's sins but my own; and if, for serving my conscience in setting down a fair course of trial, I shall lose the hands of that family,[4] I will never care to lose the hearts of any for justice sake.

Fail not to show this letter to your father-in-law, and that both of you read it twice over at least; and God so favour me as I have no respect in this turn but to please him in whose throne I sit. And so farewell, praying the author of all verity to make the clear verity be plainly manifested in this case.

JAMES R.

Lambeth Palace Library
MS. 930 (Gibson Papers,
Vol. II), Item 91

Copy, apparently of
a lost holograph

[1]Ludovic Stuart, Duke of Lennox (1574–1624), kinsman of the King.
[2]Thomas Egerton, Lord Ellesmere.
[3]The Earl of Suffolk.
[4]The Howards.

Letter 162

To the Commissioners and Judges Concerned with the Overbury Case

The first person to stand trial for complicity in the poisoning of Sir Thomas Overbury was Richard Weston, the underkeeper who had had him in his custody in the Tower. Weston was arraigned on 19 October 1615. However, as he refused to plead either guilty or not guilty, the trial could not proceed. While plans were made to subject Weston to peine forte et dure, *the torture which would end in either a plea or his death, Weston was persuaded to enter his plea without undergoing this ordeal. Accordingly, Weston was arraigned a second time on 23 October. It was during the interval between these two arraignments that James, keeping closely in touch with the proceedings, sent the following letter.*

[*Late October 1615*]

JAMES R.
Right trusty and right well-beloved counsellors, and
trusty and well-beloved, we greet you well.

In this weighty and important cause which now is in question, the discovery of the truth whereof so much concerneth the glory of God and the honour of our service, we cannot satisfy our own conscience if any course should be left unattempted whereby the foulness of so heinous a fact may be laid open to the view of the world; both that thereby the innocent may be cleared and the nocent punished, the name of our justice (against the virulent malice of slanderous tongues) both be blessed in this present age and hereafter be recommended to eternal posterity.

We therefore have thought it convenient to require you that, before Weston shall come to his second arraignment, you examine the Countess of Somerset,[1] and after confront him apart with her and Mistress Turner[2] and, if you shall find it convenient, with the Earl himself. And because a servant of ours hath this day caused this enclosed paper to be exhibited unto us, whereby he would insinuate that Weston at his arraignment did recant all his former examinations (whereunto we give no credit, the contrary being testified by the letters of you, our judges), we do require you, the commissioners, again to take the acknowledgement of Weston's former examinations from his own mouth. And you, the judges, with all conveniency to send us your opinion of this paper, that accordingly we may resolve to dispose of him who hath caused it to be put into our hand. If, for shortness of time, all these particulars cannot be performed before Monday at two of the clock in the afternoon, then are the judges to prorogue their session until such time as they shall find requisite for the performance of the service.

346

Our pleasure is that you forbear not to control the Lieutenant of the Tower[3] and Sir Thomas Monson[4] and to proceed against them as justice shall require though they be our servants, as more particularly you shall understand from our cousin the Duke of Lennox, who hath received his charge from our own mouth and with whom we have clearly confirmed of all these points.

We must earnestly require you, as you tender both our conscience and honour, to use all means for the full clearing and manifestation of the verity in this business even though you be not bound by law to do it, so that you do nothing against the law, wherein we must trust to your knowledge and integrities.

Public Record Office
SP 14/82/81

Letter and postscript are copies;
postscript is headed "Added
wth his Ma^ty owne hand."

[1]Lady Frances Howard, daughter of the Earl of Suffolk, had married Robert Carr, Earl of Somerset, on 26 December 1613, after the annulment of her marriage to the second Earl of Essex. She instigated the poisoning of Sir Thomas Overbury.

[2]Anne Turner, a pander to the vices of the court, procured for the Countess of Somerset the services of the poisoner Richard Weston.

[3]Sir Gervase Helwys, a reluctant accessory to the poisoning.

[4]Monson secured the appointment of Weston as underkeeper in charge of Overbury in the Tower.

Letter 163

To Sir Ralph Winwood

Amid his hunting and his concern over the Overbury case, King James had time to refer to Winwood, a Secretary of State, a minor case of lèse-majesté, but one which had obviously very much annoyed him.

JAMES R.

Trusty and well-beloved counsellor, we greet you well.

Being informed by our servant John Hall, one of our cupbearers, of certain unreverent and undutiful speeches of us used by Sir John Leeds and his wife on Wednesday night last past at supper, one Hawlie of our privy chamber being in company, we willed the said Hall to set down the words under his hand, which he having done, and we having willed Hawlie to declare his knowledge in the matter, he would not seem to remember any such thing. We have, therefore, thought good to send unto you herewith the said words under Hall his hand, willing you to join unto yourself the Duke of Lennox, the Earl of Pembroke, the Viscount Fenton, and Sir Thomas Lake (or so many of them as shall be there in town, in which behalf this present shall be your sufficient commission) and calling before you all the parties aforenamed, and having taken Hall his deposition, that ye bring Hawlie to a better memory than as yet we can bring him unto. What censure ye shall think fit to lay on Sir John Leeds and his wife we leave to your own judgements, and you to God. Newmarket, the 12th of November.

Above all, forget not to make Leeds tell which of my bedchamber it was that told him of my unwieldiness.

Montagu (Boughton)MSS.   *Letter under the sign manual,*
Winwood Papers, Vol. 10   *with holograph postscript*
(unpaginated)

Letter 164

To Sir Ralph Winwood

In view of James's alleged earlier unfortunate experience with Secretary Balmerino, it is curious to find him sending Secretary Winwood signed blank forms.

[1615?]

I have signed the five French letters ye sent me, but I miss letters for three, the Duc of Guise, the Prince Jenville,[1] and the Conte de Candale,[2] and because this despatch is to be sent away with all speed, I have for hastening it signed three blanks which ye are to fill for them three, and so to send away the packet. Fail not also to write to my ambassador to excuse to all these princes, upon the multitude of my affairs, that I write not to them at this time with my own hand. And so farewell.

JAMES R.

Montagu (Boughton) MSS.   *Holograph*
Original Letters, Vol. I, 1483–1688
(unpaginated)

[1]Prince de Joinville, who had been sumptuously entertained when he visited England in 1607.
[2]Comte de Candalle.

Letter 165

To Sir George More

The spring of 1616 saw both the Earl and Countess of Somerset awaiting trial for the murder of Sir Thomas Overbury.

Somerset, whose role seems to have been only that of an accessory after the fact, had apparently counted on the King's former favour to save him from being charged with murder. Awaking to his true situation, Somerset sought to blackmail James into dropping the charges against him. James undoubtedly had regarded Overbury with jealous dislike and may well have made highly unwise and prejudicial statements about him that Somerset could have used to tarnish the King's own reputation. James, to his credit, remained firm that Somerset must either confess or be tried. Endeavouring to avoid a trial by persuading Somerset to confess and throw himself upon the royal mercy, James wrote the following four highly confidential letters to Sir George More, whom he had recently appointed Lieutenant of the Tower of London, where Somerset was incarcerated.

Somerset may have tried at the last to evade trial by feigning sickness or insanity, but on 25 May he came into court, entered a plea of not guilty, and was found guilty by a unanimous verdict of the assembled lords. Sentences of death were passed on him and his wife, but these were commuted. After some six years of imprisonment under very lenient conditions in the Tower, the two were released and led a retired life in the country. On 7 October 1624, James granted a pardon to Somerset; his wife had received hers years earlier.

[May 1616]

Good Sir George,

As the only confidence I had in your honesty made me, without the knowledge of any, put you in that place of trust which ye now possess,[1] so must I now use your trust and secreatie* in a thing greatly concerning my honour and service.

Ye know Somerset's day of trial is at hand,[2] and ye know also what fair means I have used to move him, by confessing the truth, to honour God and me and leave some place for my mercy to work upon. I have now at last sent the bearer hereof, an honest gentleman and who once followed him, with such directions unto him as, if there be a spark of grace left in him, I hope they shall work a good effect. My only desire is that ye

350

would make his convoy unto him in such secreatie none living may know of it and that, after his speaking with him in private, he may be returned back again as secretly.

So, reposing myself upon your faithful and secret handling of this business, I bid you heartily farewell.

JAMES R.

Folger Shakespeare Library   *Holograph*
MS. L.b. 652

[1] The lieutenancy of the Tower of London.
[2] He was arraigned 25 May 1616.

Letter 166

To Sir George More

The second secret letter concerning Somerset.

[*13? May 1616*]

Good Sir George,

Although I fear that the last message I sent to your unfortunate prisoner shall not take the effect that I wish it should, yet I cannot leave off to use all means possible to move him to do that which is both most honourable for me and his own best. Ye shall, therefore, give him assurance in my name that if he will yet before his trial confess clearly unto the commissioners his guiltiness of this fact, I will not only perform what I promised by my last messenger, both towards him and his wife, but I will enlarge it, according to the phrase of the civil law, *quod gratiae sunt ampliandae.*[1] I mean not that he shall confess if he be innocent, but ye know how evil likely that is. And of yourself ye may dispute with him what should mean his confidence now to endure a trial, whenas he remembers that this last winter he confessed to the Chief Justice[2] that his cause was so evil likely as he knew no jury could [ac]quit him. Assure him that I protest, upon my honour, my end in this is for his and his wife's good.

Ye will do well likewise of yourself to cast out unto him that ye fear his wife shall plead weakly for his innocency and that ye find the commissioners have, ye know not how, some secret assurance that in the end she will confess of him. But this must only be as from yourself, and therefore ye must not let him know that I have written unto you but only that I sent you private word to deliver him this message.

Let none living know of this and, if it take good effect, move him to send in haste for the commissioners to give them satisfaction. But if he remain obstinate, I desire not that ye should trouble me with an answer, for it is to no end and no news is better than evil news.

And so farewell, and God bless your labours.

JAMES R.

Folger Shakespeare Library   *Holograph*
MS. L.b. 653

[1]"That favours are to be stated in detail."
[2]Sir Edward Coke.

Letter 167

To Sir George More

The third secret letter concerning Somerset.

[*May 1616*]

Good Sir George,

I am extremely sorry that your unfortunate prisoner turns all the great care I have of him not only against himself but against me also as far as he can. I cannot blame you that ye cannot conjecture what this may be, for God knows it is only a trick of his idle brain, hoping thereby to shift his trial. But it is easy to be seen that he would threaten me with laying an aspersion upon me of being, in some sort, accessory to his crime.

I can do no more (since God so abstracts his grace from him) than repeat the substance of that letter which the Lord Hay[1] sent you yesternight, which is this: if he would write or send me any message concerning this poisoning, it needs not be private; if it be of any other business, that which I cannot now with honour receive privately, I may do it after his trial and serve the turn as well for, except either his trial or confession precede, I cannot hear a private message from him without laying an aspersion upon myself of being an accessory to his crime. And I pray you to urge him, by reason, that I refuse him no favour which I can grant him without taking upon me the suspicion of being guilty of that crime whereof he is accused. And so farewell.

JAMES R.

Folger Shakespeare Library   *Holograph*
MS. L.b. 654

[1]See Letters 142, n. 2, and 168.

Letter 168

To Sir George More

The fourth secret letter concerning Somerset.

[*May 1616*]

Good Sir George,

For answer to your strange news, I am first to tell you that I expect the Lord Hay[1] and Sir Robert Carr[2] have been with you before this time, which if they have not yet been, do ye send for them in haste that they may first hear him before ye say anything unto him. And when that is done, if he shall still refuse to go, ye must do your office, except he be either apparently sick or distracted of his wits, in any of which cases ye may acquaint the Chancellor[3] with it, that he may adjourn the day till Monday next, between and which time if his sickness or madness be counterfeited it will manifestly appear. In the meantime I doubt not but ye have acquainted the Chancellor with this strange fit of his. And if, upon these occasions, ye bring him a little later than the hour appointed, the Chancellor may in the meantime protract the time the best he may, whom I pray you to acquaint likewise with this my answer as well as with the accident.

If he have said anything of moment to the Lord Hay I expect to hear of it with all speed; if otherwise, let me not be troubled with it till the trial be past. Farewell.

JAMES R.

Folger Shakespeare Library   *Holograph*
MS. L.b. 655

[1] See Letters 142, n. 2, and 167.
[2] Gentleman of the Bedchamber to Prince Charles. Evidence of the King's favour towards him is provided by a pension of £300 granted him within a year of this letter (*CSP Dom., 1611–18*, p. 444).
[3] Lord Ellesmere.

Letter 169

To John Erskine, Earl of Mar

In 1616, likening himself to a salmon with its compulsion to return to the waters where it was spawned, King James announced that he was resolved to revisit the land of his birth for the first time since he had left it for England. James was concerned that the troops of English courtiers who would travel north with him should form a good opinion of his native land. Accordingly, artificers were set to work repairing the King's palaces and houses in Scotland, and the Estates were convened to

354

determine their contribution towards the great expenses that
would be incurred.

The following appears to be a form letter sent to all those
noblemen summoned to the Edinburgh convention.

31 December 1616

JAMES R.

Right trusty and right well-beloved cousin and
counsellor, we greet you well.

Our earnest desire, the wishes of our good subjects and the
necessary affairs of that our estate having invited us to honour
that our ancient kingdom with our royal presence this approaching summer, and knowing how far it doth import the
credit and honour of our said kingdom that all things necessary
for our contented reception and entertainment be timely provided and in readiness, and that our houses (which by reason of
our long absence are become ruinous and decayed) be repaired
and meueabled* in such decent and comely order as is requisite,
so as the strangers and others who are to accompany us (of
whom there will be great numbers of all ranks and qualities)
may neither perceive any mark of incivility nor appearances of
penury and want; we therefore, out of our royal regard to the
honour of our said kingdom, have not been sparing of our coffers but have very largely bestowed great sums of money (far
exceeding the revenues of that our kingdom) upon these preparations wherein, although our treasure there be exhausted and
our coffers far emptied yet, upon examination of particulars, we
find many things resting unprovided which the rents of that our
crown are not able to furnish.

The consideration whereof hath moved us to appoint a convention of the Estates of that our realm, to be at Edinburgh the
fifth of March next, to the intent that they may advise and resolve upon the best means whereby, with least hurt to our good
subjects, all defects may be supplied and the credit and honour
of that our realm preserved. And having written to divers of our
nobility to be present thereat, we likewise require you (knowing
your good affection to the honour of that our kingdom and

willing disposition to our service) to keep that meeting and to be in Edinburgh the fourth of the said month, that in the morrow ye may be ready prepared to meet with the rest. Which undoubtedly expecting, as you regard our obedience and service, we bid you farewell. Given at our palace of Whitehall, the last of December 1616.

Scottish Record Office   *Letter under the sign manual*
GD 124/10/118

Letter 170

To the Sultan of Turkey

At this period English merchants were suffering ruinous losses at the hands of Algerian pirates. Since the Sultan of Turkey held at least nominal sovereignty over Algeria, James sent the following letter to him in an attempt to improve the situation. Apparently the letter achieved nothing, for subsequently plans were made to send a joint Anglo-Dutch expedition against Algiers.

17 January 1617[1]

James, by the grace of the most high God, King of Great Britain, France, and Ireland, Defender of the Christian Faith, to the high and mighty emperor, Sultan Achomet Cham, chief lord and commander of the Musulman kingdom, and sole supreme monarch of the Eastern Empire, sendeth health and greeting.

The many and grievous complaints which our subjects trading to your town of Argiere[2] do daily make unto us of the continual depredations and spoils done by your men-of-war upon their persons, ships, and goods, contrary to our mutual amity and capitulations of commerce, have moved us to give our ambassador there resident with Your Majesty express charge to address himself unto you, to treat in our name with you or such as you shall appoint for that purpose, as well for the restoring and releasing of our subjects, their ships and goods, which have been there taken and retained, and namely the ship called the *Grace of London*, with her men and goods, as also of all other ships, prisoners, and goods of our subjects as have been taken at sea and brought unto your said town.

And we have likewise given unto our said ambassador a further charge to treat with you in like manner of some good order to be established for the reglement [regulation] of traffic and for the safety of the goods and persons of our subjects there for the time to come; in which treaty we hope that you will have regard to the many benefits that have accrued both unto that your town and to the rest of your dominions, from us our kingdoms and people in furnishing them with such commodities as are most necessary and behooveful for them; and also in sending home many of your people which have been held captives by other nations; and that in acknowledgement thereof you will make such a grateful return of courtesies as may encourage our subjects to continue their beneficial trade unto your dominions and confirm us in our amity with Your Majesty. And so, praying you to recommend this affair in such manner to your Viceroy of Argiere and others your officers and commanders there, as it may have speedy reformation, we wish you health and happiness.

Given at our palace of Westminster, the 17th day of January, anno Domini 1616, and of our reign of Great Britain, France, and Ireland the 14th.

JAMES R.

Bodleian Library   *Illuminated letter, signed*
MS. Eng. hist. b. 172, f. 57

[1]The regnal date at the close of this letter reveals that the Anno Domini date there is Old Style. The year has, accordingly, here been given as 1617 (New Style).
[2]Algiers.

Letter 171

Apprehensive that the controversy raging in Holland between the more extreme Calvinists and the Arminians might split that country, King James wrote the following letter. It achieved little or nothing. Soon there was armed confrontation between the moderates and the extreme Calvinists, with the latter prevailing since they had Prince Maurice and his regiments on their side. Johan van Oldenbarneveldt, the leader of the "Remonstrants", was executed in 1619 after a rigged trial.

TRANSLATED FROM THE FRENCH

20 March 1617

High and mighty sirs, our good friends and allies,

When we first realized the affliction of schisms and heresies which were slipping in among you, we were so touched by the zeal that we have toward the Church of God and by the particular affection that we bear toward the welfare of your state that immediately we reached out our hand to stop the course of this evil and, by our letters expressing our desire to aid you, we earnestly gave you to understand what was our feeling and apprehension in regard to this, beseeching and exhorting you to take careful thought against letting this gangrene go any further in your body, but rather to smother the seed before it came to multiply. And, after having learned that certain of your ministers are, out of indiscretion, devoting themselves to preaching the matter of predestination in their pulpits, we wrote to you further letters on this subject, protesting to you the scanty benefit that came of such preachings, which, instead of the solid edification that they were bound to minister to your people, served only to flatter and deceive their minds with the petty details of this argument, which is too high and obscure for the ordinary people. But, after being recently informed that, instead of the profit that we expected from our good offices and protests, error and evil have made a stronger impression among your people, and that there is even a desire to use our aforesaid letters to authorize it, taking them in a sense and deduction quite contrary to our intention, we have considered ourselves obliged, as much for the glory of God as for the expression and relief of our own conscience, to represent afresh to you strongly by our letters the imminent evil and danger by which your state is threatened by these unhappy divisions, which we see ready to hatch forth in schism and faction formed among you, which are plagues all the more dangerous and pernicious to your state in that its establishment is only in its infancy[1] and that the basis of survival consists only in your union, first toward God and then toward faith among yourselves.

And this, sirs, is why we again pray and conjure you afresh, in the name of God, who until now has fortunately sustained you, to suppress these errors and partialities, which the Devil, by the artifice of your enemies, has introduced among you and already so authorized that the ruin of your state is thereby apparent and close at hand if you do not promptly apply remedies by cleaving entirely to, and holding firm, the true and ancient doctrine which you have always professed and which is approved and received by the universal consent of all the Reformed Churches, and the common profession of which has been as the first and principal foundation for establishing, as also the only solid cement that has maintained, the close friendship which has reigned for so long a time between our crown and your provinces.

If, by this time, the evil is so strong and so rooted among your people that it cannot be so promptly and readily eradicated, we beseech you at least to arrest the danger of it and by your authority to keep matters in peace, without suffering those of the true and ancient profession to be made unquiet, until you can with a common mind convoke a national synod to judge and put an end to these unhappy differences, which is in our judgement the best counsel and resolution that you can take in this matter, as being the ordinary remedy and most legitimate and efficacious means to which at all times recourse has been had in Christendom against the occurrence of such accidents. And we doubt not that, in this matter bringing about the affection and disposition required among you, God will bless its success, to the advancement of his glory and to the maintenance and strengthening of your state.

And so we pray God, high and mighty sirs, our good friends and allies, to keep you in his holy care.

From Hinchingbrooke, the 20th day of March, 1617.[2]

French text printed in
Letters from and to Sir Dudley Carleton, Knt.
during His Embassy in Holland *(London, 1757),*
pp. 122–23

[1]The Dutch confederation came into being in 1579.
[2]In diplomatic correspondence to the Continent, years were numbered according to New Style.

Letter 172

To the Council

One of the best of King James's letters, this pithy epistle was sent to "my Lords" to express his impatience at their failure to curtail his expenses according to the directive that he had given them.

[*21? November 1617*][1]

My Lords,

No worldly thing is so precious as time. You know what task I gave you to work upon during my absence and what time was limited to you for performance thereof. This same Chancellor of Scotland[2] was wont to tell me 24 years ago that my house could not be kept upon epigrams. Long discourses and fair tales will never repair my estate. *Omnis virtus in actione consistit.*[3] Remember that I told you that the shoe must be made for the foot, and let that be the square of all your proceedings in this business. Abate superfluities in all things, and multitudes of unnecessary officers wherever they be placed. But for the household, wardrobe and pensions, cut and carve as many as may agree with the possibility of my means. Exceed not your own rule of £50,000 for the household. If you can make it less, I will account it for good service. And that you may see I will not spare mine own person, I have sent with this bearer a note of the superfluous charges concerning my mouth, having had the opportunity of this messenger in an errand so nearly concerning his place. In this I expect no answer in word or writing, but only the real performance for a beginning to relieve me out of my miseries. For now the ball is at your feet, and the world shall bear me witness that I have put you fairly to it. And so, praying God to bless your labours, I bid you heartily farewell.

Your own,
JAMES R.

Folger Shakespeare Library   *Copy, apparently of*
MS. V.b. 132, p. 100   *a lost holograph*

[1]The date is supplied from a copy of this letter in the British Library (Add. 5503, ff. 96–97). This is headed "A coppie of a letter from his Matie to the Lords redd at the board the 21st of November." John Chamberlain, writing on 16 March 1618 (*Letters,* II: 149) mentioned "this late commission of reforming the household."

[2]Alexander Seton, Earl of Dunfermline.

[3]"All virtue lies in action" (cf. Cicero *De officiis* 1.19: *Virtutis laus omnis in actione consistit*).

Letter 173

To the Council

This stinging letter seems to have been provoked by the failure of Letter 172 to galvanize the Council into recommending substantial economies in the King's household and other expenses.

[*December 1617?*]

My Lords,

I received from you yesternight the bluntest letter that I think ever king received from his council. Ye write that the Green Cloth[1] will do nothing, and ye offer no advice. Why are ye councillors, if ye offer no counsel? An ordinary messenger might have brought me such an answer: "I have delivered him Your Majesty's pleasure, and he says he cannot do it." It is my pleasure that my charges be equalled with my revenue, and it is just and necessary so to be. For this a project must be made, and one of the main branches thereof is my house. This project is but to be offered unto you, and how it may be best laid then to agree with my honour and contentment ye are to advise upon, and then have my consent. If this cannot be performed without diminishing the tables, diminished they must be. And if that cannot serve, two or three must be thrust into one. If the Green Cloth will not make a project for this, some other must do it. If you cannot find them out, I must. Only remember two things: that time must no more be lost, and that there are twenty other ways of abatement besides the house, if they be well looked into. And so farewell.

JAMES R.

Folger Shakespeare Library
MS. V.b. 132, pp. 100–101

Copy, apparently of
a lost holograph

[1]The Board of Green Cloth attended to the housekeeping expenses of the King. It consisted of four officers of the Household: the Master, the Treasurer, the Cofferer, and the Comptroller.

Letter 174

To John Spottiswoode, Archbishop of St. Andrews

If the Kirk in Scotland had hoped to be relieved of the personal surveillance of James once he moved south to England, letters such as the following made it plain that this was not to be the case. The pungency of the phrasing suggests strongly that this letter was taken down from the King's dictation.

11 December 1617

After we had commanded the despatch of our other letter, we received an extract concluded (we know not how) in your Assembly and subscribed by the clerk thereof; the one concerning private communion, and the other touching the form to be used at the receiving of the holy sacrament; both so hedged, and conceived in so ridiculous a manner, as besides that, of the whole articles proponed, these two were the least necessary to have been urged and hastened, the scornful condition and form of their grant makes us justly wish that they had been refused with the rest. For in the first place, concerning the communion allowed to sick persons, besides the number required to receive with such patients and a necessity tying them upon oath to declare that they truly think not to recover but to die of that disease, they are yet farther hedged in with a necessity to receive the sacrament (in case aforesaid to be ministered unto them) in a convenient room; which what it importeth we cannot guess, seeing no room can be so convenient for a sick man (sworn to die) as his bed, and that it were injurious and inhumane from thence in any case to transport him, were the room never so neat and handsome to which they should carry him.

And as to that other Act, ordaining the minister himself to give the elements in the celebration out of his own hand to every one of the communicants, and that he may perform this the more commodiously, by the advice of the magistrates and honest men of his session, to prepare a table at which the same may be conveniently ministered—truly in this we must say that the minister's ease and commodious sitting on his tail hath been more looked to than that kneeling which, for reverence, we directly required to be enjoined to the receivers of so divine a sacrament; neither can we conceive what should be meant by that table, unless they mean to make a round table (as did the Jews) to sit and receive it. In conclusion, seeing either we and this Church here must be held idolatrous in this point of kneeling, or they reputed rebellious knaves in refusing the same, and that the two foresaid acts are conceived so scornfully, and so far from our meaning, it is our pleasure that the same be altogether suppressed and that no effect follow thereupon. So we bid you farewell.

Newmarket, the 11 of December 1617.

John Spottiswoode, The History of the Church of Scotland, *Bannatyne Club (Edinburgh, 1850), III: 249–50*

Printed text; original letter apparently lost

Letter 175

To John Erskine, Earl of Mar

A note to Mar, the High Treasurer of Scotland, to pay a large sum to the Marquess of Hamilton, who had established himself as one of James's cronies. In 1619 he was created Earl of Cambridge in the English peerage.

16 May 1618

My Lord,

It is now many months ago since I signed a precept to my Lord Hamilton of three thousand pounds sterling to be paid him out of my receipts there, and now by these presents I have thought good to revive it again and give it new strength and vigour. My pleasure is that it may be paid unto him with as convenient speed as the urgent necessity of my own particular affairs (which must be preferred before all things) may permit; and withal that it may be kept as secret as possibly may be, for eschewing the importunity of a number of suitors, and this is the reason why I write this unto you with my own hand. I know well the present wants in my estate there, but I am so fully satisfied and so much rejoiced at the conquest I have made in drawing this man to wait upon me, now that I know him as he doth me, that I assure myself his service will repay my liberality with a double interest. And thus I bid you heartily farewell.

JAMES R.

Whitehall. 16 May 1618
Scottish Record Office   *Holograph, except*
GD 124/10/149   *place and date*

Letter 176

To George Villiers, Marquess of Buckingham

Even before the ruin of Somerset, court observers were aware that a powerful new favourite was emerging who would probably supplant him. The new man was young George Villiers, the untitled and penniless son of a Leicestershire squire. His assets were remarkable good looks, a handsome figure, intelligence, grace, and charm. Introduced to the King in the summer of 1614, Villiers enjoyed a rise even more spectacular than that of Somerset. In November 1614 he was appointed a royal cupbearer, in April 1615 he was knighted, in early 1616 he was appointed Master of the Horse, in April of that same year he was made a Knight of the Garter, and in August he was created Baron of Whaddon and Viscount Villiers. In January 1617 King James promoted him to the dignity of Earl of Buckingham, and a year later to that of Marquess. Finally, in 1623, George Villiers became Duke of Buckingham. He was the last and greatest of King James's favourites. Apparently he had entered into a homosexual relationship with James at the end of August 1615.[1]

In 1617 and 1618 King James's New Year's gift for Villiers had been promotion in the peerage. His slightly delayed gift for New Year's 1619 was a little treatise he had written on the Lord's Prayer. To this "meditation" he attached this dedicatory epistle. Another gift Villiers received in January 1619 was appointment as Lord High Admiral of England.

[*January 1619*]

I might justly prefix for a preamble to this my meditation, *Ille ego qui quondam,*[2] as well as Virgil did in his poetic preamble to his Aeneid, but to a clean contrary end. For his *Ille ego* was to show how high he was mounted in his new subject, from writing of the plough to write now of princes and their wars; whereas I now, clean contrary, am come from wading in these high and profound mysteries in the Revelation, wherein an elephant may swim, to meditate upon the plain, smooth, and easy Lord's Prayer, that every old wife can either say or mumble, and every well-bred child can interpret by his catechism, having left so the solid meat that men feed upon for the milk fit for babes. But the† reason is, I grow in years, and old men are twice babes, as the proverb is; having imitated Cardinal Bellarmine herein, who of late years hath given over his bickerings in polemics and controversies, wherein he was bred all his life, and betaken himself now to set out a short meditation every year, only embellishing almost every one of them with some two or three†† fabulous miracles, wherein he shall go alone for my part.

But now, when I bethink myself to whom I can most aptly dedicate this little labour of mine, most of it being stolen from the hours ordained for my sleep, and calling to mind how

†The Trial of Wits *wisheth every man to abstain from writing any books as soon as he is past fifty.* cap. *I*

††Reiice aniles fabulas. *I. Tim.*[3]

careful I have ever been to observe a decorum in the dedication of my books: as my ΒΑΣΙΛΙ-ΚΟΝ ΔΩΡΟΝ was dedicated to my son Henry, now with God, because it treated of the office of a king, it now belonging to my only son, Charles, who succeeds to it by right, as well as to all the rest of his brother's goods; and as I dedicated my *Apology for the Oath of Allegiance* to all free Christian princes and states, because they had all of them an interest in that argument; other of my books, which treated of matters belonging to every quality of persons, being therefore indefinitely dedicated to the reader in general; I cannot surely find out a person to whom I can more fitly dedicate this short meditation of mine than to you, Buckingham, for it is made upon a very short and plain prayer and therefore the fitter for a courtier. For courtiers for the most part are thought neither to have list nor leisure to say long prayers, liking best *courte Messe & long dinner.*[4] But to confess the truth now in earnest, it is fitter for you that it is both short and plain; that it is short, because when I consider of your continual attendance upon my service, your daily employments in the same, and the uncessant swarm of suitors importunately hanging upon you without discretion or distinction of times, I can find but very little time for you to spare upon meditation; and that it is plain, it is the fitter for you, since you were not bred a scholar.

Like St. Christopher that neither could nor would fast nor pray for attaining to the service of Christ, and therefore was set to a porter's work by the hermit.

You may likewise claim a just interest in it for divers other respects. First, from the ground of my writing it; for divers times before I meddled with it, I told you, and only you, of some of my conceptions upon the Lord's Prayer, and you often solicited me to put pen to paper. Next, as the person to whom we pray, it is our

367

heavenly Father, so am I that offer it unto you not only your politic but also your economic father, and that in a nearer degree than unto others. Thirdly, that you may make good use of it; for since I daily take care to better your understanding, to enable you the more for my service in worldly affairs, reason would that God's part should not be left out, for *timor Domini* is *initium sapientiae*.[5] And lastly, I must with joy acknowledge that you deserve this gift of me, in not only giving so good example to the rest of the Court in frequent hearing the word of God, but in special in so often receiving the sacrament, which is a notable demonstration of your charity in pardoning them that offend you, that being the thing I most labour to recommend to the world in this meditation of mine. And how godly and virtuous all my advices have ever been unto you I hope you will faithfully witness to the world.

This paper-friend will not importune you at unseasonable hours, come uncalled, nor speak unrequired, and yet will he neither flatter, lie, nor dissemble.

Receive then this New Year's gift from me as a token of my love, being begun upon the eve of our Saviour's nativity and ended far within the first month of the year. Praying God tnat as you are regenerated and born in him anew, so you may rise to him and be sanctified in him forever.

Amen

Preface to A Meditation Upon the Lord's Prayer, Written by the King's Majesty for the benefit of all his subjects, especially of such as follow the Court (*London*, *1619*), *ff. A2^r – A8^r*

[1]Roger Lockyer, *Buckingham* (London, [1981]), p. 22.
[2]"I am he who formerly."

³"Neither give heed to fables." I Timothy 1:4 (literally, "Reject old wives' tales").

⁴"A short grace and a long dinner." "Messe," a variant spelling of "mass," can refer to any religious ritual.

⁵"The fear of the Lord is the beginning of wisdom." (Proverbs 9:10).

Letter 177

To Christian IV, King of Denmark

The death of James's queen, Anne of Denmark on 2 March 1619, occasioned the following letter to her brother.

TRANSLATED FROM THE LATIN

2 March 1619

James, by the grace of God, King of Great Britain, France, and Ireland, Defender of the Faith, etc., to the most serene and mighty prince and lord, Lord Christian the Fourth, by the same grace King of Denmark and Norway, the Goths and the Vandals, Duke of Schleswig, Holstein, Stormaria, Dietmarsia, Count in Oldenburg and Delmenhorst, brother, kinsman by blood, ally, and our very dear friend: health and eternal felicity.

Most Serene Prince, brother, kinsman, ally and very dear friend:

Although what has just happened was such that it has troubled our tranquillity, it must nevertheless be communicated to Your Serenity, since it is the nature of brotherly love to share the sadness of adversity no less than the joy of prosperity. She who was a most excellent wife to us and a most dear sister to you has now died, and our common loss has apportioned grief to both of us. A certain necessity has been imposed upon us that we should make this sad disclosure and desire to anticipate Rumour herself, who carries the misfortunes of princes on swifter wings.

Many pledges of both love and virtue remain after her life, whence she has left us a great longing for her. But in death itself

369

there shone forth that sanctity, that piety, which has brought us some consolation for death. Truly in this long illness which completely wore out her strength, divine goodness had already prepared her soul for the better life, and before she said farewell to these sufferings she convinced those who stood by that she had obtained a foretaste of it. She was blessed by God with a clear mind and sharp senses right up to her final breath, so that she eagerly entered upon that heavenly journey for which her entire being yearned.[1] Her death was indeed premature if her age is regarded, but because of her previous ill health not unexpected. May God, the greatest and best, grant us that we conclude the brief drama of this life with an equal felicity of departure, found in meditation upon death before it comes,[2] so that satiated with earthly pleasure we may in that moment strive for celestial glory that is without satiety.

We wanted Your Serenity to learn of these things, communicating along with proper sorrow at least some medicine for grief so that although this heroine, your sister, by whose marriage our affinity was established, has been taken away, the relationship of our descendants may endure so long as it seems good to him who dispenses length of life to sceptres. May he bestow upon Your Serenity happiness in both lives.[3]

She died in the palace of Hampton on the second of March, the third hour of the morning, 1619,[4] on which day this letter was dispatched.

Your Serenity's most loving
brother,
JACOBUS R.

Rigsarkivet, Copenhagen
England A12,
1619, 2/3

Scribal letter, with final
phrase and signature
in King James's hand.

[1]This is a thoroughly mendacious letter. When Anne was warned that her death was imminent and that she should prepare herself spiritually for it, she displayed disbelief and childish evasion.

[2] James had a neurotic dread of everything associated with death.
[3] The two lives are that in this world and that in the world to come.
[4] The year is given according to the New Style.

Letter 178

To Antonio Priuli, Doge of Venice

A letter of compliment given to a departing Venetian ambassador.

TRANSLATED FROM THE LATIN

26 April 1619

Most Serene Prince, most dear friend,

We have not been able to allow that noble man and ambassador from your renowned republic, Antonio Donato, when he disclosed to us that he had decided for serious causes to return to his fatherland (as is more fully shown in your letter), to depart without that praise which he deserves both on account of the signal courtesy of his manners and sweetness of disposition, and on account of his gravity and mature prudence, by which virtues he has shown himself equal to the duty of his embassy, which he has laudably performed at our court; and he has proved himself worthy of his most serene uncle of pious memory, Leonardo Donato, lately Doge of Venice. Wherefore we were as loath to dismiss a man most dear to us because of these gifts as we were glad to learn from your same letter that he would soon return to us.[1] Meanwhile, the patrician gentleman who by your mandate is coming to take his place at our court, Pietro Gritti,[2] we shall receive with the kindness that befits him, while we await the return of Donato when his affairs have been completed happily and with God's help. Your Serenity and the republic, which we pray will be most flourishing in peace and in arms, we commend to the protection of God, the greatest and best.

Given from our palace of Westminster, 26 April in the year 1619.

And if through this letter I had more fully disclosed how highly I esteem this your ambassador, I still could not satisfy myself without testifying to you by these lines, written by my own hand (which is not my wont), how pleasant and acceptable contact with him has been to me, since I had perceived in him an admirable prudence and modesty in a young man endowed with a mind beyond his years. And I do not doubt that you will soon send him back to me, since he is so well fortified both by my recommendation and by his own virtues.

JACOBUS R.

R. Archivio Di Stato, Venezia　　　　　　*Letter signed, with a*
Sala Diplomatica, Regina　　　　　　　*holograph postscript*
Margherita, N. 8–XXXII

[1]Upon his return to Venice, Donato was put on trial for embezzling funds while ambassador to Savoy. Found guilty, he was stripped of his ambassadorship, titles, and estates, and banished for life. He then fled in disguise to England, where King James at first received him cordially but later forbade him to appear at his court.

[2]Gritti was prevented by illness from taking up this appointment and Gerolamo Lando became Donato's successor.

Letter 179

To George Villiers, Marquess of Buckingham [?]

The opening of this letter, referring to the recipient as "my only sweet and dear child," might lead one to conclude that James was writing to Prince Charles. Actually, the King frequently spoke of Buckingham as his "child" and referred to himself as his "dad." The contents of the letter strongly suggest that it was sent to Buckingham, not Charles.

My only sweet and dear child,

    I pray thee haste thee home to thy dear dad by sunsetting at the furthest. And forget not to make Digby² give the Spanish ambassador assurance that I will leave nothing undone that I may perform with justice and honour in holding a mild hand upon the papists. Only a way must be found to make their complaints come to my ears. But as for my Lady Lake,³ I must both confess to have pronounced an unjust sentence and break my promise to my Lady Exeter in a matter of justice if I grant her any ease at this time; besides that, this cause hath no aspect to religion, except the Romish religion be composed of the seven deadly sins, for I dare swear she is guilty of them all. If Spain trouble me with suits of this nature both against my justice and honour, their friendship will be more burdensome than useful unto me. And so [the] Lord send me a comfortable and happy meeting with thee this night.

JAMES R.

British Library   *Holograph*
Harl. 6987, f. 5

¹This letter was written after the conviction of Lady Lake in February 1619 and before Digby's departure for Spain, as ambassador, in August 1620.

²John Digby, who had been created Baron Digby of Sherborne (25 November 1618) and would become Earl of Bristol (15 September1622).

³For Lady Lake's false accusations of adultery directed against the Countess of Exeter, see G. P. V. Akrigg, *Jacobean Pageant, or The Court of King James I* (Cambridge, Mass., 1962), pp. 210– 12.

Letter 180

To George Villiers, Marquess of Buckingham

On 16 May 1620, Buckingham married Lady Katherine Manners, daughter and heiress to the Earl of Rutland. The following letter was probably delivered to Buckingham on the morning after his wedding night.

[17 May 1620?]

My only sweet and dear child,

Thy dear dad sends thee his blessing this morning and also to his daughter. The Lord of Heaven send you a sweet and blithe wakening, all kind of comfort in your sanctified bed, and bless the fruits thereof that I may have sweet bedchamber boys to play me with, and this is my daily prayer, sweet heart. When thou rises, keep thee from importunity of people that may trouble thy mind, that at meeting I may see thy white teeth shine upon me, and so bear me comfortable company in my journey. And so God bless thee, hoping thou will not forget to read over again my former letter.

JAMES R.

British Library   *Holograph*
Harl. 6987, f. 180

Letter 181

To Francis Bacon, Baron Verulam

In January 1618 Bacon achieved one of his life's ambitions when he was appointed Lord Chancellor. In October 1620 he published his Novum Organum. *The following letter was sent by James after his Chancellor presented him with a copy of this work. The opinions which he here expresses are curiously at odds with a witticism attributed to him, that Bacon's book resembled the peace of God in that it "passeth all understanding."*

[16 October 1620][1]

My Lord,

I have received your letter and your book, than which ye could not have sent a more acceptable present unto me. How thankful I am for it cannot better be expressed by me than by a firm resolution I have taken: first, to read it through with care and attention, though I should steal some hours from my sleep, having otherwise as little spare time to read it as ye had to write it; and then to use the liberty of a true friend in not sparing to ask you the question in any point thereof I shall stand in doubt; *nam eius est explicare, cuius est condere;*[2] as on the other part, I will willingly give a due commendation to such places as in my opinion shall deserve it. In the meantime I can, with comfort, assure you that ye could not have made choice of a subject more befitting your place and your universal methodic knowledge. And, in the general, I have already observed that ye jump with me in keeping the middle way between the two extremes; as also in some particulars I have found that ye agree fully with my opinion. And so, praying God to give your work as good success as your heart can wish and your labours deserve, I bid you heartily farewell.

JAMES R.

British Library   *Copy, apparently*
Add. 5503, f. 101   *of a lost holograph*[3]

[1]This is the date printed by William Rawley as part of this letter (*Resuscitatio*, 3rd ed., London, 1671, Part I, "Letters," p. 69).

[2]"For it is for him to explicate who has written the work."

[3]Rawley (*Resuscitatio*, p. 69) describes this letter as "written . . . with his Majesties own hand."

Letter 182

To George Villiers, Marquess of Buckingham

The following solicitous letter appears to have been written soon after the King learned that Buckingham's wife was pregnant with their first child, Mary, who was born early in 1622.

[Mid-1621?]

My only sweet and dear child,

The Lord of Heaven bless thee this morning and thy thing my daughter, and the sweet little thing that is in her belly. I pray thee, as thou loves me, make her precisely observe these rules: let her never go in a coach upon the street, nor never go fast in it; let your mother keep all hasty news from coming to her ears; let her not eat too much fruit, and hasten her out of London after we are gone. If thou be back by four in the afternoon, it will be good time. And prepare thee to be a guard to me for keeping my back unbroken with business before my going to the progress. And thus God send me a joyful and a happy meeting with my sweet Steenie[1] this evening.

JAMES R.

British Library   *Holograph*
Harl.6987, f. 178

---

[1] A nickname for Buckingham, being a Scottish contraction for Stephen. According to one explanation, Buckingham resembled in appearance a portrait of St. Stephen owned by King James. According to another, James applied to Buckingham the description of St. Stephen in Acts 6:15—"his face [was] as it had been the face of an angel."

Letter 183

To Sir Thomas Richardson, Speaker of the House of Commons

The final weeks of 1621 saw King James embroiled with Parliament in what was perhaps the worst constitutional crisis of his reign in England.

Convening at the end of January this year, Parliament had been so eager for the punishment of English recusants that James had seen its zeal as threatening his negotiations with Spain, and in June he had rather abruptly adjourned it. Very shortly thereafter, Sir Edwin Sandys and the Earl of Southampton, who had angered the King by their speeches in Parliament, were placed under arrest. Tempers had cooled when Parliament reconvened on 20 November, but a new crisis arose when the Commons seemed about to add to an anti-recusancy petition a clause bearing directly on the projected Spanish marriage for Prince Charles and on moves in aid of James's son-in-law the Elector of the Palatinate (see headnote to Letter 187). As foreign policy had always been regarded as reserved for the Crown, the King was angered by what he saw as an infringement on his prerogative. Alerted by a secret informer (probably the Prince himself)[1] as to what the Commons were preparing, James sent the following angry letter to the Speaker. The most ominous statement in it was the King's declaration that he felt free to punish "any man's misbehaviour in Parliament." This, seen as a direct threat to the emerging principle of freedom of speech in Parliament, came as a profound shock to the House of Commons. One M.P. referred to the King's communication as "this soul-killing letter."

3 December 1621

JAMES REX

Mr. Speaker,

We have heard by divers reports, to our great grief, that the far distance of our person from the House of Parliament (caused

377

by our indisposition of health) hath emboldened some fiery and popular spirits of the House of Commons to argue and debate publicly of matters far beyond their reach and capacities, and so tending to our high dishonour and to the infringing of our prerogative royal. These are, therefore, to command you to make known in our name unto the House that none therein shall presume to treat of matters concerning government (or mysteries of state) and, namely, not to deal with the match of our dear son with the daughter of Spain, nor any ways to touch the honour of that king or any other of our friends or allies, nor yet to meddle with any man's particular which have their due motion in our ordinary courts of justice.

And whereas we understand that they have sent a message to Sir Edwin Sandys to know from him the cause of his commitment, our pleasure is that you resolve them in our name that he was not committed for any business in Parliament, although we think ourselves free and able to punish the misbehaviour of any member in Parliament as well during the sitting as after, which we mean hereafter not to spare upon any occasion of insolency there used. And further let them know that if, in the petition we hear they are sending unto us, they have touched upon any of these points (as we hear they have), that then we will not deign the hearing or answering of it. And for the conclusion of the session before Christmas, which we hear they so much desire, we will you to let them know it is through their own fault if they have it not; and that our pleasure is to give our royal assent unto such laws as are really good for the Commonwealth and so it shall appear. If such laws be not provided, it shall rest upon such turbulent spirits as do prefer their particular ends to the public weal, and so we bid you farewell.

Given at Newmarket the iij[d] December 1621.

British Library   Copy of a letter under the
Harl. 6799, f. 56   sign manual

[1]See Conrad Russell, *Parliament and English Politics* (Oxford, 1979), p. 137.

Letter 184

To Sir George Calvert

On 11 December, in consequence of the preceding letter, a delegation from the House of Commons waited on King James at Newmarket. To him they announced that the Commons renounced all claims to discuss foreign policy or the marriage of Prince Charles but must insist upon "Freedom of Speech, Jurisdiction, and Just Censure," matters which they termed "our ancient and undoubted Right, and an Inheritance received from our Ancestors." The King's reply, read to the House on 14 December, maintained that the rights alleged by the Commons were merely privileges that they enjoyed through the grace and permission of his predecessors and himself. In consternation, the Commons appointed a committee to draft a categorical declaration of their rights. Vainly attempting to head off the crisis he had brought on, the King sent by Calvert, one of the two Secretaries of State, this following message. In it he tries to be as conciliatory as possible while not conceding privileges to be rights. This and another royal letter availed nothing. Accordingly, on 18 December King James summarily adjourned Parliament, and dissolved it a few weeks later.

16 December 1621

Right trusty and well-beloved counsellor, we greet you well.

We are sorry to hear that notwithstanding our reiterated messages to our House of Commons for going on in their business, in regard of the shortness of time betwixt this and Christmas, and of their own earnest desire that we should now conclude a session by making of good and profitable laws, yet they continued to lose time. And now of late, upon our gracious answer to them, have taken occasion to make more delay in appointing a committee tomorrow to consider upon the points of our answer, and especially concerning that point in it which makes mention of their privileges. Our pleasure therefore is that you shall in our name tell them that we are so loath to have time misspent, which is so precious a thing in the well using whereof our people may receive so great a benefit, as we are thus far contented to descend from our regal dignity by explaining at this time our meaning in our said answer touching that point, that all our good subjects in that house that intend nothing but our honour and the weal of the commonwealth may clearly see our intention.

Whereas in our said answer, we told them that we could not allow of the style calling it "their ancient and undoubted right and inheritance", but could rather have wished that they then had said that their privileges were derived from the grace and permission of our ancestors and us (for most of them grew from precedents, which shows rather a toleration than inheritance). The plain truth is that we cannot with patience endure our subjects to use such antimonarchical words to us concerning their liberties, except they had subjoined that they were granted unto them by the grace and favour of our predecessors. But as for our intention herein, God knows we never meant to deny them any lawful privileges that ever that House enjoyed in our predecessors' times, as we expect[ed] our said answer should have sufficiently cleared them, neither in justice whatsoever they have undoubted right unto, nor in grace whatsoever our predecessors or we have graciously permitted unto them. And therefore we made that distinction of the most part, for whatsoever privileges or liberties they enjoy by any law or statute shall ever be inviolably preserved by us, and we hope our posterity will imitate our footsteps therein. And whatsoever privileges they enjoy by long customs and uncontrolled and lawful precedents, we will be likewise as careful to preserve them and transmit the care thereof to our posterity. Neither was it any way in our mind to think of any particular point wherein we meant to disallow of their liberties, so as in justice we confess ourselves to be bound to maintain them in their rights, and in grace we are rather minded to increase than infringe any of them if they shall so deserve at our hands.

To end therefore as we began, let them go on cheerfully to their business, rejecting their curious wrangling upon words and syllables, otherwise (which God forbid) the world shall see how oft and how earnestly we have pressed them to go on, according to their calling, with those things that are fit to be done for the weal of our crown and kingdom, and how many curious shifts have been from time to time maliciously found out to frustrate us of our good purpose and hinder them from the performance of that service which they owed to us and to our whole kingdom; whereof when the country shall come to be informed, they will give the author thereof little thanks.

Given at our court of Royston this 16th day of December 1621.

British Library   *Copy*
Sloane 1828, f. 90

Letter 185

To Lionel Cranfield, Baron Cranfield

On 30 September 1621, Cranfield became Lord Treasurer. His task of rescuing King James from his debts was hardly aided by the following note.

[*January 1622?*]

My Lord,

Shame stayed me from refreshing your memory concerning Buckingham's business upon Sunday last, having so oft and earnestly dealt with you in it before. But now, upon the occasion of his wife's going to London, his mother put him in mind of preparing things for her lying-in,[1] which I chancing to overhear, I asked earnestly and conjured him to tell me the truth of his estate, for ye know how loath he is to do it. And alas I find he must pay twenty thousand pounds for his land at "Burghlie"[2]

and these provisions for her lying-in and meubling* are like to
cost ten thousand, besides three thousand for his new house,[3]
and all this he must borrow. I need say no more; if he once run in
arrear he will ever go backward. Do quickly therefore what ye
are to do for him, and remember that a thing done in time is
twice done. Comfort me with some present good news in this
point, for till then I protest I can have no joy in the going well of
my own business; and so I conclude. Either now or never! God
bless your labours.

JAMES R.

British Library   *Holograph*
Harl. 6987, f. 1

[1]Buckingham's first child, Mary, was born in March 1622.
[2]Buckingham had a great house at Burley-on-the-Hill, Rutland.
[3]York House, bought from Bacon as a London residence after the latter's fall.

Letter 186

*To the members of the Council of Scotland, especially the
Earl of Mar, and to the "remnant Commissioners appointed
for managing our rents in our Kingdom of Scotland"*

*Further evidence of James's irresponsible extravagance in
dealing with his cronies.*

20 April 1622

JAMES R.
Right trusty and right well-beloved cousins and
counsellors and right trusty and well-beloved
counsellors, we greet you well.
    We were pleased to direct a precept to you our Treasurer for
payment be made to our cousin the Marquis of Hamilton of the
sum of ten thousand pounds sterling,[1] and also wrote to you all

to give way unto the same. And forasmuch as we were pleased to grant precepts to some others so as question may arise which should be first answered, we have thought good by these presents to require you to prefer our said cousin and cause payment be made unto him before all others whatsoever. So nothing doubting of your conformity to this our pleasure, we wish you well to fare. Given at our palace of Whitehall the 20th of April 1622.

I promised this unto him at his return from Scotland, and his service at that parliament deserved a great deal more; therefore according to his merit let him be cheerfully satisfied in this.

Scottish Record Office *Letter under the sign*
GD 124/10/230 *manual; with holograph*
postscript

[1]For instructions to Mar in 1618 to give Hamilton £3000, see Letter 175.

Letter 187

To Pope Gregory XV

On St. Valentine's Day in 1613, Princess Elizabeth, James's only daughter to survive into maturity, married Frederick, Elector of the Palatinate of the Rhine. For five happy years they resided in Frederick's capital, Heidelberg. Then Protestant rebels who had wrested control of most of Bohemia from their Catholic Hapsburg ruler appealed to Frederick for aid. After he had sent in troops who enlarged the area under the control of the rebels, the latter offered Frederick the crown of Bohemia. In September 1619 he accepted, and the coming months saw Frederick and Elizabeth, the ill-starred "Winter King and Queen," holding court in Prague.

In the summer of 1620, Catholic armies invaded both Bohemia and the Palatinate. Frederick's forces were routed and in the end he and his wife had to seek asylum in Holland. King James, with no military strength to back his position, negotiated long and fruitlessly to regain for Frederick and Elizabeth their lost territory in the Palatinate, seeking to terminate what was, in fact, the beginning of the catastrophic Thirty Years' War.

One of the unrealistic visions which James entertained was of himself, as the leader of Protestant Europe, and the Pope, as the head of the Roman Catholic Church, jointly establishing a general European settlement. To this end he wrote the following letter to the Pope, having Prince Charles and Buckingham sign it as well as himself. This letter achieved nothing.

TRANSLATED FROM THE LATIN

30 September 1622

Most holy father,

Your Holiness will perhaps marvel that we, differing from you in point of religion, should now first salute you with our letters. Howbeit, such is the trouble of our mind for these calamitous discords and bloodsheds, which for these late years by-past have so miserably rent the Christian world, and so great is our care and daily solicitude to stop the course of these growing evils betimes so much as in us lies, as we could no longer abstain (considering that we all worship the same most blessed Trinity, nor hope for salvation by any other means than by the blood and merits of one Lord and Saviour, Christ Jesus) but, breaking this silence, to move Your Holiness by these our letters, friendly and seriously, that you would be pleased together with us to put your hand to so pious a work and so worthy of a Christian prince.

It is truly to be wished, and by all means to be endeavoured, that this mischief creep on no further but that, these storms at the last ceasing and the rancour being removed by which they were at the first raised, the hearts of those princes whom it any way concerns may be reunited in a firm and unchangeable friendship and, as much as may be, knit together in stricter obligations than before, one to another. This we have always had in our desires, and to bring it to pass have not hitherto spared any labour or pains, not doubting but Your Holiness, out of your singular piety and for the credit and authority that you have with the parties, both may and will further this work in an extraordinary manner. No way can any man better merit of the state of Christendom, which if it shall take the desired effect in your days and by your assistance, Your Holiness shall worthily reap the glory and the reward due to so excellent a work.

That which remains for us further to say concerning this matter, this gentleman our subject, George Gage,[1] will deliver unto you more at large. Praying Your Holiness that you will give him in all things full credence and belief; beseeching Almighty God, from our heart, to preserve you in safety and to grant you all other happiness.

From our palace at Hampton Court, the last of September 1622.

JACOBUS R.

Bodleian Library   *Contemporary translation*
Tanner 73, f. 236

[1]An English Catholic already being used by James as an unofficial emissary to Rome in the negotiations for a marriage between Prince Charles and the Infanta Maria.

Letter 188

To George Villiers, Marquess of Buckingham

After the conclusion of the Anglo—Spanish peace treaty of 1604, the Spaniards repeatedly proposed a match between the heir to the English throne and one of their princesses. All their overtures were frustrated by Cecil, who recognized them as manoeuvres to keep England from making elsewhere a marriage that might be disadvantageous to Spain.

In 1614, several years after Cecil's death, a superbly skilled diplomat, Don Diego Sarmiento de Acuña, arrived in England as the new Spanish ambassador. Ingratiating himself with James, he renewed the marriage proposal, enchanting the King with the prospect of a Spanish dowry so immense that it would end his financial problems. Having largely immobilized England as a political force in Europe by getting its king more and more inclined towards a marriage alliance with Spain, Sarmiento was rewarded by his king with the title of Count of Gondomar.[1]

The "Spanish Match" became crucial to James after his son-in-law lost the Palatinate. He believed, fatuously, that he could make King Philip pressure the eastern Hapsburgs into restoring the Palatinate to Frederick as a condition for the marriage between Charles and the Infanta Maria. As for Charles, he had built up a romantic image of the lady, and sometime around the middle of December 1622 he and Buckingham sought James's permission to go to Madrid. Charles was bent on wooing the Infanta personally, thus ending the interminable negotiating through ambassadors.

James was appalled by the dangers to which Charles and Buckingham would expose themselves during so hazardous a journey. When the two next saw James after broaching their scheme, they were greeted with outcries and exclamations. The old king "fell into a great passion of tears, and told them that he was undone, and that it would break his heart if they pursued their resolution."[2] However, unable to deny them anything, he finally gave his consent. The following undated letter apparently belongs to this period. The prospective parting that had made James "so miserable a coward" and elicited such emotional stress must have been something much more than Buckingham's departure from the Court to visit his country house, New Hall.

[December 1622?]

My only sweet and dear child,

I am now so miserable a coward, as I do nothing but weep and mourn; for I protest to God I rode this afternoon a great way in the park without speaking to anybody and the tears trickling down my cheeks, as now they do that I can scarcely see to write. But alas, what shall I do at our parting? The only small comfort I can have will be to pry in thy defects with the eye of an enemy, and of every mote to make a mountain, and so harden my heart against thy absence. But this little malice is like jealousy, proceeding from a sweet root; but in one point it overcometh it, for as it proceeds from love so it cannot but end in love. Sweet heart, be earnest with Kate to come and meet thee at Newhall[3] within eight or ten days after this. Cast thee to be here tomorrow, as near about two in the afternoon as thou can, and come galloping hither. Remember thy picture and suffer none of the Council to come here.[4] For God's sake write not a word again and let no creature see this letter. The Lord of heaven and earth to bless thee, and my sweet daughter, and my sweet little grandchild, and all thy blessed family, and send thee a happy return, both now and thou knows when, to thy dear dad and Christian gossip.*

JAMES R.

British Library   *Holograph*
Lansdowne 1236, f. 64

[1]The present editor inclines towards the traditional view that Gondomar deliberately duped King James. For a contrary view see Charles H. Carter, "Gondomar: Ambassador to James I," *Historical Journal* VII (1964), 189–208.

[2]Edward, Earl of Clarendon, *The History of the Rebellion and Civil Wars in England Begun in the Year 1641* (Oxford, 1888), I: 18.

[3]The great mansion in Essex which Buckingham had purchased from the Earl of Sussex.

[4]"The King came to Theobalds on Monday last [16 December] and gave order that none of the Lords of the counsaile should trouble themselves to come thether" (Chamberlain, *Letters*, 21 December 1622, II: 467).

Letter 189

To Prince Charles and the Marquess of Buckingham

On 18 February 1623, Prince Charles and Buckingham, disguised as Jack and Tom Smith, started for Spain. The following letter, almost certainly written the next day, inaugurates a correspondence covering the six months of the Spanish journey. Some of Kings James's letters to Spain have been lost, but the twenty-seven that survive now follow, printed in their entirety for the first time.

[*19? February 1623*]

Sweet boys,

The news of your going is already so blown abroad as I am forced for your safety to post this bearer after you, who will give you his best advice and attendance in your journey. God bless you both, my sweet babes, and send you a safe and happy return.

JAMES R.

British Library   *Holograph*
Harl. 6987, f. 9

Letter 190

To Prince Charles and the Marquess of Buckingham

King James deals with the sensitive matter of Charles and Buckingham travelling through France incognito, informs them of noblemen travelling towards Spain, and touches on other matters.

[*27 February 1623*]

My sweet boys and dear venturous knights, worthy to be put in a new romance.

I thank you for your comfortable letters. But, alas, think it not possible that ye can be many hours undiscovered, for your parting was so blown abroad that day ye came to Dover, as the French ambassador sent a man presently thither, who found the ports stopped. But yet I durst not trust to the bare stopping of the ports, there being so many blind creeks to pass at; and therefore I sent Doncaster[1] to the French king with a short letter of my own hand to show him that respect that I may acquaint him with my son's passing unknown through his country. And this have I done for fear that, upon the first rumour of your passing, he should take a pretext to stop you; and therefore, Baby Charles, ye shall do well how soon ye come to Irun[2] in Spain to write a courteous excuse of your hasty passage to the French king, and send a gentleman with it if by any means ye may spare any.

"Uacandarie" is comed* from Spain but brings no news, save that Sim Digby[3] is shortly to be here with the list of their names that are to accompany your mistress hither; only Bristol[4] writes an earnest letter to have more money allowed him for his charges at that solemnity (otherwise, he says, he cannot hasten the consummation of the marriage); but that ye two can best satisfy him in when ye are there. Your household, Baby, have taken care to save a good deal of your ordinary charges in your absence. Kirke[5] and Gabriel will carry Georges and garters to you both with speed, but I dare send no jewels of any value to either of you by land, for fear of robbers, but I will hasten all your company and provision to you by sea. Noblemen ye will have enow, and too many: Carlisle[6] and Mountjoy[7] already gone, Andover[8] goes presently, and Rocheford[9] by land, Compton[10] goes by sea, and I think Percy[11] and Arran[12] and Denbigh[13] go by land.

I have settled Sir Francis Crane[14] for my Steenie's[15] business, and I am this day to speak with Fotherlie;[16] and by my next, Steenie shall have an account both of his business and of Kit's[17] preferment and supply in means. But Sir Francis Crane desires to know if my baby will have him to hasten the making of that suit of tapestry that he commanded him. I have written three consolatory letters already to Kate[18] and received one fine letter from Kate. I have also written one to Sue.[19] But your poor old dad is lamer than ever he was, both of his right knee and foot, and writes all this out of his naked bed.

God Almighty bless you both, my sweet boys, and send you a safe, joyful, and happy return. But I must command my baby to hasten Steenie home how soon ye can be assured of the time of your homecoming with your mistress, for without his presence things cannot be prepared here. And so God bless you both again and again.

JAMES R.

Tell Cottington[20] I have done as he desired me concerning his wife.

British Library   *Holograph*
Harl. 6987, f. 13

[1]James Hay, son of the Earl of Carlisle, assumed the title of Viscount Doncaster after his father obtained his earldom (see n. 6).

[2]A Spanish frontier town, across the river from Hendaye in France.

[3]Simon Digby, a kinsman of the Earl of Bristol, was employed by the King on various missions.

[4]John Digby, Earl of Bristol, the English ambassador to Spain.

[5]A Scot who had helped to arrange for Charles and Buckingham to cross from England to France. In 1613 George Kirk had been appointed one of the Grooms of the Prince's Bedchamber. In time he would become Master of the Robes to Charles I.

[6]James Hay, Viscount Doncaster, had been promoted to the dignity of Earl of Carlisle on 13 September 1622.

[7]Mountjoy Blount, illegitimate son of Charles Blount, Earl of Devonshire (d. 1606) had been created Lord Mountjoy in the Irish peerage.

[8]Thomas Howard, Viscount Andover, second son of the Earl of Suffolk.

[9]Henry Carey, Viscount Rochford. He was Chamberlain to Prince Charles.

[10]Lord Compton, the son and heir of William Compton, Earl of Northampton. (Sir Thomas Compton, Buckingham's stepfather, wished to go to Spain but when he came to ask permission the King, observing that he was mentally disturbed, had him return to his home.)

[11]Algernon, Lord Percy, son and heir of the Earl of Northumberland.

[12]James Hamilton, Earl of Arran, son and heir of the Marquess of Hamilton.

[13]William Feilding, Earl of Denbigh, Buckingham's brother-in-law.

[14]In 1619, under royal patronage, Crane established the Mortlake tapestry works.

[15]A nickname for Buckingham (see Letter 182, n. 1).

[16]Thomas Fotherly, Buckingham's steward (see Letters 191 and 198).

[17]Buckingham's feckless brother Christopher was created Baron of Daventry and Earl of Anglesey on 18 April 1623.

[18]Buckingham's wife, Katherine.

[19]Buckingham's sister, Susan, the Countess of Denbigh.

[20]Sir Francis Cottington, Prince Charles's secretary.

Letter 191

To Prince Charles and the Marquess of Buckingham

The King reports on those who are to travel to Spain, and on his management of Buckingham's affairs.

28 February [1623]

My sweet boys,

Yesterday I wrote an answer to your letters by young Bowie[1], whom I sent because I know he will be quickly with you, and my baby may either make use of his service there or when he hath use to make a quick despatch. I know none can carry it swiftlier than he. And this day I write these by Andover,[2] who goes by land because, he says, he is not able to go by sea. But the imperfect note that my baby left, under his hand, of his servants that should follow him hath put me to a great deal of pain, for ye left some necessary servants out in the opinion of all your principal officers; and when as I was forced to add those, then every man ran upon me for his friend so as I was torn in pieces amongst them. But now either this bearer or Sir Robert Carr[3] will bring you the note of your servants that are to go.

And now, Steenie,[4] according to my promise I took a full account of your affairs yesterday from Fotherlie.[5] To be short, he hath promised to lose no time both anent the three forests and Sedgemoor,[6] in which last I have obtained a sentence in the end of this last term; but he is of that mind to make money of them all for payment of your debts and buying of more land for you near Bewlie.[7] I have lately signed divers quillets [small

391

pieces] of land for you, in exchange for which, he says, ye shall receive eighteen thousand pounds in money. He will reduce the charges of your table to my allowance till your return, and he is now gone to despatch Kit's[8] business with the Lord Treasurer,[9] and to think upon a course for paying the Lord President[10] of his ten thousand pounds. I have commanded him to come boldly to me whenever he hath occasion for any of your businesses, for I have taken the charge of them upon me.

I have no more to say but that I wear Steenie's picture in a blue ribbon under my waistcoat next my heart. And so God bless you both and send you a joyful and happy return. From Newmarket the last of February.

JAMES R.

British Library   *Holograph*
Harl. 6987, f. 15

[1]Nothing is known of this courier.
[2]See Letter 190, n. 8.
[3]See Letter 168, n. 2.
[4]Buckingham—see Letter 182, n. 1.
[5]See Letter 190, n. 16
[6]In the final years of King James's reign the Crown undertook to reclaim 14,000 acres of marshland on Sedgemoor, the greater part to be held by private landowners. The project dragged on under Charles I and finally failed. See T.G. Barnes, *Somerset 1625–1640* (Cambridge, Mass., 1961), pp. 151–55.
[7]In July 1622, Buckingham bought from the Earl of Sussex the former royal palace of Beaulieu or Bewley, commonly known as New Hall. Probably to distinguish it from the Earl of Southampton's Beaulieu in Hampshire, it was sometimes referred to as "East Bewley."
[8]See Letter 190, n. 17.
[9]Lionel Cranfield, Earl of Middlesex.
[10]Henry Montagu, Viscount Mandeville.

Letter 192

To Prince Charles and the Marquess of Buckingham

The King reports arrangements for sending men and jewels to Spain.

2 March [1623]

My sweet boys,

I wrote to you the penult of February by Bowie, and the last thereof by Andover;[1] and now this second of March, being Sunday, I write this by Sir Robert Carr,[2] who will fully inform my baby what order his officers have taken in his affairs. Three ships are promised to be made ready within a fifteen days for transporting your men and jewels, for, as I wrote to you before, I durst not hazard your jewels by land, and fewer ships I durst not hazard for fear of pirates. I shall spur them daily till they be gone. But poor Steenie and sweet gossip,[3] thou has left no order for any of thy men to follow, so as I know not what to do in that case; as ever it be, God bless you both, my sweet boys, and send you a happy journey and a comfortable and happy return to your dear dad.

JAMES R.

British Library   *Holograph*
Harl. 6987, f. 17

[1]See Letter 190, n. 8.
[2]See Letters 168 and 191, and notes.
[3]Buckingham.

Letter 193

To Prince Charles and the Marquess of Buckingham

News concerning the Palatinate gives fresh urgency to the mission undertaken by Prince Charles.

11 March [1623]

My sweet boys,

This is now the fifth letter I have written unto you, which I send by a couple of your own family,[1] my Steenie, who are never asunder. The Emperor[2] hath now spewed the uttermost of his unquenchable malice against my unfortunate son-in-law, by giving away the Electorate to that false and unnatural Duke of Bavaria, though but during the duke's life and with a clause of reservation of my grandchildren's and other kinsmen's hereditary titles, either by way of amicable treaty or by plea in the electoral court. But if my baby's credit in Spain mend not these things, I will bid farewell to peace in Christendom during our times at least.

I have even now made choice of the jewels that I am to send you, whereof my baby is to present some to his mistress and some of the best he is to wear himself, and the next best he will lend to my bastard brat³ to wear. But of this I will write more particularly with Compton,⁴ who is to carry them. Some also I will send of a meaner value, to save my baby's charges in presents that he must give there. And so God bless my boys and send you a happy journey (for I hope ye are by this time at the furthest), and a joyful, happy, and comfortable return to your dear dad and true friend.

JAMES R.

From Newmarket the 11 of March

Bodleian Library   *Holograph*
Tanner 73, f. 287

¹I.e., of Buckingham's household.
²Ferdinand II of the Holy Roman Empire.
³Buckingham.
⁴Lord Compton, son and heir of William Compton, Earl of Northhampton.

Letter 194

To Prince Charles and the Marquess of Buckingham

King James refuses to negotiate further with the Emperor Ferdinand for the restoration of the Palatinate, but looks to the

King of Spain to act as a mediator. He fears for the Prince's
health if he remains in Spain during the hot weather.

My sweet boys,
God bless you for the welcome cordial that Grisley[1] brought
me from you yesterday. The Spanish ambassador[2] and Boiscot
from the Archduchess[3] are now agreed with me for the deposit-
ing of Frankenthal[4] in the King of Spain's and Archduchess's
hands for eighteen months (without any mention of my treating
with the Emperor, for that cannot now be done with my honour,
he having thrice broken flatly his promises unto me). All the
other conditions are very reasonable, but I hear a whispering still
that the King of Spain would have a match between my grandchild and the Emperor's daughter. But if, either that way or any
other, this business be brought to a good end, it must now be
done by the King of Spain's mediation betwixt the Emperor and
me, whom he hath so far wronged and neglected; whereas before
I did mediate between the Emperor and my son-in-law.
As to my baby's own business, I find by Bristol's[5] ciphered
letter two points like to be stucken at that ye must labour to
help by all the means ye can. The one is a long delay of finishing
the marriage; for that point I doubt not but ye will spur it on
fast enough for (though there were no other inconvenient [*sic*]
in it but the danger of your life by the coming on of the heats) I
think they have reason there, if they love themselves, to wish you
and yours rather to succeed unto me than my daughter and her
children. But for this point I know my sweet gossip Steenie will
spur and call [*sic:* gall?] them as fast as he did the post-horses in
France. The other point is that they would, if not lessen, at least
protract the terms for payment of the dowry. This were a base
thing and a breach of their promise made many years ago,
which the Conde of Gondomar,[6] I am sure, will bear witness
unto; and if your travel thither hath not earned it, as they say,
God [forbid] that ever it do me or you good.
I hear they there would be at a general peace and compre-
hend also the Low Countries. For my part, so that the business

of the Palatinate were at a good end, I wish it were so. But if the business of your match were once fully concluded, I would be glad, sweet gossip,[7] that ye felt their pulses anent the thing ye know concerning Holland, which will be fittest for you to sound, being my admiral. But I am ashamed to tell you, by the way, how many prizes belonging to you, your knavish and unthankful sea-captains have meddled with and shared amongst themselves, which are not so few as three or four as John Cooke[8] informs me. But within few days ye shall, with God's grace, have a good account of that business. In the meantime I have fully satisfied the French ambassador[9] of my baby's care to discharge honestly his promise unto him.

I send this post in haste for preparing and facilitating of the passage from the coast of Spain to the court thereof for my baby's servants and baggage, my ship now being ready to make sail, and yet will I write with her again within two or three days, in grace of God, this being the sixth letter I have written to you two, five to Kate,[10] two to Sue,[11] and one to thy mother, Steenie, and all with my own hand. And thus God bless you both, my sweet boys, and grant you after a successful journey a happy and joyful return to your dear dad.

JAMES R.

Newmarket, the 15 of March.

British Library   *Holograph*
Harl. 6987, f. 27

[1]Walsingham Gresley, a friend of Sir Francis Cottington, secretary to Prince Charles. He was steward to the Earl of Bristol.

[2]Don Carlos Coloma.

[3]Ferdinand de Boiscot, ambassador of the Archduchess Isabella, regent of the Spanish Netherlands.

[4]Frankenthal, guarded by an English garrison, was the last town in the Palatinate held by King James's son-in-law. Under the terms of the "sequestration" proposed above, it was transferred to Spanish custody on 14 April 1623.

[5]The Earl of Bristol, English ambassador to Spain.

[6]Diego Sarmiento de Acuña, Conde de Gondomar, Spanish ambassador to England 1613–1618, 1620–1622, was now in Madrid playing an important part in the marriage negotiations.

[7]Buckingham.

[8]John Coke, one of Buckinghams' followers, was the most important member of the board that attended to the administration of the navy. Knighted in 1624, he became a Secretary of State the following year.

[9]Tanneguy Le Veneur, Comte de Tillières.

[10]See Letter 190, n. 18.

[11]See Letter 190, n. 19.

Letter 195

To Prince Charles and the Marquess of Buckingham

In this amusing letter King James not only lists the jewels that he is sending Charles from England but coaches him in the timing of their presentation to the Infanta and instructs him in a ponderous compliment that Charles is to pay her.

17 March [1623]

My sweet boys,

I write now this seventh letter unto you upon the seventeenth of March, sent in my ship called the *Adventure* to my two boys adventurers, whom God ever bless. And now to begin with him, *a Jove principium,*[1] I have sent you, my baby, two of your chaplains fittest for this purpose, Mawe[2] and Wren,[3] together with all stuff and ornaments fit for the service of God. I have fully instructed them so as all their behaviour and service shall, I hope, prove decent and agreeable to the purity of the primitive church and yet as near the Roman form as can lawfully be done, for it hath ever been my way to go with the Church of Rome *usque ad aras.*[4] All the particulars hereof I remit to the relation of your before-named chaplains.

I send you also your robes of the order,[5] which ye must not forget to wear upon Saint George's Day and dine together in them, if they can come in time, which I pray God they may, for it will be a goodly sight for the Spaniards to see my two boys dine in them. I send you also the jewels as I promised, both some of mine and such of yours (I mean both of you) as are worthy the

397

sending. For my baby's presenting his mistress, I send him an old double cross of Lorraine, not so rich as ancient, and yet not contemptible for the value; a goodly looking-glass with my picture in it, to be hung at her girdle, which ye must tell her ye have caused it so to be enchanted by art magic as, whensoever she shall be pleased to look in it, she shall see the fairest lady that either her brother or your father's dominions can afford. Ye shall present her with two fair long diamonds set like an anchor, and a fair pendant diamond hanging at them. Ye shall give her a goodly rope of pearls; ye shall give her a carcanet or collar of thirteen great balas rubies[6] and thirteen knots or cinques of pearls; ye shall give her a head-dressing of two and twenty great pear pearls; and ye shall give her three goodly pear pendant diamonds, whereof the biggest to be worn at a needle on the midst of her forehead and one in every ear. And for my baby's own wearing, ye have two good jewels of your own, your round broach of diamonds and your triangle diamond with the great round pearl; and I send you for your wearing "The Three Brethren," that ye know full well but newly set; and "The Mirror of France," the fellow of the Portugal diamond, which I would wish you to wear alone in your hat with a little black feather. Ye have also good diamond buttons of your own to be set to a doublet or jerkin. As for your "I," it may serve for a present to a don.

As for thee, my sweet gossip, I send thee a fair table diamond which I would once have given thee before, if thou would have taken it, and I have hung a fair pear pearl to it for wearing in thy hat or where thou pleases; and if my baby will spare thee the two long diamonds in form of an anchor with the pendant diamond, it were fit for an admiral[7] to wear, and he hath enough better jewels for his mistress. Thou has of thine own thy good old jewel, thy three Pindar's[8] diamonds, the picture case I gave Kate, and the great diamond chain I gave her, who would have sent thee the least pin she had if I had not stayed her. If my baby will not spare the anchor from his mistress, he may well lend thee his round broach to wear and yet he shall have jewels to wear in his hat for three great days.

And now for the form of my baby's presenting of his jewels

to his mistress, I leave that to himself with Steenie's advice and my Lord of Bristol's. Only, I would not have them presented all at once, but at the more sundry times the better. And I would have the rarest and richest kept hindmost. I have also sent four other crosses, of meaner value, with a great pointed diamond in a ring, which will save charges in presents to dons according to their qualities. But I will send with the fleet divers other jewels for presents, for saving of charges whereof we have too much need; for till my baby's coming away there will be no need of giving of presents to any but to her.

Thus ye see, how as long as I want the sweet comfort of my boys' conversation, I am forced (yea, and delights) to converse with them by long letters. God bless you both, my sweet boys, and send you after a successful journey a joyful and happy return in the arms of your dear dad.

JAMES R.

From Newmarket on Saint Patrick's Day, who of old was too well patronised in the country ye are in.

British Library   *Holograph*
Harl. 6987, f. 29

[1] Properly "*ab Jove principium*" (Virgil *Eclogues* 3. 60: "From Jove is the beginning").
[2] Leonard Mawe, later Bishop of Bath and Wells.
[3] Matthew Wren, later Bishop of Ely.
[4] "Even unto the altars."
[5] The Order of the Garter, whose feast day is St. George's Day, 23 April.
[6] A kind of ruby that comes from the Persian province of Badakhshan.
[7] Buckingham was Lord High Admiral of England.
[8] Sir Paul Pindar, a wealthy merchant, had acquired some remarkable jewels during his residence in Turkey, where he served as English ambassador.

Letter 196

To Prince Charles and the Marquess of Buckingham

Philip IV's first response to news of the totally unexpected arrival in Madrid of Charles and Buckingham was to kneel before a crucifix and swear not to let the Prince's presence draw him into anything concerning the Catholic religion without the consent of the Pope. (The Infanta herself detested the very thought of marrying a heretic.) In the following letter King James, having learned that difficulties could stand in the way of a papal dispensation for the marriage, shows his first realization of what a quagmire he had got himself into by seeking this totally unsuitable match, one which the Spaniards themselves had never seriously contemplated.

25 March [1623]

My sweet boys,

God bless you both and reward you for the comfortable news I received from you yesterday (which was my coronation day)[1] in place of a tilting. And God bless thee, my sweet gossip, for thy little letter all full of comfort. I have written a letter to the Conde D'Olivares[2] as both of you desired me, as full of thanks and kindness as can be devised, as indeed he well deserves.

But in the end of your letter ye put in a cooling card anent the Nuncio's averseness to this business and that thereby ye collect that the Pope[3] will likewise be averse. But first ye must remember that in Spain they never put doubt of the granting of the dispensation, that themselves did set down the spiritual conditions, which I fully agreed unto and by them were they sent to Rome, and the consulto there concluded that the Pope might, nay ought, for the weal of Christendom grant a dispensation upon these conditions. These things may justly be laid before them; but I know not what ye mean by my acknowledging the Pope's spiritual supremacy. I am sure ye would not have me to renounce my religion for all the world. But all I can guess at your meaning is that it may be ye have an allusion to a passage in my book against Bellarmine,[4] where I

400

offer, if the Pope would quit his godhead and usurping over kings, to acknowledge him for the chief bishop, to whom all appeals of churchmen ought to lie *en dernier resort*.[5] The very words I send you here enclosed,† and that is the furthest that my conscience will permit me to go upon this point; for I am not a monsieur who can shift his religion[6] as easily as he can shift his shirt when he cometh from tennis.

I have no more to say in this, but God bless my sweet baby and send him good fortune in his wooing, to the comfort of his old father, who cannot be happy but in him. My ship is ready to make sail and only stays for a fair wind. God send it her. But I have, for the honour of England, curtailed the train that goes by sea of a number of rascals. And my sweet Steenie gossip, I must tell thee that Kate was a little sick within these four or five days of a headache, and the next morning, after a little casting, was well again. I hope it is a good sign[7] that I shall shortly be a gossip over again, for I must be thy perpetual gossip.[8] But the poor fool Kate hath by importunity gotten leave of me to send thee both her rich chains; and this is now the eighth letter I have written to my two boys, and six to Kate. God send me still more and more comfortable news of you both, till I may have a joyful, comfortable, and happy meeting with you; and that my baby may bring home a fair lady with him, as this is written upon Our Lady's day.

JAMES R.

†And for myself, if that were yet the question, I would with all my heart give my consent that the Bishop of Rome should have the first seat. I, being a western king, would go with the patriarch of the west. And for his temporal principality over the seigniory of Rome, I do not quarrel it neither. Let him, in God's name, be *primus episcopus inter omnes episcopos et princeps episcoporum*,[9] so it be no other ways, but as S. Peter was *princeps apostolorum*.[10]

British Library   *Holograph*
Harl. 6987, f. 41

[1]James refers not to 15 March, the day of his coronation in Westminster Abbey, but to 24 March ("The King's Day"), the anniversary of his accession to the throne. Tilting generally marked the latter occasion.

[2]Gaspar de Guzman, Conde de Olivares, favourite and chief minister of Philip IV.

[3]Gregory XV.

[4]*A Premonition to All Most Mighty Monarchs, Kings, Free Princes, and States of Christendom* (1609).

[5]This statement goes beyond what James said in the *Premonition,* as a glance at the King's appended excerpt from the latter reveals.

[6]An echo of Henri IV's conversion because "Paris is worth a mass."

[7]Buckingham's wife presented him later this year with their second child, Jacobina, who died soon after birth.

[8]King James wanted to be godparent to all of Buckingham's children. See Glossary, *gossip.*

[9]"First bishop among all bishops and chief of the bishops."

[10]"Chief of the apostles." For this passage from the *Premonition,* see *The Political Works of James I,* ed. C. H. McIlwain (Cambridge, Mass., 1918), p. 127.

Letter 197

To Prince Charles and the Marquess of Buckingham

As this letter amusingly indicates, King James had difficulty preserving the confidentiality of the letters from his son and his favourite.

1 April [1623]

My sweet boys,

I hope before this time ye are fully satisfied with my diligent care in writing unto you upon all occasions, but I have better cause to quarrel [with] you, that ye should ever have been in doubt of my often writing unto you, especially as long as ye saw no post nor creature was comd* from me but Michael Andrew; and yet by Carlisle,[1] in whose company he parted from me, I wrote my first letter unto you. And I wonder also why ye should ask me the question if ye should send me any more joint letters or not. Alas, sweet hearts, it is all my comfort in your absence that ye write jointly unto me—besides the great ease it is both to me and you. And ye need not doubt but I will be wary enough in not acquainting my council with any secret in your letters. But I have been troubled with Hamilton,[2] who, being present by chance at my receiving both of your first and second packet out of Madrid, would needs peer over my shoulder when I was reading them, offering ever to help me to read any hard words. And, in good faith, he is in this business as in all things else as variable and uncertain as the moon.

But the news of your glorious reception there makes me afraid that ye will both miskenne[*] your old dad hereafter. But in earnest, my baby, ye must be as sparing as ye can in your spending there, for your officers are already put to the height of their speed with providing the five thousand pounds by exchange; and now your tilting stuff, which they know not how to provide, will come to three more—and God knows how my coffers are already drained. I know no remedy, except ye procure the speedy payment of that hundred and fifty thousand pounds which was once promised to be advanced, which my sweet gossip, that now is turned Spaniard, with his golden key will be fittest to labour in, who shall have a fine ship to go thither with all speed for bringing him home to his dear dad. But I pray you, my baby, take heed of being hurt if ye run at tilt. As for Steenie, I hope thou will come back before that time, for I hope my baby will be ready to come away before the horses can be there well rested, and all things ready for running at tilt; which must be my baby's parting blow, if he can have leisure to perform it there. I pray you in the meantime keep yourselves in use of dancing privately, though ye should whistle and sing one to another, like Jack and Tom,[3] for fault of better music.

As for the main business, I hope the dispensation will come speedily and well; if otherwise, ye must put that king bravely to it, as I wrote in my last unto you; for the Archduchess's ambassador here says that my son's going there in this fashion hath obliged that king, in honour, to bestow his sister upon him, whether the dispensation come or not; and that there are numbers of Catholic Romans and Protestants married in the world without the Pope's dispensation. This the Baron de Boiscot[4] said to myself. I send you, according to your desire, a letter of thanks to that king which, my sweet Steenie, thou shall deliver unto him in my name with all the best compliments thou can; and, when thou wants, Carlisle can best instruct thee in that art. And I have sent a letter for the Conde d'Olivares in the last packet.[5]

And thus God keep you, my sweet boys, with my fatherly blessing, and send you a happy successful journey, and a joyful and happy return in the arms of your dear dad. From Theobalds, the first of April.

JAMES R.

British Library   *Holograph*
Harl. 6987, f. 50

[1] James Hay, Earl of Carlisle.
[2] James Hamilton, Marquess of Hamilton.
[3] The aliases used by Charles and Buckingham when they slipped out of England en route to Spain were Jack and Tom Smith. For the poem King James wrote on the Journey of Jack and Tom, see *Poems of James VI of Scotland*, ed. J. Craigie, II: 192–93.
[4] The ambassador from the Spanish Netherlands, the "Archduchess's ambassador" referred to above.
[5] See Letter 196, n. 2.

Letter 198

To Prince Charles and the Marquess of Buckingham

An important indication of Spanish attitudes was the reception given to the two "heretic" Church of England chaplains attending upon Prince Charles. In the following letter, King James instructs the Prince how to react if these clergymen are not allowed to conduct services in the quarters allocated to Charles in the King of Spain's palace.

My sweet boys,

I now send you by this young married man my tenth letter, who hath left a tythe in his wife's belly as I hear. I pray God bless her with it. My ship with my baby's servants and the jewels hath made sail with a fair wind five days ago. I hope in God they shall be with you before this letter.

The Spanish ambassador here let a word fall to Gresley,[1] as if there would be some question made that my baby's chaplains should not do their service in the king's palace there; but he concluded that that business would be soon accommodated. Always, in case any such difficulty should be stucken at, ye may remember them that it is an ill preparation of giving the Infanta free exercise of her religion here to refuse it to my son there, since their religion is as odious to a number here as ours is there. And if they will not yield, then, my sweet baby, show yourself not to be ashamed of your profession but go sometimes to my ambassador's house and have your service there, that God and man may see ye are not ashamed of your religion. But I hope in God this shall not need.

And now my sweet Steenie and gossip, I must give thee a short account of many things. First, Kate and thy sister supped with me on Saturday night last and yesterday both dined and supped with me, and so shall do still, with God's grace, as long as I am here. And my little grandchild[2] with her four teeth is, God be thanked, well weaned, and they are all very merry. I look hourly for the warrant for Kit's honour[3] to be brought to me, and likewise for that of his land, for Fotherly[4] assures me it is at a point. And he shall also have more than two thousand pounds of money that was due to me of the rents of Pewcame, which in truth the Treasurer[5] found out for him, who now so-licits me to make thee a duke in thy absence. Thou knows I am ready when thou will give the word. I stay not upon thy request but upon thy consent. Sue[6] hath gotten her ward and thanked me for it. Fotherly hopes within eight days to put a good end to the business of Barnwood Forest and within a fortnight to have a return of a survey of Hatfield Chase. We are presently in hand about Sedgemoor,[7] and I hope it shall be shortly brought to a good conclusion. I have signed a warrant which Fotherly is in hope will enable me to pay my Lord President's[8] debt. Dick Graham[9] is hastening all things here, and my gossip shall have two of my ships to bring him home. I pray God ye may procure the hastening of all things there as well.

And so God bless you, my sweet boys, and after a happy success in your business grant that ye may happily and comfortably return and light in the arms of your dear dad.

JAMES R.

From Whitehall the seventh of April.

British Library   Holograph
Harl. 6987, f. 63

[1]Walsingham Gresley (see Letter 194, n. 1).
[2]Lady Mary Villiers ("Mall").
[3]The creation of Buckingham's brother, Christopher Villiers, as Earl of Anglesey.
[4]See Letter 190, n. 16.
[5]Lionel Cranfield, Earl of Middlesex.
[6]Buckingham's sister Susan, the Countess of Denbigh.
[7]See Letter 191, n. 6.
[8]Henry Montagu, Viscount Mandeville.
[9]Sir Richard Graham, Buckingham's Master of the Horse.

Letter 199

To Prince Charles and the Marquess of Buckingham

Impatient for the return of his "sweet boys," James was now hastening the preparation of a naval squadron to bring Prince Charles and his bride to England. Since Buckingham was expected to return rather earlier, two other ships were assigned for his passage.

10 April [1623]

My sweet boys,

God ever bless and thank you for your last so comfortable letters. It is an ease to my heart now, that I am sure ye have received some of my letters. As for the fleet that should, with God's grace, bring my baby home, they are in a far greater readiness than ye could have believed, for they will be ready to make sail before the first of May if need were, and the smallest of six, besides the two that go for Steenie, are between five and six hundred tons. Their names and burden, Dick Graham[1] shall bring to you, who is to follow two days hence. It is now, therefore, your parts to advertise by the next post how soon ye would have them to make sail, for the charge and trouble will be infinite if their equipage stay long aboard, consuming victuals and making the ships to stink. My gossip shall come home in the *George,* and the *Antelope* wait upon him; and of their readiness Dick Graham will bring you word. The Treasurer[2] hath likewise made that money ready which my baby desired. I must bear him witness he spares not to engage himself and all he is worth for this business. As for your tilting stuff, these roaguie* bearers will give you an account, as likewise they will acquaint you with some other things from me. But I must bear witness to my baby's cofferer, without whose extreme diligence, besides his engaging of himself, ye had seen no tilting stuff at this time. God bless my sweet boys and send them, after a happy conclusion there, a comfortable and happy return to their sweet and dear dad.

JAMES R.

The 10 of April

[1]See Letter 198, n. 9.
[2]Lionel Cranfield, Earl of Middlesex.

Letter 200

To Prince Charles and the Marquess of Buckingham

Yearning for his favourite, the King despatched one of his ships, the George, *to bring Buckingham home, leaving Prince Charles to proceed with his courtship of the Infanta. Ignoring James's wishes, Buckingham remained in Spain with the Prince.*

18 April [1623]

My sweet boys,

I send you now the first sea-captain of our Admiral's[1] choice, who I hope shall ever prove worthy of such a patron. I begin now to long sore to hear more news from you, for this is the eleventh day since your last packet came to my hands. My baby shall receive his tilting stuff now bravely set forth and fit for a wooer; but in good faith the weather will be so hot there before ye can use it, that I would wish you rather to forbear it, for I fear my baby may catch a fever by it, and my Steenie gossip must be coming home before the horses can be ready to run. My sweet babies, for God's sake and your dear dad's, put not yourselves in hazard by any violent exercise as long as ye are there.

I am presently to go in hand with the providing of jewels for my baby to give in presents, which I hope shall save him a good deal of money. In the meantime, because my gossip is to come away in this ship, I send him six jewels to give in presents there at his parting. And my baby shall have his with the fleet, for sooner than at his parting he is not to give presents to any but to his mistress. How to dispose of these six, I leave it to thy discretion, my Steenie, but the watch is the richest and fittest for some old lady, in my opinion, but the ring is the far noblest. And thus, God bless you, my sweet boys, and after a happy success there send you comfortably and happily back again (every one in his own time) in the arms of your dear dad.

JAMES R.

From Windsor the 18 April.

British Library   *Holograph*
Harl. 6987, f. 71

¹I.e, Buckingham's own choice (he was Lord High Admiral of England).

Letter 201

To George Villiers, Marquess of Buckingham

One of the King's few letters to Spain not addressed jointly to Prince Charles and Buckingham.

18 April [1623]

My sweet Steenie gossip,

The bearer hereof had so great a longing to see you as I was forced to give him leave. I forgot in my former letters to tell you that, the Star Chamber process being ready for Oxford,¹ my attorney² told me it was fit he should be set at liberty how soon the process were served upon him; but the Lord Treasurer,³ coming to Newmarket, advised me rather to suspend the process than let him out before the return of my baby. "Except," quoth he, "ye would provide a ringleader for the mutineers" — which advice I followed.

For news, your bay Spanish mare with the black mane and tail hath an exceeding fair and fine horse-foal of ten days old, just of her own colour but that he hath the far foot white; and there is another of them ready to foal. God send my sweet baby the like luck with his Spanish breed before this time twelvemonth. Thus hoping that ye will give a good advice to the bearer hereof to lead a good life in times coming, I pray the Lord send my sweet Steenie gossip a happy and comfortable return in the arms of his dear dad.

JAMES R.

Kit is now an earl[4] and hath also the patent of his land; thus was thou born in a happy hour for all thy kin.

From Windsor the 18 of April.

British Library   *Holograph*
Harl. 6987, f. 69

[1]Henry de Vere, 18th Earl of Oxford, an opponent of the Spanish Match, was sent to the Tower on 22 April 1622 for "unfit speaches touching the King and his government" (Chamberlain, *Letters,* 27 April 1622, II: 433). According to one account, he attacked Buckingham; according to another, Gondomar. Both reports may be true. One version says that Oxford was in his cups when he spoke so indiscreetly.

When Oxford's supporters argued that he should either be brought to trial or released, a bill was filed in the Court of Star Chamber declaring that he had scandalously abused the government. Although the charge was not proceeded with, Oxford was not released until December 1623.

[2]The Attorney-General, Sir Thomas Coventry.

[3]Lionel Cranfield, Earl of Middlesex.

[4]Christopher Villiers was created Earl of Anglesey the day that this letter was written.

Letter 202

To Prince Charles and the Marquess of Buckingham

On 24 April a courier arrived at Madrid bringing from Rome the papal dispensation required for the marriage of Prince Charles and the Infanta. Unfortunately, far-reaching conditions were attached to this dispensation, ones that would require concessions that King James had already refused. Prince Charles promptly asked his father for plenary powers to negotiate a revised marriage treaty. In this letter James gives his consent. A week after writing this and the following letter, James made his "Steenie" Duke of Buckingham.

My sweet boys,

Yesterday in the afternoon I received two packets from you, after my coming hither, by two several posts, and the day before I wrote to you my opinion[1] from Theobalds anent the three conditions annexed to the dispensation. I now send you, my baby, here enclosed the power you desire. It were a strange trust that I would refuse to put upon my only son and upon my best servant. I know such two as ye are will never promise in my name but what may stand with my conscience, honour, and safety, and all these I do fully trust with any one of you two. My former letter will show you my conceit, and now I put the full power in your hands with God's blessing on you both, praying him still that after a happy success there ye may speedily and happily return and light in the arms of your dear dad.

JAMES R.

Greenwich, the 11 of May

British Library   *Holograph*
Harl. 6987, f. 94

[1]This letter has been lost, apparently with several others written between 18 April and 11 May.

Letter 203

To Prince Charles

The following is the authorization for Prince Charles to bind King James to any terms the former might conclude with the Spaniards.

My dearest son,

I do hereby promise, in the word of a king, that whatsoever ye my dearest son shall promise there in my name, I will punctually and faithfully perform, and so God bless you.

Your loving father,
JAMES R.

Greenwich the 11 of May.

Bodleian Library   *Holograph*
Tanner 73, f. 317

Letter 204

To Prince Charles

Further evidence as to how a burned-out James was surrendering authority is provided by his promise in this letter not to convene a parliament during the absence of Prince Charles.

11 May [1623]

My sweet baby,

Since the ending of my last letters unto you I have received a letter of yours from the Lord Keeper[1] which tells me the first news of a parliament (and that in a strange form) that ever I heard of since your parting from me. By such intelligence, both ye and my sweet Steenie gossip may judge of their worth that make them unto you, and ye may rest assured that I never meant to undertake any such business in your absence if it had been propounded unto me; as in good faith I never heard of it. And so, with God's blessing to you both, I pray God that after a happy conclusion there ye may both make a comfortable and happy return in the arms of your dear dad.

JAMES R.

Greenwich the 11 of May.

Bodleian Library   *Holograph*
Tanner 73, f. 316

¹John Williams, Bishop of Lincoln, the Lord Keeper of the Great Seal.

Letter 205

To Prince Charles and the Marquess of Buckingham

*Besides the royal menagerie which the kings of England had
kept in the Tower of London for centuries, King James maintained collections of exotic birds and animals in St. James Park
and at Theobalds. Knowing of his special zoological interests,
the Duke of Savoy presented him with a tiger and a lion, and
Henri IV sent him two ostriches. In this letter he refers to a gift
of six camels and an elephant from the King of Spain.*

[*Late May 1623*]

My sweet boys,

If the Dutch post had not been robbed and sore beaten in
Kent three days ago,[1] ye had sooner received the duplicate of the
power[2] I put in my sweet baby's hand, which I send you for the
more security, seeing the expedition of your return depends
upon it. But it rejoiceth my heart that your opinion anent the
three conditions annexed to the dispensation agreeth fully with
mine, as ye will find by one of my letters, dated at Theobalds,
which Gresley will deliver unto you.[3] Carlisle came yesterday
morning, *todos Castillanos*[4] and a devoted servant to the
Conde d'Olivares.

But my sweet Steenie gossip, I heartily thank thee for thy
kind drolling letter. I do herewith send thee a kind letter of
thanks to that king for the elephant,[5] as thou desired, wherein I
likewise thank him for a letter of his which Carlisle delivered
unto me, which is indeed the kindest and courtesest* letter that

413

ever I received from any king. I have likewise received from Carlisle the list of the jewels which ye have already received, and which of them my baby means to present to his mistress. I pray you, sweet baby, if ye think not fit to present to her the collar of great balas rubies[6] and knots of pearls, bring it home again and the like I say of the head-dressing of great pear pearls which ye have, and other three head-dressings which Frank Stewart[7] is to deliver unto you, for they are not presents fit for subjects. But, if ye please, ye may present one of them to the Queen of Spain. Carlisle thinks that my baby will bestow a rich jewel upon the Conde d'Olivares but, in my opinion, horses, dogs, hawks, and such like stuff to be sent him out of England by you both will be a far more noble and acceptable present to him.

And now, my sweet Steenie gossip, that the poor fool Kate[8] hath also sent thee her pearl chain, which by accident I saw in a box in Frank Stewart's hand, I hope I need not to conjure thee not to give any of her jewels away there, for thou knows what necessary use she will have of them at your return here; besides that it is not lucky to give away anything that I have given her. Now, as for mules, the more strong mules for carriage that ye can provide me with, I will be the better served in my journeys and the better cheap. If ye can get deer brought handsomely hither, they shall be welcome. I hope the elephant, camels, and asses are already by the way.

And so God bless you both and after a happy success there send you speedily and comfortably home in the arms of your dear dad.

JAMES R.

British Library   *Holograph*
Harl. 6987, f. 80

[1]This robbery is noted by John Chamberlain: "There was a Spanish post lately robd of goode store of monie about Shooters-hill. The fellowes that did yt and the postillon that set the match are since taken by their owne folly and brought to court before the King, beeing like to pay for yt with their neckes" (*Letters*, 14 June 1623, II: 502).

[2]Letter 203.

[3]This letter has been lost.

[4]"Entirely Castilian." Chamberlain, writing on 30 May, speaks of Carlisle as back from Spain (*Letters*, II: 409).

[5]"The king of Spaine hath sent hither five camells and an elephant, which going throughe the towne this day sevenight after midnight could not yet passe unsene" (Chamberlain, *Letters*, 12 July 1623, II: 507). King James ordered that the public not be permitted to look at the elephant before he himself had seen it.

The arrival of the elephant in London inspired the Venetian ambassador to quip in a despatch home: "The King of Spain has sent his Majesty the present of an elephant. I do not know whether it comes as an earnest of the Infanta or instead of her" (*CSP Venetian, 1623–25*, p. 75).

[6]See Letter 195, n. 6.

[7]Sir Francis Stewart, a naval officer who had Buckingham for his patron, had been given command of the two vessels sent to bring him home.

[8]Buckingham's wife.

Letter 206

To Prince Charles and the Duke of Buckingham[1]

The Pope had attached to his dispensation a major condition: that the King of Spain guarantee that the King of England would fulfil the terms of the marriage treaty. Philip IV asked a junta of Spanish theologians to decide the circumstances under which he could give such a guarantee. The theologians in their reply advised that any marriage be merely one per verba de præsenti[2] *and its consummation postponed for a year, during which time the English Catholics must be seen to have received all the benefits provided for them by the treaty. Meanwhile, King James had become increasingly unhappy about the long delays that had held Charles and Buckingham in Spain. News of the junta's decision filled him with agitation and despair and elicited the following letter.*

14 June [1623]

My sweet boys,

Your letter by Cottington[3] hath strucken me dead. I fear it shall very much shorten my days, and I am the more perplexed that I know not how to satisfy the people's expectation here, neither know I what to say to our Council, for the fleet that

415

stayed upon a wind this fortnight (Rutland[4] and all aboard) must now be stayed, and I know not what reason I shall pretend for the doing of it. But as for my advice and directions that ye crave in case they will not alter their decree it is, in a word, to come speedily away if ye can get leave, and give over all treaty; and this I speak without respect of any security they can offer you, except ye never look to see your old dad again, whom I fear ye shall never see, if ye see him not before winter. Alas, I now repent me sore that ever I suffered you to go away. I care for match nor nothing, so I may once have you in my arms again. God grant it! God grant it! God grant it! Amen, amen, amen. I protest ye shall be as heartily welcome as if ye had done all things ye went for, so that I may once have you in my arms again. And so God bless you both, my only sweet son and my only best sweet servant, and let me hear from you quickly with all speed, as ye love my life. And so God send you a happy and joyful meeting in the arms of your dear dad.

JAMES R.

From Greenwich the xiiii of June.

British Library   *Holograph*
Harl. 6987, f. 100

[1]On 18 May 1623, George Villiers was created Duke of Buckingham.
[2]See Letter 216.
[3]See Letter 190, n. 20.
[4]Francis Manners, Earl of Rutland, had been made admiral of the fleet that was to bring Prince Charles home.

Letter 207

To Prince Charles and the Duke of Buckingham

Early June found King James tormented by doubts concerning acceptance of the marriage treaty as revised by the Pope. Finally, on 20 July, he acquiesced. The treaty ceremoniously signed in the Chapel Royal at Whitehall that morning was, however, in-complete. Supplementing it were four secret clauses (which James signed that evening), so favourable to James's Catholic sub-jects that Protestant England would have exploded with anger had their contents become known. Contemplating the extraordi-nary concessions which he had made, the King could find but one consolation–Phillip IV had reduced to eight months the year that the junta of theologians had recommended should pass be-fore the consummation of Prince Charles's marriage with the In-fanta. Even so, if Charles married her forthwith, he would not be able to enjoy her until the following March. James was depressed at the prospect of having to send two fleets, expensively and elab-orately outfitted, to Spain–the one to bring Prince Charles home this summer, the other to fetch the Infanta in the spring of 1624.

21 July [1623]

My sweet boys,

Even as I was going yesterday in the evening to the ambassa-dors to take my private oath, having taken the public before noon in great solemnity, Andover[1] came stepping in at the door like a ghost and delivered me your letters. Since it can be no better I must be contented; but this course is both a dishonour to me and double charges if I must send two fleets—but if they will not send her till March let them, in God's name, send her by their own fleet. The ambassadors speak broadly against this de-lay, and plainly say that it is senseless and swear they will write earnestly with Cottington[2] to persuade the change of that reso-lution. But if no better may be, do ye hasten your business. The fleet shall be at you as soon as wind and weather can serve, and this bearer will bring you the power to treat for the Palatinate and the matter of Holland. And, sweet baby, go on with the contract and the best assurance ye can get of sending her the next year; but, upon my blessing, lie not with her in Spain ex-cept ye be sure to bring her with you. And forget not to make them keep their former conditions anent the portion, other-wise both my baby and I are bankrupts forever. And now I must tell you miracles: our great primate[3] hath behaved himself wonderful well in this business, insomuch as my Lord Keeper[4] says he will love him the better while he lives for it; and my Lord Chamberlain[5] hath gone beyond all the Council in clear and honest dealing in this business. All other things I remit to the sufficiency of this bearer whom Steenie hath so earnestly recommended unto me.

And so God bless you, my sweet children, and send you a happy, joyful, and speedy return in the arms of your dear dad, amen.

JAMES R.

Whitehall the xxi of July.

British Library   *Holograph*
Harl. 6987, f. 123

[1]See Letter 190, n. 8.
[2]See Letter 190, n. 20.
[3]George Abbot, Archbishop of Canterbury, whose strong Protestantism would have been expected to make him hostile to the Spanish Match.
[4]John Williams, Bishop of Lincoln.
[5]The Earl of Pembroke.

Letter 208

To George Villiers, Duke of Buckingham

The King reports that he has obtained £2000 from the East India Company for his favourite.

31 July [1623]

My sweet Steenie,

Thou remembers that among many other particulars whereof I gave thee an account in my last letter to thee, by Gresley,[1] I told thee that Mildmay[2] had put me in hope that the East Indian Company would present thee with twelve hundred pounds sterling; but I found he hunted upon so cold a scent as

418

thy best steward was forced to labour in it himself, and now I can assure thee they will presently present thee with two thousand pounds and deliver it to thy wife as thy nearest friend. And so God bless thee, my sweet Steenie, and send thee a quick and happy return, with my sweet baby, in the arms of thy dear dad and steward.

JAMES R.

Bromame[3] the last of July.

British Library   *Holograph*
Harl. 6987, f. 135

[1]See Letter 194, n. 1.
[2]Sir Henry Mildmay, Master of the Jewel House.
[3]Bromham (near Devizes), the Wiltshire home of Sir Edward Baynton.

Letter 209

To Prince Charles and the Duke of Buckingham

In this letter James broaches, for the first time, the possibility of Charles marrying the Infanta by proxy.

31 July [1623]

My sweet boys,

In your last letter by Clerke[1] ye keep me still, as formerly ye did, betwixt hope and despair of the Infanta's coming this year. I like well two of the three ways ye have offered them for hastening her coming home; but the third, of sending to the Pope, will delay all this year and lose the season, especially considering that the Pope is dead,[2] and God knows how long they will be of choosing another and how he will be affected when he is chosen. And therefore, I pray you, put us out of this lingering pain one way or other. But, if she come not this year, the disgrace and my charges will prove infinite.

All is performed and put in execution here to the ambassadors' full satisfaction. If ye can bring her home with you, strive by all means to be at home before Michaelmas, for after it will be dangerous being upon the sea; if otherwise, I hope ye will hasten you home for the comfort of your old dear dad. But yet, after the contract, go as far as ye can before your parting upon the business of the Palatinate and Holland, that the world may see ye have thought as well upon the business of Christendom as upon the codpiece point. I protest I know not what to do if she come not this year, for this very refreshing of my fleet with victuals hath cost me eight thousand pounds, and therefore ye had need to hasten the payment of the dowry after the contract. And if ye come without her, let the marriage at least be hastened as soon as can be after your parting to be performed by commission in your absence, but I pray God ye may bring her with you.

And so God bless you, my sweet children, and send you a happy and comfortable return in the arms of your dear dad, and that quickly.

JAMES R.

Bromame[3] the last of July.

British Library   *Holograph*
Lansdowne 1238, f. 35

[1]Edward Clarke, Extraordinary Clerk of the Council.
[2]Gregory XV died on 8 July 1623. His successor, Urban VIII, was elected a month later.
[3]See Letter 208, n. 3.

Letter 210

To Prince Charles and the Duke of Buckingham

The Spanish ambassadors, ordinary and extraordinary, in England constantly urged James to show greater and greater leniency in applying the penalties to which his Catholic subjects were liable. Their uncollected fines meant, of course, a very considerable loss in revenue for the Crown.

5 August [1623]

My sweet boys,

I write to you now upon the good fifth day of August[1] in the afternoon. Secretary Calvert's[2] moving the ambassadors to have a sight or copy of what they wrote hath produced this effect: that I find their letter leaner and drier than either I expected or deserved. What course I have taken with them hereupon, at their coming hither to this feast, Secretary Conway's[3] letter will inform you at large. To be short, I have given order to put in present execution all that I have promised and more, as themselves confess—and had been done before this time if themselves, by new unreasonable motions, had not hindered it. And this much more than I promised have I granted unto them, at their earnest suit, which is a discharge of all debts already owing to me by recusants. And therefore, if they cast up now the great dowry that they are to give, remember that by this deed I quit six and thirty thousand pounds of good rent in England and Ireland, which, in good account, will strike down the third part at least of their dowry.

If Killigrew[4] be not already gone, he will deliver this letter unto you; but, if he be gone, Clerke[5] will give you it, who shall immediately be despatched after the sealing of that pardon and privy seal which is presently to be drawn up.

I have no more to say but if ye hasten you not home I apprehend I shall never see you, for my extreme longing will kill me. But God bless you, my sweet boys, upon this good day; and he that delivered me from so great a danger upon it preserve you and grant you a speedy, happy, and comfortable return in the arms of your dear dad. Amen. Amen. Amen.

JAMES R.

Carlisle hath told me a tale of this marquis[6] that shows him to be a slim* man and my Steenie's small friend; and the devil take

421

them all that are so, except my baby, who I know can never love
Steenie! But, in earnest, he broke off a crafty discourse to Carlisle, but he choked him too soon; therefore keep this to yourselves till ye hear more of it.

British Library   *Holograph*
Harl. 6987, f. 137

¹The anniversary of James's escape from the Gowrie Plot, 5 August 1600.
²Sir George Calvert was one of the two Secretaries of State between 1619
and 1625.
³Sir Edward Conway had become a Secretary of State on 16 January 1623.
⁴Peter Killigrew, who had arrived from Spain on 7 July.
⁵See Letter 209, n. 1.
⁶The reference may be to the Marquis of Inojosa, the Spanish ambassador
extraordinary.

Letter 211

To Prince Charles and the Duke of Buckingham

A brief note urging their return.

10 August [1623]

My sweet boys,

I can now assure you that the ambassadors are either more
than fully satisfied or they are worse than devils, if worse can
be; but, in good faith, I believe they are really well pleased.
What labour I had in it, Secretary Conway¹ will inform you at
large. It only rests now to pray you for God's sake to haste,
haste, haste; but do as much of your great businesses as ye can,
as I wrote in my first letter by Killigrew² (I mean of these two
that he now carries). If ye hasten not ye will get no more letters
from me; for I protest to God I have written mine eyes almost
dry, and in my last letter and this every stroke of my pen seems
two. If any other thing come in my mind, I will commit it to this

bearer's relation, and never cease to pray the Lord to bless my
sweet boys and send you a happy, comfortable, but speedy return in the arms of your dear dad.

JAMES R.

From Cranborne the 10 of August.

British Library   *Holograph*
Harl. 6987, f. 139

[1] See Letter 210, n. 3.
[2] See Letter 210, n. 4.

Letter 212

To George Villiers, Duke of Buckingham

*Reluctance to send bad news has kept James from telling
Buckingham of his wife's illness.*

10 August [1623]

My Steenie,

Even as I had written my joint letter to my baby and thee,
Apsley[1] came with his good news. I have written a letter to my
baby and another to thee, as ye desired, which ye may show and
make use of, if need shall require it. As for the recusants' by-
past fines, I have already granted it, at the ambassadors' suit, in
the name of my baby's mistress, and so thou and I thought one
thought. It is true I did not write to thee of thy wife's sickness,
for I hope in God never to write evil news unto thee, but now I
thank God she is very well. Some feared a consumption, but
Mayerne[2] assured me it was but a vapour that came from her
spleen. Commend me to my sweet baby, and the Lord to bless
you both and send you a happy, joyful, and speedy return in the
arms of your dear dad, gossip, and steward.

JAMES R.

Cranborne the 10 of August.

British Library   *Holograph*
Harl. 6987, f. 141

[1]Probably Sir Allen Apsley, who was connected, through marriage, with the Villiers family (see Lockyer, *Buckingham*, p. 39).
[2]Theodore Turquet de Mayerne, knighted in 1624, was a French physician held in particularly high regard by King James.

Letter 213

To Prince Charles

A letter commanding the prince to return home. On 30 August Charles and Buckingham left Madrid for England. Negotiations for a marriage with the Infanta dragged on for months, but to all intents and purposes the project was dead.

10 August [1623]

My dearest son,

I sent you a commandment long ago not to lose time where ye are, but either to bring quickly home your mistress, which is my earnest desire, but if no better may be, rather than to linger any longer there, to come without her, which for many important reasons I am now forced to renew. And therefore I charge you, upon my blessing, to come quickly either with her or without her. I know your love to her person hath enforced you to delay the putting in execution of my former commandment. I confess it is my chiefest worldly joy that ye love her, but the necessity of my affairs enforceth me to tell you that ye must prefer the obedience to a father to the love ye carry to a mistress. And so God bless you.

JAMES R.

Cranborne the 10 of August.

British Library   *Holograph*
Harl. 6987, f. 143

Letter 214

To George Villiers, Duke of Buckingham

Although clearly addressed to Buckingham in Spain, the following letter supplies no evidence as to its exact date.

[1623]

My sweet Steenie and gossip,

Thy single letter was so sweet and comfortable unto me as I cannot forbear to pray God ever to bless and reward thee for it.

Praying God I may never have comfort of my sweet baby longer than I shall remain a true friend to my sweet Steenie and gossip, to whom God grant a comfortable and happy return to his dear dad.

JAMES R.

British Library   *Holograph*
Harl. 6987, f. 147

Letter 215

To George Villiers, Duke of Buckingham

During the period that Charles and Buckingham were in Spain, they concerned themselves with negotiations relating to the marriage and the Palatinate, while other matters were left to the Earl of Bristol, the regular English ambassador. The Spanish ban on imports of wool from England, that country's principal export, was so serious a matter, however, that King James asked Buckingham to take up the matter directly with Philip IV. With this and the preceding undated letter, we reach the end of King James's correspondence with his son and his favourite in Spain.

[1623]

My sweet Steenie and gossip,

Thou must deal as vigorously and effectually as thou can with that king and his ministers for either recalling or making a good interpretation of their new pragmatic against perpetua-noes[1] and all sorts of woollen stuffs; otherwise our trade will be undone here.

God bless thee and all thy labours, my sweet gossip, and send thee quickly and happily home to thy dear dad.

JAMES R.

British Library   *Holograph*
Harl. 6987, f. 145

[1]Also termed "perpetuanas." The "pragmatic against perpetuanoes" signifies an ordinance against durable wool fabrics of a particular kind.

Letter 216

To John Digby, Earl of Bristol

Prince Charles and Buckingham arrived in England on 5 October 1623, to the acclaim of a nation that rejoiced to have King James's heir restored to them safe, single, and Protestant. Hopes for the match with Spain died hard with the old king. In the following letter he suggests Christmas for the betrothal of Prince Charles and the Infanta, making it also the ultimate date for undertakings that Philip IV could never give.

We have received yours brought us by Gresley[1] and the copy of yours to our dear son, and we cannot forbear to let you know how well we esteem your dutiful, discreet, and judicious relation and humble advice to ourself and our son. Whereupon, having ripely deliberated with ourself and communicated with our dear son, we have resolved with the great liking of our son to rest upon that security (in point of doubt of the Infanta's taking a religious order)[2] which you in your judgement shall think meet. We have further thought meet to give you knowledge that it is our special desire that the betrothing of the Infanta with words *de præsenti*[3] should be upon one of the days in Christmas (New Style), that holy and joyful time best fitting so notable and blessed an action.

But first we will that you repair presently to that king and give him knowledge of the safe arrival of our dear son to our court, so satisfied and taken with the great entertainments, personal kindness, favour, and respect he hath received from that king and court as he seems not able to magnify it sufficiently, which makes us not know how sufficiently to give thanks. But we will by all means that you endeavour to express our thankfulness to that king and to the rest to whom it belongs, in the most ample and best manner you can. And hereupon you may take occasion to let that king know that according to our constant affection to make a firm and indissoluble amity between our families, nations, and crowns, and not seem to abandon our honour nor (at the same time we give joy to our only son) to give our only daughter her portion in tears, by the advice of that king's ambassadors [which] they have offered themselves as our counsel, we have entered a treaty concerning the restitution of the Palatinate, as will more particularly appear to you as by the copies herewith sent.

Now we must remember you that we ever understood and expected that upon the marriage of our son with the Infanta we should have clear restitution of the Palatinate and electoral dignity to our son-in-law, to be really procured by that king according to the obligation of our honour as you have well expressed in your reasons why the person of our son-in-law should not be left out of the treaty but that the Emperor should find out a greater title or by increasing the number of electoral styles wherewith to satisfy the Duke of Bavaria. We now, therefore, require you that presently in your first audience you procure from that king[4] a punctual answer what course that king will take for the restitution of the Palatinate and Electorate to our son-in-law and, in case that either the Emperor or the Duke of Bavaria will oppose any part of the expected restitution, what course that king will take to give us assurance for our content in that point whereof we require your present answer, and that you so press expedition herein that we may together receive the full joy of both in Christmas, resting ourself upon that faithful diligence of yours we have approved in all your service. Though almost with the latest, we must remember to you as good a ground for you to work on: that our son did write us out of Spain that that king would give us a blank in which we might form our conditions concerning the Palatinate, and the same our son confirms to us. Now what observation and performance that king will make we require you to express and give us a speedy account.

British Library   *Copy*
Harl. 4761, f. 57

[1] Walsingham Gresley, Bristol's steward.
[2] A constant anxiety was that the Infanta, to avoid marriage to a heretic, would become a nun.
[3] *Sponsalia de præsenti* took effect immediately; *sponsalia de futuro* did not.
[4] Philip IV.

Letter 217

To Frederick, Elector of the Palatinate of the Rhine

Prince Charles and Buckingham having returned from Spain unsuccessful in their attempts to arrange the return of the Palatinate to King James's son-in-law, the King had to fall back on

your possessions and enjoying of all according to the contract which is presently to be made, and also to serve for a preparation for the bettering of the said conditions to your person (which will be in all likelihood when the marriage will be resolved and concluded), that a marriage be made betwixt your eldest son, our grandchild, and one of the Emperor's daughters; in contemplation whereof they have approached a degree nearer, to wit that the electoral dignity shall come again to your person after the Duke of Bavaria's death. In which treaty of marriage to clear the principal difficulty, which consisted with the education of your son with the Emperor, we have taken from them all hope therein (wherein we assure ourselves you will be content) and have purposed that he shall have his education with our son and with and in the presence of the Infanta when she shall be in our court.

We have exactly showed you the state of this negotiation which chiefly concerns you and yours to the end you may fix your eyes upon your necessity and bare condition and manner of living, which dependeth upon the courtesy and assistance of others, and that you may judge advisedly whether your ready entrance into the possession of your own and with a kind of present liberty of living (with insurance in time to recover the possession of it) shall not be more convenient for you than a hazardous long expectation upon other uncertain means, the former whereof I prefer before the latter. We pray you to consider what probable and feasible means we may undertake to reduce your condition to that estate as you promise yourself, wherein we doubt not but you will weigh our forces and those of our allies and such others whereof we may hope or be assured, to the end that if it should happen that we cannot obtain to the entire of that we desire by way of treaty, or that we should take another course, you may be partakers of councils as well as the issues and uncertain events. And forasmuch as we are desirous to consider with you for your personal estate, and as we are obliged to have regard to the right of our only daughter and to the inheritance of your children with the hope of their posterity, by what way it may be most easily established and by what fit

430

means provision may be made best to that effect. And herein we remain your most affectionate father.

JACOBUS REX

From Whitehall, the 20 of November 1623.

British Library
Sloane 1775, f. 59

Apparently a contemporary
translation of a Latin
original

Letter 218

To George Villiers, Duke of Buckingham

King James declares his love for Buckingham.

[*December 1623?*][1]

My only sweet and dear child,

Notwithstanding of your desiring me not to write yesterday, yet had I written in the evening if, at my coming out of the park, such a drowsiness had not come upon me as I was forced to sit and sleep in my chair half an hour. And yet I cannot content myself without sending you this present, praying God that I may have a joyful and comfortable meeting with you and that we may make at this Christmas a new marriage ever to be kept hereafter; for, God so love me, as I desire only to live in this world for your sake, and that I had rather live banished in any part of the earth with you than live a sorrowful widow's life without you. And so God bless you, my sweet child and wife, and grant that ye may ever be a comfort to your dear dad and husband.

JAMES R.

Bodleian Library
Tanner 72, f. 14

Holograph

[1]This undated letter was first printed in 1839 by J. S. Brewer in his edition of

Bishop Goodman's *The Court of King James the First* (II: 379). Brewer's date for this letter, 1625, was subsequently accepted by J. O. Halliwell in his *Letters of the Kings of England* (II: 236). However, since King James died in March of 1625, this year made no sense for a letter mentioning plans for "this Christmas." In 1956, D. H. Willson in his *King James VI and I* (p. 445) gave, without comment, December 1624 as the date of this letter.

Willson was quite possibly correct in his dating, but the contents of the letter may indicate a date either in late 1622 or in late 1623. The former would fit if the reference to physical separation was made when the Spanish journey was first proposed. The latter would be consonant with a royal resolve, when Buckingham had recently returned after an eight months' absence, to celebrate "a new marriage ever to be kept hereafter." Similarly, James's readiness to "live banished in any part of the world" with Buckingham may tie in with a resolution, now that Buckingham was back, never to endure again such pangs of separation as he had suffered while his favourite was in Spain.

Letter 219

To Sir Edward Conway[1]

On 19 February 1624, King James opened his fourth and last parliament. It met amid "a clash of generations in the royal family."[2] Prince Charles and Buckingham, having decided that further marriage negotiations with Madrid were pointless, both urged war with Spain as the only means left to get restitution of the Palatinate. James, more aware of how ill England could afford a war, clung to vestigial hopes for a diplomatic settlement.

Pressured by his son, his favourite, and an ardently anti-Spanish parliament, James gradually weakened before demands that he break off negotiations with Spain. On 20 March the Commons committed themselves to levy three subsidies and three fifteenths once the treaties with Spain were broken. A most unhappy King James dithered while Charles and Buckingham built up pressure. From Parliament came an anti-recusant petition with a clause calling on James to declare he would not, as part of any marriage treaty, slacken the laws against English Catholics. A commitment of this sort would inevitably signal a break with Spain, and James knew as much. In this letter to Conway, the King puts his agonized question: can he be sure of the money from Parliament once he has broken with Spain?

In the end Charles and Buckingham got their war. James sim-
ply had not the energy to stand up to them for long, allied as
they were with Parliament.[3]

[*4 April 1624*]

Pardon me the breaking of this hour, for it is a fault I seldom commit; but my son's being here and a number of people that came with him so plied me with business as I had never leisure till now to write unto you. My son will inform you as he finds the lower house inclined in this business, that ye may advertise me accordingly—I mean whether they will go on with the subsidies according to their promise, and trust to my wisdom and discretion in answering their petition; or if they will make it in effect a condition *sine qua non,* though not say it plainly. I hope ye will likewise do all ye can to discover this, for if I may be sure that they mean to keep their promise to me, let the packet go on.[4] Otherwise it were no reason I should be bound and they leap free and leave me naked and without help.

Though I have commanded my son to acquaint you with what he can discover, yet knows he not of these my private directions unto you. All this I must commit to your secrecy, discretion, and diligence. The short and the long is that if I may be sure that their passing of the subsidies will not depend upon my answer to their petition, let the post go, post haste post. But if they will not move without first having their will in that, no reason they should break their promise and I still be bound. Farewell.

JAMES R.

Public Record Office   *Holograph*
SP 14/163/30

---

[1]Sir Edward Conway had become a Secretary of State on 16 January 1623. He was entirely Buckingham's creature (James observed that "Steenie" had given him a secretary who could not write), and there is something pathetic about James making him his confidant as he tries to manœuvre without the knowledge of the Prince or the Duke.

[2]Conrad Russell, *Parliaments and English Politics 1621–29,* p. 145.

[3]Russell, *Parliaments,* p. 190, points out that Parliament, although vehemently

anti-Spanish, was much less keen on actual war with its attendant cost than has been recognized.

⁴The previous day, in a letter very similar to this, James in great apprehension had secretly written to Conway to detain the messenger who was to have left for Spain to break off the treaties. (See Appendix, letter of 3/4/24.)

Letter 220

To Louis XIII, King of France

On 17 April 1624, Buckingham revealed to a parliamentary committee that King James had written to Philip IV dissolving the marriage treaty signed with Spain the previous year. Unofficial overtures had already been made to the French for a match between Prince Charles and Princess Henrietta Maria. By July negotiations for that marriage were well along, with the arrival from France of a new ambassador, the Marquis d'Effiat, and the despatch to Paris of Henry Rich, Lord Kensington.

TRANSLATED FROM THE FRENCH

21 July 1624

Most high, most excellent, and most mighty Prince,
our most dear and well-beloved good brother, cousin,
and ally of long standing:

When we consider the evils which threaten the present age, we foresee likewise the happy deliverance that God is preparing by the conjunction of our friendships, for the hope of which we are urged by your letters, of which each word is a sentence which silently conveys more than it expresses. For our part, there is so little that you would have cause to blame in us that we should rather bear witness to our promptitude to join ourself with you in all your good and great designs and to confirm and complete the perfect friendship that exists between our persons, of which this paper is not capable of expressing the affection, any more than the impatience with which we await the effects.

And accordingly we have commanded that lord the Baron of Kensington[1] (whose affection and fidelity are, we presume, sufficiently known to the two of us) to dilate more particularly on this subject, waiting for time to give us occasion to confirm it in effect. And we are of the opinion that it will be agreeable and acceptable to you, for the judgement that we make of your good affection toward us, by the choice that you have made of so gallant a gentleman as the Lord Marquis d'Effiat[2] to employ him near us, who is not only a wise and confidential pledge between us but also a great hunter and good company, whom, because of the intimate friendship of our mutual affections, and according to his own desire, we are treating as one of our household, communicating to him our counsels and satisfactions in the house and making him a part of our recreations in the fields. In these matters he serves us with such good grace that we cannot hide our gratitude any more than the emotion with which we await the accomplishment of our designs and reciprocal affections.

And on this we shall pray God to keep you, most high, most excellent and most mighty Prince, our very dear and well-beloved good brother, cousin, and ally of long standing, to keep you in his sure and worthy care.

Written from Bletsoe,[3] this 21 of July, 1624.

Your very affectionate brother,
cousin, and ally of long standing,
JAQUES R.

Huntington Library	*Scribal letter, with last*
HM 28569	*phrase and signature in*
	King James's hand

[1]Henry Rich, created Baron Kensington on 5 March 1623 and Earl of Holland on 24 September 1624.

[2]Antoine Coiffier de Ruzé, Marquis d'Effiat. James had known the newly arrived ambassador less than two weeks when he delivered the fulsome compliments in this letter.

[3]The Bedfordshire home of Lord St. John.

Letter 221

To George Villiers, Duke of Buckingham

Buckingham's health was not robust, and under stress it was likely to falter. In the spring of 1624 Buckingham was under great strain, guarding himself against hostile Spanish ambassadors and a rival faction at court, manipulating Parliament, and maneuvering a suspicious and unhappy King James into reversing his foreign policy. Not surprisingly, all this told on his health. Buckingham took to his bed early in May, apparently afflicted with jaundice. Sent by King James to Greenwich to convalesce, Buckingham improved; but overwork brought on a relapse and he retired to his mansion of New Hall in Essex, whither James sent him "loving letters," possibly including the three undated ones which follow.

In mid-August, continuing ill health led Buckingham to visit the spa at Wellingborough.[1]

[*1624?*]

Alas, sweet heart, thy letter yesternight made my heart to bleed. For God's sake be as wary as thou can with drugs and physicians, for they are but for cases of necessity. I can take no pleasure in Theobalds Park till thou come, and yet the thistle is here. If thy health may permit thee to be here tomorrow night, it will be a great comfort unto me that thou and thy "cuntis"[2] may see me hunt the buck in the park upon Friday next. And if thou show me not all the devices in this park before I go from hence, I shall never have comfort in it. I have sent Conway[3] to thee as thou desired. God ever bless thee and all thine, and send thee health and heart, to the comfort of thy dear dad.

JAMES R.

I have found another tale in the book of a calf, like that of the cow.[4]

British Library   *Holograph*
Harl. 6987, f. 186

[1]On Buckingham's health problems, see Lockyer, *Buckingham,* pp. 194–203 passim. For contemporary references to his illness in the spring and summer of 1624, see Chamberlain, *Letters,* II: 558 and *CSP Venetian 1623–25,* p. 364.

[2]Countess? Cunts? See Letter 225, n. 6, and Letter 226.

[3]Sir Edward Conway, appointed Secretary of State 16 January 1623.

[4]Like the preceding reference to "the thistle," a private allusion now lost beyond recall.

Letter 222

To George Villiers, Duke of Buckingham

Another letter to Buckingham during convalescence.

[1624?]

Sweet heart,

Blessing, blessing, blessing on my sweet Tom Badger's[1] heart roots and all his, for breeding me so fine a kennel of young hounds, some of them so fair and well shaped, and some of them so fine pretty little ones, as they are worthy to lie on Steenie and Kate's bed, and all of them run together in a lump both at scent and view. And God thank the Master of the Horse[2] for providing me such a number of fair useful horses, fit for my hand—in a word, I protest I was never master of such horses and hounds! The bearer will tell you what fine running we had yesterday. Remember now to take the air discreetly "and peece and peece."[3] And, for God's sake and mine, keep thyself very warm, especially thy head and thy shoulders. Put thy park of Bewlie[4] to an end, and love me still and still. And so God bless thee, and my sweet daughter, and god-daughter,[5] to the comfort of thy dear dad.

JAMES R.

Thy old purveyor sent thee yesternight six partridges and two leverets. I am now going to hawk the pheasant.

British Library   *Holograph*
Harl. 6987, f. 184

[1]One of James's sportive names for Buckingham.
[2]Buckingham was Master of the Horse from 1616 until his death.
[3]Apparently meaning "a bit at a time"—a warning to Buckingham not to overdo things.
[4]See Letter 191, n. 7.
[5]Presumably the sweet daughter is Buckingham's wife and the god-daughter their first child, Mary.

Letter 223

To George Villiers, Duke of Buckingham

The third of the King's letters to a convalescent Buckingham.

[*1624?*]

My only sweet and dear child,

Blessing, blessing, blessing on thy heartroots and all thine. This Tuesday morning here is great store of game, as they say, especially partridges and stone curlews. I know who shall get their part of them. And here is the finest company of young hounds that ever was seen. God bless the sweet master of my harriers, that made them be so well kept all summer—I mean Tom Badger.[1] I assure myself thou will punctually observe the diet and journeys I set thee down, in my first letter from

Theobalds. God bless thee, sweet Kate, and little Mall to the comfort of thy dear dad.

JAMES R.

Let my last compliment stick to thy heart till we may have a sweet and comfortable meeting, which God send and give thee grace to bid the drugs adieu this day.

British Library   *Holograph*
Harl. 6987, f. 182

¹See Letter 222, n. 1.

Letter 224

To George Villiers, Duke of Buckingham

Amid his hunting, James has received good news about the marriage negotiations with France.

[Early September 1624]

Sweet heart,

When I made little Dick write my excuse to thee yesterday for not writing myself, I was very sick of a great flux that morning. But now I thank God I am well, in spite of thee, and having changed my purpose in resolving to stay here¹ till Monday, so earnest I am to kill more of Zouche's great stags.

I summon thee to come here tomorrow, and let Kate and Sue go to Windsor and meet me on Monday afternoon at Harrison's Heath hard with their bows. My Lord Percy is comde* out of France² with better news than before: our standing to it hat[h] made them more reasonable; they are contented now with a letter and no mention of the Holy Evangels in it. Thy letter did great good. How soon my son comes from Guildford I will send thee the paper. I send thee an excellent Barbary melon. In good faith I had no melons since thy parting till yesternight. God bless thee and thine.

JAMES R.

British Library   *Holograph*
Harl. 6987, f. 192

[1]Presumably at Lord Zouche's country seat at Bramshill, Hants.
[2]"I heare now the Lord Percie came last night out of Fraunce, with goode newes as is presumed, els wold they not make him the messenger" (Chamberlain, *Letters*, 4 September 1624, II: 580). Lord Percy was Algernon Percy, the eldest son of the Earl of Northumberland.

Letter 225

To George Villiers, Duke of Buckingham

A note concerning miscellaneous matters.

[*October? 1624*]

Sweet heart,

I thank thee for thy sweet kind letter. I have passed the President's bill,[1] for it is reasonable. As to Holland's suit,[2] I have according to my custom put the note in the Master of Requests' hand; and when the party shall be convicted, I will do in it as the worth of the thing shall prove and as thou shall advise me. As to the Dunkirkers' business,[3] it seems my captain of my ship complains of the Hollanders' behaviour; if that prove so I must have reparation of them or else mend myself. It is thy office[4] to try this. I am glad thou will keep thy set day and I hope thou will not fail to be at Bewlie[5] tomorrow, and at thy return I would have thee to bring all the "cuntis"[6] with thee (I mean both thy

440

wife, thy mother, and thy sister) that our joy may be the more full at our happy meeting, which God grant, and bless thee and all thine, to the comfort of thy dear dad.

JAMES R.

Thy old purveyor sent thee yesternight three pheasants, three sucking rabbits, and a fat leveret, all of his own catching.

British Library   *Holograph*
Harl. 6987, f. 190

[1]In September 1621, Henry Montagu, Viscount Mandeville, was named to fill the long-vacant office of Lord President of the Council.
[2]Henry Rich, Baron Kensington, was created Earl of Holland on 24 September 1624.
[3]In May 1624, after a sea fight, four Dunkirk ships sought refuge in the Downs, where they were blockaded by twelve Dutch ships. They finally escaped in a tremendous gale on 13 October, thanks in part to an English man-of-war interposing itself.
[4]As Lord High Admiral.
[5]See Letter 191, n. 7.
[6]See Letters 221 and 226 for other occurrences of this word. King James is almost certainly being bawdy. For parallel examples of Buckingham calling women "cunts" in his letters to the King, see *Harl. 6987*, ff. 230, 232, 236. It is hard to read "cuntis" as "countesses." Although Buckingham's mother received a life peerage as Countess of Buckingham in 1618 and his sister became Countess of Denbigh in 1622, his wife was first a marchioness, then a duchess—never a countess.

Letter 226

To George Villiers, Duke of Buckingham

A familiar note to the royal favourite.

[*October 1624?*]

My sweet dear child, scholar and friend,
St. Paul, thou knows, commands us to examine ourselves before we go to the sacrament,[1] but yet he commands [not] to go

and receive it. So, though I put thee in mind to speak as thou promised to the Spanish agent,[2] yet did I surely expect thy coming here and this night. Thou may make the big Irishman bring him hither to thee, or thou may take occasion to go any day in this week to dine in London and meet with him there if he cannot be brought to thee tomorrow morning. Alas, sweet heart, I find by this how precise thou are to keep thy word to me, when thou prefers it to thy own greatest comfort in coming to me. God reward thee for it! But I must quarrel [with] thee that, though in both my former letters I prayed thee to bring the "cuntis"[3] with thee, thou has not so much as sent me word whether they can come or not. I would gladly have them here but, however it be, fail not to be here thyself tomorrow before supper time. And so God bless thee and all thine, to the comfort of thy dear dad.

JAMES R.

Your old purveyor sends you a kid for your dinner tomorrow, and thou shall find another here.

British Library   *Holograph*
Harl. 6987, f. 188

[1] I Corinthians 11:28.

[2] After the Spanish ambassador extraordinary, the Marquis of Inojosa, had left England at the end of June 1624, and the ordinary or lieger ambassador, Don Carlos Coloma, had followed him in mid-October, Spain was represented only by an agent, Giacomo Brunio (Jaques Bruneau), whom James refused at first to allow in his presence. Mention of an agent, not an ambassador, gives some indication of the date of this letter.

[3] See Letter 225, n. 6.

Letter 227

To Princess Henrietta Maria

King James assures her that he desires her coming as much as Prince Charles does. James died on 27 March 1625; Henrietta Maria arrived in England in June.

TRANSLATED FROM THE FRENCH

[*December 1624?*][1]

Madame my most dear daughter,

Each day that has passed since my son wrote his last letter to you has only redoubled the grief by which he is constrained, not being able to find any rest in his soul without his being able to do you the service of writing again, by the messenger whom you have already seen, in order to show you his languishing until he shall be able to have the honour and the fortune to enjoy your presence. Nevertheless I shall pray you to believe that, in this languishing, second place to him will never be taken by

Your most affectionate father,
J. R.

Bodleian Library   *Copy*
Clarendon State Papers,
Vol. 97, f. 1

[1]This letter presumably postdates the ratification of the marriage treaty by King James and Prince Charles on 12 December 1624.

GLOSSARY

A

accomplots: plots
acsistaire: assister
adoes, adoos, adoose (pl. of "ado"): concerns, affairs, business
advert: to inform
afauld: sincere, true, faithful
afauldlie: sincerely, faithfully, honestly
affectuislie: earnestly
after checcis: after-checks
afterhend: afterwards
agreation: agreement
aggrege, agredge: to aggravate, make worse
allane: alone
allainerlie, allanerlie, alaneerlie, alanerlye: only
alluterlie: entirely (all utterly)
always, alluaye: in all events, on all occasions
anis: once, for some time, sometime
appardon, appardone: to pardon
appearandlie: apparently
assertis: assarts, pieces of forest land cleared and made arable
ay: always

B

bairn: child
band: bond

beis: is
boutades: sudden outbursts
brangled: shaken
buddit: bribed
burstin: bursten, burst
by: beyond

C

cassin: to cast
checce, cheece: check
chirurgie: surgery
claggit: clogged, laden
colere: choleric
comd, comde, comed: come (past participle)
commountie: land possessed in common
complots: plots
componer: composer
compte: account, reckoning
concety: flighty
concredited: entrusted
contempne: to condemn, scorn
contentation: satisfaction, contentment
courtesest: most courteous
cummid: *see* comd
cunn: to know, know how

D

dalie: dally, to converse idly
dayet: meeting, session, day or time appointed, date
declairaitoure: declarature, judicial declaration, statement of decision
delaitid: informed
dependeris: dependents
descrive, descryve: describe, to set down in writing
diet, dyet: *see* "dayet"
domine: to rule, have authority
doole weede: mourning garment

E

ee: eye
effectuous: urgent
enpaunde, empawnde: to give in pledge

F

facon: fashion, manner
faconis: factions
faillie: failure
faine: to feign
fairde, fard: force, impetus, onset
fascherie: trouble, annoyance
faschous, fashouse: troublesome, annoying
faschit, fashit: bothered, troubled
faulteris: those who commit faults
feinzeid: feigned
fensid: fortified, fenced
ficht, fichte: fight
flaine: flayed
fra: since, by, from
fyling: staining with dishonour

G

gar, garr [past: gart]: to do, cause, instruct, take measures
garrne wearie: to grow weary (?)
ghooke: fool
gif: to give
gossip: godparent, chum
grandie: grandly
gurne: to bare the teeth, snarl

H

hained: kept
hairtelie: hearty, wholehearted

hardill: pack (of dogs)
horneris: outlaws (men "put to the horn")

I

infame: to belittle, slander
inlayke: to be lacking
intercommoun: to be in communication with, consult with
interpone: to interpose
intromet, intromit: to concern oneself with, interfere with

K

kythe: to make known, show oneself, appear

L

laiked: looked
langsum, longsum: wearisome, lengthy
levingis: livings
lightled: slighted, scorned
lippen, lippin: to confide, trust
loadenit: laden, loaded
longsum, langsum: wearisome, lengthy
longsumnes: tedious lengthiness, verbosity
louping: leaping, jumping, escaping

M

marrow: comrade, associate, equal
maun: must
meat: meeting
meditat: to meditate upon
mekill, mekle: much

mee: more
mell: to deal in, have to do with
menid: intended, purposed
meubling: providing with furniture
meueabled: furnished
middes: middle course
mintid: ventured
miskenne: to refuse to recognize, not to know
mote, mott, motte: may

N

nathing: nothing
naturall: nature
nor: than
nouelles (novelles): news

O

onfreindis: enemies (unfriends)
ornit: ornamented
otherwayes: in another way, manner or case; otherwise
oulke: week
outgait: outgate, way out
ower: over
owin, owne: own

P

patrie: country
pegral, pigraill: commonplace, petty, mean
praeveine: to come before
prejudge: to prejudice, affect injuriously
promouid (promovid): promoted
propone: to suggest, propose, purpose

Q

quhilkis: which
quhill: till
quhylis: at times, at other times

R

rathest (cf. "rather"): most particularly, especially
reciproke, reciproque: reciprocal
redding: saving, relieving, clearing
refuse: refusal
reiking: fitting, rigging
relaxit: released, removed the outlawry on a man
relayed: laid once more
ressett: to receive, protect, harbour (usually criminals)
roaguie: pertaining to rogues
rou: roll, list

S

sa: so
secreatie: secrecy
sen: since
sensyne: since then
sho: she
sic: such
siclike: similar, similarly
skansit: scanned, looked upon
skarrid: caused apprehension
skath: (1) injury, trespass; (2) scarcely
slim: crafty, of little substance
souertie (sovertie): surety, security
speciallis: special persons
speire: to enquire
sperable: to be hoped for
stark: strong
steiring: stirring

stoup: post, pillar, whipping-post
stow: place
streighting: confining
subduced: withdrawn
suiting: sitting
supplant: to trip
sute: suit, retinue
swearnesse, swearenes: indolence, sloth
sylid, syled: deceived, betrayed
syne, sine: after, afterward

T

taiken: token
then: after
thir: these
thoch: though
thraw: throe, death-throe
teinds: tithes
till: at
timous: timely
timously: in good time, at the right time
tint: lost
tocher: dowery
toone: tune
torts: wrongs (esp. in the breaking of agreements)
traist: tryst, meeting
trow: trust
trucheman, truchman: interpreter
tua (twa): (1) two or more, a couple; (2) thitherward
tuition: protection, care
turn: piece of business
twiche: touch
tyne: lose

U

unabill: impossible
unhap, unhapp: misfortune, disaster

unquhile (umquhile): erstwhile, former, late
unsell: worthless
unspearid: not asked about, not enquired for
unspirring: not asking
untimous, untimously: untimely

V

vanterie: vaunting, boasting
viflie, vifly, vivelie: lively, in an energetic manner

W

wairde: ward, custody, imprisonment
warenes: wariness
wed: pledge, something deposited as security
well: weal
wrangous: wrongful
wyte: blame

Y

yestereen: last night

APPENDIX
A Finding-List for Other Letters of James VI & I Available in Print

NOTE: Excluded are many hundreds of letters of appointment, of credence, of recall, of leave of absence, of instructions, as well as warrants, commissions, summons and orders, etc.—items that are essentially pieces of governmental paperwork. Also excluded are thousands of short notices such as those in the *Calendar of State Papers (Domestic)* and paraphrases such as those in the *Calendar of State Papers (Venetian)*.

SOURCES CITED

BannCl—Publications of the Bannatyne Club, Edinburgh:

BannCl 18—*Memoirs of His Own Life by Sir James Melville of Halhill*, 1827.

BannCl 26—*Papers Relative to the Marriage of King James VI*, 1828.

BannCl 81—*Acts and Proceedings of the General Assemblies of the Kirk of Scotland*, 3 vols., 1839–45.

BannCl 92—*Original Letters Relating to the Ecclesiastical Affairs of Scotland*, 2 vols., 1851.

BannCl 93—John Spottiswoode, *History of the Church of Scotland*, 3 vols., 1850–51.

BannCl 104—*Original Letters of Mr. John Colville 1582–1603,* 1858.

Bruce—John Bruce, ed., *Letters of Queen Elizabeth and King James VI of Scotland* (Camden Society, Vol. 46), London, 1849.

CCAL—*Catalogue of the Collection of Autograph Letters . . . formed . . . by Alfred Morrison,* 13 vols. [London], 1883–97.

Cldwd—David Calderwood, *The History of the Kirk of Scotland,* 8 vols., Edinburgh (Wodrow Society), 1842–49.

Coke—Roger Coke, *Detection of the Court and State of England,* 2nd ed., 2 vols., London, 1696.

CSP(S)—*Calendar of the State Papers Relating to Scotland and Mary, Queen of Scots 1547–1603,* 13 vols., Edinburgh, 1898–1969.

EgerPprs—J. Payne Collier, ed., *The Egerton Papers* (Camden Society, Vol. 12), London, 1840.

Ellis—Henry Ellis, ed., *Original Letters Illustrative of English History including Numerous Royal Letters,* 3 series, London, 1824, 1827, 1846.

Facs.—Sir Henry James, ed., *Facsimiles of National Manuscripts of Scotland,* 3 parts, Edinburgh, 1867–72.

Goodman—Godfrey Goodman, *The Court of King James the First,* John S. Brewer, ed., 2 vols., London, 1839.

Gordon—William Gordon, *The History of the Ancient, Noble, and Illustrious Family of Gordon,* 2 vols., Edinburgh, 1727.

Hailes—Sir David Dalrymple, Lord Hailes, *Memorials and Letters Relating to the History of Britain in the Reign of James the First,* Glasgow, 1762.

Hal—James Orchard Halliwell, ed., *Letters of the Kings of England,* 2 vols., London, 1848.

Har—Sir John Harington, *Nugæ Antiquae,* 2 vols., London, 1804.

HMC—Reports of the Historical Manuscripts Commission, London (particularly the volumes devoted to the Buccleuch, De L'Isle, Downshire, Hamilton, Hastings, Home, Laing, Mar, Ormonde, Portland, and Salisbury manuscripts). The most important of these being:

HMC Sal. MSS.—Historical Manuscripts Commission, *Calendar of the Manuscripts of the Most Hon. the Marquess of Salisbury, Pre-*

served at Hatfield House, Hertfordshire, 24 parts, London, 1888–1976 (published as part of the Ninth Report).

KJS—Robert S. Rait and Annie I. Cameron, eds., *King James's Secret: Negotiations between Elizabeth and James VI Relating to the Execution of Mary Queen of Scots, from the Warrender Papers,* London, [1927].

MaitCl—Publications of the Maitland Club, Edinburgh:

MaitCl 25—*Miscellany of the Maitland Club,* Vol. I, 2 parts, 1833–34.

MaitCl 35—*Letters to James VI,* 1835.

MaitCl 50—*Letters to the Argyll Family,* 1840.

MaitCl 51—*Miscellany of the Maitland Club,* Vol. II, 2 parts, 1840.

MaitCl 57—*Miscellany of the Maitland Club,* Vol. III, 1843.

MaitCl 71—*Selections from the Family Papers Preserved at Caldwell,* 3 vols., 1854.

Murdin—William Murdin, ed., *Collection of State Papers Left by William Cecil, Lord Burghley,* London, 1740–59.

Nichols—John Nichols, *The Progresses, Processions, and Magnificent Festivities of King James the First,* 4 vols. London, 1828.

RIA—William Bruce, "Original Letters from James VI of Scotland and Chancellor Maitland to Robert Bruce, Minister of the Gospel," *Transactions of the Royal Irish Academy,* Vol. XV, (Dublin, 1828), Part 3, pp. 243–91.

Rushworth—John Rushworth, *Historical Collections,* 8 vols., London, 1659–80.

Rymer—Thomas Rymer, *Foedera,* 20 vols., London, 1704–35.

Sanderson—William Sanderson, *A Compleat History of the Lives and Reigns of Mary, Queen of Scotland, and of her Son and Successor, James the Sixth, King of Scotland,* London, 1656.

SHR—J. D. Mackie, "A Secret Agent of James VI," *Scottish Historical Review,* Vol. IX, pp. 376–86.

"Two Unpublished Letters of James VI," *Scottish Historical Review,* Vol. XVI, pp. 141–43.

SpaCl—"The Gordon Letters," *Miscellany of the Spalding Club,* Vol. III (Aberdeen, 1846), pp. 213–16.

Spedding—James Spedding, *The Letters and the Life of Francis Bacon,* 7 vols., London, 1868–74.

STC 14361—*The Copie of His Maiesties Letter Sent on Tuesday the 26 of June 1604 to the Commons,* London, 1604.

STC 14362—*The Copie of the K. Maiesties Letter to the L. Maior of London,* [Edinburgh, 1603].

STC 14378—*His Maiesties Gracious Letter to the Earle of Southampton, Treasurer, and to the Councell and Company of Virginia Here,* London, 1622.

WarrIllus—Margaret Warrender, ed., *Illustrations of Scottish History . . . Letters and Documents . . . from the Originals in the Possession of Sir George Warrender,* Edinburgh, 1889.

WarrPprs—Annie I. Cameron and Robert S. Rait, eds., *The Warrender Papers,* 2 vols., Edinburgh, 1931–32.

Winwood—*Memorials of Affairs of State . . . from the Original Papers of the Rt. Hon. Sir Ralph Winwood,* ed. Edmund Sawyer, 3 vols., London, 1725.

Date	Recipient	Written from	Printed in	Contents
16/3/1578	Elizabeth	Stirling	CSP (S) V: 278	Thanks for declaration of Thos. Randolph. James has assumed govt. from E. of Morton.
1/7/78	"	"	CSP (S) V: 301–2	Thanks for letter of 28 May. Steps to end troubles which have disturbed her. Morton added to Council.
Sept./78	Cts. of Argyll	"	HMC Rpt. 6, 655	Renews request concerning J.'s godson, James Crichton.
12/2/79	Laird of Wedderburn, Wn. East March	Holyrood House	HMC Rpt. 15, App. Pt. 67 (Home), 49–50	In Cranston affair it "were to small purpose to spare the father and prosecute the sons." Other Border affairs.
29/3/79	Elizabeth	Stirling	HMC Rpt. 17, App. Pt. 8, (Laing), 29–30	Recent letters show her affection and care during his minority. J. has communicated his mind concerning "intended practices."
3/7/79	Burghley	"	CSP (S) V: 340	Asks B. to aid James Murray, J.'s messenger to Q. E.

457

Date	Recipient	Written from	Printed in	Contents
5/7/79	Gen. Assembly Edinburgh	"	BannCl 81, II: 428–29	Not to make innovations which may cause unrest but leave various matters to Parl.
5/10/79	Elizabeth	?	CSP (S) V: 352–54	Asks surrender of Ld. Claude Hamilton, a fugitive in England, wanted with his brother for murder of E. of Lennox and E. of Moray. Complains about English wardens of East and Middle Marches.
9/4/80	Wedderburn, Wn. E. March	Stirling	HMC Rpt. 15, App. Pt. 67 (Home), 50	Q. E. having agreed to meeting of Border commissioners, W. to come to Stirling to advise J. and Council of all matters needing redress.
28/3/81	E. of Mar	HH	HMC Rpt. 15, App. Pt. 1, (Mar), 32–33	Warned of coming troubles by M.'s letter, J. will be careful to see him preserved.
19/4/81	Mary Q. of Scots	Edinburgh	CSP (S) VI: 9	J. will show her duty and honour as long as he lives. E. of Lennox will answer points in her letter. J. hopes she can get French assistance for him if needed.

458

Date	Correspondent	Place	Reference	Summary
17/8/81	"	Dalkeith	CSP (S) VI: 45	Has received her letter of 10 July. Will shortly reply to her requests sent by George Douglas. Assurances of obedience to her commands.
17/6/82	Mary Q. of Scots	?	CSP (S) VI: 133	Q.E.'s refusal to let M. send a messenger to J. is consequence of J.'s refusal to receive Q.E.'s messenger.
2/7/82	E. of Argyll	Stirling	MaitCl 50, p. 20	Summons to consult at Perth. Not more than 24 hours of his time required. Request for deer hounds.
29/9/82	Elizabeth	"	CSP (S) VI: 183	Thanks for friendly messages by Sir George Carey and Robt. Bowes. He has communicated freely with Sir. G. Proximity of blood and common benefit make J. look to her for favour.
11/11/82	"	HH	CSP (S) VI: 208–10	Wardens of the Marches having failed to cope, J. asks Q.E. to appoint persons who may decide with him and his council how good order may be maintained this winter. Suggestions for improving Border situation.

Date	Recipient	Written from	Printed in	Contents
17/11/82	"	"	CSP (S) VI: 211–12	Asks passport for Lennox from England to France. Storms have hindered L.'s departure from Scotland. Release of E. of Arran could not affect J's warm feelings for Q.E.
29/12/82	"	"	CSP (S) VI: 229–30	Bearer, John Colville, to declare to Q.E. the loving mind of J.
1/1/83	"	"	CSP (S) VI: 285–86	Good reception Q.E. has given Colville and her treatment of D. of Lennox require heartfelt thanks.
12/2/83	"	"	CSP (S) VI: 295	Asks Q.E. to protect J's Italian servant Pocho de Bonettis from enemies while he attends to business in London. (*Holograph postscript*)
29/3/83	"	"	HMC Rpt. 9 Sal. MSS. XIII: 218	Bearer has behaved discreetly. He and next messenger, Col. Stewart, will declare J's mind. (*Holograph*)
23/4/83	"	"	Bruce, p. 6	Desires her to trust words of the two bearers. His wish for a perfect union and friendship. (*Holograph*)

Date	Addressee	Place	Reference	Note
24/4/83	"	"	CSP (S) VI: 407–8	Colville has reported how well Q. E. took the suit of James Hudson, whom J. had recommended to her.
"	"	"	CSP (S) VI: 408	Asks favourable hearing for his messengers, Col. Wm. Stewart and John Colville.
"	Council (Eng.)	HH	BannCl 104, p. 25	Asks support for Stewart and Colville (*v. supra*).
"	Burghley	"	HMC Rpt. 13, App. Pt. 2 (Portland), II: 15	" " "
"	Walsingham	"	CSP (S) VI: 415	" " "
"	Wm. Davison	"	CSP (S) VI: 415–16	" " "
9/7/83	Elizabeth	St. Andrews	Bruce, pp. 7–9	Expressions of gratitude for Q. E.'s kindness. (*Holograph*)
12/9/83	"	?	CSP (S) VI: 612	J. has conferred with the bearer, whose report may be trusted as also his promises in J.'s name. (*Holograph*)
4/10/83	Walsingham	Falkland	CSP (S) VI: 631	At W.'s request, J. has freed the Abbot of Dunfermline. He trusts W. to explain to

Date	Recipient	Written from	Printed in	Contents
				Q.E., more fully than set down, the points agreed upon at recent conference of J. and W. Thus W. can frustrate "crafty and unquiet spirits" who conspire against Anglo-Scottish amity.
9/10/83	Robt. Bowes	"	CSP (S) VI: 631	B. and Walsingham concurring in being "gude instrumentis," all things will turn out to the contentment of Q.E.
20/10/[83]	Walsingham	Edinburgh	BannCl 104, pp. 35–36	Thanks for favours shown to Colville on his recent mission. W. has shown both fidelity to Q.E. and affection for Anglo-Scottish friendship.
31/10/83	Elizabeth	Stirling	CSP (S) VI: 645	Archbp. of St. Andrews going to Plombières for his health, J. makes him his messenger to Q.E.
[c. Oct. 1583]	William the Silent	?	WarrPprs I: 159–61	Thanks W. for intelligence of plots against J. but is confident of God's protection. He will seek help of all Christian princes and always prize a good relationship with Q.E.

Date	Recipient	Place	Source	Summary
12 calends of Nov. 1583	Foreign Protestant ministers	Falkland	Hal II: 68–70	Takes opportunity of Continental tour of "our beloved noble" to solicit views as to how the Scottish church may be further reformed.
[1583]	Elizabeth	?	BannCl 18, pp. 297–99	J. accepts her admonishing quotation from Isocrates. Comments upon circumstances when he was prisoner of Ruthven lords. He will not try to punish those who forcibly kept the late D. of Lennox from his presence. (Letter, drafted by Sir James Melville, copied in J's *holograph*.)
8/1/84	Walsingham	HH	CSP (S) VII: 6	Asks W.'s favour for bearer, who seeks to bring to Scotland "expert men in the minerall" so that he can perform contract made with J.
15/3/84	Mary Q. of Scots	"	WarrIllus, p. 13	Reconfirms that earlier letter was held up by delay in Fontenay's departure.
4/5/84	Elizabeth	Stirling	CSP (S) VII: 111–12	Time has disclosed "the restless minds and lurking malice" of J.'s rebellious subjects who seized Stirling. J. has regained town and castle, and hopes Q.E. will return to Sc. for punishment any rebels who fled to Eng.
19/6/84	Burghley	Falkland	CSP (S) VII: 192–93	Thanks B. for past help. Asks present aid.

463

Date	Recipient	Written from	Printed in	Contents
14/10/84	Walsingham	HH	CSP (S) VII: 364	Asks W. to forward the mission of Master of Gray.
24/10/84	Sir E. Hoby	"	CSP (S) VII: 378	Thanks for conveying J.'s ambassador to Durham.
23/11/84	Leicester?	"	CSP (S) VII: 425	J. hears good reports of him from his ambassador and will show himself an honest friend. (*Holograph*)
[1584?]	Secretary (Maitland)	?	CSP (S) VII: 514–15	J. asks M. to expedite bearer's business so that he can return quickly to J. (*Holograph*)
16/2/85	Elizabeth	HH	CSP (S) VII: 565	Recommends his ambassador, Sir Lewis Bellenden, who will discuss with Q. E. the Scottish rebels in Eng.
13/3/85	Sir Lewis Bellenden	"	HMC Rpt. 17, App. Pt. 8 (Laing), I: 46–47	The heinous treason, lately detected, against Q.E.'s person, may make her more understanding of J.'s trouble with rebels. Lenience of princes inflames cancer of treason. B. must seek arrest of all Sc. traitors in Eng. and must remain until after trials, especially that of Black Jack Home, who is to

Date		Place	Reference	Summary
				be returned to Sc. Q. E. may send observer to see he is treated fairly. Nothing prejudicial to J. is to be permitted in the new parliament.
13/4/85	"	"	Ibid., I: 53–54	Pledge by J., who is neither forgetful nor ungrateful. (Largely duplicates Akrigg, Letter 13.)
27/6/85	Elizabeth	Dunfermline	HMC Sal. MSS. XIII: 268–69	Praises her ambassador, Wotton, and messenger, Alexander. Will look into report about Ld. Maxwell. (*Holograph*)
19/7/85	"	Falkland	HMC Sal. MSS. XIII: 281–82	To assure Q. E. of J.'s constancy and to counterpoise false reports. Always keep one ear open for J. (*Holograph*)
13/8/85	"	Stirling	HMC Sal. MSS. XIII: 282–83	Thanks for trust. Will investigate latest mishap. (*Holograph*)
24/9/85	"	"	CSP (S) VIII: 110–11	Asks redress for Sc. merchants (bearer, Adam Fullerton, is their agent) robbed by Eng. pirates.
"	Walsingham	"	CSP (S) VIII: 111	Asks W. to support bearer (apparently Adam Fullerton, *v. supra*) in suit to Q. E.
20/12/85	Elizabeth	Linlithgow	Bruce, pp. 24–25	Reasons for sending messenger, who will tell her "my secret intention in all things."

Date	Recipient	Written from	Printed in	Contents
"	Walsingham	"	Bruce, p. 25	Asks W. to assist bearer in his mission to Q.E.
"	Leicester	"	Bruce, p. 26	Hearing L. has not yet departed [for Low Countries], J. sends bearer to declare a message to him.
[c. Apr. 1586]	Elizabeth	?	Bruce, p. 32	J. had postponed writing pending treaty of alliance. He has now signed this. Desires her seal to be attached to the instrument.
16/6/86	T. Randolph	Falkland	CSP (S) VIII: 444–45	J. will use R.'s counsel. Encloses holograph letter for Q.E. Wants meeting of commissioners to continue for a short time. Commits R.'s old bones to God's protection.
30/6/86	Elizabeth	Dunfermline	CSP (S) VIII: 488	Problem of setting date for redress of Border affairs.
5/7/86	E. of Rutland	Falkland	CSP (S) VIII: 504	Asks him to use influence to help Sir Cuthbert Collingwood, now a prisoner in Eng.
[July 1586]	Archibald Douglas	"	CSP (S) VIII: 509	The Carrs are to be delivered without delay. J. is the same man as when he last spoke to D.

466

Date	Recipient		Reference	Description
6/8/86	Mary Q. of Scots	"	CCAL II: Pl. 91	Lack of trustworthy messengers and uncertainty about her place of residence have kept J. from writing. He now uses opportunity provided by French ambassador to assure her of devotion. She must disregard false reports. (*Holograph*)
13/8/86	Sir Chr. Hatton	"	HMC Sal. MSS. III: 168	Asks H. to advise Archibald Douglas in negotiations with Q.E. (*Holograph*)
22/9/86	Ld. Hunsdon	HH	HMC Sal. MSS. XIII: 310	Recommends Robt. Ker for Q. E.'s pardon and asks H. to let him cross the border unsearched.
24/9/86	Archibald Douglas	"	CSP (S) IX: 46–47	D. to seek recall from exile in Sc. for the three Wallace brothers who murdered a Sc. fugitive in Eng.
[Oct. 1586]	"	?	HMC Sal. MSS. XIII: 315	J. so busy writing to others he has to leave Master of Gray "to write my ample mind unto you." (*Holograph*)
9/11/86	Elizabeth	HH	CSP (S) IX: 150–51	Having appointed E. of Angus lieut.-gen. over all the Marches, J. asks Q. E. to make similar appointment. Requests extradition of Lady Johnstoun.
17/12/86	Master of Gray	?	KJS, pp. 107–15	A lengthy letter setting forth reasons why Mary's life should be saved and attempting

Date	Recipient	Written from	Printed in	Contents
"	Burghley	HH	HMC Sal. MSS. XIII: 321	rebuttal of alleged reasons for her execution. (Partly parallels Akrigg, Letter 26)
20/12/86	Ld. Scrope, Eng. Wn. of W. March	"	CSP (S) IX: 199	J's ambassadors, Master of Gray and Sir Robt. Melville, have been wronged by misreports. Both should be believed as one would believe J. himself. (*Holograph*) Asks aid for Ld. Hamilton, Lieut. of Sc. W. March, in punishing rebels and fugitives.
[1586]	Claude Nau	?	Murdin II: 568	Regrets that Mary has quarrelled with Cts. of Shrewsbury and urges reconciliation.
[1586?]	Elizabeth	?	HMC Sal. MSS. XIII: 323–24	Thanks for so discreet an ambassador and money. Help bearer, your returning ambassador, with problems arising out of death of his uncle. (*Holograph*)
[Jan. 1587]	Archibald Douglas	?	Ellis, Ser. 1, III: 14	Exhortation to save Mary from execution. (Identical with Akrigg, Letter 25 to Master of Gray.) (*Holograph*)

Date	Recipient	Place	Reference	
10/3/87	Mrs. Carmichael	?	CSP (S) IX: 331–32	She is to explain to Ld. Hunsdon why, after the execution of his mother, J. cannot receive messenger from Q. E.
20/4/87	E. of Huntly	Edinburgh	SpaCl *Misc.* III: 214–15	Concerned at cruelties and disorders in the Isles, J. sends directions for H. in his lieutenancy.
14/8/87	Laird of Cesford	Falkland	CSP (S) IX: 477	J. is sending E. of Angus to reinforce Cesford. Meanwhile, C. is to seek meeting with Eng. warden, his counterpart.
1587	Frederick II of Denmark	?	Hal II: 79–81	Peter Junius has told J. much of F.'s "very sweet children" and brought answers to J.'s enquiries. He sends Junius and Sir Patrick Vaux now as ambassadors.
[c. 1587]	Elizabeth	?	HMC Rpt. 17, App. Pt. 8, (Laing), 72	Q. E.'s anger at J.'s refusal to receive Robt. Carey is unjustified. How else could he behave in light of preceding "heavy accidents" [execution of Mary]? If she will repair damage to his honour, he will accommodate self and realm to accord with "equity and good intelligence." *(Draft only)*
[1587?]	Chancellor Maitland?	?	CSP (S) IX: 529	J. has conferred at length with "yone erl of ouris," who dealt very plainly with him. Patrick Murray will call on Chancellor. *(Holograph)*

469

Date	Recipient	Written from	Printed in	Contents
[Aug. 1588?]	Chancellor Maitland	?	CSP (S) X: 89–90	Bothwell and the shooting of "oliphaire" [Oliver?]. Arrangements about Ld. Maxwell's imprisonment. (*Holograph*)
[*c.* Sept. 1588]	Catherine de Bourbon	?	WarrPprs II: 80–81	Reports of her virtues fill J. with admiration. She is to think of him as one who hopes to assure her of his love.
Dec./88	Duke of Parma	Dalkeith	WarrPprs II: 93–94	Announces arrest and subsequent escape of Wm. Semple, who abused Parma's credit in stirring rebellion in Sc.
18/3/89	Elizabeth	HH	HMC Sal. MSS. XIII: 408	Thanks for acquainting him with intercepted letters. He sends Laird of Weems to discuss strengthening Britain against invasion. (*Holograph*)
15/4/89	Burghley	?	CSP (S) X:40	Compliments. J. asks B.'s assistance for his ambassador. Low Country commissioners. (*Holograph*)
19/7/89	"	Canonry of Ross	CSP (S) X: 121	Asks B. to aid Robt. Jowsie and Thos. Fulie [Foulis?], who are to purchase ornaments

[c. July 1589]	Henri of Navarre	?	WarrPprs II: 107–108	for J.'s wedding. (*Holograph postscript:* "the occasion is extraordinary.") J. glad to hear of H.'s accord with K. of France. He desires H.'s prosperity more than that of any man alive.
15/8/89	Burghley	Edinburgh	CSP (S) X: 138–39	Now, more than ever, J. needs Q.E.'s friendship. Asks B. to help in this matter. (*Holograph*)
[c. 2/10/89]	Q. Anne	?	WarrPprs II: 109–10	Anxious because of storms since she embarked, J. sends messenger to Norway for news of her.
17/10/89	Elizabeth	Leith	CSP (S) X: 171–73	Writes to support claim of Francis Dacre, who has arrived from Eng., to title of Ld. Dacre and estates.
22/10/89	Scottish subjects	"	BannCl 26, pp. 4–11	(A proclamation rather than a letter; cf. Akrigg, Letter 36.) Motives for marriage. Reasons for Anne's delay in reaching Sc. and J.'s decision to bring her from Norway personally. Precedent showing resident monarch not essential if due provision for govt. be made. D. of Lennox to be president of Privy Council in J.'s absence. Ld. Admiral (E. of Bothwell) to be his coadjutor. Gentry

Date	Recipient	Written from	Printed in	Contents
"	Ld. Scrope?	"	CSP (S) X: 178	to attend on them in rotation. Lords who are to assist Ld. John Hamilton keep order on Border. Other arrangements.
"	Wm. Asheby	"	CSP (S) X: 177–78	While fetching bride from Norway, J. leaves Ld. Hamilton in charge of Borders.
26/11/89	Sophia, Q. Dowager of Denmark	Oslo	BannCl 26, pp. 23–25	Announces decision to go to Norway for bride. Since Q.E. approves the match, he assumes she will approve voyage. Will write to Q.E. when time serves for a long letter.
2/12/89	Robt. Bruce	Oslo	RIA XV, Pt. 3:279	On advice of S. and all his counsellors, J. has decided to remain in Denmark until winter is over. He would like to visit her and royal children at Elsinore [Kronborg Castle]. Proposes to go there in early Dec.
15/2/90	Council (Sc.)	Kronborg Castle	Rymer XVI: 41–42	Reminds B. of "the prosecution of this platt anent the sustenation of the ministerie." B. must spare no labour on this while J. is in Scandinavia.
				Writes with own hand to tell of heartiness of Danish reception. Thanks Council for

Date	Sender	Place	Reference	Summary
				diligence. Hasten repair of Holyrood Abbey. Send no more lords or gentlemen hither "for I am already overchargeable to these Folks here." End discords so no quarrels will be seen by Danes returning with him. Provide good hunting against his return. He will hasten home, not losing a good wind by sitting or drinking. (*Holograph*)
21/2/90	Sir Pat. Vans	"	MaitCl 25, Vol. I, Pt. 2: 279–80	Summons for help in entertaining "gentlemen designed for our convoy" from Denmark to Sc.
4/3/90	Council (Sc.)	Copenhagen	Rymer XVI: 51–52	Ships for J.'s return voyage. Imprisonment ordered for three Spaniards and pilot. Care of park at Holyrood. J. will purge from Council any who seek release of Spaniards in his absence.
31/3/90	"	Kronborg	CSP (S) X:261	Obey directions entrusted to bearer. J.'s return close.
4/4/90	Robt. Bowes	[Kronborg]	CSP (S) X: 265	Q. E. likes the overture he made. Will do utmost to further it during brief time left in Denmark. (*Holograph*)
21/4/90	Elizabeth	Elsinore [Kronborg]	CSP (S) X: 277–78	Requests duty-free export of 1200 pieces of Eng. cloth for use of Queen Anne.

Date	Recipient	Written from	Printed in	Contents
25/5/90	Lord Deputies of Denmark	?	Hal II: 82–83	Announces safe return to Sc. Thanks for warmth of reception in Denmark.
3/6/90	Sir Pat. Vans	HH	MaitCl 25, Vol. I, Pt. 2: 280–81	Request for payment of levy to entertain Danes who accompanied J. home to Sc.
6/6/90	Burghley	"	CSP (S) X: 313	J. has concerned self with German affairs. Urges B. to expedite matters. (*Holograph*)
[June 1590]	Ambassadors to Denmark & Germany	?	CSP (S) X: 337-40	Extended directions concerning their mission.
[Early June? 1590]	Burghley	?	CSP (S) X: 320–21	J.'s messenger to Q. E. to use B.'s advice. Mutual amity desired. "I need not use any longer harangue for that matter." (*Holograph*)
17/8/90	Robt. Erskine	Stirling	HMC Rpt. 5, App. Pt. 1: 636–37	Expresses shock that E. has frustrated royal bounty intended for the widow of E.'s suicide son by appropriating the estate himself.

Date	Correspondent		Reference	Summary
1/10/90	Robt. Muir	HH	MaitCl. 71, Pt. I: 83–84	Renewed request for hackney coach for use of Q. Anne's ladies. J. hopes he will not have to requisition it.
20/11/90	?	"	CSP (S) X: 422–23	Declares Archibald Douglas is no longer authorized to act for J. Action to prevent future misrepresentation.
[c 26/12/90]	Vicomte de Turenne	"	WarrPprs II: 146–48	Thanks for report on French affairs. J. wishes he had T. here to advise him but realizes crisis keeps him in France. His king can count on J.'s total support in this most just and holy war.
[c. Mar. 1591?]	E. of Huntly	?	Gordon II: 615–16	J. busy about business between H. and E. of Moray. Argyll says he will no longer be a head of this quarrel. Moray's honest friends want him to agree. Moray has promised J. a direct answer by 15 April. Whatever happens, matters will end well for H.
15/5/91	Elizabeth	HH	CSP (S) X: 515	Determination to preserve peace on Border. Bothwell's "restraint" will not affect Liddesdale.
16/10/91	"	"	CSP (S) X: 577–78	Asks Q.E. to see that Wm. Reynolds goes through with promised marriage to Agnes Swinton.

Date	Recipient	Written from	Printed in	Contents
13/11/91	"	"	CSP (S) X: 587–88	Asks restoration of Irish estates of Garrett Carew, who entered J.'s service in Denmark.
Nov./91	Burghley	"	HMC Rpt. 13, App. Pt. 2 (Portland Vol. II), 18	Asks B. to solicit Q. E. to mediate so that Scottish captain, prisoner in Russia, may be released.
23/12/91	Lady Arabella Stuart	"	CSP (S) X: 605	J.'s satisfaction at hearing of her virtues. Certain knowledge of her abode will make him visit her more frequently with letters.
3/1/92	Elizabeth	"	WarrPprs II: 166–67	After late accident [Bothwell's "besetting" Holyrood], J. sends particulars and request for aid.
"	Burghley	"	CSP (S) X: 616	Bearer can inform B. better than a public messenger of the last villainous act attempted here.
[c. Feb. 1592]	E. of Huntly	?	Cldwd V: 146–47	J. has never been in such danger [because of mutinous guard and rioting in Edinburgh] as since H. left. He had to dissemble but

476

remains constant. Come armed for your own protection. Send a letter to pacify minister.

Date	To	Repository	Reference	Description
13/6/92	Burghley	HH	HMC Rpt. 13, App. Pt. 2 (Portland Vol. II), 19	Desires Q.E.'s favour for Englishman J. diverted from intended visit to Denmark and Germany, and took into his own service.
20/6/92	"	"	CSP(S) X: 702	Asks pardon for Walgrave [Waldegrave], printer.
31/10/92	E. of Essex	"	CSP (S) X: 799–800	Letter to Burghley having failed, he writes now to Essex on behalf of bearer, a victim of pirates.
3/2/93	Chancellor Maitland	Stirling	CSP (S) XI: 276–77	Asks M. to attend to complaint of John Acheson that he has not been paid money due to him. (Holograph P.S. jokes about M. not acting like a hunter.)
31/5/93	Burghley	HH	CSP (S) XI: 95	Asks B. to secure speedy payment of J.'s annuity from Q.E. (Holograph P.S. refers to annuity as so small as scarcely to be worth receiving.)
4/6/93	Elizabeth	"	CSP (S) XI: 95	J.'s Treasurer, Sir Robt. Melville, to give Q.E. information and assurances.

Date	Recipient	Written from	Printed in	Contents
"	Burghley	"	CSP (S) XI: 95	Asks help for his ambassador's speedy despatch. B.'s dutiful respect for his sovereign. (*Holograph*)
19/6/93	Sir Robt. Melville	"	HMC Rpt. 77 (DeLisle), II: 139	M. should not worry because of any reports which may reach him. "James Stewart, the late Chancellor," is not being granted any more favour than in December last. J. merely allows him to take up causes in law.
[19/6/93?]	Ld. John Hamilton	?	HMC Rpt. 11, App. Pt. 6 (Hamilton), 66	When H. comes to the "day of law" he is to disband his followers except for his ordinary attendants. (*Holograph*)
[Before 21/7/93]	Sir Robt. Melville	?	CSP (S) XI: 129	Bothwell has been seen publicly in Northumberland. M. is to complain to Q. E. and secure punishment of those to blame.
31/7/93	Ld. Paisley	HH	MaitCl 71, Pt. I: 87	Seeks to induce P. to settle dispute with Ld. Sempill.
7/12/93	Elizabeth	"	HMC Sal. MSS. IV: 430–32	J. has received Q. E.'s advice about lords involved in "Spanish Blanks" affair. Trusts she finds his actions conform with that advice. Tells of actions taken, and justifies

his moderation. Will Eliot and the "late attempt of Liddisdale." (*Holograph*)

Date	Recipient	Place	Source	Description
23/12/93	Ld. John Hamilton	"	CSP (S) XI: 248	Q. Anne is with child. H. summoned to attend meeting at Holyrood House on 11 Jan.
[Feb. 1594]	Prince Ulric	?	Hal II: 85–86	Letter, sent by Peter Junius, announcing birth of Prince Henry.
[Apr. 1594]	James Colville & Edw. Bruce	?	CSP (S) XI: 312–14	Detailed instructions to follow in upcoming interview with Q.E.
[Apr. 1594]	James Colville	?	CSP (S) XI: 314–15	Instructions for his coming meeting with K. of France.
1/5/94	"	Edinburgh	CSP (S) XI: 328	Take up the case of the Fosters, Eng. horsethieves, with Q. E. or her Council.
[c. 5/5/94]	States Gen. of United Provinces	?	WarrPprs II: 240–41	Invitation delivered by Sir Wm. Keith and Capt. Wm. Murray to send representatives to baptism of Prince Henry. J. numbers the Dutch among his best friends.
26/7/94	Elizabeth	Edinburgh	Hal II: 89–91	Pleased at her response to his last letter, J. will no longer listen to siren excuses of his Spanish lords.

479

Date	Recipient	Written from	Printed in	Contents
31/7/94	Laird of Glenurquhy	Stirling	BannCl 100, p. 431	Uncertainty of times of arrival of remaining foreign ambassadors requires postponement of Prince's baptism until 18 Aug. G. to be on hand by 15 Aug. Supplies for festivity to be delivered in previous week.
3/8/94	Sir Pat. Vans	"	MaitCl 25, Vol. I, Pt. 2: 281–82	Summons to attend baptism of Prince Henry.
31/8/94	Chancellor Maitland	"	CSP (S) XI: 425	J.'s financial problems. (Their urgency stressed in a *holograph* P.S.)
16/10/94	Ministers of Evangel, Edinburgh	Aberdeen	Cldwd V: 354–55	Having left Edinburgh with troops, J. has encountered floods in North and finds rebels evasive. Based at Aberdeen, he seeks to subjugate area. Asks money to pay troops for second month so that "this good and necessary work" not be left undone.
3/11/94	Robt. Bowes	"	HMC Sal. MSS. V: 17–18	Though Bothwell seeks J.'s life, he and accomplices are received in Eng. Asks arrest of James Douglas and Thos. Cransoun, two of Bothwell's agents.

480

Date	Recipient		Reference	Summary
15/1/95	States Gen. of United Provinces	HH	CSP (S) XI: 514	Wm. Stewart is J.'s ambassador. J. calls on Dutch to resist Spaniards actively in present crisis.
14/2/95	Col. Wm. Stewart	?	CSP (S) XI: 531–33	Instructions for his embassy to United Provinces.
1/3/95	Burghley	HH	CSP (S) XI: 541–42	Reasons for earlier pardoning of J. Colville, J.'s present envoy to Q. E. B. asked to assist Colville.
"	Robt. Bowes	"	BannCl 104, pp. 142–44	Colville to be paid £1266 due to J. from Q. E., his earlier disloyalty being forgiven. J. explains his unexpected clemency: "Mercy is the anchor of our conscience." Irish matters.
[Early 1595?]	E. of Huntly	?	SpaCl, *Misc.* III: 213	J. will see H. in Edinburgh as soon as possible, meanwhile is not to be troubled with requests on behalf of Spanish lords. (*Holograph*)
"	"	?	SpaCl, *Misc.* III: 213	Having no answer to opinion he sent H. by his friends, J. asks him to listen to what this gentle minister tells him. Alex. Lindsay will inform H. of time for latter's coming rendezvous with J. (*Holograph*)

Date	Recipient	Written from	Printed in	Contents
"	"	?	SpaCl, *Misc.* III: 215	J. thinks of H. every hour of the day and would have seen him ere now if not detained by bearer's business. (*Holograph*)
"	"	?	SpaCl, *Misc.* III: 215–16	H. must fight friends as he would enemies in a foreign war. He may count upon J. during his own absence. (*Holograph*)
"	"	?	SpaCl, *Misc.* III: 216	Let H. follow J.'s advice, no matter what his friends say to contrary. J. and the bearer are constantly attending to H.'s business. (*Holograph*)
"	"	?	SpaCl, *Misc.* III: 216	J. will send directions as to how H. should conduct himself. Let him remember vow made at his bridal. (*Holograph*)
[*c.* 3/4/95]	Chancellor Maitland	?	CSP (S) XI: 567–68	Informer has given E. of Mar bad reports of Maitland, but J. will not suspect the latter pending a meeting. Maitland has been fed bad reports of Mar. Knaves seek to injure J. (*Holograph*)
[Aug?]/95	"	?	Sanderson, p. 184	Sorrow at hearing of M.'s illness. When God calls M., J. will show his widow and children the same favour he has shown M. himself.

Date		Place	Source	
24/10/95	Elizabeth	Linlithgow	CSP (S) XII: 48	J. is moving swiftly to attend to Q. E.'s complaints re Sc. borderers.
20/12/95	"	HH	CSP (S) XII: 94–95	After two years of failure of peas and beans in Sc., J. asks licence to import grain from Eng.
24/1/96	James Hudson	"	CSP (S) XII: 133–34	H. to seek a licence to bring 30 tuns of beer from Eng. for provision of J.'s house.
30/6/96	David Foulis	Falkland	CSP (S) XII: 256	Q. E. withholding his annuity, J. may rightly break their league. The annuity "being of so small quantity and so malignly paid", J. is amazed at this nonpayment. F. to find Q. E.'s mind and determination of her Council.
7/7/96	Elizabeth	Edinburgh	EgerPprs, pp. 226–27	Border affairs. J. replies to Q. E.'s complaint of delay while he sought advice: "Were I not a father, but a Nestor Kynge, I were but a starke foole yf in matters of such importance, I would take all upon me, unspiringe* the advise of any."
[19/8/96]	Secretary (John Lindsay of Balcarres)	?	SHR IX: 378	J. asks Secretary to hasten Frenchman's despatch. He believes latter (M. de la Jessé) wants to serve him all he can. (*Holograph*)
[6/9/96]	"	?	SHR IX: 379	J. shares Secretary's view of Frenchman. Let him have general letters of recommendation.

Date	Recipient	Written from	Printed in	Contents
				He can blow abroad J's claim to the [Eng.?] title. (*Holograph*)
2/10/[96]	E. of Huntly	?	WarrPprs II: 299–301	H. must choose to obey Kirk or go into exile and never be a Scotsman again. His wife and family may enjoy his patrimony.
17/10/96	Secretary (John Lindsay of Balcarres)	?	Facs. Pt. III: Pl. LXXIII	J. cannot accept answer that there is not available the small amount of silver needed for the Isles. J. marvels Secretary has not kept him better informed about "ministeriall maitteris." J. will have to come to Edinburgh and himself sift the chaff from the corn. (*Holograph*)
1/3/97	Laird of Philorth	Perth	CSP (S) XII: 480	Requests a gift of his gyrfalcon, which J. understands is the best in the country.
22/4/97	Elizabeth	HH	CSP (S) XII: 512–13	Our commissioners create fear in the lawless borderers. Let Q. E. beware of partiality in Eng. officers and keep ear open for Scots. She shall not lack satisfaction. (*Holograph*)

Date	Recipient	Place	Source	Description
25/4/97	Laird of Wester Wemyss	?	HMC Rpt. 3, p. 422	Archie Armstrong and other trouble-makers transferred to custody in J.'s houses and castles.
[July? 1597]	Elizabeth	?	CSP (S) XIII, Pt. 1: 68–69	Default of others made J. fail to keep promises. Has received pledges from wardens and wants date set for handing them over. Proposes joint proclamation for Borders. (*Holograph*)
3/9/97	Henri IV	Falkland	SHR XVI: 143	Late arrival of H.'s ambassador has caused delay in renewing ancient friendship of France and Scotland.
27/9/97	Sir Robt. Cecil	Linlithgow	CSP (S) XIII, Pt. 1:92	Recommends Robt. Jowsie, who is to receive annuity paid J. by Q.E.
5/10/97	Robt. Bowes?	"	CSP (S) XIII, Pt. 1: 94–95	J. is going in person to attend to the failure of Buccleuch or his pledges to hand selves over to Q.E.
6/10/97	Sir Wm. Bowes	"	CSP (S) XIII, Pt. 1: 95	Buccleuch having surrendered to Eng., J. hopes he will be released on bond to find his delinquent pledges.
13/10/97	Robt. Bowes	"	CSP (S) XIII, Pt. 1: 101	Displeasure at late accident concerning Border pledges. (*Holograph P.S.* blames knavery of "one or two of my seditious subjects.")

Date	Recipient	Written from	Printed in	Contents
20/10/97	Sir Wm. Bowes	"	CSP (S) XIII, Pt. 1: 106–7	Asks B. to support application for Buccleuch's release on bond.
"	Robt. Bowes	"	CSP (S) XIII, Pt. 1: 108–9	B. asked to cooperate in investigation of tumult arising out of Buccleuch affair.
29/10/97	"	"	CSP (S) XIII, Pt. 1: 116–17	Asks that Buccleuch be kept at Berwick and not moved south.
21/12/97	Ld. John Hamilton	HH	HMC Rpt. 11, App. Pt. 6 (Hamilton), 67	J. does not mean to disgrace H. by seeking Dumbarton from him; he is ready to let H.'s son have Arbroath. (*Holograph*)
22/12/97	E. of Tyrone	"	CSP (S) XIII, Pt. 2: 1138	After death of Q. E., J. will gladly accept T.'s offered service. J. will use his credit with Q. E. to secure for T. hearing of any complaints he wishes to make.
[1597]	Secretary (John Lindsay of Balcarres)	?	HMC Rpt. 6, App. Pt. 1: 669	Should J. send a private man or a Councillor as envoy to Eng.? (*Holograph*)
22/3/98	Ld. Gray	HH	CSP (S) XIII, Pt. 1: 179	Arrangements for entertainment of J.'s brother-in-law, the Duke of Holstein.

Date	Correspondent	Place	Source	Summary
1/4/98	Edw. Bruce	?	CSP (S) XIII, Pt. 1: 184–85	B. to discover why Q. E. treats so rigorously Sir Robt. Kerr and Buccleuch, entrusted to her as pledges.
7/8/98	Elizabeth	Falkland	CSP (S) XIII, Pt. 1: 252–53	Latest Border troubles caused not by Border thieves but by Q. E.'s officers. J. asks that principal offenders be turned over to him.
26/9/98	"	Dalkeith	CSP (S) XIII, Pt. 1: 297–98	J. thanks Q. E. for not believing Valentine Thomas's slanders and trusts she will see J.'s name cleared.
"	Council (Eng.)	"	CSP (S) XIII, Pt. 1: 301–2	Thanks for preserving J.'s honour from "malicious calumny of a debauched villain" (V. Thomas). Asks that some public form be used to efface all scandal.
8/1/99	Elizabeth	HH	CSP (S) XIII, Pt. 1: 378–79	Expostulates at delay in reparation for Eng. borderers' raid on Sc. Attackers penetrated six miles.
29/5/99	"	?	CSP (S) XIII, Pt. 1: 476–77	Need for candour. False complaints have been presented to Q. E. Sir Robt. Kerr has been wrongly blamed by her and means "to quit all his wild Border fashions."
13/6/99	Ld. Newbottle	Falkland	Hal II: 96–97	Orders money owing to George Heriot be paid so that Q. Anne's jewels can be taken out of pawn.

487

Date	Recipient	Written from	Printed in	Contents
1/7/99	Master of Elphinstone (Treas.)	"	MaitCl 57, III: 343	Orders immediate despatch of deerhounds to K. of Denmark.
14/8/99	Elizabeth	"	CSP (S) XIII, Pt. 1: 527	Trusts Q. E. will acquit him of all imputations of dishonour after hearing James Sempill deliver truth.
24/9/99	Clement VIII	HH	Rushworth I: 166	Gratitude that Pope has not sought to use his authority against him. Recommends Bishop of Vazion for cardinal's hat. He is an honest Catholic from whom Clement can learn truth concerning J.'s policies.
30/1/1600	Ld. Gray	"	CSP (S) XIII, Pt. 2: 619	Seeks to reconcile G. with his son.
9/7/1600	Master of Elphinstone (Treas.)	Falkland	HMC Rpt. 9, App. Pt. 2: 195	Orders immediate start on "reparation" of Holyrood House.
4/8/1600	Elizabeth	"	CSP (S) XIII, Pt. 2: 674–75	Appoints James Hamilton to attend upon her as his agent.

Date	Recipient	Place	Source	Summary
"	Sir Robt. Cecil	"	CSP (S) XIII, Pt. 2: 675	James Hamilton to be J.'s agent in London.
[Sept. 1600]	Elizabeth	?	HMC Sal. MSS. X: 331–32	Thanks for congratulations on failure of Gowrie Plot. Q.E. holds first place in his heart. He does not, as slander reports, prepare for her funeral. (*Holograph*)
21/9/1600	"	Linlithgow	CSP (S) XIII, Pt. 2: 710	On behalf of an old man who served J.'s father and grandfather.
11/11/1600	Master of Gray	HH	CSP (S) XIII, Pt. 2: 726–27	Rebukes G. for busying himself with matters above his reach. Wills him to withdraw from Eng. to inland France.
14/12/1600	"	"	CSP (S) XIII, Pt. 2: 751–52	J. will think well of G. if he returns from Eng. to clear his name in Sc. (*Holograph* P.S.: Good service will be rewarded. "As I have ever been to all my good subjects, I will be gladder of your doing well than yourself can be.")
5/2/01	E. of Mar & Abbot of Kinloss	"	HMC Rpt. 15 App. Pt. 1 (Mar, 47–48	Steps J. has taken to remove suspicion he is dealing with Pope and K. of Spain. M. and K. are to learn why Q.E. treats such reports seriously. Cases of Edw. Drummond and Poury Ogilvy. Rumour-mongers are seditious enemies.

489

Date	Recipient	Written from	Printed in	Contents
20/2/01	Laird of Johnston & Robt. Scott	"	HMC Sal. MSS. XIV: 172	E. of Mar having gone on embassy, they are to prevent Border violence and cooperate with Ld. Scrope.
31/3/01	Laird of Johnston & Buccleuch deputy	"	CSP (S) XIII, Pt. 2: 795–96	Since they have failed to punish Sc. borderers who invaded Eng., J. has authorized Eng. wardens to cross into Sc. to punish same.
9/4/01	E. of Mar	Linlithgow	HMC Rpt. 15, App. Pt. 1 (Mar), 48–49	J., as is his custom in weighty matters, has already written to Mar, his ambassador, in his own hand. Now he has ordered this letter written about Border affairs, especially the late hunting accident.
19/4/01	George Nicolson (Q.E.'s agent in Sc.)	Huntingtower	CSP (S) XIII, Pt. 2: 806–808	Excuses broken promise, justifies course taken with Dunkirker with an Eng. prize. Denies he has countenanced help for traitor Tyrone. N. must speak and write with greater civility.
28/4/01	E. of Mar	Dalkeith	CSP (S) XIII, Pt. 2: 811–12	Recent raids of Sc. borderers due to absence of Ld. Scrope. Hanging of Abyis Richie.

490

Date				
				Mar to seek appointment of new Eng. Wn. of W. March, replacing Ld. Scrope, who is a lesser man than his father.
21/11/01	Elizabeth	HH	CSP (S) XIII, Pt. 2: 900–901	Renewed offer to assist in Ireland. J. has learned who secretly supplied Irish rebels from Scotland and will deal sternly with them.
[Nov. 1601?]	"	?	Bruce, pp. 139–40	Asks her kind offices for bearer, whom she may cross-examine on his journey to France. All J.'s foreign negotiations are open to her. (*Holograph*)
4/12/01	"	HH	CSP (S) XIII, Pt. 2: 909–10	Complains of shelter in Eng. for murderers of Wn. of W. March. Other outrages. Corrupted ministers may have sinisterly dazzled her eyes. Punishment demanded.
[1601]	Shah Abbas	Edinburgh	Facs. III: Pl. LXXX	Sir Anthony Shirley has made known Shah's splendour. J. hopes to see hateful ensigns of the Turks overthrown, but, since death of "that hero the Earl of Essex," Eng. aid must not be looked for. English oppose present embassy. J. can do more against Turks when, as K. of England, he commands its very powerful fleet.

Date	Recipient	Written from	Printed in	Contents
[c. Jan. 1602]	Elizabeth	?	CSP (S) XIII, Pt. 2:935	Thanks for welcoming D. of Lennox. J. passes on report of Spanish armaments. (*Holograph*)
18/2/02	Elizabeth	HH	Rymer XVI: 427	Having learnt peril of using unfit instruments, J. has chosen the trusted E. of Mar and the Abbot of Kinloss (a Privy Councillor) as ambassadors to Q. E.
[c. Feb. 1602]	Capt. Robt. Elliott	?	CSP (S) XIII, Pt. 2: 942–44	Spaniards are no longer a threat. J. not a persecutor of Catholics. He thinks well of Pope but will not deal with him. J. is no K. of France to forsake religion for a kingdom, but "will maintain the religion that I now profess to the death." Kings are ruined by priests.
7/3/02	Elizabeth	Dumfries	CSP (S) XIII, Pt. 2: 958	Visiting the W. March, J. finds Eng. warden most cooperative.
16/5/02	Ld. Roxburghe	Falkland	CSP (S) XIII, Pt. 2: 991	R. to deal firmly with the pledges who slipped away from York Castle.

492

Date	Person	Place	Reference	Description
22/5/02	E. of Caithness	Dunfermline	CSP (S) XIII, Pt. 2: 991–92	Orders arrest of Jeremy Luif, pirate. (*Holograph P.S.*: C. must prove his affection to J. and justify latter's trust in this matter.)
16/7/02	Henri IV	Falkland	CSP (S) XIII, Pt. 2: 1024–25	J. sends letter with special envoy to congratulate H. on escaping Duc de Biron's conspiracy.
[July 1602]	Duc de Mayenne?	?	WarrPprs II: 390–91	Invoking the bond between M's house and Sc. crown, J. asks for assistance for Ld. Home on present embassy.
19/9/02	Ld. Scrope	Dunfermline	HMC Sal. MSS. XII: 384–85	J. announces intended visit to W. March to remedy "enormities and insolences" caused by S's rash and unadvised proceedings.
[Sept. 1602?]	Elizabeth	?	Bruce, pp. 151–53	Reports French king thinks Low Countries should join France, England, Scotland in alliance. Lindsay's alleged message from Pope requests Pr. Henry be reared a Catholic. J. has dealt stiffly with this unauthorized ambassador.
12/10/02	"	Dumfries	Bruce, pp. 147–48	The English having made a Border arrest in Sc., J. wants the criminal transferred to Sc. for trial.

493

Date	Recipient	Written from	Printed in	Contents
31/10/02	Ld. Scrope	Edinburgh	HMC Sal. MSS. XII: 458–59	J. glad to learn S. means to cooperate with Sc. warden. Authority to pursue outlaws and fugitives.
[Oct.? 1602]	Elizabeth	?	Bruce, pp. 149–51	J. reports on conversation with Fr. ambassador concerning common front against Spain. Spain expected to propose marriage between Infanta and Pr. Henry. J. distrusts such siren songs.
8/12/02	"	HH	CSP (S) XIII, Pt. 2: 1087–88	Detailed accusation against Ld. Scrope, who, instead of preventing Border raids, actually leads them himself. Asks Q. E. to hand him over.
[1602]	"	?	Bruce, pp. 145–47	Q. E.'s acceptance of J.'s honest intentions makes him happier than if he had won the Golden Fleece. Delay in hearing from France about proposed alliance. Frank Mowbray's message about K. of Spain and Archduke offering friendship. Q. E. to be his oracle in answering. (Holograph)

[1602?]	"	J. will report to Q. E. on future negotiations for alliance of France, England, and Scotland against Spain. Henri IV is favourably inclined. Assurances of faithfulness. (*Holograph*)	Bruce, pp. 143–44
[1602?]	?	Though personally unacquainted with person who has written to him, J. thanks him for stationing self close to border. J. will not need his services, but will reward him in due time. (*Holograph*)	CSP (S) XIII, Pt. 2: 1125
[Late 1602]	Elizabeth	Having sent this messenger to collect his pension, J. takes the opportunity to report on negotiations with Fr. ambassador. K. of France told Ld. Home of coming proposals from Rome for religious toleration in Sc. J. will not accede, but do Q. E.'s will. (*Holograph*)	Bruce, pp. 153–54

Date	Recipient	Written from	Printed in	Contents
Undated letters, probably written before James ascended English throne	Ld. John Hamilton	?	HMC Rpt. 11, App. Pt. 6 (Hamilton), 66	J. gives thanks for brach and promises H. two or more hounds from royal kennels. (*Holograph*)
	"	?	HMC Rpt. 11, App. Pt. 6 (Hamilton), 67–68	The new wine being unwholesome, J. wants H. to brew Dutch beer for his visit to H. (*Holograph*)
	"John Slates" (E. of Mar)	?	HMC Rpt. 15, App. Pt. 1 (Mar), 37	J. desires a visit from him, hopes the Duke will not hinder one. (*Holograph*)
	"	?	HMC Rpt. 15, App. Pt. 1 (Mar), 37	J. must see him as soon as possible. (*Holograph*)

Date	To	Place	Reference	Description
27/3/03	D. of Lennox	HH	HMC Rpt. 3, App., 396	Summons to accompany J. to England.
28/3/03	Robt. Lee, Ld. Mayor of London	"	STC 14362	Appreciation for L.'s prompt proclamation of J. as King of Eng. Assurances of favour.
29/3/03	John Dalston	"	HMC Sal. MSS. XV: 20–21	Thanks for message of support. Instructs D. to proclaim him at Carlisle if he has no message from Ld. Scrope.
[Late Mar. 1603]	Council (Eng.)	?	HMC Sal. MSS. XV: 345–46	Having learnt of Q. E.'s death, J. thanks them for their services to her and confirms them in office.
3/4/03	Sir John Harington	HH	Har I: 335	Acknowledges gift of lantern and accompanying verses.
6/4/03	Council (Eng.)	Berwick	Ellis, Series 1, III: 64–67	Money received. Hopes to see Council at Burghley. Intends state entry into York. Funeral arrangements for Q. E. Items for Q. Anne.
10/4/03	Sir David Carnegie	Newcastle	HMC Rpt. 7 App. (Vol. II), 722	Because of shortness of time, J. could not have C. travel to Eng. with him. However,

Date	Recipient	Written from	Printed in	Contents
				English long to see Q. Anne and royal children, and C. can accompany her.
11/4/03	Cecil	"	HMC Sal. MSS. XV: 43	C. to repair to J. to discuss letters from abroad and other matters not to be trusted to paper. He is to show this letter to Council as warrant for a quick short trip to meet J.
12/4/03	Council (Eng.)	?	MaitCl 35, p. xlii	Send forward jewels, coaches, horses, and litters in readiness for Q. Anne's arrival from Sc.
13/4/03	"	Newcastle	Ellis, Series 1, III: 67–69	C. to order coronation coinage from mint. J. specifies form for new royal coat of arms.
15/4/03	Ld. Keeper & other officers of state	Topcliff	Ellis, Series 1, III: 69–71	Councillors are to remain at their posts. Jewels for Q. Anne. Choice of ladies to attend her. Litters and coaches for her journey.
"	Council (Eng.)	"	MaitCl 35, p. xlii	Further to letter of 12 Apr, he does not want principal jewels of state among those sent for Q. Anne.

498

Date	To/From	Place	Reference	Summary
[Apr.]/03	[E. of Kent]	?	HMC Sal. MSS. XV: 65	Lady Arabella Stuart to be freed from unpleasant life with grandmother and live in J.'s household as befits her station.
[Apr.?]/03	Cecil	?	HMC Sal. MSS. XV: 87–88	Matters on which he wants C.'s advice. No other king alive will rely more confidently on a counsellor than J. on C. (*Holograph*)
11/5/03	E. of Kent	?	HMC Sal. MSS. XV: 82	Lady Arabella Stuart permitted to travel to Greenwich with Cts. of Shrewsbury to meet J.
14/5/03	E. of Mar	Greenwich	HMC Rpt. 15, App. Pt. 1 (Mar), 50	Letters both from his dearest bedfellow Q. Anne and Sir George Douglas have informed J. of recent incident at Stirling. M. to conform himself to J.'s wishes as communicated by D. of Lennox.
17/5/03	"	"	HMC Rpt. 15, App. Pt. 1 (Mar), 50–51	M. to come to Eng. and report more fully on plot to seize Prince Henry. He is to return Q. Anne's letter to her.
[22?/5/03]	Council (Eng.)	?	HMC Sal. MSS. XV: 99	Policy about granting suits for lands, reversions, titles etc. Council to be limited to 24 members in future.
9/8/03	Presbytery of Edinburgh	Hampton [Court]	BannCl 92, I: 2	Thanks for their declaration of joy at his accession to Eng. throne.

Date	Recipient	Written from	Printed in	Contents
12/1/04	Privy Council (Sc.)	"	MaitCl 35, pp. lv–lvii	Plague having abated in Eng., J. can proceed with project to unite Eng. and Sc. A parliament to be convened in Sc., its sole business to be the Union. Selection of commissioners. Procedures.
8/2/[04?]	E. of Argyll	"	MaitCl 50, pp. 32–33	A., being pledge for Laird of Auchinbrek, will be held responsible for Laird's oppression of J.'s poor tenants of Bute.
9/2/04	E. of Montrose (Chanc., Sc.)	Whitehall	MaitCl 50, p. 34	Sc. Council to be told Argyll deserves commendation. Nature of reward to be decided when Sc. Secretary comes to Eng. for consultation.
26/6/04	House of Commons	?	STC 14361	Why J. is not asking his first parliament to vote him a subsidy.
25/9/04	Privy Council (Sc.)	Windsor	BannCl 92, I: 353*–54*	Huntly not to be excommunicated for failure to receive communion, provided he attends Kirk, hears sermons.
[1604?]	E. of Mar	?	HMC Rpt. 15, App. Pt. 1 (Mar), 52	Reminds him of his cousin Fenton's errand and recommends him as one of those who preserved J.'s life. (*Holograph*)

Date	Recipient	Place	Source	Summary
22/1/05	Robt. Cecil, Visc. Cranborne	Hinchingbrooke	HMC Sal. MSS. XVII: 29–30	Need for a treaty with France to protect merchants. Fr. king's complaint about Eng. ambassador in Venice.
11/2/05	Privy Council (Sc.)	Whitehall	BannCl 92, I: 354*–55*	Although J. advised great moderation in use of excommunication against noblemen, action should be taken against those who are irreconcilable.
[5/3/05?]	Certain noblemen	?	Hal II: 124–25	Measures to be used to discover probable imposture by a woman who goes into trances. Miracles must be tested.
6/3/05	French Protestants	Royston	Hal II: 111–12	Their envoy has been welcome. J.'s concern for injuries to which they are exposed. Determination to aid them.
8/6/05	Robt. Cecil, E. of Salisbury	Windsor	HMC Sal. MSS. XVII: 244–45	£300 to be allowed to the victim of Eng. pirates on whose behalf Christian IV wrote. Lord Chandos. Sir Oliver Cromwell's petition.
13/6/05	E. of Wigton	Greenwich	MaitCl 51, Vol. II, Pt. 2: 396–97	W. is to give assistance to E. of Dunbar, charged with state and church affairs in Sc.
26/6/05	Ralph Winwood	Westminster	Winwood II: 78–81	J.'s policy towards Dutch intrusion into Eng. ports in pursuit of Spanish ships. W. to follow J.'s *via regia* between the two enemies.

Date	Recipient	Written from	Printed in	Contents
19/7/05	Ld. Balmerino (Sec., Sc.)	Havering-at-Bower	BannCl 92, I: 355* – 57*	J. has learnt of contemptuous, seditious meeting of ministers at Aberdeen. These gangrened members who usurped authority of a General Assembly must be cut off.
[Nov. 1605]	Cecil	?	HMC Sal. MSS. XVII: 529–30	Suspicious circumstances about Northumberland and Gunpowder Plot. Questions to be put to Carleton. (Holograph)
2/12/05	Archd. Albert of Austria	Westminster	HMC Sal. MSS. XVII: 537–38	Thanks A. for his concern at Gunpowder Plot. The part played by Owen and Baldwin.
17/12/05	Ld. Spynie	Waltham Abbey	BannCl 92, I: 455* – 56*	S.'s compensation for surrender of lands of Bishopric of Moray.
[1605?]	Cecil	?	HMC Sal. MSS. XVIII: 372–73	E. of Home unwilling to accept foreign employment, to anger of Don Diego. J. cannot move him. J. on dealing with "inconstant and coy fools." (Holograph)
22/1/06	Privy Council (Sc.)	Whitehall	BannCl, 92, I: 360* – 64*	Instructions concerning "contemptuous and rebellious ministers" involved in unauthorized "General Assembly" at

				Aberdeen. P.C. to prepare a royal proclamation.
8/4/06	"	"	MaitCl 25, Vol. I, Pt. I: 149–50	Earls must not wear crimson velvet robes at next parliament, only at coronations, creations, and similar solemnities. Only royal children may wear crimson velvet to parliament.
21/5/[06]	William Scott	Greenwich	BannCl 92, I: 48–50	Though letters show J.'s attachment to Kirk, enemies malign him. S. and others are to appear before J. on 15 Sept. and give him benefit of their learning and experience.
24/6/06	Privy Council (Sc.)	"	BannCl 92, I: 365*–66*	Learned and experienced ministers have been summoned to appear before J. by 15 Sept. to inform him of the divisions in the Kirk so that he can remedy them.
19/9/[06]	"	Theobalds	MaitCl 25, Vol. I, Pt. 2: 353	Noblemen are to accept precedence as laid down in Decree of Ranking.
20/10/06	Presbytery of Dunfermline	Newmarket	BannCl 92, I: 67–68	Failure of ministers seeking the causes of dissension in the Kirk requires summoning of nobles and ministers at Linlithgow on 10 Dec. to decide remedies.
[Oct. 1606]	Justice Deputy (Sc.)	?	BannCl 93, III: 181–82	Orders banishment of those Scottish ministers convicted of treason who have not shown contrition.

Date	Recipient	Written from	Printed in	Contents
[1606?]	Cecil	?	HMC Sal. MSS. XVIII: 373–74	J. knows himself a man inferior to many in many things. Discusses union of Eng. and Sc. He could wait a Methuselah's age for a perfect Union. (*Holograph*)
3/1/07	Privy Council (Sc.)	Whitehall	BannCl 92, I: 371*	How to proceed if those addicted to anarchy cause trouble at the coming General Assembly.
21/2/07	Ld. Balmerino (Sec. Sc.)	"	BannCl 92, I: 371*–72*	Some ministers continue to pray for those convicted for their part in the Aberdeen "General Assembly." Council must immediately stop this.
[Mar. 1607]	Archbp. of Canterbury (Richard Bancroft)	"	HMC Sal. MSS. XIX: 83–84	J. wants Archbp. to attempt to reconcile Sir John Paginton and his wife.
5/3/07	Ld. Balmerino	"	BannCl 92, I: 373*–74*	J. is keeping 7 Sc. ministers in Eng. for further consultation. B. is to have substitutes look after their parishes.
20/4/07	Privy Council (Sc.)	Royston	BannCl 92, I: 374*–76*	How P.C. is to deal with consequences of late misbehaviour at Synod of Perth.

Date	Recipient	Place	Source	Content
3/6/07	E. of Huntingdon	Westminster	HMC Rpt. 78 (Hastings), IV: 192	H. is to assemble gentlemen and justices and suppress demonstrations against enclosures. He may "invade, destroy or disperse," or use mercy, according to circumstances.
6/7/07	Cecil	"	HMC Sal. MSS. XIX: 174	J. gives two brace of bucks to the farmers of the customs.
19/7/07	Ld. Scone	Whitehall	HMC Rpt. 6, App, 615	As a reward for good service against Clan Gregor, E. of Argyll to be rewarded with 20,000 marks and land at Kintyre.
24/7/07	D. of Lennox	Oatlands	BannCl 92, I: 382*	Sets precedence of lords and prelates in procession for opening of Sc. Parliament.
6/9/07	Privy Council (Sc.)	Windsor	BannCl 92, I: 383*–84*	Rooms of Andrew Melville, dismissed as Provost of New College, St. Andrews, are to be unlocked and emptied for successor.
[Sept.? 1607]	Philip III	?	HMC Rpt. 75 (Downshire), II: 457–58	The Dutch instigated the action by Scots of whom Philip complains; J. is not responsible. J. gives much more attention to Philip's complaints than Philip gives to J.'s.
[22?/10/07]	Council (Eng.)	?	HMC Sal. MSS. XIX: 291–92	J.'s pleasure at aldermen and people making loan. Genoa bankers will be impressed. Thanks Council for diligence in this matter. Never a king since Christ's time has been more happy than J. in his Council. (*Holograph*)

Date	Recipient	Written from	Printed in	Contents
[1 Dec.? 1607]	Cecil	?	HMC Sal. MSS. XIX: 351–53	How to deal with Dutch and French. If the Dutch cannot survive without Eng. aid, let them stop claiming title of a free state. Fuller's case. (*Holograph*)
7/3/08	Privy Council (Sc.)	Newmarket	BannCl 92, I: 391*	J. has seen John Murray's seditious sermon and wants him punished.
20/3/08	"	Whitehall	BannCl 92, I: 391*–92*	Stinging rebuke for delay in punishing offending minister, John Murray.
30/4/08	"	"	BannCl 92, I: 392*–93*	Rebuke for inadequate investigation of distribution of John Murray's seditious sermon.
20/7/08	General Assembly, Linlithgow	Theobalds	BannCl 92, I: 143–45	J. wants free speech but no impertinent or insolent discourses. Inveighs against malign dispositions of some who attended "that Conventicle of Aberdeen." The E. of Dunbar will report how each member behaves.
14/11/08	Ld. Scone	Whitehall	HMC Rpt. 17, App. Pt. 8 (Laing, Vol. I), 112	S. is to keep Lord Balmerino close prisoner in tower at Falkland pending trial for his heinous offence against J.'s honour. Dunbar

506

Date	Recipient	Place	Source	Content
24/11/08	Sir J. Houston	Thetford	BannCl 92, I: 169–70	will hand over Bal. to S. Bal. not to receive or write letters.
26/11/08	Sir R. Spencer & Sir Ralph Winwood	"	Winwood II: 451	Joy at commissioners' reports of concord at General Assembly. Summons to a Convention of the Estates, 26 Jan.
[Dec. 1608?]	Henri IV	?	HMC Sal. MSS. XX: 285	Sir Archibald Erskine having been slain, command of his troops in Low Countries is to pass to his brother.
23/1/09	Convention of Estates (Sc. Parl.)	Royston	BannCl 92, I: 402*–4*	Thanks for gracious reception of Cecil's son.
[28?/2/09]	Sir John Herbert et al.	Westminster	HMC Sal. MSS. XXI: 22–23	Agenda for the Estates. Supervision of foreign travel of young noblemen a necessary guard against Catholicism.
5/3/09	Privy Council (Sc.)	Whitehall	BannCl 92, I: 405*–6*	They are to be a screening committee reporting to Privy Council on applications for royal bounty. No king is more eager than J. to reward merit but he must preserve for his posterity the revenues of Crown.
				They must stop releasing convicted ministers without first obtaining J.'s permission.

Date	Recipient	Written from	Printed in	Contents
24/3/09	Sir Thos. Hamilton (Ld. Advocate)	"	BannCl 92, I: 406*–7*	As Ld. Advocate he is to further J.'s project of restoration of the Sc. episcopate.
23/4/09	E. of Mar	"	HMC Rpt. 15, App. Pt. 1 (Mar), 60–61	J.'s reliance on Mar and Dunbar in Sc. matters. He wants them, with other councillors, to advise how he should act on excommunicated lords.
31/5/09	"	Greenwich	HMC Rpt. 15, App. Pt. 1 (Mar), 63	Dunbar will manage affairs in coming Sc. parliament. M. is to take his cue from him.
"	Privy Council (Sc.)	"	BannCl 92, I: 409*–10*	They are to approve the anti-Catholic actions of the Archbishop of Glasgow.
7/6/09	E. of Mar	"	HMC Rpt. 15, App. Pt. 1 (Mar), 63–64	Dunbar will brief M. on various matters to be brought up in Sc. parliament. J. wants to be told who furthers his service in parliament, who crosses it, and who is lukewarm.
[7 June? 1609]	Archd. Albert of Austria	?	HMC Sal. MSS. XXI: 64	Letter with presentation copy of J.'s *Premonition to All Christian Monarchies, Free Princes and States*.

6/7/09	E. of Mar	Whitehall	HMC Rpt. 15, App. Pt. 1 (Mar), 64	Dunbar and another have reported Mar's great care and dexterity in handling Sc. parliament. J.'s thanks.
15/9/09	Sir Ralph Winwood	Theobalds	Winwood III: 69	W. to be ready to mediate between Dutch and Q. Anne's kinsman the Count of Oldenburgh.
8/10/09	Ld. Commissioners on Benefices (Sc.)	Royston	BannCl 92, I: 413*–14*	J. having laid out great sums to restore the Sc. dioceses, they must see that the bishops properly maintain them.
12/10/09	E. of Mar	"	HMC Rpt. 15, App. Pt. 1 (Mar), 65	M. may marry his son to the second daughter of E. of Errol despite Errol's Catholicism. Lady to receive religious instruction and profess Protestantism.
10/11/09	Ld. Commissioners on Benefices (Sc.)	Whitehall	BannCl 92, I: 418*–19*	Archbp. of St. Andrews is claiming many things that belong to the Crown. Stop his "impertinent pretences."
20/11/09	Cecil	Royston	HMC Sal. MSS. XXI: 160	After a disputed election, J. supports Valentine Carey for mastership of Christ College, Cambridge.
[1609?]	"	?	HMC Sal. MSS. XXI: 172	J. will speak again to Lady Anne Home. No word of Poolie. Lumsden's fall. Thanks for enlarging Theobalds Park. (*Holograph*)

Date	Recipient	Written from	Printed in	Contents
20/1/10	Privy Council (Sc.)	Royston	BannCl 92, I: 422*	Rebuke for permitting confined ministers to travel outside their parishes.
8/5/10	General Assembly (Glasgow)	Thetford	BannCl 92, I: 248–50	Formerly some people sought to maintain "a sort of headless government in Scotland," but J. remedied the situation, partly through use of General Assemblies. Because of "our duty to Our God, being his Lieutenant here," J. has summoned this Assembly to advance peace of Kirk.
"	E. of Dunbar	"	BannCl 92, I: 425*	Preparing for the General Assembly at Glasgow, D. is to distribute 10,000 marks among fitting persons.
24/6/10	Cecil	Westminster	HMC Sal. MSS. XXI: 225	The Emperor having arrested English Hanseatic merchants and seized goods, his subjects and their goods are to be held likewise.
30/7/10	"	"	HMC Sal. MSS. XXIV: 188–89	C. to fetch young Ld. Mordaunt from his mother to the Bishop of London, who will direct his education.

510

Date	Recipient	Place	Source	Content
[Aug. 1610]	"	?	HMC Sal. MSS. XXI: 236	Now that Juliers is won, the adverse party will be more ready to negotiate. May J.'s ambassador be as successful as General Cecil and his soldiers. (*Holograph*)
24/10/10	Auditors of Exchequer (Sc.)	Whitehall	BannCl 92, I: 429*	Dunbar to be credited with £3010 he gave Moderator of General Assembly, Linlithgow, to distribute among certain ministers.
[1610?]	Cecil	?	HMC Sal. MSS. XXI: 275	A matter in which Ld. Chamberlain must satisfy J. J.'s son did not receive the intelligence from C.'s nephew. (*Holograph*)
29/4/11	Laird of Weem	Greenwich	HMC Rpt. 6, App, 694	He is to assist E. of Argyll, who has been commissioned "to pursue that barbarous race of the name of McGregour with fire and sword."
29/9/11	Cecil	Hampton Court	HMC Sal. MSS, XXI: 313	Regulation of Anglo-Scottish trade.
6/10/11	Sir Ralph Winwood	Theobalds	Winwood III: 295	Alarmed at strength of Vorstius's supporters, J. has written accompanying letter. W. to urge Dutch to remove this "blasphemous Monster." If they will not, J. will publish to the world their defection from true religion.

Date	Recipient	Written from	Printed in	Contents
10/4/12	Archbp. of Glasgow	Whitehall	BannCl 92, I: 282–83	Wm. Birney to replace Mr. Dunbar as minister of Ayr because of latter's enormities. Birney also to be Dean of restored Chapel Royal of Scotland.
17/6/12	Privy Council (Sc.)	"	BannCl 92, I: 442*–43*	Books on divinity or devotions, history, and law to be published only after licensing.
26/9/12	E. of Mar	Hampton Court	HMC Rpt. 15, App. Pt. 1 (Mar), 68	J. declines to make Laird of Findlater a baron at M's request. Creation of many noblemen is doing more harm than good to the state and alienating hearts from the Union.
[c. 1612]	Convention of Estates (Sc. Parl.)	?	HMC Rpt. 17, App. Pt. 8 (Laing, Vol. I), 127–28	Parliament to make an act cancelling all assignations of Kirk revenues to ministers not actually serving parishes.
[1612?]	Bishops & clergy of Scotland	?	BannCl 93, III: 215–16	Fugitives from law have been improperly excommunicated. Bishops and ministers must abandon their citations which bid offenders come and be hanged.

Date	Recipient	Place	Source	Description
11/3/13	Commissioners of Rents, (Sc.)	Thetford	HMC Rpt. 6, App., 615	E. of Argyll not to be penalized for failure to build town at Kintyre. His service against Clan Gregor prevented him doing so.
29/8/13	Ld. Deputy of Ireland	Farnham	HMC Rpt. 14, App. Pt. 7 (Ormonde, Vol. I), 74–75	Outlines quarrel between E. of Ormonde and his son-in-law and heir. Ld. Deputy to seek reconciliation. J.'s anger against those who incite Ormonde.
[1613?]	Privy Council (Sc.)	?	BannCl 92, I: 306–8	The late Ld. Spynie improperly extorted 10,000 marks from the Bishop of Moray before giving him lands of his bishopric. J. directs action to be taken.
[1613]	Viscount Butler	?	HMC Rpt. 14, App. Pt. 7 (Ormonde, Vol. I), 5	B. is not to be discouraged by malign "ministers about the Earl of Ormonde" (whose heir he is) but to rely on J.'s favour.
28/3/14	Archd. Albert of Austria	Westminster	HMC Rpt. 75 (Downshire), IV: 352	Emperor's designs on Aix-la-Chapelle can cause a great conflagration. J. cannot be indifferent to what concerns the Palatinate. Asks A. and Elector of Cologne to abstain from action.
[April 1614]	Archbp. of Canterbury	?	HMC Rpt. 75 (Downshire), IV: 393	At request of his daughter, J. asks Anglican bishops to raise funds to build a church at Frankenthal for Protestant refugees there.

Date	Recipient	Written from	Printed in	Contents
20/5/14	E. of Mar	Whitehall	HMC Rpt. 15, App. Pt. 1 (Mar), 70	J. wants M. and Sir James Lockhart to choose "an indifferent neighbour" to arbitrate their quarrel.
22/8/14	Sir Henry Wotton	Castle Ashby	HMC Rpt. 77 (De L'Isle), V: 228	Sorrow at learning Spinola has won Aix and concern at reports of Wesel besieged. If reports are true, Wotton is to seek aid for city from Dutch.
17/9/14	E. of Ormonde	?	HMC Rpt. 14, App. Pt. 7 (Ormonde, Vol. I), 6	Commends suit of a gentleman (Ld. Dingwall?) who wishes to marry a lady (O.'s widowed daughter?). (*Holograph P.S.*)
27/2/15	Ld. Binning (Secr., Sc.)	Whitehall	HMC Rpt. 10, App. Pt. 1: 40–41	J. dislikes seeing titles pass out of lineal descent and accordingly refuses to let Sir Alex. Montgomery inherit title of E. of Eglinton. He will, however, newly create him E. of Eglinton by royal investiture.
14/3/15	E. of Ormonde	Newmarket	HMC Rpt. 14, App. Pt. 7 (Ormonde, Vol. I), 6–7	Sets London as place for arbitration of differences between O. and his kinsman by marriage, Ld. Dingwall.

Date	Addressee	Place	Source	Description
28/5/15	"	Greenwich	HMC Rpt. 14, App. Pt. 7 (Ormonde, Vol. I), 77	Peremptory summons to come to London, where J. will arbitrate differences between O. and Ld. Dingwall.
16/10/15	Sir Ralph Winwood	Royston	HMC Rpt. 15, App. Pt. 18 (Buccleuch, Vol. I), 161–62	Urges Council members to whom "this great matter" (Overbury case?) has been committed to move swiftly so as to stop spread of rumours prejudicial to innocent.
26/10/15	Archbp. of Canterbury et al.	"	HMC Rpt. 15, App. Pt. 18 (Buccleuch, Vol. I), 162	Seize Sir Robt. Cotton's state papers and find if he has communicated them to Spanish ambassador.
[Oct.? 1615]	Chief Justice Coke	?	HMC Rpt. 15, App. Pt. 18 (Buccleuch, Vol. I), 162	Overbury Case. C. to decide about bail for Mrs. Turner. He is to send his opinion of the case to J. secretly.
13/11/15	Sir Ralph Winwood	?	HMC Rpt. 15, App. Pt. 18 (Buccleuch, Vol. I), 165	Archbp. of Canterbury and Chancellor may replace Pembroke, Fenton and Lake in Leeds hearing. (See Akrigg, Letter 163.)
25/2/16	Thos. Egerton, Ld. Ellesmere (Chanc., Eng.)	Newmarket	Sanderson, p. 432	J. rejoices at E's recovery, for which he has prayed. His determination to defend the Court of Chancery. (Holograph)

Date	Recipient	Written from	Printed in	Contents
14/4/16	Privy Council (Sc.)	"	BannCl 92, II: 803–4	In Scotland as in England and Ireland, *God and the King*, containing the Oath of Allegiance, is to be a book taught in all the schools.
21/4/[16?]	Sir Edw. Coke and other judges	"	HMC Rpt. 9, App. Pt. 2: 374	The command given them by the Attorney-General did not proceed from wrong information. Royal prerogative has been treated with unprecedented boldness in Westminster Hall. They are not to touch so tender a case until J. returns to London.
10/6/16	Univ. of St. Andrews	Greenwich	BannCl 92, II: 805–6	J. confirms the university's privileges while calling on it to reform itself according to the directions of the Dean of Winchester.
22/6/16	Archbp. of St. Andrews	Wanstead	BannCl 81, III: 1113–14	Approves High Commission's imprisonment of Huntly. Follow through with other actions against Catholics. Devilish disposition of C. Gordon's wife.
19/10/16	E. of Eglinton	Hinchingbrooke	HMC Rpt. 10, App. Pt. 1: 41	J. does not want to deny honest recreation to his lords, but only to preserve game in

				reasonable quantity, so E. can use long-winged hawks in W. Scotland (except against partridges and moorhens). He can hunt hares, but not with greyhounds.
2/11/16	Privy Council (Sc.)	Whitehall	BannCl 92, II: 811	P.C. to pass an act requiring parents to obtain a religious education for their children.
9/2/17	Thos. Egerton, Visc. Brackley (Chanc. Eng.)	Newmarket	Sanderson, pp. 432–33	J's letter of a year ago having proved so effective a medicine, this one may likewise prove a remedy. E. to fight disease knowing "how evil I may want you." (Holograph)
13/3/17	Bishops & ministers, Edinburgh	Whitehall	BannCl 92, II: 497–99	Rebukes them for scruples about figures of patriarchs and apostles in redecorating chapel at Holyrood House. These are not papistical.
16/7/17	Sir Ralph Winwood	Falkland	HMC Rpt. 15, App. Pt. 18 (Buccleuch, Vol. I), 206	Discover why wife of Sir Edw. Coke so unexpectedly opposes the match Sir Edw. has planned for daughter. Coke to have full backing of law in disposing of his children.
"	Archbp. of Canterbury et al.	"	HMC Rpt. 15, App. Pt. 18 (Buccleuch, Vol. I), 205–6	Call wife of Sir Edw. Coke and Lady Withipole before you and investigate their conveyance of Frances Coke away from her father's possession. If they do not return her to him they are to be taken in custody.

Date	Recipient	Written from	Printed in	Contents
16/8/17	E. of Mar (Treas., Sc.)	Houghton Tower	HMC Rpt. 15, App. Pt. 1 (Mar), 80-81	Urgent appeal for "two couple of excellent terriers or earth dogs." Perhaps E. of Menteith can supply these.
[25?/8/17]	Sir Francis Bacon	Nantwich	Spedding VI: 243–45	B. rebuked for opposing Coke's proposed match for his daughter. J. accuses B. of jealousy towards Buckingham and tells him he is officious.
6/12/17	Archbps. of St. Andrews & Glasgow	Newmarket	BannCl 92, II: 524	As for their letter, J. wants them to know that, having come of age, he is not content to be fed with broth. Peremptory orders to preach on Christmas Day.
"	"	"	BannCl 93, III: 248–49	Proceedings of Assembly at St. Andrews are disgraceful. They are to keep Christmas precisely, preaching that day. They will find what it is to anger a king. (*Holograph P.S.*)
10/7/18	General Assembly (Perth)	Theobalds	BannCl 93, III: 252–54	J. had decided against any more assemblies but granted wish of the bishops. He expects simple acceptance of articles he has sent them. Royal scolding, Dean of Winchester will report to him what happens at Perth.

[July? 1618]	Archbp. of St. Andrews?	?	BannCl 92, II: 565–66	Stinging rebuke for having given a letter of commendation to Thos. Ross, a "malicious, uncounselable fool."
29/9/18	Privy Council (Sc.)	Hampton [Court]	BannCl 92, II: 583	J. greatly pleased with conduct of General Assembly at Perth. He ratifies and confirms articles agreed upon there.
19/2/19	Ld. Deputy of Ireland	Newmarket	HMC Rpt. 14, App. Pt. 7 (Ormonde, Vol. I), 79	Sends his award arbitrating between E. of Ormonde and Lady Dingwall, and orders Ld. Deputy to see that its provisions are carried out.
[17/5/19]	Privy Council (Sc.)	Greenwich	BannCl 92, II: 600–1	There must be no more opposition to recently ratified Kirk articles, and no more libels.
31/5/19	E. of Mar & Sir Gideon Murray	Theobalds	HMC Rpt. 15, App. Pt. 1 (Mar), 86	Although J. may never see Inverness Castle again, he wants it put in proper repair for possible use by his successors.
6/7/19	Privy Council (Sc.)	Windsor	BannCl 92, II: 613–14	Let Sir James Skene receive the communion kneeling and J.'s suspicions will end.
17/7/19	Ld. Deputy of Ireland	Theobalds	HMC Rpt. 14, App. Pt. 7 (Ormonde, Vol. I), 80–81	Since E. of Ormonde has failed to pay the £100,000 which J. ruled he must pay Ld. and Lady Dingwall, his castles, manors and lands are to be seized.

Date	Recipient	Written from	Printed in	Contents
[Dec.? 1619]	Archbp. of St. Andrews	?	BannCl 92, II: 620	Ld. Scone sent with confidential message about dispossessing unruly ministers.
30/3/20	Privy Council (Sc.)	Theobalds	BannCl 92, II: 623–24	Out of "peevish humour," many in Edinburgh receive communion from silenced or deprived ministers. Ringleaders are to be banished from the city.
17/4/20	E. of Mar	Whitehall	HMC Rpt. 15, App. Pt. 1 (Mar), 88–89	Since J. plans to revisit Scotland next year, M. is to see"Moore Eumont" is in good condition for hunting. He must improve hawk breeding in Sc., "for if we be unfurnished from thence we shall forget to cause pay your pension."
12/6/20	Adam Loftus (Chanc., Ireland)	Westminster	HMC Rpt. 14, App. Pt. 7 (Ormonde, Vol. I), 81–82	To enforce the arbitration award in the Ormonde–Dingwall case, L. is to issue an order upon a bill being exhibited by E. of Desmond and wife.
18/7/20	E. of Mar	Theobalds	HMC Rpt. 15, App. Pt. 1 (Mar), 89–90	Asks M. to act with E. of Angus in "a deed of Christian charity," saving Sir Hugh Carmichael from rapacious son.

14/3/21	Philip IV	"	Rushworth I: 57	Letter of condolence on death of Philip III.
	Philip IV	"	Rushworth I: 57–58	Now, at brink of old age, J. brings up project, broached in Philip's father's time, of match between Pr. Charles and Philip's youngest sister. Ld. Digby is sent to negotiate. Concern about Palatinate.
"	Balthazar de Zuñiga	"	Rushworth I: 59–60	J. asks him to use his influence with Philip IV and so advise Ld. Digby that his mission may succeed.
5/7/21	E. of Mar (Treas., Sc.)	Windsor	HMC Rpt. 15, App. Pt. 1 (Mar), 95	M. to complete work on Linlithgow Palace since J. means to revisit Scotland in summer of 1622.
13/7/21	E. of Mar	Theobalds	HMC Rpt. 15, App. Pt. 1 (Mar), 96–97	J. wants M. to work closely with the Marquess of Hamilton in furthering royal interest in the coming parliament. J. will "mark every man's carriage" there.
"	Convention of Estates (Sc. Parl.)	"	Hailes, pp. 81–86	Asks subsidy to help regain Palatinate. Vindicates his conduct of German affairs.
12/8/21	Archbps. & Bishops, (Sc.)	Rufford?	BannCl 92, II: 662–64	How untimely was their jeremiad just when Parliament had strengthened them against that "rebellious and disobedient crew," the

Date	Recipient	Written from	Printed in	Contents
				Puritans. The sword is in their hands. If they prove faint-hearted, they can be replaced.
29/9/21	Privy Council (Sc.)	Hampton [Court]	BannCl 92, II: 671	Since J. will have reforms begin "at our elbow," all councillors and law officers must conform to the Perth Assembly's orders or face dismissal.
30/10/21	E. of Mar	Theobalds	HMC Rpt. 15 App. Pt. 1 (Mar), 103	M. to send 4000 or 5000 young firs for transplanting at Buckingham's estate of Burley-on-the-Hill.
7/1/22	John Digby, E. of Bristol	?	HMC Rpt. 8, App. Pt. 1: 214–15	J. approves of what D. has done. He wants to know what Philip IV has written to the Emperor.
27/5/22	Privy Council (Sc.)	Theobalds	BannCl 92, II: 686–87	Archbps. are to report semi-annually on Catholic sympathizers. J. strikes Catholics and Puritans equally.
28/5/22	E. of Mar	"	HMC Rpt. 15, App. Pt. 1 (Mar), 111	Financial benefits for Lady Lyon now that she has allied her son according to J.'s wish.

Date	Sender	Place	Reference	Description
[June 1622?]	Ld. Advocate (Sir Wm. Oliphant)	?	HMC Rpt. 15, App. Pt. 1 (Mar), 112–13	J. concerned that neither E. of Mar nor Ld. Elphinstone improperly allege royal authorization in their dispute.
9/7/22	Virginia Company	Westminster	STC 14378	Orders cultivation of silk in Virginia, a richer and more solid commodity than tobacco. John Bonoeil's treatise on sericulture to be their guide.
4/8/22	Archbp. of Canterbury	Windsor	Rushworth I: 64	Orders greater care in keeping unsuitable preachers from pulpits.
17/8/22	Sir Rich. Houghton	Aldershot	Nichols IV: 776	J. calls H. to court for a personal interview.
12/9/22	Privy Council (Sc.)	Havering-at-Bower	BannCl 92, II: 694–95	Heavily diseased Jesuit prisoner, Mortimer, to be expelled from J.'s dominions.
[c. Sept. 1622]	E. of Mar (Treas., Sc.)	?	HMC Rpt. 15, App. Pt. 1 (Mar), 115	So that J. can pay £12,000 to Marquess of Hamilton and buy in various pensions, he must ask M. to borrow on his own credit and that of his friends. The burden may seem hard at first.
21/10/22	"	Royston	HMC Rpt. 15, App. Pt. 1 (Mar), 116	A year having passed during which J. has heard nothing from Mar about suggested appointment of a deputy treasurer to assist him, J. has given the post to Sir Archibald

Date	Recipient	Written from	Printed in	Contents
				Napier, whom he trusts M. will cherish. Assurances of regard for M.
25/10/22	E. of Bristol	Huntingdon	HMC Rpt. 8, App. Pt. 1: 214	If certain conditions are observed, B. can wait a month longer for the papal dispensation. (*Holograph*)
28/10/22	Ld. Montagu	Hinchingbrooke	HMC Rpt. 15, App. Pt. 18 (Buccleuch, Vol. I), 257	J. wants to talk to him as soon as convenient and sets appointment for interview at Royston.
30/10/22	Privy Council (Sc.)	"	BannCl 92, II: 700–2	Recent leniency towards Catholics proceeded from "reasons of State, in the deep and mystery whereof every man is not to dive or wade." Religious tolerance is not intended.
[Oct.? 1622]	E. of Bristol	?	Rushworth I: 68	Philip IV is to be told that if Emperor does not cease hostilities in Palatinate, Philip must assist in recovery of it. B. to allow only two months after audience with Philip so "we may understand that King's final resolutions before Christmas."

24/11/22	"	Newmarket	HMC Rpt. 8, App. Pt. 1: 214	B. to press Philip IV for effective resolution of Palatinate problem. Children of Pr. Charles and Infanta may be educated by mother until age nine, though B. may concede age ten. Supervision of Infanta's priests.
[Feb.?] 1623	Philip IV	?	Goodman II: 260	J. sends his son, the sworn King of Scotland. J., his son, and his kingdom are at Philip's service.
6/3/23	E. of Mar (Treas., Sc.)	Theobalds	HMC Rpt. 15, App. Pt. 1 (Mar), 117–18	J. having decided to create a new royal park in Glenalmond, he orders M. to pay compensation to landowner.
22/6/23	"	Wanstead	HMC Rpt. 15, App. Pt. 1 (Mar), 120–21	J. tries to convince M. that recent order that uncommitted royal revenues be paid to the new deputy treasurer does not show loss of confidence in M.
30/8/23	Infanta Maria	?	Hal II: 227	J., like Pr. Charles, has an ardent desire for the pleasure of her presence.
[Aug.?] 1623]	E. of Bristol	?	Hal II: 228	B. to thank Philip for entertainment of Pr. Charles and get his decision about the Palatinate.
21/7/24	Privy Council (Sc.)	Houghton Lodge	BannCl 92, II: 760–61	P.C. to hunt out conventicles and see that people kneel when receiving the communion.

Date	Recipient	Written from	Printed in	Contents
22/9/24	"	Theobalds	BannCl 92, II: 837	J. gives Robt. Bruce permission to return from exile at Inverness. If, however, he stirs from his home he must return to Inverness, no matter how bad the weather. "We think it neither convenient nor tolerable that he who opposeth himself against all bishops should play the part of an universal bishop, and like an Apostle go from place to place preaching the gospel."
[Sept. 1624]	Sir Geo. Hay (Chanc., Sc.)	?	BannCl 92, II: 764–65	Wm. Rig is to be fined. Punishment or pardon lies only in the King.
1/11/24	"	Royston	BannCl 92, II: 768	J.'s surprise that prisoners have been released without his knowledge.
"	E. of Mar	"	MaitCl 57, III: 344–45	Despatch four or five couple of terriers. J. wants to send them to France.
26/11/24	Privy Council (Sc.)	Newmarket	BannCl 92, II: 771–72	Having ever wished Edinburgh well, J. does not wish to undo the town, but the enclosed articles will have to be enforced to prevent further turmoil there.

Date	Recipient	Place	Reference	Summary
[3/4/24]	Secretary Conway	?	Rushworth I: 140–41	C. must have heard of House of Commons's "stinging petition against papists." C. also knows J. opposed to a war of religion. He is to detain Spanish post until after J. has spoken to Pr. Charles. Keep this secret.
12/1/25	Marquess of Huntly	Theobalds	HMC Rpt. 15, App. Pt. 1(Mar), 129	If H. is not content to receive from Mar the same discharge as Hamilton and Angus received, disinterested friends can arbitrate.
"	Chanc., Sc. (Sir Geo. Hay)	"	BannCl 92, II: 774	The Fr. ambassador having asked favour for Roman Catholics at this time of Pr. Charles's marriage, J. is ordering a stay of proceedings against them.
9/2/25	Louis XIII	Newmarket	Coke I: 118–19	J. has been vanquished by L.'s last two affectionate letters. He and kingdom are at L.'s disposal. He will never countenance disloyal Frenchmen, but will tell L. of those who forget their allegiance.
Undated	Ld. John Hamilton	?	HMC Rpt. 11, App. Pt. 6: 67	Requests loan of two or three hounds and a horse. (*Holograph*)
"	"	?	HMC Rpt. 11, App. Pt. 6: 68	The bearer, your servant, will correct all such misreports as have reached you. (*Holograph*)

527

Date	Recipient	Written from	Printed in	Contents
"	"	?	HMC Rpt. 11, App. Pt. 6: 68	Give heedful hearing to bearer, who will relate truth of business creating a stir. (*Holograph*)
"	E. of Mar	?	HMC Rpt. 15, App. Pt. 1 (Mar), 37	Bearer will inform M. of matters touching his honour. M. should trust J. as he would any other friend. (*Holograph*)
"	"	?	HMC Rpt. 15, App. Pt. 1 (Mar), 38	Since M.'s "heavy sickness" may proceed from unhappiness, bearer will give him reassurance. (*Holograph*)

528

INDEX

Designer: Janet Wood
Compositor: Innovative Media Inc.
Text: VIP Sabon
Display: Phototypositor Sabon
Printer: Braun-Brumfield, Inc.
Binder: Braun-Brumfield, Inc.